PRAISE FOR

The Traveler's Guide to American Crafts

EAST OF THE MISSISSIPPI

"When I travel I'm always searching for something more than fudge, T-shirts, and the junk that passes for antiques. Here at last are the books that will take me to the heart of Americana."

—Michael Spring, Editorial Director, Fodor's Travel Guides

"The ideal guide for combining travel with the discovery of the best in American crafts. Easy to use, and authoritative."

—Elizabeth Harryman and Paul Lasley, hosts of The Travel Show, KABC Radio, Los Angeles

"Thorough and accurate. Her guides will enable me to pack the maximum of craft pleasure and learning into my limited travel time."

—Martha Garrott, Director, Mississippi Crafts Center, Craftsmen Guild of Mississippi

"An excellent presentation of wonderful discoveries and treasures. . . . Exemplary and much needed publications."

—Marlene Gabel, Executive Director, Contemporary Crafts Gallery, Portland, Oregon

SUZANNE CARMICHAEL is a widely published freelance writer who has traveled extensively along the back roads of the United States and Canada. Her own craft collection includes Native American jewelry, traditional tribal masks, and Inuit native stone carvings, plus contemporary ceramics and baskets. She lives in the Puget Sound area of Washington.

D1372381

THE TRAVELER'S GUIDE TO
AMERICAN CRAFTS

East of the Mississippi

A Traditional and Contemporary Selection

SUZANNE CARMICHAEL

DUTTON · New York

DUTTON
Published by the Penguin Group
Penguin Books USA Inc., 375 Hudson Street,
New York, New York 10014, U.S.A.
Penguin Books Ltd, 27 Wrights Lane,
London W8 5TZ, England
Penguin Books Australia Ltd, Ringwood,
Victoria, Australia
Penguin Books Canada Ltd, 2801 John Street,
Markham, Ontario, Canada L3R 1B4
Penguin Books (N.Z.) Ltd, 182–190 Wairau Road,
Auckland 10, New Zealand

Penguin Books Ltd, Registered Offices:
Harmondsworth, Middlesex, England

First published by Dutton, an imprint of Penguin Books USA Inc.
Published simultaneously in Canada by Fitzhenry & Whiteside, Limited.

First printing, April, 1990
10   9   8   7   6   5   4   3   2   1

Library of Congress Cataloging-in-Publication Data

Carmichael, Suzanne.
  The traveler's guide to American crafts east of the Mississippi:
a traditional and contemporary selection / Suzanne Carmichael.—
1st ed.
    p.   cm.
  ISBN 0-525-24859-5.—ISBN 0-525-18551-1 (pbk.)
  1. Handicraft—Northeastern States—Directories.   2. Handicraft—
Southeastern States—Directories.   3. Artisans—Northeastern
States—Directories.   4. Artisans—Southeastern States—directories.
1. Title.
TT12.C37   1990
680'.25'74—dc20   89-27963
                                                     CIP

Printed in the United States of America
Set in ITC Cheltenham Light
Designed by Stanley Drate/Folio Graphics Co. Inc.

Jacket illustrations: Peter M. Petrochko (Oxford, Conn.), Window Sculpture. Mahogany, bloodwood, ebony, ipe, curly maple, shedua, bubinga, wenge, ash, and purpleheart. H. 30″; W. 15″; L. 20″. FRANK POOL; Lester Breininger (Robesonia, Pa.), Redware storage jar with sgraffito decoration. H. 12″; Diam. 11½″; Manuel Albalate (Miami, Fla.), Venezuelan mask; Susan Denson (Mississippi Crafts Center, Ridgeland, Miss.), Choctaw double-weave hamper. Swamp cane. H. 25″; Diam. 21″; TOM JOYNT; Ethel Wright Mohamed (Belzoni, Miss.), Fourth of July Picnic. Embroidered pictorial. H. 18″; L. 26″; Steven M. Lalioff (Deming, Ind.), Reproduction c. 1790–1830 trunk with grain-painted interior. Poplar, calfskin, brass, tacks, paint. Irvan J. Perez (St. Bernard, La.), Decoy of green-wing teal hen and drake. Life-size.

For CB,

The perfect companion for traveling all of life's byways,
in the Deep Woods and outside. . . .

FGB

CONTENTS

ACKNOWLEDGMENTS

Above everyone else my gratitude goes to the craftspeople, gallery owners, museum directors, and craft event sponsors who took the time to answer my inquiries and send me information and illustrations. Without their assistance there would be no book.

Equally important were the people who helped me locate these artisans and places, including craft collectors, museum curators, gallery owners, state folklorists and art commission directors, editors of craft publications, craftspeople themselves, and many, many others. Some people went so far out of their way to assist me in this regard that they deserve special thanks and recognition: Deborah A. Bedwell, Baltimore Clayworks; Merri Belland, Florida Folklife Programs; Kim Rogers Burdick, Delaware's unofficial state folklorist; Mrs. Alice B. Carpenter (Vermont); Mrs. Hillary Rodham Clinton, wife of the governor of Arkansas; Nancy Fisher, Panaca Gallery (Bellevue, Washington); Florene Fratcher (Missouri); Marlene Gabel, Contemporary Crafts Association (Portland, Oregon); Martha Garrott, Craftsmen's Guild of Mississippi; Ruth Greenberg (California); Phyllis A. Harrison, Institute of the NorthAmerican West; Carolyn A. Hecker, Maine Crafts Association; Ron Kent (Hawaii); Joanne Kliejunas (California); Melanie LaBorwit-Cohen, South Dakota state folklorist; Robert K. Liu, *Ornament* magazine; Penny Loucas (Montana); Richard Marsh, Wisconsin Arts Board; Claude Medford, Jr. (Louisiana); Alice C. Merritt, Tennessee Artist-Craftsmen's Association; Pennsylvania Bureau of Travel Development; Margie Shurgot and Bill Hynes (Colorado); Jaune Quick-To-See Smith; Willie Smith, State Arts Council of Oklahoma; Susan L. Steinhauser (California); Rebecca A. Stelling, West Virginia Department of Culture and History; Elaine Thatcher, Western Folklife Center; Gerard Tsonakwa (everywhere); Cynthia Wayburn (Colorado); and Jo Luck Wilson, Arkansas Department of Parks and Tourism.

Special thanks and love go to Christopher Lydon, who said I should write books, not just magazine articles (and whose caring wisdom has been an important part of my life for many years). Thanks also to Susan Biskeborn, who gave me tremendous support and invariably helpful suggestions when the idea for this book was in its infancy. I also owe an enormous debt of gratitude to the women who operate the Tacoma Public Library's Quick Information telephone line. Their prompt, friendly, and accurate answers to requests for addresses and phone numbers, unusual spellings, and a myriad of other questions saved me considerable time and money. Also, a tip of the craft hat to Fred Tausend, friend and attorney, for introducing me to Bob Lescher, my agent; and to Bob for his assistance in nailing down all the particulars that make a book contract a positive document.

Writers tend to become antisocial animals, especially when deadlines threaten, so friends who persevere and continue to call (and provide a link with the outside world) are particularly precious. Thanks in this regard go to Scott, my stepson and friend, for his support and interest; to Zia for her bubbly, upbeat phone conversations (and for Fuller); and to Sandi, whose quiet support, sense of humor, and intelligent advice made such a tremendous difference.

It is impossible to adequately thank Sandra Soule, my editor. Sandy is truly an author's editor. A partner, not a dictator (or is that dictatress?); an adviser, not a nag; Sandy's unflagging support, quick intelligence, irreverent humor, and wise counsel made every interaction a delight.

The single most important person in the life of this book is my husband, Don, a talented craftsman in his own right. Born as an idea during one of our travel adventures, sustained by his belief in me and my abilities, this book is as much his as it is mine. For the entire twenty months this book took from inception to completion, Don was always available to engage in a debate on some obscure aesthetic point or grammatical construction, supply the word that couldn't get past the tip of my tongue, or cheer me up with a phone call in the middle of the day. Don's love made the difference in this book, as it does daily in every aspect of my life.

INTRODUCTION

If you prefer back roads to interstates, country inns to chain motels, and local delicacies to fast food, you're likely to reject mass-produced souvenirs in favor of mementos that tap local creative talent. Serving as an artistic diary of your trip, craft purchases can recall the colors of a Southwestern desert, Florida's ethnic diversity, or a shopping artstravaganza in Soho. In fact, pursuing local crafts can change your entire itinerary, taking you down bumpy dirt roads to visit traditional potters, dropping you off at snazzy upscale galleries, plopping you down in the midst of a gigantic quilt festival, or keeping your children fidget-free as they visit a carousel museum or watch a coppersmith ply his centuries-old craft.

This book is for the traveler who wants unique keepsakes or special gifts for friends back home, for neophytes as well as experienced collectors, for armchair travelers, and for craftspeople who want to explore other artisans' work. Whether you have $5 or $20,000 to spend; prefer traditional crafts or cutting-edge contemporary work; like to visit craftspeople in their studios and homes or prefer to browse in galleries, at craft festivals, and in museums, this book will introduce you to some of the country's finest craftspeople and their work.

Throughout American history, crafts have served as both a reflection of current culture and a window to the past, a mirror of each region's natural environment and an abstract portrait of its people. Spawned originally by necessity, functional crafts quickly gained decorative aspects, from the earthenware vessels made by ancient Pueblo Indians to the housewares and furnishings of American colonists. Created from local fibers and wood, native clay, minerals, and dyes, crafts were produced for family use, were used in bartering, served as an economic base for utopian religious communities, and offered a continuing link with immigrants' ethnic heritages.

Increasingly displaced beginning in the mid-1800s by cheap, mass-produced goods, American crafts nevertheless retained a tenuous foothold. Although average Americans had little contact with crafts during the ensuing "dark ages," a few farsighted individuals and groups such as Boston's Society of Arts & Crafts encouraged craftspeople by displaying their work and providing limited marketing. The late nineteenth-century English Arts & Crafts Movement, which advocated combining beauty with the utilitarian necessities of everyday life, also found advocates in the United States. The influence of these advocates

1

can be seen in period crafts and remnants of utopian artists' communities such as Roycroft in western New York State.

In the 1920s and 1930s, a number of farsighted individuals, particularly in Appalachia, established schools and cottage industry networks to keep local crafts alive. During this same time Bauhaus devotees in the United States argued for a closer relationship between craft techniques and pure art, spurring a new interest in architectural crafts, furniture design, and textiles. Even the Depression helped. The Works Progress Administration employed craftspeople to create a variety of items for use in national park hotels and visitors' centers.

The current resurgence of crafts, however, can be laid directly at the sandaled feet of the flower children of the 1960s. Rejecting plastic Americana, creating their own (often crude) crafts, they successfully focused public attention on the importance of creative energy and individual vision. From the spotty outdoor 1960s craft fairs with tables of poorly crafted (generally brown) pottery and interminable racks of macramé plant hangers, current craft events have grown to include prestigious indoor shows that can pull in over $10 million in wholesale and retail sales during a single five-day session.

Unfortunately, threats remain to the continued existence of some crafts, particularly traditional ones. Sources of natural fibers are increasingly extinguished as developers drain swamps and pave open spaces, forcing craftspeople, particularly basket makers, to travel hundreds of miles to find and harvest materials. Several multigenerational crafts are also under siege. Children and grandchildren seem unlikely to take over crafts that are extremely time-consuming and provide a relatively low monetary return, such as intricate Native American beadwork, Hmong story quilts, and East European needlework.

Ironically, the increasing popularity of these crafts may revive interest and assure their continuance while also sowing new threats. As folklorists and traditional craft specialists are quick to point out, strong public demand and rising prices sometimes conspire to dilute or destroy a craft, pressuring individual artisans to increase production at the expense of detail, quality, and craftsmanship itself.

To an overwhelming extent, however, American crafts are thriving. Spurred on by the American Craft Council and its marketing arm, by a host of craft organizations and publications, and even by a few supportive state governments, more and more Americans are purchasing crafts as gifts or starting personal collections. Some interest in crafts can also be attributed to the increasing numbers of people with disposable income who cannot afford the astronomically priced world of fine art.

Which brings us to the ongoing debate of whether any given item is actually a "craft," "fine art," or, in the case of Native American work, "tribal art." Although the arguments are all somewhat unconvincing and any distinctions ultimately artificial, it is a controversy taken very seriously by many craftspeople and galleries. In the cultural wasteland of the 1950s, "craft" was often used interchangeably with "hobby" to refer to work produced from kits or that required little formal instruction or skill. Further blurring the issue is the fact that "craft," in its customary usage, referred to items that were primarily functional: a chair that could be sat upon; a bowl used at mealtime; textiles for clothing, drapes, and rugs. During the last twenty years, however, decorative aspects became increasingly important, sometimes so dominant that the original function was obscured or lost: a wood sculpture that suggests the outlines of a chair but cannot be used as one, a purely decorative ceramic vessel, textiles meant only as wall hangings. Are these items "crafts"? Or are they "art"?

Other pressures have added fuel to the debate. Art galleries were (and many still are) loathe to sully their collections with anything that wasn't "Art." So craftspeople began marketing their work *as* art in order to be shown in the most prestigious galleries. Likewise, many Native American artisans, wanting their work to be taken seriously and not be confused with ersatz "Indian" trinkets, also reject the "craft" label, preferring the term "tribal arts" to denote authentic work based on centuries-old cultural traditions, designs, and techniques.

This book excludes paintings, sculpture, prints, photography, and other "fine arts." Included are works that retain a suggestion of function or are based on traditional craft materials such as ceramics, glass, textiles, and natural fibers. Many contemporary crafts, however, straddle the crafts/fine arts fence, and only individual, subjective judgments have been made.

To find the crafts and artisans mentioned in this book I cast a wide net, asking for input from gallery owners, collectors, curators, state folklorists, crafts guilds, and other sources. I also reviewed major craft periodicals for the last twenty years. Since time and finances did not permit personal visits, the initial list was winnowed down and almost 4,000 detailed questionnaires were mailed to craftspeople, galleries, museums, and craft event sponsors. Recipients were asked to provide slides or illustrations of their work and were invited to submit as much additional information as they wished. No fees of any type were ever charged to anyone.

The final choices provide travelers with a wide range of traditional and contemporary crafts, all individually made, often one-of-a-kind. By exploring the entries, readers will discover each state's or region's most distinctive contemporary and traditional crafts as well as Native American, immigrant/ethnic crafts, and crafts handed down for generations. Some traditional crafts cross geographical boundaries, particularly those crafts created by the Amish/Mennonites and the Shakers, who formed communities in several states. Because contemporary artisans are as mobile as other Americans, and often find the best markets outside their own locales, travelers will find such anomalies as Amish quilts in Washington State, Iroquois pottery in New Mexico, and Southwestern crafts in San Francisco.

Traditional crafts were chosen for both their authenticity and their quality. Contemporary crafts also had to meet strict criteria. Excluded were many excellent contemporary crafts that did not significantly differ from ones found in other parts of the country. Included are pieces of exceptional design, showing unique vision, often incorporating imagery, materials, and colors unique to the artisan's locale. When in doubt I gave myself the "itinerary detour test": Would I, when traveling, be willing to make a substantial detour to see this work? Those that passed the test are included.

Other criteria were also used to choose the entries. In addition to creating top-notch crafts, individual artisans had to have their work regularly available for visitors to see and purchase, either through their home/studio, a nearby gallery/shop, or, in rare instances, exclusively through the mail. Unfortunately, this forced the exclusion of some very talented craftspeople who have very limited output or extremely restricted marketing outlets.

The artisans included range from people in their twenties to several in their nineties, from internationally recognized craftspeople to those who are little known even within their own communities. Informally collected statistics concerning these craftspeople show that

49 percent are male, 35 percent are female, and 16 percent work together as either couples or families. Seventy-five percent of the artisans listed themselves as full-time craftspeople, 6 percent are retired, and the remaining 19 percent hold a variety of jobs from crafts instructor and gallery owner to auto mechanic, commercial fisherman, secretary, barber, attorney, cowboy, pastry chef, stockbroker, farmer, and factory worker. Forty-eight percent of the craftspeople are self-taught, 22 percent learned their craft from parents or grandparents, and 30 percent acquired their skills through apprenticeships or course work. A significant number of artisans said their parents taught them the craft as a young child to keep them busy, and others said they initially taught themselves their craft in order to make an item they couldn't afford to purchase.

Public interest in crafts has generated a deluge of craft galleries, events, and even museum craft collections. The quality and staying power of these activities and art forums, however, vary tremendously. Included here are galleries that seem likely to still be in business five years hence and that display top-notch American crafts of particular appeal or unusual quality. Although some specialize in regional work, most galleries display work by a national roster of artisans. Craft events that exercise strong quality control and offer something unique are also listed, as are museums that specialize in regional crafts or have a significant American craft collection. Because watching crafts being made is part of the fun, museum, event, and gallery demonstrations are also mentioned. Some individual artisans are also willing to demonstrate their techniques to potential purchasers—just ask.

If you have a favorite craftsperson, place, or event that is not listed, please use the Craft Report Card at the back of the book to tell me about it. I also welcome comments on your visits to the people and places listed in the book. Did they live up to your expectations? Has ownership and quality of a gallery changed? Were the directions accurate? Is there something I should add or delete in a subsequent edition? I look forward to your comments and suggestions, and when possible I will respond with a personal note. Send all correspondence to: Suzanne Carmichael, P.O. Box 7604, Tacoma, Washington 98407-7604.

Visiting Craftspeople's Studios/Homes

Visiting craftspeople in their studios or homes is a special treat, offering an opportunity to both purchase crafts and get to know the artisans personally. A trip to a craftsperson's studio/home is, however, quite different from visiting a commercial gallery or shop. Don't be shy about visiting craftspeople, but do realize you are a guest in their homes. To help you understand the etiquette of such a visit (and know what to expect) here are some basic do's and don'ts, including some recommendations from craftspeople.

Do visit artisans whose work sounds like something you may be interested in purchasing. Although a visit does not imply you will definitely buy their work, *do not* take up a craftsperson's time if the work is out of your price range or you have absolutely no intention of purchasing anything. Remember that artisans' time and skill are their only stock in trade. If you are merely curious, send for a catalog or brochure, or visit a gallery that displays the artisan's work. (NOTE: Entries stating "work also available through . . ." list only galleries/ shops near an artisan's hometown. Many craftspeople also show their work in galleries throughout their states and around the country; call the artisan for additional locations.)

4

Do read the entry carefully. If it says "Visitors: by appointment," "please call first," or asks you to "call for directions," definitely telephone in advance. *Do not* stop by unannounced. The best bet is to call several days ahead to arrange for a mutually convenient time. If you have trouble reaching the craftsperson during the day, call in the evening before 10 P.M. Remember to check which time zone you're calling so you won't call at an inconvenient hour.

If the entry says "Visitors: Yes," an appointment is not required, but *do* use common sense. Plan your visit during daylight hours (but not before 9 A.M.), avoid the dinner hour, and don't drop by too early on weekends. If possible, out of courtesy, phone ahead to ask what time would be most convenient for a visit.

A few craftspeople sell their work only through the mail. These entries will state "mail order only." *Do not* visit these craftspeople; use their address only for correspondence.

Do realize that you are visiting a private residence or studio. Keep your children under control (or leave them in the car), leave your pets outside, and don't smoke.

Do not expect any craftsperson to welcome more than three or four people at a time. If you are traveling with a larger group, call ahead to see if all of you can be accommodated.

Do not expect craftspeople to accept credit cards or personal checks (although a few do). Be prepared to pay cash, especially for less expensive items.

What to Expect: Don't expect a formal showroom with hundreds of samples. At some studios/homes you will find a large assortment of items, in others the selection will be more limited. Sometimes the demand for an artisan's work is so high that very little work is available for display. In this case craftspeople will be happy to show you what they're presently working on as well as slides and photographs of their other work.

Do realize that an artisan's work continually evolves. Few craftspeople find satisfaction in merely producing one type or style of work. Instead, their craft is continually changing, sometimes subtly, at other times more radically. Between the time this book was written and your visit, the specific work described in the entries or shown in the illustrations may no longer be available. Chances are, however, if you like what you read about or see, you'll enjoy equally an artisan's latest endeavors.

Catalogs/Brochures: A substantial number of craftspeople sell their work through the mail. The types of catalogs and brochures they offer vary from multiple-page, color-illustrated catalogs to photocopied price lists. When sending for mail-order information, be sure to enclose a self-addressed, stamped envelope (SASE) where requested and a check to cover any listed cost.

Commissions: Although most craftspeople do accept commissions (special orders) there are generally limits as to what they are willing to produce. Some will customize an item to your color, design, and other specifications, but most will create only pieces consistent with their current work. To avoid any misunderstandings, follow a few simple rules. Put everything in writing (a simple letter will do) so there will be no questions later about size, color, cost, approximate delivery date, and other details (including which party will pay for packing and shipping, insurance, and other costs). If possible, commission a work only after seeing a similar piece in person or in a color illustration.

One advantage to commissioning work is that you often pay wholesale rather than gallery prices. Although it is perfectly appropriate to contact craftspeople personally to discuss commission work, if you first see their work in a gallery, it is considered bad form to do an end run directly to the craftsperson. Consult your conscience.

Other Information

Glossary: Starting a craft collection also means acquiring a new vocabulary. The glossary at the back of the book defines some of the technical craft terms used in this book.

Prices and Hours: All prices mentioned in the book are listed only as general guidelines and are subject to change (and do not include any applicable taxes). Use these prices merely as a guide to see whether the crafts (or events) are within your budget. Gallery, museum, and craft event hours may also vary, particularly during the Christmas season. Where listings indicate "Closed major holidays," this will generally include Easter, Memorial Day, July 4th, Labor Day, Thanksgiving, Christmas, and New Year's Day. Call for specifics.

Getting Your Crafts Home: Unless you can't bear to part with a new craft purchase, it may be best to ship it directly to your home. That way you avoid the prospect of losing it, having it stolen, or damaging it in transit. Galleries and shops are experts at wrapping and mailing your work, but expect to pay for the service. If you buy items from individual craftspeople, do not expect them to ship the items for you but do ask for their advice on packaging. Remember to insure the package; if you're not planning to be home soon, ship it to yourself in care of a friend.

Displaying and Taking Care of Your Craft: Displaying a craft to its best advantage is an art itself, and the expert is the craft's creator. Ask the craftsperson or gallery owner for suggestions concerning placement, lighting, pedestals, and other considerations. Ask also what protections the work needs (from dust, humidity, sunlight, and other hazards) and what type of care and cleaning is advised. Since textiles are particularly fragile and subject to deterioration, they need regular care. An excellent how-to booklet by a recognized expert is *Textiles: Home Care and Conservation*, by Audie Hamilton. For a copy send $6 plus $1.50 postage to Audie Hamilton, 408 West Main Street, Kerrville, Texas 78028.

Planning to Start a Craft Collection: This can be an exciting endeavor requiring many decisions: Should you specialize? How can you learn to determine quality? Should you make decisions based on investment potential or enjoyment? How do you add to your collection? How do you document, insure, display, and conserve your collection? An excellent book that offers insight on these and many other questions is *Contemporary American Craft Art, A Collector's Guide*, by Barbara Mayer (1988). Available currently only in hardcover from Peregrine Smith Books (P.O. Box 667, Layton, Utah 84041; 801-544-9800), the book has a $45 price tag—but it's worth every penny (or save your coins and borrow it from your local library). A paperback edition may be issued in the future; inquire care of Peregrine Smith Books.

NEW ENGLAND

Steeped in history and tradition, New England is fertile ground for travelers who want to retrace colonial America, experience the grace of fine country inns, discover small prim towns, or wander along deserted winter beaches in Maine or Cape Cod. Once the bastion of traditional crafts such as pewtersmithing, the region is now a pleasant mix of historical and contemporary work. Maine, Massachusetts, and New Hampshire also boast a handful of Shaker villages and museums that display this nineteenth-century religious community's meticulous craftsmanship from baskets and textiles to furniture and metal crafts.

During the last twenty years increasing numbers of craftspeople have been drawn to New England, particularly Maine, New Hampshire, and Vermont, for its slower pace of life, great beauty, and accessibility to urban centers and galleries. Primarily contemporary craftspeople, these new artisan/immigrants have added to the eclectic artistic mix of the area. Visitors are as likely to find avant-garde jewelry and nonfunctional ceramics as more traditional metal or textile crafts. New England also offers museums that trace the region's other craft legacies, excellent galleries, and a sprinkling of craft shows.

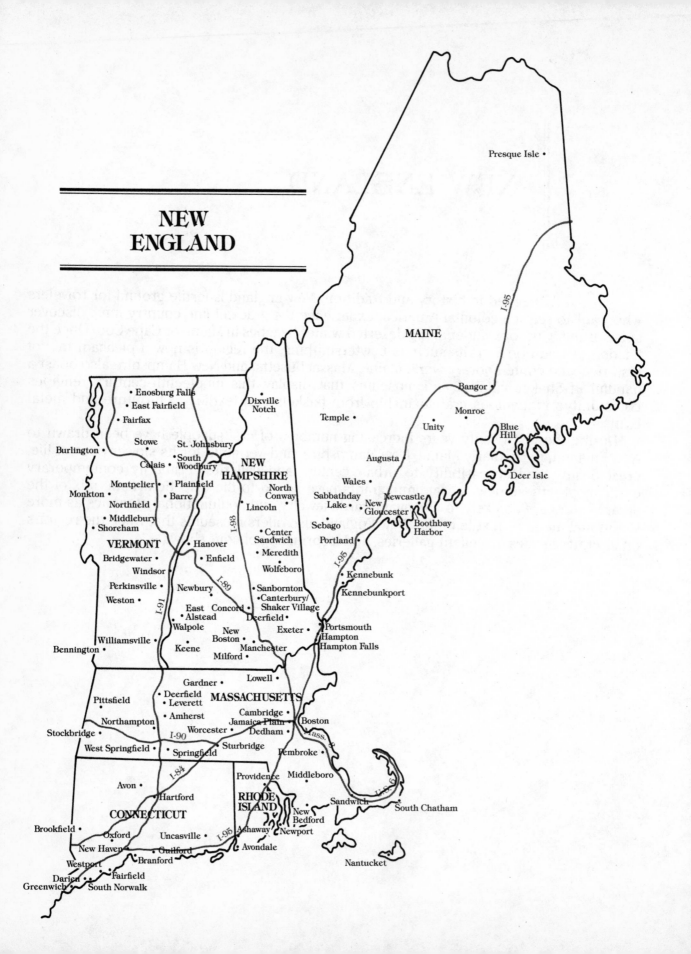

NEW ENGLAND

CONNECTICUT

Whether you're whizzing through Connecticut from New York City to Boston or you're on a leisurely jaunt along the coast or up the Connecticut River valley, design your route to include some of the state's craft offerings. Contemporary craft galleries range from Greenwich's top-notch Elements Gallery to craft centers that combine artists' studios with galleries and sales shops. More interested in traditional work? See Appalachian crafts in Darien and a small museum exhibiting rare Mohegan Indian crafts in Uncasville. For a special treat visit artisans who create intricate papercuttings or stunning contemporary wood vessels. Annual craft shows include one exhibiting only hooked rugs and another that combines quality crafts with classical music and gourmet food.

AVON

Farmington Valley Arts Center
CRAFTS STUDIOS AND SHOP

Mature trees and plush lawns form a parklike setting for this converted nineteenth-century factory. Once home to a safety fuse manufacturer, this two-story stone building now houses crafts studios, classrooms, and a gallery shop. Guests are welcome to visit the studios, where forty artists work in a variety of media: paper marbling, pottery, jewelry, leather, fiber arts, painting, printmaking, and many others.

You might be able to visit the Chair Clinic to see Jan Bennet weave cane and rush chair seats. The third generation of her family to practice this craft, she and her father also restore antique chair seats for private collections. Interested in exotic leathers? Then watch William Julian Niemczyk transform these rare skins into innovative briefcases, pocketbooks, and accessories. Or stop by Judee Kaufman's studio, where metals from fine gold to plumber's copper pipes become unusual jewelry.

Sometimes foreign craftspeople are also in residence. In the past the center hosted a Russian repoussé technician, a Jamaican sculptor, and a Japanese artist. The Gallery Shop exhibits the work of all studio artisans as well as pieces from over one hundred other regional and national craftspeople.

PRICES: $2–$400. Accepts MasterCard, Visa. Gallery and some studios are wheelchair accessible.

OPEN: Gallery Shop open Wed.–Sat., 11 A.M.–4 P.M.; studios have no regular hours.

LOCATION: Northwest of Hartford. 25/27 Bunker Lane, Avon Park North, P.O. Box 220, Avon, CT 06001; 203-678-1867. From Hartford, go south on I-84 to exit 39, Rte. 4. North on Rte. 4 to Farmington, then north on Rte. 10/202 for 6 miles. Left on Rte. 44, 1 mile to Avon Park North. Right at traffic light near town offices onto Ensign Drive. Left on Bunker Lane.

MORE: Bring a picnic lunch to eat on the parklike grounds around the center.

BRANFORD

Martha Link Walsh
PAPERCUTTINGS

Martha Walsh cuts paper snowflakes in her sleep. The rest of the time she creates intricate paper designs, from a delicate flower to an entire village, with every line interconnected. Beginning with a single sheet of white paper, she uses only scissors and a scalpel to "paint" her pictures. Like Escher, the famous Dutch graphic artist, her work makes one aware of the distinction between positive and negative space: the paper is uncut for sky, but removed from building interiors except for detail work. Tiny windowpanes on a church—did she cut out the pane or the frame?

Martha stumbled onto her craft through illness.

"I was recuperating from an illness that left my eyesight fuzzy," Martha recalls. "I couldn't read or watch television, so I began to cut paper. Mother always said something good would come from that illness! Later I researched the craft and studied under several European masters."

The results range from simple cuttings for birth announcements or graduation cards to extremely complex pieces that tell a story. *Forest Menagerie* includes a tree with every leaf defined. Birds, squirrels, and a fluffy cat explore its branches; underneath, deer graze, a bird pulls a worm from the ground, and rabbits hide under a bush. In Martha's *Floral Alphabet* letters are linked to each other in a continuous flow, each lending itself to a nearby flower. A daffodil sprouts from the *D,* the *M* is intertwined with a morning glory, and the *W* sits next to a water lily.

PRICES: Custom, from $60 to $5,000; others, from $25; silk-screened reproductions, $15–$30; notecards, $6.75 for set of ten. "The bulk of my business is custom work." Free catalog/brochure.

Martha Link Walsh: *Peace,* papercutting. H. 14″; W. 15″.
CRAIG HELMRICH

LOCATION: 10 miles east of New Haven. Branford Craft Village, second-floor studio; 779 East Main Street, Branford, CT 06405; 203-481-3505. From I-95, take exit 56. North on Rte. 1 toward Guilford. 1 mile on the right. (NOTE: Branford Craft Village includes twenty-five other shops and studios.)

MORE: In summer, take a cruise through the nearby Thimble Islands, twenty-seven dots of land in the Atlantic. For more information, call the cruise operators at 203-481-4841 or 203-488-9978.

BROOKFIELD

Brookfield Craft Center
CONTEMPORARY AND TRADITIONAL CRAFTS

Offering craft courses from boatbuilding to metalsmithing, Brookfield also has a good gallery and artist studios open to the public. With two campuses, one in South Norwalk and one here, there is always something new to see. The monthly exhibits add focus to the gallery, which seems to have a little bit of everything. Past exhibits have focused on Amish folkcraft, sculptured baskets, weathervanes, and prominent art glass.

PRICES: $5–$500. Accepts American Express, MasterCard, Visa.

OPEN: Tues.–Sat., 11 A.M.–6 P.M.; Sun., noon–5 P.M. Closed major holidays. Partially wheelchair accessible.

LOCATION: Western Connecticut. P.O. Box 122, Brookfield, Connecticut 06804; 203-775-4526. From I-84 to Hawleyville, Rte. 25 exit. Go north on Rte. 25. The center is located on Rte. 25.

MORE: See the South Norwalk listing for information on Brookfield's SoNo Craft Center.

DARIEN

Appalachian House
APPALACHIAN CRAFTS

If you can't travel to Appalachia, Appalachia will travel to you, at least as far as Darien. Run by a nonprofit group to provide income for craftspeople from six Appalachian states, this shop is filled with high-quality, authentic items. Rugs from Hendersonville, North Carolina, are handwoven of mill end pieces from the local sock factory. From Gatlinburg, Tennessee, and Berea, Kentucky, come a variety of handmade brooms. In Elkins, West Virginia, craftspeople send their pottery, including pieces with lovely blue quilt patterns stenciled on the surface.

PRICES: $1–$500 (average, $25–$100). Accepts MasterCard, Visa.

OPEN: Mon.–Sat., 10 A.M.–5 P.M. Closed major holidays. Wheelchair accessible on first floor only.

LOCATION: Southwest corner of Connecticut. 1010 Boston Post Road, Darien, CT 06820; 203-655-7885. From I-95, take exit 11, then go north on Rte. 1. The house is on the right in downtown shopping area.

FAIRFIELD

Annual Hooked Rug Exhibit

Since 1959, rug hookers nationwide have gathered in Fairfield every April to exhibit and sell their work. From 150 to 250 rugs are shown each year, with styles as diverse as the regions and ages of their creators. Abstract and geometric, floral and pictorial, the rugs present a riot of colors, loops, and designs.

EVENT: One day in mid-April. For information, call United Methodist Women of Fairfield–Grace United Methodist Church, 1089 Fairfield Woods Road, Fairfield, CT 06430; 203-374-6528. Admission is $2.50 per adult, but anyone bringing five rugs of his or her own making will be admitted free.

LOCATION: Southwest of Bridgeport. Fairfield Woods Middle School, 1116 Fairfield Woods Road, Darien, CT. From I-95, take exit 22 and turn north on North Benson Road. Turn right on Fairfield Woods Road to next traffic light at school driveway.

MORE: Hooked rug door prizes, cake sale, lunch/snacks prepared by church members.

GREENWICH

The Elements
CONTEMPORARY CRAFTS GALLERY

Innovation, humor, and striking design are touch-stones of quality at The Elements. This is a collectors' gallery, with high-quality pieces often on the cutting edge of modern creativity. Representing over 150 artists from throughout the country, the collection includes well-known masters as well as emerging talent.

Josh Simpson, one of the foremost glass artists in the country, offers elegant stemware, glass sculptures, and pieces from his planet series: lush glass globes of fantasy seas and unworldly land-scapes. Eschewing jewelry that is uncomfortable or "only for black turtlenecks," Lisl Potter, former associate fashion editor at *Vogue*, combines silver and precious stones into pieces that flatter the wearer. In the humorous but practical category, Barry Norling creates copper-and-brass weather-vanes that burst with primal energy. In one, a dog runs eternally toward a ball just out of reach.

PRICES: $15–$4,000 + (average, $50–$300). Accepts Master-Card, Visa.

OPEN: Tues.–Sat., 10 A.M.–5 P.M. Closed Thanksgiving, Christmas, New Year's. Wheelchair accessible.

LOCATION: Southeast Connecticut. 14 Liberty Way, Green-wich, CT 06830; 203-661-0014. From New York City, take I-95 to exit 3. At end of ramp, go left on Arch Street and continue across Greenwich Avenue. At the first light turn left on Mason Street. At next light turn left on Elm Street. In middle of block on right turn into large parking lot. Gallery is in the middle of the parking lot, in an old stable.

GUILFORD

Guilford Handcrafts, Inc.
CONTEMPORARY AND TRADITIONAL CRAFTS

Many of the finest craftspeople exhibiting at this Guilford gallery also teach courses here. If you're lucky, you may be able to watch Myrna Brunson, of Niantic, Connecticut, create one of her "Porcupine"

baskets. Made from dyed Torrey Pine needles coiled with waxed linen, the prickly result is just like its namesake: made to look at but not touch. Also from Connecticut are Joe Ferola, whose hand-turned maple bowls resemble paper more than wood, and Melissa Greene, whose ceramic pieces often borrow Southwest Indian themes.

PRICES: $1–$800 (average, $25–$50). Accepts MasterCard, Visa.

OPEN: Mon.–Sat., 10 A.M.–4 P.M.; Sun., noon–4 P.M. Closed major holidays. Limited wheelchair accessibility.

LOCATION: 15 miles east of New Haven. 411 Church Street, P.O. Box 589, Guilford, CT 06437; 203-453-5947. From I-95, take exit 58 to Rte. 77, then go north on Rte. 77 to the Handcrafts center, on the right.

NEW HAVEN

Celebration of American Crafts
ANNUAL CRAFTS EXHIBITION

Serious collectors go elbow to elbow with holiday gift shoppers at this high-quality, juried craft show. Since its inception in 1968, this event has offered a wide array of items from toys to furniture. "The prices are fair, there is something for everyone on your gift list, and you also get to see what is new in glass, ceramics, jewelry, and other media," says Roz Schwartz, chairperson of the Celebration. Craftspeople come from throughout the country for this show, some of them returning each year to show a new phase of their work. Profits support the Creative Arts Workshop, which offers crafts studios, classes, and a year-round sales shop.

EVENT: The six and a half weeks prior to Christmas. Open Mon.–Sat., 11 A.M.–5 P.M.; Sun., 2–5 P.M. Free admission.

LOCATION: Creative Arts Workshop, 80 Audubon Street, New Haven, CT 06511; 203-562-4927. Take I-91 north to exit 3. At bottom of ramp, go left on Orange Street to light, then right on Audubon.

OXFORD

Peter M. Petrochko
CONTEMPORARY WOOD VESSELS

Peter's bandsaw bowls (see illustration on cover) are subtle plaids of exotic woods, often pairing ebony or walnut with a flash of red padouk or a stripe of purpleheart. Some bowls seem to have two colorful skins, one peeled back here and there to provide a glimpse of the other. "Much of my work is experimental," Peter says. "It is influenced by listening to jazz and my study of architecture and fine arts in college. In fact, I carved my first block of wood in 1967, in an architectural design class."

Exploring new forms, patterns, colors, and textures is Peter's forte. "I love the media in which I work: nature in general, trees in particular," Peter comments. "Although in the past I created wood furniture and sculptural wood carvings, my work is now concentrated in wooden bowls. I am challenged by the many possibilities of what a bowl might be, from natural shapes which I hand carve from a single log to more complex, laminated pieces. Since I'm always trying new designs and techniques, I never lose interest in my work. It's all flexible from the initial design stage through the finishing work."

PRICES: $150–$5,000. Commissions accepted. No catalog/brochure.

VISITORS: Welcome.

LOCATION: Between Bridgeport and Waterbury. 370 Quaker Farms Road, Oxford, CT 06483; 203-888-9835. Take Rte. 8 to exit 19 and Rte. 334. Continue northwest on Rte. 334 to the traffic circle. Go around the traffic circle and continue north on Rte. 188 (which is also Quaker Farms Road). Peter's studio will be on the left about 2.9 miles past the traffic circle.

MORE: Peter's work is also available through The Elements (see listing under Greenwich).

SOUTH NORWALK

Brookfield Sono Craft Center
CONTEMPORARY CRAFTS

Like its counterpart in Brookfield, the center in "SoNo" offers classes and a gallery, this time from an alley in a restored riverfront historic area swarming with art galleries, specialty boutiques, and wonderful seafood restaurants. Of note are the gallery's monthly exhibits featuring artisans of national repute. Claiming to have "the largest selection of handmade American work in the state," the gallery is next to working studios that are open to the public.

PRICES: $1–$25,750. Accepts American Express, MasterCard, Visa.

OPEN: Tues.–Sat., 11 A.M.–6 P.M.; Sun., noon–5 P.M. Closed major holidays. Wheelchair accessible.

LOCATION: Southwestern corner of Connecticut. Brookfield Alley, 127 Washington Street, South Norwalk, CT 06854; 203-853-6155. Take I-95 to exit 14, Rte. 136. Follow Rte. 136 to South Norwalk, then drive toward the water.

UNCASVILLE

Tantaquidgeon Indian Museum
MOHEGAN INDIAN CRAFTS

Serious students of Native American crafts will appreciate this small family museum, one of the only museums in the country exhibiting Mohegan crafts. Built originally in 1931 by John Tantaquidgeon, a direct descendant of Uncas, chief of the once powerful Mohegan Nation, the museum consists of three rooms behind the Tantaquidgeon home. In the first are excellent examples of Northeastern Woodland Indian crafts, including Mohegan baskets, bowls, and ladles. Some of these were made by John Tantaquidgeon, last of the Mohegan basket makers, others by his ancestors.

Once interviewed by scholars concerning the now lost Mohegan language, John's wife, Gladys, became interested in anthropology herself and later conducted her own research among other tribes. Some of the items she collected, which are in the museum's other two rooms, are examples of the craftsmanship of the Southeast, Southwest, and Northern Plains nations.

OPEN: May–Oct., Tues.–Sun., 10 A.M.–4 P.M. Free admission, donations welcome.

LOCATION: Southeast Connecticut. Rte. 32, Norwich-New London Road, Uncasville, CT 06382; 203-848-9145.

MORE: Two hundred yards from the museum is the Mohegan Congregational Church, built in 1831 and still in use. Nearby is the site where Samson Occum was born in 1723. Occum went on to become the most outstanding Christian Indian leader of his time and was instrumental in raising funds used in the founding of Dartmouth College. Not far away is Cochegan Rock, a secret meeting place for Uncas and his councillors, said to be the largest boulder in New England.

WESTPORT

Westport Handcraft Show

Combining high-quality crafts, classical music, and gourmet food, this annual craft show provides a welcome change of pace from most Memorial Day weekend events. For over twenty years, this event has been the major fund-raiser for a cooperative nursery school, but it isn't child's play. Every year jurors travel throughout the country to select the work of 125 top-notch craftspeople. Visitors to this show may find Shaker reproduction furniture, contemporary jewelry, floorcloths, bookbinding, children's furniture, decoys, and many other functional and decorative crafts.

EVENT: Memorial Day weekend. Sat., 10 A.M.–6 P.M.; Sun., 10 A.M.–5 P.M. Admission is $4 for adults, $3 for seniors, children under 12 free. For more information, call Fenton Barnes, Westport-Weston Cooperative Nursery School, 21 Deer Run Trail, Weston, CT 06883; 203-227-6799.

LOCATION: Southwest Connecticut, southwest of Bridgeport. Staples High School, North Avenue, Westport, CT. Take I-95 to exit 18, follow directional arrows. Or take the Merrit Parkway to exit 42, follow directional arrows.

MORE: To keep the children happy while you shop, there are magicians, clowns, and other entertainment.

MAINE

After you're visited Maine's beaches, pursue a craft discovery route that will lead you from south of Portland into Maine's lake country, up the coast to Blue Hill and Deer Isle or even to remote Presque Isle in Aroostook County. As you travel, be alert for small homemade signs reading POTTERY, WOODCARVING, or WEAVING. Tacked next to a cabin in the woods or pointing down a dirt road, these craft beacons can lead to talented artisans who use their spare time to create innovative, unsung treasures.

Begin your explorations with craftspeople who create everything from classic furniture to miniature Shaker and American country pieces, fantasy woodcarvings to traditional Maine baskets. Save room on your craft intinerary for a production pottery partially inspired by Gandhi, contemporary crafts galleries, Micmac Indian baskets, a renowned crafts school, and a glass and ceramics museum.

BLUE HILL

Rowantrees Pottery
CERAMIC DINNERWARE, ACCESSORIES

In 1898 Adelaide Pearson inherited a house in Blue Hill and immediately became involved in the community. Wealthy, well-traveled, and a natural benefactress, she revived the library, brought in art exhibits, and offered summer handicraft classes. Seeing how much children liked to "play in clay," she founded Rowantrees Kiln in 1934. Five years later, however, during a visit to India, Mahatma Gandhi tartly informed her that pottery was much too serious to be left to children and she should do it right or not do it at all. Taking his comments to heart, she visited potteries from England to China, then returned to Blue Hill and established a production pottery.

Although Miss Pearson died in 1954, the pottery continues to make dinnerware and accessories in the same style, using many of the same glazes that were used during her lifetime. "If someone has a

Rowantrees Pottery: Heather blue jam jar with blueberries.

15

set of dishes they bought thirty years ago and needs a new piece, we can always make one for them," says current owner Sheila Varnum. Rowantrees potters hand-shape each piece using local clays and glazes, including one called "ducks-head," which produces a lustrous color resembling a mallard's feathers.

"A lot of people buy our dinnerware for informal entertaining," Sheila says. "President Eisenhower had a set, in a soft gray glaze with black edging, which he usd at Gettysburg. But our most famous piece is the jam jar set, a plain blue saucer and bowl with a sculpted lid of Maine blueberries or strawberries."

PRICES: $4–$300+. Does not accept commissions. Accepts American Express, MasterCard, Visa. $1 charge for catalog/brochure.

OPEN: Summer—Mon.–Fri., 7 A.M.–5:30 P.M.; Sat. & Sun., noon–5:30 P.M. Winter—Mon.–Fri., 7 A.M.–3:30 P.M.

LOCATION: Penobscot peninsula, about 47 miles south of Bangor. Box C, Blue Hill, ME 04614; 207-374-5535. Take coastal Rte. 1 to junction with Rte. 15, 4 miles north of Bucksport, then turn south on Rte. 15 to Blue Hill. Rowantrees is on the main street.

MORE: While in Blue Hill, visit Rackliffe Pottery, a third-generation endeavor using clay dug from its own land, a unique blue glaze, and the familiar blueberry and strawberry motifs. Prices $5–$135, free brochure. Open Mon.–Sat., 8 A.M.–4 P.M. Box 393, Blue Hill, ME 04614; 207-374-2297.

After visiting Blue Hill, follow Rte. 15 to Stonington, a picturesque seaside town on Deer Isle where you can embark on a ferry for Isle au Haut, a prototypical Maine island including a relatively deserted part of Acadia National Park.

BOOTHBAY HARBOR

Abacus Gallery
CONTEMPORARY CRAFTS

Boothbay Harbor is one of those typical split personality Maine seacoast towns: charming, peaceful, and a bit dotty in winter; mobbed, noisy, but offering a glimpse of its winter self in summer. Try to visit in the off-season but still within this gallery's season, which extends from May 15 to December 24.

Offering a variety of good contemporary crafts, this gallery's specialty is jewelry, particularly the 18K hollowware of Michael Good, the gold pieces by Patty Daunis, and the precious stone designs of Neal Rosenblum, Margaret Barnaby, and Lee Angelo Marraccini. For total whimsy, and a change of medium, see Carey Armstrong-Ellis's soft sculptures. Originally trained as a biologist and zoologist, she has a Gary Larson–type view of the world: a family of carrots dines on roast rabbit, pigs fly, and beach potatoes play Frisbee and drink beer.

PRICES: $6–$6,000 (average, $15–$1,000). Accepts American Express, MasterCard, Visa.

OPEN: May 10-June 30, Mon.–Sat., 10 A.M.–5 P.M.; Sun., noon–5 P.M. July 1–Labor Day, daily, 9:30 A.M.–9:30 P.M. Labor Day–mid-Oct., Mon.–Sat., 9:30 A.M.–6 P.M.; Sun., 10 A.M.–6 P.M. Mid-Oct.–Dec., Mon.–Sat., 10 A.M.–5 P.M. Gallery is closed Jan. 1–early May. Visitors have to negotiate two steps, but the gallery staff will assist those who need help.

LOCATION: Central Maine coast, about 52 miles northeast of Portland. 8 McKown Street, Boothbay Harbor, ME 04538; 207-633-2166. Take I-95 north from Portland to Brunswick, then Rte. 1 east to Wiscasset. South on Rte. 27 to Boothbay Harbor. Go into center of village to first complete stop sign. The town library will be on your right. Turn right at that corner; the gallery is half a block on the left.

MORE: Abacus also has a superb Portland gallery. 44 Exchange Street, Portland, ME 04101; 207-772-4880. Open Mon.–Sat., 9:30 A.M.–6 P.M.; Sun., noon–5 P.M.

DEER ISLE

Haystack Mountain School of Crafts

Founded in 1950 by a small community of crafts-people interested in the Bauhaus concept of inter-locking design, function, and architecture, Haystack offers summer studio workshop programs in ten different media. Considered one of the preeminent craft schools in the country, Haystack's intense summer sessions unite craft professionals and students in an atmosphere crackling with crea-tivity. Studios are open twenty-four hours a day and are often occupied even in the middle of the night.

Nestled in a pine grove on picturesque Deer Island, the school is definitely worth a visit if you're already in the Blue Hill–Bar Harbor area. Although crafts are only sold at the school's annual end-of-session auction, works by instructors and students are on display throughout the summer at the Haystack gallery. Visitors are also welcome to peek through windows and entrances to observe workshops, and to attend free evening lectures and slide presentations.

VISITING HOURS: June–early Sept., daily, 10 A.M.–4 P.M. Evening lectures generally begin at 8 P.M. (call for details).

LOCATION: Mid-coastal region, about 35 to 40 miles south of Bucksport. Deer Isle, ME 04627-0087; 207-348-2306. Take Rte. 1 north of Bucksport 5 miles to Rte. 15. Then Rte. 15 south past Blue Hill and across the bridge over Eggemoggin Reach to Deer Isle. Continue on Rte. 15 for 5 miles, past the village of Deer Isle. Turn left at the Gulf gas station (there is a blue state highway marker here). Follow the small HAYSTACK signs 7 miles to the school.

James Hastrich: Miniature five-drawer chest with decoration typical of New England's itinerant painters, c. 1825. ELLEN MESERVE

KENNEBUNK

Renee Bowen and James Hastrich
SHAKER AND AMERICAN MINIATURES

As an adult, Queen Mary, grandmother of the present Queen Elizabeth, would lock herself in a palace room and play for hours with her dollhouse, turning doorknobs, flushing toilets, and running miniature Hoover vacuums. Now you can also escape to the world of miniatures with exquisite furniture and accessories.

"Jim started out making full-size furniture," Renee says, "while I did miniature replicas. One day he made a salesman's sample in miniature and decided that was the scale he wanted to work in too." Now, doing business as the Tin Feather, they produce two lines, the Shaker Collection and the American Country Collection. Patterned after classic New England furniture, all are exact 1"-to-1' scale reproductions of quality museum pieces and are made using the same techniques and decoration as the full-size piece.

From their Shaker Collection you can purchase a lilliputian sewing desk, an herb chopping table, a ladderback chair and footstool, or even three tiny Shaker boxes. More interested in the American Country pieces? Then take home a tiny decorated dower chest, or a five-drawer chest whose drawers each have hand-painted scenes of trees, houses, ships, and people. Want something even more un-

usual? Buy a child's potty chair or a weathervane of a mariner holding a brass telescope.

PRICES: $10–$950. Commissions accepted. Send $1 plus SASE for catalog/brochure.

VISITORS: Yes. Daily (except Wed.), 10 A.M.–5 P.M.

LOCATION: Southern Maine, about 20 miles south of Portland. The Tin Feather, 28 York Street, Kennebunk, ME 04043; 207-985-6279. From the Maine Turnpike, take exit 3 east for 1.6 miles. Turn south on Rte. 1 for half a mile. The shop is on the left side of street.

MORE: Work can also be seen at the Kansas City Miniature Museum and at the Christmas exhibit of the Abby Aldrich Rockefeller Folk Art Collection in Williamsburg (see listing under Virginia).

KENNEBUNKPORT

Craftsman Studio
HOOKED RUG DISPLAY

One of the largest collections of fine hooked rugs in this country, perhaps in the world, can be seen at Craftsman Studio, a supply house for the craft. Over 100 rugs are exhibited, including a very old

E. S. Frost, many rugs from the Old Sturbridge Village/McGown collection, and originals by Joan Moshimer and many others. Although these famous rugs are not for sale, visitors can purchase their own supplies here, watch a hooking demonstration, receive a free lesson, and take home a copy of the studio's publication, *Rug Hooker News & Views.*

OPEN: Mon.–Fri., 10 A.M.–4 P.M.. Closed holidays.

LOCATION: Southern Maine coast. Craftsman Studio, North Street, P.O. Box 351, Kennebunkport, ME 04046; 207-967-3711. Take Maine Turnpike to exit 2. Follow Rte. 9 to Kennebunkport. Go straight through Dock Square. When Rte. 9 branches to the right, bear left instead. Follow for 150 yards, then go over a bridge. Studio is third building on right after the bridge (there is a sign on the barn).

KENNEBUNKPORT

Claudia and Carroll Hopf
SCHERENSCHNITTE

*S*cherenschnitte is a Swiss-German word meaning scissor-cut paper designs. Snipped from a single piece of paper, these elaborate compositions formed borders on eighteenth- and nineteenth-century birth and baptismal certificates, house blessings, and personal love letters. Later, in the Victorian era, housewives used them as decorative shelf paper and doilies. Although continued in this country by the Pennsylvania German community, the craft generally fell into disuse until Claudia revived it in 1967.

"I lived in Pennsylvania at the time," she recalls, "and was researching lost crafts for presentation at a museum workshop. I came across Scherenschnitte and decided it was something I wanted to try. Since no one was doing it, I studied the old work and taught myself." Today Claudia creates intricate cuttings, paints each one in delicate earth colors, then carefully mounts them in a hand-grained frame made by her husband, Carroll. The result? A garden scene of flowers with a rabbit perched nearby, Noah coaxing his menagerie aboard the ark, or a woman hanging colorful items on her wash line.

PRICES: $35–$2,500. Commissions accepted (write Hopf, 13 Mechanic Street, Kennebunk, Me 04043). No catalog/brochure.

VISITORS: No.

MORE: The Hopfs' work is available through the Priscilla Hartley Gallery, Wharf Lane, Box 70, Kennebunkport, ME 04046 (summer only). For a list of other shops selling the Hopfs' work, send an SASE to the Mechanic Street address.

MONROE

Ron Garfinkel
POTTERY

*R*on studied pottery at the famous Penland School of Crafts in North Carolina before moving to Maine and founding the Monroe Salt Works. His studio uses traditional salt-glazes in combination with simple forms and colorful botanical motifs. Mugs have a rough-textured, stippled brown-and-white border surrounding bouquets of dainty, hand-painted Maine wildflowers. These pieces are somehow reminiscent of cups your great-grandmother might have used for her morning coffee.

PRICES: $6–$200. Commissions accepted. No catalog/brochure.

VISITORS: Yes. Mon.–Fri., 8 A.M.–4:30 P.M.

LOCATION: Central Maine, about 25 miles south of Bangor. Stovepipe Alley, Monroe, ME 04951; 207-525-4471. From Bangor, take Rte. 1A south 15 miles to Frankfort. Turn west on Rte. 139 to Monroe (8 miles), then north on Rte. 141 for 2 miles, bearing right at the fork. Go another 2 miles, then turn right. The pottery is the first place on the left.

NEWCASTLE

Marion D. Berry
PYSANKY

*U*krainian Easter eggs, called Pysanky, come from the verb *pysaty* ("to write"), because the designs are actually written on the eggs with a stylus and melted beeswax. The egg is then dyed in a variety of colors and the beeswax is removed by gently rubbing the egg near a candle flame. "There are many stories about the origin of Pysanky," Marion says. "My favorite is that Mary decorated eggs and offered them to Pontius Pilate while pleading for her son's life. As she prepared them, tears fell on the eggs, making dots which the dyes couldn't cover."

Marion learned this ancient craft from an elderly woman at a Ukrainian church in Pennsylvania. "In Ukrainian homes, a bowl of Pysanky is kept not only as a decoration, but to ward off evil," Marion recounts. "In western Ukraine, they believe an evil monster's power is limited by Pysanky. He is chained in a cave while attendants go out and count the number of Pysanky that have been made each year. If there aren't enough, the monster's chains are loosened and evil spreads throughout the world."

Marion won't guarantee her eggs will ward off demons, but she can tell you the meaning of every color and symbol she uses: brown means happiness and pink signifies success, a deer indicates prosperity, crosshatched lines represent Peter's fishnets, and pine branches represent youth and vigor. "There are so many colors and symbols," Marion says, "that I give each customer a sheet which explains them all."

PRICES: Individual eggs, $7–$15; collection of eggs, $50–$75. No commissions. No catalog/brochure.

VISITORS: Yes. May–Oct., Wed.–Sat., noon–5 P.M.

LOCATION: Central coast, about 40 miles northeast of Portland. P.O. Box 272, Hopkins Hill Road, Newcastle, ME 04553; 207-563-8975. Take I-95 from Portland to Brunswick, then travel 28 miles on Rte. 1 to Newcastle. Go left on Hopkins Hill Road; the house is a yellow Cape Cod immediately on the right.

NEW GLOUCESTER

Christian H. Becksvoort
CLASSIC FURNITURE

Even Christian's business card is made of wood. "I'm a second-generation cabinet maker," he says, "and in my designs I try to maintain a link with the past. Like much of the Shaker work I've seen at nearby Sabbathday Lake Museum, I emphasize function and simple lines."

Most of Christian's pieces are of American black cherry, which is a pale pink-tan when freshly sawn and then colors rapidly to a rich, reddish brown patina. "I take great care in matching the wood,"

Christian points out. "I match grain along the edges of boards, horizontal rows of drawers are always cut from one board, door panels above each other have continuous grain, and adjacent door panels are bookmatched."

Although he builds only thirty-five to fifty pieces each year, Christian offers a wide range of styles, from trestle tables to laminated cherry chandeliers and narrow fifteen-drawer collector's cabinets. Want your child surrounded by fine furniture? Then

Christian H. Becksvoort: Fifteen-drawer collector's cabinet. Black cherry. H. 50"; W. 14"; D. 15½". KIP BRUNDAGE

choose a graceful cherry cradle or a unique snow glider. The glider, patterned after an old-fashioned coach, has a body of polished blue-lacquered ash, an upholstered leather seat, and runners and bells of solid brass.

PRICES: $160–$17,000. Commissions accepted. Custom design services are also offered. The catalog/brochure costs $2.

VISITORS: Yes.

LOCATION: South-central Maine, about 30 miles north of Portland. P.O. Box 12, New Gloucester, ME 04260; 207-926-4608. Take Rte. 202 north from Portland for about 27 miles, then Rte. 231 to New Gloucester. Follow signs from Rte. 231 to workshop.

PORTLAND

The Stein Glass Gallery
CONTEMPORARY GLASS

Since 1970 this excellent glass gallery has exhibited some of the finest and most unusual glasswork being created today. Claiming to have the largest selection of functional, decorative, and sculptural glass in the Northeast, this gallery represents over thirty-five artists, including Bruce Pizzichillo. Bruce creates multilayered vessels of blown and constructed glass that also incorporate telephone wire, brass, aluminum, and other metals. Many of his pieces suggest whimsical renditions of space aliens, bizarre robots, or functional containers come to life.

PRICES: $25–$2,500. Accepts MasterCard, Visa, personal checks.

OPEN: Mon.–Sat., 11 A.M.–6 P.M.; Sun. (summers only), noon–4 P.M. Not wheelchair accessible.

LOCATION: In downtown Portland's historic district. 20 Milk Street, Portland, ME 04101; 207-772-9072. Take I-295 north to exit 4 (waterfront). Go across bridge, through circle, on Rte. 1A (truck route) to Commercial Street. Follow about half a mile to Market Street (DiMillo's Floating Restaurant is on the right). Turn left onto Market Street, proceed two blocks to intersection with Milk Street. Gallery is on left corner.

PRESQUE ISLE

Aroostook Micmac Council "Basket Bank"
TRADITIONAL MICMAC INDIAN BASKETS

Aroostook, Maine's northernmost county, is very unlike the more familiar coastal region. Sparsely populated, its land owned primarily by timber companies, it nonetheless rewards travelers who pass through it on their way to Quebec or New Brunswick. More French-Canadian than American, much of the population is bilingual, and travelers will sometimes come upon menus written only in French.

But before any European transplants came to Aroostook, Micmac Indians lived here and throughout eastern Canada. Once hunters and expert canoers, they transported their belongings in brown ash baskets. Later, when settlers began cultivating potatoes, the Micmacs produced sturdy baskets for harvesting the crop. Although machines now do the harvesting, Micmas continue to create these pleasing, functional baskets, as well as several modern adaptations.

"We still pound trunks of brown ash until they separate into thin layers by year rings," says David Sanipass, director of the Basket Bank. "Then we weave them into potato, picnic, backpack, and other baskets. But brown ash trees are getting harder to find, others are dying off, and someday our baskets may no longer be made." The Micmacs also weave specialty baskets, including fishing creels, laundry hampers with covers and handles, and small jewelry baskets embroidered with splints.

PRICES: $12–$64 (best-selling basket, $25). Accepts Master-Card, Visa. Catalog/brochure available.

OPEN: Sun.–Fri., 8 A.M.–4 P.M. Closed holidays. Limited wheelchair accessibility (no ramp).

LOCATION: Far northern Maine, 290 miles northeast of Portland, 160 miles north of Bangor. 8 Church Street, P.O. Box 930, Presque Isle, ME 04769; 207-764-1972. Follow Rte. 1 into Presque Isle. Located just off Main Street, first building on right, across from police station and fire department.

SABBATHDAY LAKE

Shaker Museum

The United Society of Believers in Christ's Second Appearing is the formal name for the religion that became known as the Shakers because its adherents danced and moved about during religious services. Today the Shaker Village at Sabbathday Lake is the only active Shaker community in the world. Diminished in number by its rule of strict celibacy, this community has recently attracted several young members.

Subsisting on homegrown vegetables and the income they derive from selling herbs, timber, and wool, the Shakers live a simple life even though they do not disdain modern appliances such as televisions and dishwashers. Although they no longer produce the range of fine crafts for which Shakers are known, excellent examples of these pieces can be seen in the museum's four buildings.

OPEN: Memorial Day–Columbus Day, 10 A.M.–4:30 P.M.; closed Sundays. Open on limited basis by appointment during off-season. Woodcrafts and hand-knit goods are available at the museum shop. Admission is $3 for adults, $1.50 for children. Tours are available. Not accessible for wheelchairs.

LOCATION: South-central Maine. Rte. 25, Sabbathday Lake, Maine. The mailing address is R.R. #1, Poland Spring, ME 04274; 207-926-4597. Take I-495 (Maine Turnpike) to exit 11, then go north on Rte. 26 to Sabbathday Lake.

MORE: The Shaker Library, located in the restored schoolhouse, has an excellent collection of Shaker books, ephemera, and resource materials. It also has a special collection of items concerning radical religious sects and communal groups worldwide.

SEBAGO

Jones Museum of Glass and Ceramics
TRADITIONAL AND CONTEMPORARY WORK

The ambitious mission of this museum is to "collect, preserve, and interpret the full range of glass and ceramics art, with pieces from all time periods and geographic areas." Although admitting that it still has gaps in its collection, the museum already owns over 6,000 pieces ranging from Roman pottery to contemporary American art glass.

"To us," says museum registrar Nancy Eaton, "the measure of man is very clearly illustrated by the objects he surrounds himself with and uses on a daily basis, from the upper-class items to Woolworth-type wares." Carrying out this philosophy, the museum exhibits rare antique glass as well as souvenir production pottery. As part of its promise to show the full array of ceramic and glass creations, there is an extensive collection of miniatures and toys, as well as an entire room devoted to reproductions and fakes. The museum also annually sponsors a schedule of lectures and several special exhibits.

OPEN: May 1–mid-Nov.; Mon.–Sat., 9:30 A.M.–5 P.M.; Sun., 1–5 P.M. Antique glass and ceramics are available at the museum shop. Admission is $2.50 for adults, $1.50 for students, and 50¢ for children. Tours are available. First-floor temporary exhibition spaces and library are wheelchair accessible; main galleries on second floor are not.

LOCATION: Southern Maine, 28 miles northwest of Portland. Douglas Hill, Sebago, ME 04024; 207-787-3370. From Portland, take Rte. 25 to Gorham, then right on Rte. 114 to museum sign in East Sebago.

MORE: An easy twenty-minute climb up nearby Douglas Hill provides a spectacular view of the White Mountains' Presidential Range.

TEMPLE

Stephen Zeh
TRADITIONAL MAINE BASKETS

When Stephen was teaching himself to make baskets, he sought advice from an old Penobscot Indian basket maker, Eddie Newell. "The best advice I can give you," Eddie said, "is to make them the hard way." Stephen took the advice to heart, and each basket he makes takes over thirty separate steps. "And every step is important," he notes. "You can't take shortcuts and still end up with a superior basket. For example, you can't use just any tree. Probably only one brown ash tree in a hundred is good for baskets."

A former woodsman who once supported his family by trapping, Stephen found the commercial pack baskets he used were unwieldy and fragile. "I wanted to make ones," he recalls, "which were both pleasing to the eye and had a solid feel of quality. Some commercially available baskets are made from splints that are cut *across* the grain of the wood; mine are cut *with* the grain, making them very strong." His baskets, which are made in a heavier weave than Indian ones, include traditional Maine potato baskets, an open carrier, and a swing-handle gathering basket.

PRICES: $85–$3,450. Commissions are taken "occasionally." Send $2 for the catalog/brochure to Stephen at P.O. Box 381, Temple, ME 04984; or call 207-778-2351.

VISITORS: No, mail order only.

MORE: Stephen's work is also available through Family Tree Antiques (6 Pleasant Street, Bridgton, ME 04009; 207-647-2874), Victorian Stable Gallery (Water Street, Damariscotta, ME 04543; 207-563-1991), and Thos. Moser Cabinetmakers (415 Cumberland Avenue, Portland, ME 04101; 207-774-3791).

UNITY

Perry Smith Terry Collection
Unity College
MAINE INDIAN BASKET COLLECTION

With over 500 baskets from the Micmac, Maliseet, Passamaquoddy, and Penobscot Indian nations, this museum's basket collection is the finest in the state. Although exhibits change annually, displays always include baskets from each tribe made from different fibers and for a variety of purposes. There are sweet grass and brown ash work baskets, birch bark and porcupine quill containers, and a variety of special-purpose baskets. Look for the Passamaquoddy "handkerchief" basket (a squat, flat basket whose wide splints are interwoven with narrow, braided sweet grass) or the "curly" basket (a fancy, round container covered with rows of tightly curled splints).

OPEN: Summer, Mon.–Fri., 8 A.M.–4 P.M. No museum shop. Free admission. No tours. Wheelchair accessible.

LOCATION: Central Maine, 85 miles north of Portland, 30 miles south of Bangor. Unity College, Unity, ME 04988;

207-948-3131. Take I-95 to the Fairfield exit, north of Waterville, then Rte. 139 to Unity.

WALES

Amy Pact
FANTASY WOODCARVING

Amy's woodcarvings always make you look twice. A three-paneled, carved wood screen appears to show a forest scene, but closer inspection reveals some whimsical surprises: a tree trunk becomes the head of a deer, a tiny flying dinosaur slips between branches, a curved line can only be an elephant's trunk, and an upper limb supports a beguiling female nude.

"Fantasy is an important part of my work," Amy says. "I studied art and design at Gothenburg University in Sweden, then apprenticed to Swedish and Swiss masters. Swedish woodcarving is much freer and more whimsical than traditional European work, and even ancient Egyptian carving is full of fantasy." Amy also creates wooden creatures

Amy Pact: *Midsummer Dream,* screen. American black walnut. H. 60″; W. 63″; D. 2″. JOHN TANABE PHOTOGRAPHY

(painted animals covered with brilliant splotches of color) and fantasy furniture, functional pieces that immediately became the center of attention.

Although much of her work adds a light touch to any room, she also accepts major commissions such as the 10′ risen Christ figure installed in St. Pius V Church, Queens, and ceiling moldings used in the restoration of City Hall in New York City.

PRICES: $50–$10,000 + . Commissions are accepted. No catalog/brochure is available, but she will send slides and other information on request.

VISITORS: Yes, by appointment only.

LOCATION: South-central Maine, about 45 miles north of Portland. R.R. #1, Box 1220, Station Road, Wales, ME 04280; 207-375-8094. Directions will be provided when appointment to visit is made.

DIRECTORIES

Members of the Maine Crafts Association are listed in its *Traveler's Guide.* Arranged geographically by region, each entry includes the member's address and phone number as well as a description (and sometimes a photo) of the member's work. The guide also includes information about a variety of Maine cultural events. Handy regional maps pinpoint the location of each member's studio and event. Send $2 to Maine Crafts Association, P.O. Box 228, Deer Isle, ME 04627. (NOTE: The association also has a slide file of its members' work, available for viewing at the group's office. Call 207-348-9943 for details.)

Directions, a statewide organization of professional craftspeople, also publishes a directory. Issued each spring, the directory is arranged by region and includes traditional and contemporary artisans: blacksmiths, potters, fiber artists, jewelry makers, and many more. Tiny print, however, means you need to include a magnifying glass in your ditty bag. For a free copy, write to Directions, c/o Nick Humez, P.O. Box 8763, Portland, ME 04104.

MASSACHUSETTS

From Cape Cod to the Berkshires, travelers will find contemporary and traditional crafts exhibited in museums, for sale in galleries, or offered by individual artisans. Galleries include one in business since 1900 and another housed in a former chicken coop. Museums display glass from the state's nineteenth-century art glass and pressed glass producers as well as quilts and textile embroidery. Other nineteenth-century crafts are demonstrated daily at Old Sturbridge Village. For a more initimate experience, visit Boston craftspeople who create contemporary stained glass, wall quilts, and unusual furniture; Nantucket Islanders who fashion traditional "lightship baskets," and other artisans who specialize in everything from pine needle basketry to Hebrew calligraphy.

AMHERST

River Valley Crafts
CONTEMPORARY AND TRADITIONAL CRAFTS

Have you ever hesitated to purchase a craft because you didn't know how to display it or how it would go with your decor? If so, this is the gallery for you. With an interior design consultant always on hand, River Valley Crafts can answer these questions and also suggest proper care of any item you purchase.

Featuring handcrafted contemporary and traditional furniture and one-of-a-kind 14K gold and sterling silver jewelry, the gallery also shows George Thiewes's fantasy garden glasswork and Mark and Melvin Lindquist's turned, spalted wood vessels. If you're looking for something even more unusual, see Nick Nicholson's small, inlaid wood boxes, which hold a collection of miniature brass toys including a rocking horse, a soldier with cannon, a teddy bear, ducks, and even a jack-in-the-box.

PRICES: $10–$3,000. Accepts American Express, Master-Card, Visa. Not wheelchair accessible.

LOCATION: West-central Massachusetts, downtown Amherst. 236 North Pleasant Street, Amherst, MA 01002; 413-253-7919. Take I-91 to Northampton, then go east on Rte. 9 to Amherst. Go to center of Amherst, take a left at the commons. Continue straight through two lights to fork. The gallery is directly on the left at the corner of Pleasant and Hallock.

MORE: Also worth seeing in Amherst are the Mead Art Museum's seventeenth-to-twentieth-century paintings and sculpture. The museum is located on the Amherst College campus, one block south of Rte. 9.

BOSTON

Society of Arts & Crafts
CONTEMPORARY FURNITURE AND CRAFTS

The oldest nonprofit crafts gallery in the United States unites an impressive legacy with a dedication to promoting today's emerging talent. Sponsor of America's first crafts exhibit, the society has maintained a gallery since 1900. Included in the list of craftspeople who have displayed their work here are craft immortals Louis Comfort Tiffany, Gustav Stickley, John LaFarge, and Will Bradley.

Continuing its original mission to identify and assist future master craftspeople, the society now represents over 150 artisans, 60 percent of whom are from New England. Located in a charming nineteenth-century bowfront building in the heart of Boston's cultural district, the gallery specializes in handcrafted furniture, including pieces by Everett Bramhall. A recent graduate of the Rhode Island School of Design, Everett creates furniture that redefines function and line. In one of his dinner tables, the legs extend resolutely above the surface, making them dominant and the surface a mere support.

PRICES: $15–$15,000 (average, $50–$150). Accepts American Express, MasterCard, Visa. Not wheelchair accessible.

OPEN: Mon.–Fri., 10 A.M.–5:30 P.M.; Sat., 10 A.M.–5 P.M. Closed Thanksgiving and Christmas.

LOCATION: Downtown Boston. 175 Newbury Street, Boston, MA 02116; 617-266-1810. Take I-90 (Massachusetts Pike east) to Copley Square exit, then Dartmouth Street south to Newbury Street. Gallery is located on Newbury between Dartmouth and Exeter.

MORE: Membership in the society provides 10 percent purchase discounts, invitations to exhibits and special events, and free access to a furniture slide viewing system where the work of more than fifty artists can be seen.

CAMBRIDGE

Lyn Hovey
STAINED GLASS

To many Americans, stained glass is associated with churches, Tiffany lamps, and even ersatz renditions in fast-food restaurants. Although modern techniques have made the craft more accessible to hobbyists, there are still a few superbly skilled artisans producing exquisite work. One of these is Lyn Hovey.

"I began drawing as a very young child," Lyn says, "then started formal drawing lessons at age ten. By age thirteen I was studying with an Impressionist and by fifteen I was a student at the Cleveland Institute of Art. The type of painting and drawing I developed led quite naturally to stained glass as my main medium." Lyn is equally adept at creating an elaborate pictorial church window, designing an abstract geometric skylight, or making a

dining room window sport Jack-and-the-Beanstalk-dimension morning glories.

Lyn is also one of the few people in the world who creates bent glass lampshades. "We bend the glass in our own kiln," he says, "and the result is a perfect combination of form and design." Sometimes the eye doesn't even see the lampshade, but focuses instead on an Art Nouveau iris or a sinuous peacock.

PRICES: $300–"unlimited." Commissions are accepted. The catalog/brochure costs $2.

VISITORS: Yes. Mon.–Fri., 9 A.M.–5 P.M.

LOCATION: Across the Charles River from Boston. 266 Concord Avenue, Cambridge, MA 02138; 617-492-6566. Take I-95 to Rte. 2 east. Follow Rte. 2 to its end. Bear right past Alewife Station and continue straight over the railroad bridge to Freshpond Circle. Concord Avenue is off the second traffic circle you will encounter, between Sozio Electric and the Citgo gas station. Go three-quarters of a mile; studio is on right side, just past Walden Street.

MORE: Lyn's work can be seen in many public and private buildings. A bronze lantern with stained-glass inserts hangs outside the main entrance of Boston's Old City Hall at 45 School Street, Boston; and there are nineteen of his windows at Saint Ambrose Church, 240 Adams Street, Dorchester (south of Boston, north of Milton).

CAMBRIDGE

Ten Arrow Gallery
CONTEMPORARY CRAFTS

Harvard University attracts not only some of the country's preeminent scholars but also any number of tony shops and galleries in the surrounding streets. Although there are other craft galleries in the area, one with staying power is Ten Arrow Gallery, which reflects the eclectic taste of owner Elizabeth Tinlot. Customers will find unusual jewelry by Yoshiko Yamamoto, Josh Simpson's blown glass, and Nancee Meeker's burnished topographic vases. For sleight of eye, see the trompe l'oeil furniture by Silas Kopf. On the closed front of one Kopf cabinet, seemingly open doors reveal a cat sound asleep on a pile of books.

PRICES: $10–$1,000 (average, $25–$200). Accepts Master-Card, Visa. Not wheelchair accessible.

OPEN: Mon.–Wed. and Fri. & Sat., 10 A.M.–6 P.M.; Thurs., 10 A.M.–9 P.M.; Sun., 1–5 P.M. Closed major holidays and Sun. in July & Aug.

LOCATION: Several blocks off Harvard Square. 10 Arrow Street, Cambridge, MA 02138; 617-876-1117. Park anywhere you can find a nearby space. Arrow is a short, one-way street between Massachusetts and Bow streets, near Putnam Circle.

DEDHAM

Judith Larzelere
CONTEMPORARY WALL QUILTS

"**I** turned from painting to quilt design in 1978," Judith says, "because I felt so much more at home with fabric and its visually accessible color than with mixing paints to apply on canvas. I incorporate as many as sixty colors in a single quilt, distributing them in tiny, mosaiclike bits of pieced cloth." Influenced by Seminole Indian strip-piecing, where many different colors are torn into strips, stitched into bands, and then sewn on to solid backgrounds, Judith uses narrow strips of color punctuated horizontally with tiny contrasting bands (see color plate #1).

"I try to use color to evoke a mood," Judith explains. "My designs aren't variations of traditional patterns, nor are they pictorial, although they do sometimes suggest images to the viewer." Indeed they do. Her quilts act as a virtual Rorschach test. A quilt with muted grays and blues banded in bright orange suggests the sparkle of sunshine on the ocean. In others, strips of green, yellow, and blue suggest a cubist butterfly, and bright alternating reds and blues might be an infrared satellite map.

PRICES: $2,000–$10,000. Commissions accepted. The catalog/brochure is free with an SASE.

VISITORS: By prior appointment only.

LOCATION: Immediately southeast of Boston. 254-C Westfield Street, Dedham, MA 02026; 617-329-4936. Directions will be provided when appointment to visit is made.

MORE: Judith's work is also available through the Randall Beck Gallery, 168 Newbury Street, Boston, MA 02114; 617-226-2475.

DEERFIELD

Memorial Hall Museum
TEXTILES

Deerfield Academy's original 1798 schoolhouse displays some important New England antiquities, including schoolgirl art, quilts, textiles, and Bangwell Putt, purportedly the oldest rag doll in America. But the highlight of this museum is work by the Deerfield Society of Blue and White Needlework.

In 1896 two Deerfield ladies visiting the museum came across a few fragile eighteenth-century embroideries. Realizing this superb work was being replaced by poorly designed, mass-produced, and aniline-dyed pieces, they decided to re-create the old needlework. First they experimented with natural dyes until they matched the old colors, then they dyed background linens as well as threads. Next, they painstakingly transferred old designs onto linen and provided a number of local women with detailed instructions and a bundle of carefully counted threads. As one of the first successful cottage industries in the United States, this work continued until the group disbanded in 1926. Many of these pieces are on display, including the more experimental designs.

OPEN: May 1–Oct. 31, Mon.–Fri., 10 A.M.–4:30 P.M. Sat. & Sun., noon–4:30 P.M. Open all holidays during six-month season. Museum shop on premises. Admission is $2 for adults, 75¢ for children. Self-guided tours. Wheelchair accessible by prior appointment (an elevator in an adjoining building is used).

LOCATION: Northern Massachusetts near the Connecticut River. Memorial Street, Deerfield, MA 01342; 413-774-7476. Take exit 24 off I-91 north, then go 6 miles north on Rte. 5. Museum is on corner of Rte. 5 and Memorial Street in Old Deerfield.

MORE: Visit old Deerfield's restored eighteenth-century homes. Many are open to the public on guided tours, including the Helen Geier Flynt Textile Museum, which displays period coverlets, needlework, and clothing. For more information call historic Deerfield, Inc., at 413-774-5581.

GARDNER

Peter Erickson
*STERLING SILVER FLATWARE,
HOLLOWWARE, AND JEWELRY*

If it's important to have a quickly recognized name stamped on the back of your silverware, head to Tiffany's. But if you want personalized quality and tradition that date back to colonial times, ask Peter to create a set of sterling silver flatware or individual serving pieces. "I'm one of the few independent silversmiths left who make anything other than jewelry," Peter says. "And I'm continuing work begun by colonial silversmiths. In fact, the flatware and hollowware patterns I use were passed down to me from my grandfather, with whom I apprenticed for five years. He, in turn, received the designs from the man who had the shop before him, and some may even go back to Paul Revere's time."

Starting with a small piece of sterling silver, Peter forges, shapes, and polishes it to create knives, forks, spoons, and serving pieces as well as bowls and cups. "I do make some jewelry," Peter admits, "but my main interest is in carrying on tradition. I want to create silverware you'll set next to your finest china, use on special occasions, then pass on to your children and grandchildren."

PRICES: $20–$2,000. Commissions accepted. A catalog/brochure is available.

VISITORS: Yes.

LOCATION: North-central Massachusetts. 119 Green Street, Gardner, MA 01440; 508-632-0702. Take Rte. 2 west to the first Gardner exit. Bear right, then go past three gas stations to light. Bear right at light on Elm Street. Follow Elm about 1 mile to the traffic circle. Go straight through traffic circle to Green Street.

GARDNER

Gardner Heritage State Park
CHAIRMAKING

Known as the "chairmaking capitol of the world," Gardner has a furniture heritage that began in 1805 with a single craftsman. A century later there were thirty-nine companies producing over four million chairs annually—now there are eighteen. If you're already in north-central Massachusetts, this unusual state park is worth a visit. Spotlighting Gardner's chair history, the Visitors' Center provides a variety of exhibits including locally crafted chairs, chair seats made from cattails and reeds found in nearby swamps, and an 8' chair kids can climb upon. There are also regular demonstrations of how to make fiber-rushed chair seats.

OPEN: Mon.–Wed. and Fri. & Sat., 9 A.M.–4:30 P.M.; Thurs., 9 A.M.–8 P.M.; Sun., noon–4:30 P.M. Closed Thanksgiving, Christmas, and New Year's. Free admission. Ask about tours at reception desk. Wheelchair accessible.

LOCATION: North-central Massachusetts. 26 Lake Street, Gardner, MA 01440; 508-630-1497. Take Rte. 2 to the Rte. 68 (Hubbardston/Baldwinville) exit. Follow Rte. 68 (Main Street) north three-tenths of a mile to the center of Gardner. At the five-way intersection, take a hard right, then follow Lynde Street to municipal parking lot. Small street straight ahead leads to the Visitors' Center.

JAMAICA PLAIN

Dale Broholm
CONTEMPORARY FURNITURE

"My aim," says Dale, "is not only to create furniture which is fully functional, but also to have it be visually challenging and stimulating." Influenced by seventeenth- and eighteenth-century American furniture, Dale reinterprets those designs

Peter Erickson: Sterling silver tomato server, pie/cake server, cake server, and pie server.

with exaggerated lines, spurts of color, and contradictory elements. A classic arched cabinet perches on legs resembling a ballerina "en pointe." Chairs surrounding a breakfast bar have graceful scooped backs of exotic wood and lightning bolt legs edged in bright colors. The sections of a drop leaf table are triangular rather than rectangular. No matter what Dale makes, the work always asks questions: Sculpture or furniture? Traditional or contemporary? Serious statement or whimsy? The answer? It's up to you.

Dale Broholm: Side chair. Curly maple, Bird's-eye maple veneer, pearwood. H. 48″; W. 20″; D. 18″. ANDREW DEAN POWELL

PRICES: $1,000–$16,000. Commissions accepted. A catalog/brochure is available for $2.

VISITORS: By appointment only.

LOCATION: Greater Boston. Box 653, Jamaica Plain, MA 02130; 617-524-0958. Directions will be provided when appointment to visit is made.

LEVERETT

Peggy H. Davis
HEBREW CALLIGRAPHY

Referring to herself as "your personal scribe," Peggy combines calligraphy and illumination to create a variety of ceremonial documents. "I particularly like creating Jewish marriage contracts [*ketubot*]," Peggy says. "I can make them very special, very personal. Although there's always been interest in Hebrew lettering, recently people have begun to accept it as an art form, a way to instill a document or invitation with special meaning and a connection to tradition."

Sometimes adding flourishes of gold leaf, delicate watercolor borders, or a scene of Jerusalem, Peggy also calligraphs sabbath blessings, Bat Mitzvah wishes, baby amulets, and even greeting cards. Putting additional meaning into a specific piece, she may write the words in flowing lines that suggest mountains and valleys, or shape the message in the form of a wine goblet. "I particularly enjoy designing a piece with a customer," Peggy notes. "I can incorporate their ideas and intention about an event by subtle use of colors, or the way I form a word."

Although Peggy specializes in Hebrew calligraphy, she also maintains a studio in Minnesota, where she used to live, that does not specialize in this. Her Minnesota assistants both work in English lettering, although "one also does Hebrew calligraphy and the other specializes in Chinese."

PRICES: $100–$3,000. Commissions accepted. Free catalog/brochure.

VISITORS: Yes.

LOCATION: Western Massachusetts. Studio: Leverett Crafts & Arts, Montague Road, P.O. Box 298, Leverett, MA 01054; 413-548-9070. Her home phone is 413-367-2096 (please do not call from Fri. evening through Sat. evening). Follow studio logo signs from Rte. 63 near Leverett. The Minneapolis studio is located at 3249 Hennepin Avenue South, Suite 257, Minneapolis, MN 55408; 612-822-5709.

Peggy H. Davis: Jewish marriage contract with papercut border designs. H. 29″; W. 23″. VISUAL TECHNOLOGY, INC.

LEVERETT

Leverett Crafts & Arts
CONTEMPORARY CRAFTS

First a chicken coop, then a box factory, and now snazzy digs for a crafts complex—all different reincarnations of the same building. Nestled in the hills of western Massachusetts, this structure now houses Leverett Crafts & Arts' two galleries, a spacious gift shop, and ten artists' studios. The work exhibited here is so diverse, and of such high quality, that all visitors should find something to suit their tastes and budgets.

Gallery director Liz Canali's miniature games in precious metals make perfect gifts. Who wouldn't like to shoot carnelian beads in a tiny, sterling silver pinball game? More interested in ceramics?

Look for resident artist Marilyn Coplin's pit-fired vessels or Mary von Blake's porcelain platters that resemble intricate hooked rugs. Leverett Crafts & Arts also offers jewelry, wood accessories, glass, and fiber, including traditionally inspired pattern weaving by Lisa Glantz. Can't make up your mind? Then just drop by the various studios to watch Leverett's top-notch craftspeople at work.

PRICES: $1–$4,500 (average, $40–$150). Accepts Master-Card, Visa.

OPEN: Tues.–Sun., noon–5 P.M. Not wheelchair accessible.

LOCATION: Western Massachusetts. Montague Road, P.O. Box 298, Leverett, MA 01054; 413-548-9070. Follow studio logo signs from Rte. 63 near Leverett.

LOWELL

New England Quilt Museum

Since Lowell was the first great textile manufacturing city in America, and the source of many fabrics used in making quilts, it is only appropriate that this museum decided to locate here in a former silk mill. Although definitely the new kid on the museum block, it already presents excellent exhibits as well as a full program of workshops and lectures. In the future there will also be quilting demonstrations and an archive for New England quilt documentation projects.

Textiles are too fragile to be permanently exhibited, so all displays are rotated at least every two months, providing repeat visitors with something new to see. Using part of their own collection as well as touring and specially curated shows, the museum has recently displayed New England and contemporary Canadian quilts and hosted an invitational show of famous quiltmakers' first and most recent quilts.

OPEN: Tues.–Sat., 10 A.M.–4 P.M.; Sun., noon–4 P.M. Closed major holidays. There is a museum shop, but it does not sell quilts. Admission is $2 for adults, $1 for seniors and children. Tours can be arranged; call for an appointment. Wheelchair accessible.

LOCATION: Northeastern Massachusetts. 256 Market Street,

Lowell, MA 01852; 508-452-4207. From I-495, take Lowell connector to Thorndike Street exit. Turn right on Thorndike and continue to stoplight at Dutton Street. Turn right on Dutton. First right is entrance to parking lot of Lowell National Historical Park. Museum is across courtyard from Visitors' Center.

MORE: Lowell National Historical Park includes restored mills, workers' homes, and the canal system of this former textile center. For more information write to 169 Merrimack Street, Lowell, MA 01852; or call 617-459-1000.

MIDDLEBORO

Anita G. Nielsen
WAMPANOAG INDIAN CRAFTS

A member of the Wampanoag tribe, Anita creates a variety of crafts, the finest of which are her finger-twined bags and belts. "I got interested in the crafts of my people," Anita says, "by watching elders at powwows. Relatives in my tribe always made beautiful things and I wanted to continue the tradition. I always tell my customers something about my culture so the items will have more meaning to the purchasers."

Finger-weaving is a traditional craft of Eastern Woodland Indians. In fact, colonial portraits of Indian leaders often show them regaled in wide, brilliantly colored, finger-twined belts. Finger-weaving is actually a unique version of flat braiding. Rather than using separate warp and weft threads, as is common in loom weaving, there is only one set of fibers, which take turns being the weft. Using this process, Anita creates hemp belts with decorative chevrons and fully lined bags with red borders and designs on a black background. In addition to finger-twining, Anita does beadwork and makes deerskin pouches.

PRICES: $8–$175. Allow at least 6 to 8 weeks for commissions. Send an SASE for catalog/brochure.

VISITORS: Yes, with prior appointment.

LOCATION: Southeastern Massachusetts, about 40 miles southeast of Boston, 15 miles north of New Bedford. 190 Wood Street, Middleboro, MA 02346; 508-947-4159. Directions will be provided when appointment to visit is made.

MORE: For a more detailed explanation of finger-weaving, see *Threads* magazine, no. 12, Aug./Sept. 1987, pp. 46–49.

Nantucket Lightship Baskets

Nantucket Island is a vegetated sandbar thirty miles south of Cape Cod. Once a fishing center and whaling port, it is now a destination for a deluge of summer tourists and a source for lightship baskets. Over 150 years ago, sailors were stationed on lightships off the island to warn against dangerous shoals and shifting sands. Spending months at a time on these floating lighthouses, sailors used the enforced solitude to craft sturdy, elaborate, rattan baskets with wood bottoms and swinging handles. Each basket was formed around a mold, made originally from wood ship masts.

Today Nantucket has almost as many basket makers as inns, and lightship baskets have become a pricey collector's item. Based on the sailors' designs, the baskets often come in "nesting" groups or with a lid that converts them into stylish purses. Although still functional for their original purposes of storing food, holding knitting, and carrying potatoes, they're much more likely to be seen on a fashionable arm in New York or Paris.

All Nantucket lightship baskets are not, however, created equal. Purchasers should look for tightly woven, evenly colored rattan on baskets that are perfect circles or ovals. Handles and rims should be smoothly finished; handles and lids should swing freely on strong hinges. Since many of the purse lids have ivory designs or scrimshaw, check for well-executed carvings and pleasing designs, and, to salve your environmental pangs, ask about the origin of the ivory.

Our recommendations: Visit in the off-season if possible and shop around before purchasing a basket. Although there are numerous basket makers on the island, here are several that offer something a little different.

NANTUCKET

Nantucket Basketworks

If you want to watch baskets being made, as well as see an array of styles, this is the place to start. "Ninety percent of our work is custom ordered," says Alan S. W. Reed, owner. "People want their baskets personalized or of a special shape. One couple even ordered a twenty-seven-inch oval basket to be used as a bassinet for their grandchildren."

For something a little different, buy one of Alan's picnic baskets or see Nap Plank's miniature lightship baskets. Adding a unique touch to some of the baskets, scrimshander Lee Ann Papale decorates ivory and whalebone handles and medallions with Nantucket wildflowers and landscapes. "I don't ever want our work to lack in diversity," says Reed. "That's a way we can keep interested and offer unique, top-quality work to our customers."

PRICES: $100–$15,000 (average, $1,500–$4,000). No credit cards.

Alan S. W. Reed: Nesting Nantucket lightship baskets. Maple, oak, ivory, whalebone. Diam. 2½″–11½″. Color scrimshaw by Lee Ann Papale. JACK WEINHOLD

OPEN: Mon.–Sat., 9 A.M.–5 P.M. Wheelchair accessible.

LOCATION: 14 Daves Street, Nantucket, MA 02554; 508-228-2518. 1 mile from downtown Nantucket, 2 miles from airport.

NANTUCKET

Chin Oo Manasmontri

A silk weaver as a young boy in his native Bangkok, Chin is now chef at his own restaurant and a craftsman of fine Nantucket baskets. He first visited the island in 1972, working as a gardener during a college vacation. His employer had signed up for a lightship basket–making course but became ill, so Chin took her place. "That was it," he says. "I loved making them and I sold my first one before it was even finished." Like other basket makers, Chin uses a mold to assure a precise shape for each basket. Unlike others, he returned to his native Thailand to have teak molds made.

In addition to more traditional sizes and shapes, Chin makes a shoulder bag with a woven leather handle, square purses, and even a tall narrow wine carrier.

PRICES: $400–$2,500. Commissions accepted. No catalog/ brochure.

VISITORS: Yes. June–Sept., daily, 10 A.M.–5 P.M., at 29 Center Street, Nantucket. Appointment needed, Oct.–May.

LOCATION: Summer sales—29 Center Street, Nantucket, MA. During the rest of the year contact Chin at 49 Miacomet Avenue, Box 2057, Nantucket, MA 02584; 518-228-4300.

NANTUCKET

Gerald L. Brown

"I made my first basket when I needed a present for a girlfriend," Gerald recalls. "My father made them part-time so I learned from him. I use white oak ribs and handles with exotic wood or ivory for the tops and bottoms. I make really nice baskets. You have to here—the competition between makers is so intense." Gerald's open baskets have either one or two small fixed handles, and one or two hinged handles or no handles. Bottoms can be of ebony, rosewood, black walnut, or even whalebone. But if you want Gerald's popular set of eight nesting baskets, you may have a five-to-six-year wait.

PRICES: $100–$1,850. Commissions accepted. Free catalog/brochure.

VISITORS: Yes.

LOCATION: 1 Old South Wharf, P.O. Box 1452, Nantucket, MA 02554; 508-228-4894.

NEW BEDFORD

New Bedford Glass Museum

To travelers casually passing by on I-195, New Bedford may look like an aging, depressed, industrial city. It is. But glass aficionados shouldn't let that stop them from seeing this museum's collection of local glass. Site of the longest continuous glass production in New England, New Bedford was a leader in the art glass movement and one of the first production centers to make electric lamps.

In 1878, New Bedford's Mt. Washington Glass Works created America's first art glass, called lava glass. Mount Etna volcanic ash was used to create its almost black color. Pieces of lava and samples of locally produced glass from 1866 to the present are on exhibit at the museum along with some oddities: one of only two glass violins in existence, and a vase designed for Queen Victoria, which was the first to combine uranium and gold oxides to produce a range of shaded colors.

OPEN: Mon.–Sat., 10 A.M.–5 P.M. (closed Mon., Jan.–April); Sun., 1–4 P.M. Closed Thanksgiving, Christmas, and New Year's. Art glass and contemporary crafts are available in the museum shop. Admission is $2 for adults, $1.50 for seniors, and 50¢ for children. Tours are available. Wheelchair accessible.

LOCATION: Southeastern Massachusetts. 50 North Second Street, New Bedford, MA 02740; 508-994-0115. Take I-195 to exit 15, bear right at "Downtown" exit. Right on Elm Street, left on William Street, left on Second Street.

MORE: Museum visitors can watch glassblowing and glass-cutting next door at New Bedford Glass Works, the city's only extant glass studio. Also worth visiting is the Whaling Museum, one and a half blocks away at 18 Johnny Cake Hill, New Bedford, MA 02740; 617-997-0046.

Northampton/Pioneer Valley Area

Over the last decade the woods and rolling hills of Massachusetts's Pioneer Valley have attracted over 1,000 professional craftspeople. Drawn to the quiet country along the Connecticut River and to the cultural offerings of the nearby Amherst, Hampshire, Mount Holyoke, Smith, and University of Massachusetts campuses, artisans have moved into renovated mills, refurbished industrial buildings and small studios. Inevitably, a spate of craft galleries has opened, many centered in Northampton, others an easy drive away. Although the shops vary in quality and longevity, the two below are a good starting point. For a list of other galleries (with map and restaurant list), contact Pioneer Valley Convention/Visitors Bureau, 56 Dwight Street, Springfield, MA 01103; 413-787-1548.

NORTHAMPTON

Artisan Gallery
CONTEMPORARY CRAFTS

Eyes glazed from seeing too many ceramics? Mind blown by hunting for just the right art glass? Attention splintered by contemporary furniture? Collect yourself and refocus on this gallery's sixty-five kaleidoscope artists. Decide how you want to view the world by choosing a scope with interchangeable handmade marbles, stained-glass wheels, oil-encased objects, or one that multiplies what you see by twenty-four. Exteriors of these wonderful adult toys range from wood, brass, and chrome to glass and painted paper.

Been following the beat of another drummer

too long? Then change pace with a porcelain ocarina or flute by Northampton's own Doug Deihl. Although the exterior of these unique instruments is a crackled glaze, the tone is pure and sweet. Doug also makes double penny whistles, double ocarinas, and a long flute that plays more than two octaves.

Artisan also offers the work of over seventy jewelers, a major jewelry box collection, and other ceramic, glass, and wood items.

PRICES: $10–$1,000 (average, $25–$65). Accepts American Express, Discover, MasterCard, Visa.

OPEN: Mon.–Wed. & Sat., 9:30 A.M.–5:30 P.M.; Thurs. & Fri., 9:30 A.M.–9 P.M.; Sun., noon–5 P.M. Closed most holidays.

LOCATION: West-central Massachusetts. 150 Main Street, Thornes Market "B" Level, Northampton, MA 01060; 413-586-1942. From I-91 take exit 18 (if headed north) or exit 20 (if headed south), then continue on Rte. 5 to center of town. Thornes Market is a large former department store now housing forty shops and galleries.

NORTHAMPTON

Pinch Pottery/Ferrin Gallery
CONTEMPORARY CERAMICS

Every autumn Leslie Ferrin throws a tea party that lasts almost two months. It's not a Mad Hatter happening, but an invitational exhibit where 200 artisans are asked to submit teapots, teacups, and tea sets. Since 1979, the gallery has been steeped with the largest variety of tea paraphernalia ever assembled: oversized and miniature; teapots in the form of cows, pyramids, or flying fish; rococo cups; austere minimalist tea settings. There's always something that will be your cup of tea.

During the rest of the year visitors will find contemporary crafts, including Mara Superior's unusual platters and cavorting animals wearing classic porcelain glazes, and husband Roy Superior's fantasy machines, so bizarre they make sense.

PRICES: $1–$10,000 (average, $25–$50). Accepts American Express, Discover, MasterCard, Visa.

OPEN: Mon.–Wed. & Sat., 10 A.M.–6 P.M.; Thurs. & Fri., 10 A.M.–9 P.M.; Sun. noon–5 P.M. Closed on national holidays. Wheelchair accessible.

LOCATION: West-central Massachusetts. 179 Main Street, Northampton, MA 01060; 413-586-4509. From Rte. 91 north,

take first Northampton exit. Go left off the ramp 1 mile to town, then left on Main Street.

PEMBROKE

Foster S. Campos
REPRODUCTION CLOCKS

Ticked off with modern clocks that don't rhythmically tock off the minutes or chime the hours? Yearn to actually *hear* the hours pass by? Toss out that boring digital timepiece and replace it with one of Foster's replica nineteenth-century banjo or shelf clocks. Faithfully rendered reproductions, Foster's clocks are made from mahogany or maple with hand-carved cases, hand-painted glass insets, and brass detailing and finials. Tastefully ornate, most have solid brass weight-driven pendulum movements that produce a soothingly audible march of time.

A clock maker for over thirty years, Foster began his career in 1946 as a furniture finisher. "But I met a Weymouth clock maker and started working as his assistant. I found it much more interesting work because I did a little bit of everything. At the furniture company they assign you one function and that's all you ever do." After working for the clock maker for over twenty-five years, Foster set out on his own. Now an award-winning clock maker, Foster sells his work through museum shops and from his home workshop.

If you're looking for an elegant shelf clock, consider Foster's replica 1810 David Wood featuring a solid mahogany case, crotch-veneered door, satin wood inlay, and hand-painted dial. For something more ornate, choose a banjo clock with intricately painted glass insets and gold leaf detailing, or a reproduction 1830 Lemuel Curtis Lyre Clock with a carved leaf motif.

PRICES: $500–$2,700. No commissions. Send $2 and an SASE for the catalog/brochure.

VISITORS: Yes.

LOCATION: About 35 miles southeast of Boston. 213 Schoosett Street, Pembroke, MA 02359; 617-826-8577. From Boston, take I-93/Rte. 3 south. Follow Rte. 3 to the Rte. 139

exit (Marshfield/North Pembroke). Take Rte. 139 west to Rte. 53, then Rte. 53 south to North Pembroke. Turn right on Rte. 14 to Pembroke.

PITTSFIELD

Hancock Shaker Village

Hancock offers a superb introduction to Shaker architecture, crafts, and life-style. Established in 1790, the village reached its peak in 1830 with over 300 residents who made their living farming, selling seeds and herbs, manufacturing medicines, and producing crafts. Over twenty of the original buildings have been restored and most are open to visitors.

Craft highlights include artisans who demonstrate traditional Shaker crafts including oval box making, basketmaking, tinsmithing, furniture crafting, and textile production. Highly recommended is a stop at the Sisters' Dairy and Weave Shop, where artisans transform wool shorn from village sheep and flax harvested from local fields into a variety of Shaker textiles. Many visitors are surprised at the bright colors and intricate designs used in Shaker weaving, especially in the finely woven rag rugs, which sometimes include vibrant oranges, blues, and greens. One thing that makes these demonstrations particularly appealing is that visitors can purchase all items produced by craftspeople.

OPEN: Memorial Day–Oct. 31, daily, 9:30 A.M.–5 P.M.; April, May, & Nov., 10 A.M.–3 P.M. Closed Thanksgiving. Museum shop on premises. Admission is $7 for adults, $6.25 for seniors, $3 for children over 6, free for children under six. Guided tours are available Memorial Day–Oct. 31, daily at 10:30 A.M. and 2 P.M.; April, May, & Nov., daily every hour on the hour.

LOCATION: Western Massachusetts. P.O. Box 898, Pittsfield, MA 01202; 413-443-0188. Take Massachusetts Turnpike to exit 1. North on Rte. 41 9 miles to Rte. 20. Turn left on Rte. 20 to village entrance.

SANDWICH

Sandwich Glass Museum

With plenty of woodlands for fuel and a small harbor providing transportation, Deming Jarves chose Sandwich as the site for his new glass factory. Operating from 1825 to 1888, the Boston and Sandwich Glass Works was one of the first companies to make glass by pressing it into a mold. Mechanical pressing meant cost reductions through mass production, so average families could afford glassware for the first time.

This well-organized museum directs visitors through rooms chronologically displaying Sandwich glass from early handmade pieces through pressed glass and on to patterned work made late in the company's history. There is also an entire room of glass candlesticks. A catalog/brochure is available for 50¢.

OPEN: Apr. 1–Oct. 31, daily, 9:30 A.M.–4:30 P.M.; Nov., Dec., Feb., & March, Wed.–Sun., 9:30 A.M.–4 P.M. Closed Jan. Sandwich glass reproductions are available in museum shop. Admission is $2.50 for adults, 50¢ for children. There are no tours, but docents are available for questions. Wheelchair accessible.

LOCATION: Southeastern Massachusetts, gateway to Cape Cod. 129 Main Street, P.O. Box 103, Sandwich, MA 02563; 508-888-0251. Take Rte. 3 across the Sagamore Bridge, then Rte. 6 to exit 2. Left on Rte. 130 to Sandwich. Bear left at island in town; museum is directly across from Town Hall.

SOUTH CHATHAM

Kathy & Robert Loring
PINE NEEDLE BASKETS

Like tiny shafts of wheat, intricate pine needle designs climb the sides and tops of the Lorings' unique basket-purses. Circling the lower sides are elaborate needlework designs made with thin strands of rafia. A carved ivory handle, lid medallion, and closing bolt and peg complete these unique collector pieces.

"The pine needle baskets we make are based on the coiled Pre-Columbian Indian ones," Kathy says. "It's one of the oldest forms of basketry in this hemisphere." Each of the Lorings' pine needle bas-

Kathy E. Loring: Large pine needle basket with Victorian rose scrimshaw. ROBERT O. LORING

kets is individually designed and takes four months to make. "First I design the basket," Kathy explains, "then Robert makes a wire form I cover with Madagascar raffia. With a sewing needle and thinner raffia strands I next weave the intricate inner designs. Then I shape Florida slash pine needles around the circumference of the wire forms. Finally, I line the basket with supple leather and coat the outside with several layers of shellac."

Although the Lorings also make well-crafted Nantucket lightship baskets, their pine needle basket-purses are what earn them a seat in the top ranks of America's craftspeople.

PRICES: Pine needle basket-purses, $2,800–$3,600; Nantucket lightship baskets, $125–$1,540. No commissions. The catalog/brochure costs $1.

VISITORS: By appointment only.

LOCATION: Far southeastern Cape Cod. Heirloom Baskets of Chatham, P.O. Box 1145, South Chatham, MA 02659; 508-432-8746. Directions will be provided when appointment to visit is made.

STOCKBRIDGE

Holsten Galleries
CONTEMPORARY GLASS

Whether you are a serious glass collector or just want an introduction to the virtuosity of today's top glass artists, redesign your itinerary to include Holsten Galleries. All of the contemporary Amer-

ican glass giants are here. Even if you can't afford the prices, just seeing the work of Harvey Littleton, father of the studio art glass movement, may well be the highlight of your trip.

Prepare yourself for brilliant colors, fluid shapes, frozen interiors, a slice of outer space, molten yolks. These glass sculptures will assault your emotions, soothe your eyes, and, above all, motivate you to succeed financially so you can take one home. John Lewis's pieces resemble masterful carvings from a subzero iceberg, Dale Chihuly creates nesting shell shapes, Vladena Klumpar captures blocks of underworld activity, Bob Dane combines blown and plate glass, and Michael Pavlik works with cast and laminated glass. There are so many others: Tom Patti, Gary Beecham, Molly Stone. . . . Discover the rest for yourself, but take a notepad. You'll want to remember these names!

PRICES: $1,000–$35,000 (average, $2,000–$4,000). Accepts American Express, MasterCard, Visa.

OPEN: Apr. weekends; May & June, Fri.–Tues.; July & Aug., daily; Sept.–Dec., Fri.–Tues. Closed Jan.–March. Wheelchair accessible.

LOCATION: Western Massachusetts, about 55 miles west of Springfield. Elm Street, Stockbridge, MA 01262; 413-298-3044. Take I-90 to Rte. 102, then Rte. 102 south to Rte. 7. In Stockbridge turn left from Rte. 7 on Elm Street. Gallery is located behind the post office.

MORE: Holsten Galleries has an equally superb gallery in Palm Beach, Florida; see the Florida chapter for details. While in Stockbridge there are two other art-related sites worth visiting. The first is Chesterwood, the studio of Daniel Chester French, who sculpted Abraham Lincoln for the Washington D.C. Lincoln Memorial. The plaster cast used for the monument is on display. The studio is located two miles south of the junction of Rtes. 102 and 183. Call 413-298-3579 for information. The second site is the Reuss Audubon Galleries, which has a large collection of Audubon lithographs. It's located at Pine and Shamrock streets; 413-298-4074.

STURBRIDGE

Old Sturbridge Village
DEMONSTRATIONS OF NINETEENTH-CENTURY CRAFTS

With over forty buildings, 200 acres of land, and costumed interpreters, Old Sturbridge recreates the daily life of an early nineteenth-century New England community. Although in summer a sea of Bermuda shorts may somewhat obscure your vision of the past, everyone should visit either Old Sturbridge Village or Historic Williamsburg in Virginia at least once.

In addition to the inevitable farm, blacksmith shop, and pottery, there are several unusual craft demonstrations which make the steep admission price seem almost reasonable. A village exclusive is strawbraiding, which once provided an alternative source of income to hundreds of New England households; rye straw was braided into strips, then used to decorate bonnets and hats. Visitors can also watch the entire coopering process, an accurate re-creation of a preindustrial shoemaking shop, and a bonnet maker fabricating both cloth and straw bonnets.

OPEN: Apr. 29–Oct. 30, daily, 9 A.M.–5 P.M.; Oct. 31–Apr. 28, daily, 10 A.M.–4 P.M. (*Except* Mon., Nov. 28–March 27). Closed Christmas and New Year's. There is a museum shop, but items produced by most demonstrators are not for sale. Admission is $12 for adults, $5 for children 6–15, children under 6 free (prices subject to change). No tours. Not wheelchair accessible.

LOCATION: South-central Massachusetts. One Old Sturbridge Village Road, Sturbridge, MA 01566; 508-347-3362 (hearing-impaired TDD number is 508-347-5383). From I-90 (Massachusetts Turnpike) take exit 9, then follow Rte. 20 west to village. From I-84, take exit 2 and follow Rte. 20 to village.

MORE: For quiet accommodations away from the village hubbub, try the Colonel Ebenezer Crafts Inn, c/o Publick House, P.O. Box 187, Sturbridge, MA 01566; 617-347-3313.

WEST SPRINGFIELD

ACC Craft Fair
CONTEMPORARY CRAFTS

People from all over the world plan their vacations to coincide with this fair, one of the premier craft events in the country. Sponsored by a subsidiary of the American Craft Council, this fair was first held in 1965 and has been located in West Springfield since 1983. Exhibitors are juried in by a highly selective process, with only the very finest crafts accepted. The fair features established master craftspeople as well as emerging talent, and an annual visit will keep you abreast of new trends in every medium. Our recommendation? Don't try to see it all in one day; take time to savor the array and chat with the artisans.

EVENT: Third weekend of June. Fri., 11 A.M.–8 P.M.; Sat., 11 A.M.–6 P.M.; Sun., 11 A.M.–5 P.M. Admission is $5 for adults, children 12 and under free.

LOCATION: South-central Massachusetts. Eastern States Exposition Center, 1305 Memorial Avenue, West Springfield, MA. Take I-90 (Massachusetts Turnpike) to exit 4. Proceed south on Rte. 5 about 4 miles to Rte. 147. Right on Rte. 147 for 1 mile to fairgrounds.

MORE: For information, write or call American Craft Enterprises, Inc., P.O. Box 10, 256 Main Street, New Paltz, NY 12561; 914-255-0039.

WORCESTER

Worcester Center for Crafts
CONTEMPORARY CRAFTS

The oldest nonprofit crafts institution in the United States, Worcester Center began in 1856 with classes for women who wanted to learn sewing, lacemaking, and weaving. Today the center continues to offer classes and workshops in addition to exhibits in both its main and atrium galleries and a gift shop representing hundreds of regional artisans. Particularly strong in textiles and ceramics, the center also features superb metalwork by Sarah Nelson, wood creations by Robert March, and a variety of glass, leather, and mixed-media pieces. If you're near Worcester during the third weekend in May, plan a visit to the center's annual juried craft fair.

PRICES: $15–$600. Accepts MasterCard.

OPEN: Mon.–Sat., 9 A.M.–5 P.M. Closed all major holidays. Wheelchair accessible.

LOCATION: Central Massachusetts. 25 Sagamore Road, Worcester, MA 01605; 508-753-8183. Take I-290 to exit 17 (going east) or exit 18 (going west). Follow to Sagamore Road.

NEW HAMPSHIRE

As you roam New Hampshire's lake and mountain regions, drop by local studios to see some of the state's finest traditional craftspeople: pewtersmiths and colonial coverlet makers, artisans who create authentic Shaker baskets or reproduction Shaker furniture. For contemporary pieces, meet the creators of vivid, kaleidoscopic wall quilts, sculptural furniture, and acquatically inspired mobiles. Bridging the gap is a Deerfield shoemaker who combines historic techniques with classic yet modern styles.

Prefer to see the crafts of many artisans all at once? Visit one of the League of New Hampshire Craftsmen's eight shops scattered across the state from Manchester to North Conway. Farther north, at Dixville Notch, watch artisans fashion crafts in the lobby of the luxurious Balsams resort.

CANTERBURY

Shaker Village

Begun with a singular vision of serving God, nineteen Shaker villages once dotted the East Coast from Maine to Kentucky. Fated to extinction by strict celibacy rules and increasing secularization, there are now only two centers where a few Shakers survive. One of these is peaceful Canterbury Shaker Village, now open to visitors.

Shakers were renowned for their crafts, which were both innovative and simple. At Canterbury, visitors can watch daily demonstrations of these special Shaker skills: oval box making, weaving, carpentry, and broommaking. Of particular note are this community's poplarware handkerchief and sewing boxes, which are made from woven strips of poplar wood. All items are available for sale in the shop.

OPEN: Early May–late Oct., Tues.–Sat., 10 A.M.–5 P.M. Open holiday Mondays. Admission is $6.50 for adults, $3 for children. Ninety-minute tours leave every hour on the hour. Not wheelchair accessible.

LOCATION: Twenty minutes north of Concord. If northbound, take I-93 to exit 15E, then I-393 to Rte. 106. Go north on Rte. 106 7 miles. Left on Shaker Road 3 miles. If southbound, take I-93 to exit 20. Go left on U.S. 3, right on Rte. 140 to Belmont. Left to Shaker Village (follow signs).

MORE: After shopping here, visit Martha Wetherbee in nearby Sanbornton for top-quality reproduction Shaker baskets (see entry under Sanbornton).

CENTER SANDWICH

Ayotte's Designery
HANDWEAVING

Nestled beneath the Squam and Sandwich mountain ranges, Center Sandwich was once a favorite retreat for poet John Greenleaf Whittier. Now a summer resort area, it is also the home and studio of an unusually productive husband-and-wife weaving team.

Robert and Roberta Ayotte met while attending the Rhode Island School of Design and have been textile design collaborators since 1958. Operating out of a rambling 1856 structure that once served as the local high school, the Ayottes' weaving studio is located in a former shop classroom. Visitors can watch workers at six large floor looms produce a variety of fabrics. In another area of the shop, colorful yardage may be transformed into sweeping capes, tailored vests, skirts, or other apparel. The Ayottes also produce a full line of rugs, pillows, and other items. Look for their colonial coverlets, woven with traditional fibers and colors, then finished with hand-knotted wool fringe. Although the Ayottes sell a variety of crafts, the textiles are the draw, including drapery, upholstery, and other fabric by the yard.

PRICES: $1–$495 (average, $25–$35). Commissions accepted.

VISITORS: Thurs.–Sat., 10 A.M.–5 P.M. Closed for vacation in spring and fall.

LOCATION: East-central New Hampshire. Center Sandwich, NH 03327; 603-248-6915. Take I-93 to Rte 3 (south of Plymouth), then Rte. 3 east to Rte. 113. Go north on Rte. 113 to Center Sandwich.

MORE: The Ayottes also sell a home-study course called "Handweaving with Robert and Roberta." Details are available upon request.

CENTER SANDWICH, CONCORD

See the League of New Hampshire Craftsmen listings at the end of this chapter.

DEERFIELD

Cordwainer Shop
FINE LEATHER FOOTWEAR

Ever wished for perfect-fit walking shoes to take on your next trip to Europe? Shoes that will go with everything, look superb, wear well, and are comfortable from the first day? Then these cordwainers may have the answer. "Cordwainer" originally meant a person who worked with cordovan, a soft, fine-grained leather. Later the word became synonymous with "shoemaker." Both definitions apply to the Mathews family, which has crafted fine footwear for three generations. "We hand-cut choice leather for each individual order," Barbara Mathews says, "then we hand-stitch everything, use veg-

etable-tanned leather linings and oak-tanned soles."

"Although our designs have changed over the years," Barbara adds, "they all emphasize total foot comfort. It's important your toes can wiggle and spread, but we also know that if you don't like the look of your shoes, you'll never wear them."

Both men and women have choices of sandals or sleek continental-style walking and dress shoes. Most come in either smooth leather or suede in a full range of colors. Problem feet? At a nominal extra charge, the Mathewses will do custom fitting. In fact if you're not satisfied with the fit, the Mathewses will replace without charge any order returned "unsoiled."

PRICES: $185–$295. The catalog costs $2.

VISITORS: By appointment only. Mon.–Sat., 9 A.M.–5 P.M.

LOCATION: Between Portsmouth and Concord. P.O. Box 10, 67 Candia Road, Deerfield, NH 03037; 603-463-7742 (days) or 603-463-7181 (evenings). Directions will be provided when appointment to visit is made.

DIXVILLE NOTCH

Crafts Gallery at the Balsams

Far northern New Hampshire has rugged remote mountains, a sparse population, and plentiful wildlife. This isn't a place where you would expect to find a grand old hotel set next to a crystal lake. But the Balsams Grand Resort Hotel, opened originally in the late nineteenth century, is full of surprises. With its white walls, red-roofed towers, and 15,000 acres of land, it manages to please all of your senses, even your aesthetic ones. In addition to cozy rooms, fine cuisine, and activities from croquet to golf and canoeing, the Balsams boasts a resident silversmith and a summer craft gallery.

Each week during July and August, a different visiting craftsperson sets up shop. One week it might be a quilter, the next week a wood carver or a Shaker basket maker. Guests can watch an item being created, chat with the craftsperson about technique and history, then purchase the perfect travel memento. Throughout the year, visitors can pause between a dip in the pool and a gourmet meal to watch Peter Lear create silver jewelry in his studio space.

DETAILS: From July 4th weekend through Labor Day, the visiting craftspeople rotate every Monday. Their hours are irregular, but they are generally present during the hours meals are served. Resident silversmith Lear is open during the summer season, Mon.–Sat., 9 A.M.–5P.M.; during winter, Sat.–Thurs., 3 P.M.–8 P.M. Nonresident guests are welcome to watch craft demonstrations.

RATES: Summer rates for double accommodations range from $105 to $140 per person per night and include all meals and activities (rates are subject to change).

LOCATION: The Balsams Grand Resort Hotel, Rte. 26, Dixville Notch, NH 03576; 603-255-3400.

EAST ALSTEAD

Tafi Brown
CONTEMPORARY WALL QUILTS

Multiple blue kaleidoscope images bordered by bursts of red form unusual wall quilts that marry photography with textiles. Using cyanotype, the original archival method of blueprinting, Tafi first photographs trees, wild flowers, or unusual objects. Then, instead of printing them on paper she prints them on cloth. "Afterwards," Tafi explains, "I piece and quilt."

The images, always blue, often appear as abstract designs until closer inspection reveals repeated, recognizable objects. Since Tafi is also a freelance architectural designer interested in timber frame house construction, some of the objects she photographs are house frames or workers atop rafters. Certainly not part of your standard quilt pattern!

"How long it takes to make a quilt varies with the seasons," Tafi adds. "Since the print is exposed and printed with natural sunlight, it may take me forty-five minutes in the winter to expose a print that would only take seven minutes in July." Tafi's work is getting good exposure year-round; some of

Tafi Brown: *1121 Pecos,* quilt. Cyanotype prints on cotton. H. 54″; W. 43″.

her quilts are displayed in corporate collections, including the collections of IBM, Bank of Boston, and Chubb Life America.

PRICES: $85 (small piece, not a quilt) to $10,000 (average, $1,000–$3,000). Commissions accepted. No catalog/brochure.

VISITORS: By appointment only, to clients seriously interested in purchase.

LOCATION: East of I-91, north of Keene. HC 63, Box 48, East Alstead, NH 03602; 603-835-6952. Directions will be provided when appointment to visit is made.

MORE: Tafi's work is also available through McGowan/Knipe Fine Arts (10 Hills Avenue, Concord, NH 03301; 603-225-2515) and the League of New Hampshire Craftsmen shops in Hanover, Manchester, and North Conway (see information on these shops at end of chapter).

ENFIELD

Museum at Lower Shaker Village

From 1793 to 1923 Shakers lived beside Mascoma Lake, supporting themselves with a packaged seed industry, an herbal medicine business, and through craft sales. They also invented the "Eclipse" corn seeder, a turbine water wheel, and the sulfur match. Some of the crafts are displayed in this new museum, but the real draws are the craft demonstrations and one-day workshops held here, which are perfect for travelers who want a peaceful day off the road. Visitors can learn basic tinsmithing, traditional rug hooking, Shaker woodworking, or even take two hours to explore the lush hillsides for Shaker medicinal herbs. The museum shop sells very good quality Shaker reproduction tin, textiles, poplarware, and furniture.

OPEN: May 15–Oct. 15, Mon.–Sat., 10 A.M.–5 P.M.; Sun., noon–5 P.M. During the rest of the year, open weekends only. Closed Christmas Day. Admission is $3 for adults, $2 for seniors, $1 for children 10–18. Tours during summer season only. Difficult wheelchair accessibility.

LOCATION: West-central New Hampshire. Rte. 4A, Enfield, NH 03748; 603-632-4838. Take I-89 to exit 17. Turn right on Rte. 4, then take another right on Rte. 4A to museum.

ENFIELD

Dana Robes Wood Craftsmen
SHAKER FURNITURE

Shakers created practical yet graceful furniture by using excellent joinery to assure durability and natural grain to emphasize simple lines and symmetrical designs. Now visitors can watch craftsmen create custom furniture using these same Shaker techniques. Located in the original 1813 laundry and dairy complex at Lower Shaker Village, Dana Robes and his craftspeople fashion everything from pegboards to cherry armoires.

"We encourage visitors to ask questions," says Robes. "They'll smell and hear the wood being cut, watch finishes being applied by hand. It's an opportunity to glimpse a time when perfection and quality were important. We try to duplicate this. For example, all of our drawers are made with dovetail joints in the front as well as the rear and are divided by dust panels. As a quality test, we put the drawers in upside down to check for squareness."

For armchair travelers, Robes produces a well-illustrated catalog showcasing his furniture, books on Shaker crafts, and a few other high-quality Shaker reproduction crafts including tinware, baskets, and stoneware featuring the Shaker Tree of Life pattern.

PRICES: $24–$3,900. Commissions accepted. For the catalog/brochure, send $1 to Dept. TGAC.

VISITORS: Mon.–Fri., 8 A.M.–5 P.M.; Sat., 9 A.M.–3 P.M.

LOCATION: West-central New Hampshire. P.O. Box 707, Enfield, NH 03748; 603-632-5385. Take I-89 to exit 17. Turn right on Rte. 4, another right on Rte. 4A to museum.

EXETER

See the League of New Hampshire Craftsmen listings at the end of this chapter.

HAMPTON

J. Donald Felix
WEATHERVANES

Sassy donkeys, delicate butterflies, a down-winged goose, a moose, and fat pigs are just some of the animals who will tell you which way the wind blows. Each individually handcrafted weathervane has its own personality. "I enjoy trying to capture these images as they appear in real life," Don says. "And by doing each one freehand, every weathervane is different."

For over twelve years, starting when he was in high school, Don worked in a high-production copper shop making lanterns and other items. Since 1970 he has been crafting weathervanes as they were originally made. "Not in molds or mass produced in Taiwan like so many that pass for 'folk art' today," he adds. "And all of mine tell true wind direction." Don also makes wall sconces and

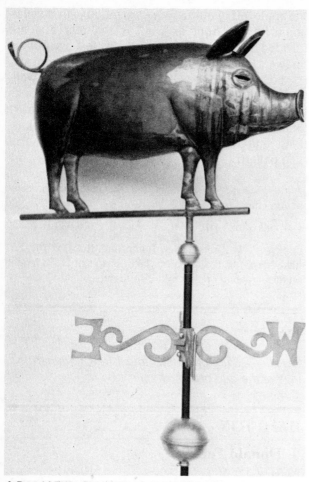

J. Donald Felix: Pig weathervane. Copper. H. 23″; W. 30″.

sculptures and specializes in custom work. "From a picture," he says, "I can make any style weathervane. Just ask!"

PRICES: $29–$1,000. Commissions accepted. The catalog/brochure costs $1.

VISITORS: By appointment only.

LOCATION: East of I-95 south of Portsmouth. P.O. Box 995, Hampton, NH 03842; 603-474-2225. Directions will be provided when appointment to visit is made.

HAMPTON FALLS

John Starvish, Jr.
PEWTERSMITH

John Jr. has big shoes to fill, big pewter shoes. His dad, John Starvish, Sr., began learning trades at the age of fourteen and became an accomplished silversmith, coppersmith, jeweler, shoemaker, and watch and clock repairman, but his specialty was always pewter. Recognized nationally as a master pewtersmith and repairman, he passed this trade on to his son, who continues the family business. "Our showroom," John Jr. says, "has always been a room in the house, the source of virtually all our sales."

John Jr. emphasizes that his pieces are meant to be used, rather than act as "shelf pieces." "I carefully roll all edges, then back solder them," he points out, "so after table use they can be washed without drawing soap and water into seams." Using tools his father made, John Jr. makes some modern designs, but his specialties are the traditional pewter classics: plates, tankards, goblets, and porringers (small dishes with a handle on the side used for porridge or as a child's bowl).

PRICES: $6–$250. Commissions accepted "occasionally." No catalog/brochure.

VISITORS: Yes.

LOCATION: East of I-95, 10 miles from the Massachusetts border. 64 Drinkwater Road, Hampton Falls, NH 03844; 603-772-5712. Take I-95 to Rte. 107, Rte. 107 east to Seabrook, then north on Rte. 1 to Rte. 88. Go west on Rte. 88, over I-95, and left on Drinkwater Road. Starvish Pewter is on the left.

MORE: John Jr.'s work is also available through Valley Artisans, Goboro Road, Epsom, NH 03234.

HANOVER

See the League of New Hampshire Craftsmen listings at the end of this chapter.

LINCOLN, MANCHESTER, & MEREDITH-LACONIA

See the League of New Hampshire Craftsmen listings at the end of this chapter.

MILFORD

The Woodworkers Gallery
CONTEMPORARY FURNITURE

Few galleries complement their exhibits as well as this one does. Owner Michael Ciardelli designed the building as a showcase for New England woodworkers. Carefully constructed of oak, using cabinetmakers' joints and wooden pegs, the gallery sports a winding staircase, arched windows, and a cathedral ceiling. "It ended up more elaborate than it started out to be," Michael says. "It turned into a finished work, like a piece of furniture."

In addition to running the gallery and helping out with the family's fuel oil business, Michael creates contemporary furniture using fine woods and simple lines. His gallery also displays the work of other regional furniture makers, all of whom accept custom orders and have portfolios at the gallery.

PRICES: Average, $100–$3,000. Accepts MasterCard, Visa. Commissions accepted.

OPEN: Tues.–Sat., 10 A.M.–5 P.M. Closed Mon. and holidays. Not wheelchair accessible.

LOCATION: 13 miles southwest of Manchester. 161 Nashua Street, Milford, NH 03055; 603-673-7977. From Rte. 3, travel west on Rte. 101A 10 to 12 miles to Milford. The gallery is seven-tenths of a mile past the stoplight at Lorden Lumber Co., on the left next to Woodman's Florist and before the railroad crossing.

NEW BOSTON

Jon Brooks
SCULPTURAL FURNITURE

When is a chair not a chair? When Jon suggests its form and function but provides no seat. Although it would be possible to sit on his *Cyclone* stool or

rest your glass on his *Gordon Below Franklin, Dam vs. No Dam* table, they're more likely to challenge your concept of what they were and have become. A brilliant yellow zigzag circle tops a natural three-pronged branch. An abstract flower? Yes, but also a

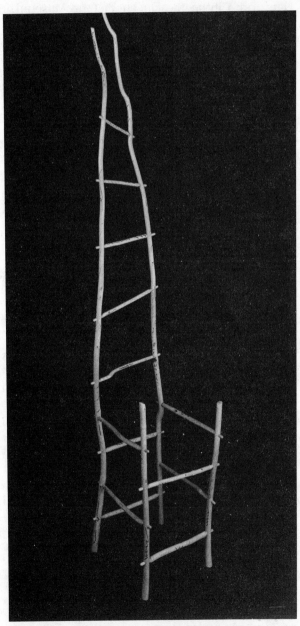

Jon Brooks: *Styx,* ladderback chair. Maple, colored pencil, gold, lacquer. H. 96"; W. 18"; D. 18". GEOFFREY KATZ

music stand. Spots of color appear on the black rungs of a chair; closer inspection shows they are stickmen and squiggles. Did Jon put them there? Or are they a visiting child's precocious scribbles?

Internationally acclaimed for his innovative explorations of furniture, Jon has pieces in public collections from the American Craft Museum in New York City to the Queen Victoria Museum in Australia. "I became interested in wood as a child," Jon says, "and was initially quite influenced by Brancusi's sculptures. Now I'm more often affected by seeing a tree branch, or by political/ecological issues." Whatever the motivation, Jon's furniture is provocative and innovative with a touch of humor just below the surface.

PRICES: $500–$5,000. Commissions accepted. No catalog/brochure.

VISITORS: By appointment only.

LOCATION: About 13 miles west of Manchester. Art Kamp, Pine Road, New Boston, NH 03070; 603-487-2780. Directions will be provided when appointment to visit is made.

NEWBURY

Annual Craftsmen's Fair

Over 450 craftspeople participate in America's oldest crafts fair. Since 1934, artisans and collectors have gathered for this nine-day event, which includes children's activities and craft demonstrations from glassblowing to lacemaking. Wear old clothes and be prepared to roll up your sleeves—this is a place where you can try your own skill at throwing clay, spinning, woodcarving, and other crafts. Don't know where to put all the items you've purchased? Stop by the "Living with Crafts" exhibit and let experts give you display tips.

EVENT: First Sat. to second Sun. in Aug., daily, 10 A.M.–5 P.M. Admission is $5 for adults, children under 12 free.

LOCATION: South-central New Hampshire. Mt. Sunapee State Park, Newbury, NH. The park is on Rte. 103, 3 miles west of Newbury.

MORE: For information, contact the League of New Hampshire Craftsmen Foundation, 205 North Main Street,

Concord, NH 03301; 603-224-1471. The last Sat./Sun. of fair is Folk Arts Weekend, featuring regional/ethnic crafts. Also, while you're here, take the triple chair lift (or hike on trails) to Mt. Sunapee's 2,700-foot summit for panoramic views of mountains and Lake Sunapee.

NORTH CONWAY

See the League of New Hampshire Craftsmen listings at the end of this chapter.

PORTSMOUTH

Strawbery Banke
OUTDOOR HISTORY MUSEUM

Portsmouth was originally called Strawbery Banke, named by English settlers for the abundance of wild berries growing along nearby Piscataqua River. With ten acres and forty-two historic homes, this outdoor museum may be too large and busy to be your cup of tea, especially on weekends in summer and early fall. On hand are a cooper, weaver, potter, and other "period artisans" common to such museums, with one addition not often featured—a boat maker. If period boats are your passion, brave the crowds and head directly for the Boat Shop, where craftsmen produce a variety of boats and dories (you can even take one home).

OPEN: Daily, 10 A.M.–5 P.M., holidays included. Admission is $6 for adults, $5 for seniors, $3 for children 6–17, children under 6 free. There are tours throughout the day; ask at front entrance. Not wheelchair accessible.

LOCATION: 454 Court Street, Portsmouth, NH 03801; 603-433-1100. Take I-95 to exit 7 (Market Street) and follow signs to museum.

SANBORNTON

Martha Wetherbee
AUTHENTIC SHAKER BASKETS

Martha Wetherbee removed the art of Shaker basketmaking from the list of lost crafts. "When I became interested in making them, I discovered there were no texts, no authorities," Martha recalls. "Since I was once New Hampshire's only licensed

Martha Wetherbee: Mt. Lebanon Shaker fruit basket with captured lid. Brown ash. O.H. 10″; H. 5½″; W. 9½″.

Martha's *Handbook of New Shaker Baskets* provides a brief history of each basket she reproduces and discusses the techniques she uses. Beautifully illustrated, the booklet may become a collector's item itself in the future.

PRICES: $60–$1,250. Commissions not accepted. There is a $4 charge for her *Handbook of New Shaker Baskets.*

VISITORS: Mon.–Fri., 9 A.M.–5 P.M.

LOCATION: 20 miles north of Concord. Eastman Hill Road, Box 116, Sanbornton, NH 03269; 603-286-8927. From I-93 take Sanbornton exit (exit 22). If going north, take left at end of ramp toward Gaza; if going south, take a right. Follow road for 3 miles to stop sign at Gaza corner. Turn left going north on Rte. 132 toward New Hampton. Follow for 2.25 miles, then turn right onto Hermit Woods Road (road will turn to dirt). Bear right on Eastman Hill Road. At the top of the hill look for BASKET SHOP sign, turn right to shop.

female private investigator," she says with a laugh, "I decided to put my skills to a new use."

Martha read old Shaker journals, studied baskets in museums, and took old baskets apart and reconstructed them. Slowly, she began to piece together the Shaker technique, which was originally learned from local Indians. Martha then worked on some of the finer details as the resident basketmaker at Canterbury Shaker Village (see entry at the beginning of New Hampshire chapter). Here the surviving Shaker eldresses let her use old molds and encouraged her efforts.

The legacy of this hard work is a collection of small, delicate, authentic Shaker baskets that begin with a brown ash log. Martha first removes the bark, then pounds the log until a year's growth is loosened. These layers are then cut into splints for weaving. "This takes two or three days of constant pounding," Martha says, "and leaves me with enough splints for thirty baskets, as well as some very sore muscles!" Martha then makes cat head (upside down they resemble their name), tatting, cheese, or other Shaker-style baskets.

WALPOLE

Jonathan J. Clowes
WOODEN MOBILES

A splash from the top of a wave, the skeleton of a long, curling comber—delicate, fluid, with constantly changing positive and negative spaces—Jonathan's mobiles reflect his love of boats and the rhythms of the sea. A boat builder and cabinetmaker, Jonathan has borrowed from each discipline for his mobiles. He incorporates the laminating techniques of boats with the subtle lines of exquisite furniture. Influenced by the playful sense of humor in Calder's mobiles, Jonathan bends and laminates hardwoods into gentle abstractions of the sea.

PRICES: $200–$10,000. Commissions accepted. Catalog/ brochure available.

VISITORS: Only for those commissioning work.

LOCATION: Southwest New Hampshire, along the Connecticut River. P.O. Box 610, Walpole, NH 03608; 603-756-3220 (please call only between 4 and 9 P.M. EST). Directions will be provided when appointment to visit is made.

WOLFEBORO

Hampshire Pewter

Producing a line of elegant pewterware, Hampshire uses a special alloy called Queen's Metal™. Formulated from tin, copper, antimony, bismuth, and silver, this alloy was considered so superior that British royalty at first reserved it for their own exclusive use. Now the common folk can also purchase this pretty but durable pewter. Although Hampshire makes everything from baby cups to table lamps, it is best known for pewter Christmas ornaments. These delicate decorations annually adorn the official New Hampshire State tree in front of the White House. Visitors can purchase reproductions of these ornaments and other items at the store.

PRICES: $4–$175. Commissions accepted. The catalog/brochure costs $2.

OPEN: Shop hours are Mon–Sat., 9 A.M.–5 P.M. Factory tours are given Mon.–Fri., 9 A.M.–8 P.M. (May 30–Labor Day), and 4 times daily Labor Day–Columbus Day.

LOCATION: East-central New Hampshire. 9 Mill Street, P.O. Box 1570, Wolfeboro, NH 03894; 603-569-4944. Follow Rte. 28 to Wolfeboro. Hampshire is located on Back Bay in downtown Wolfeboro.

WOLFEBORO

See the League of New Hampshire Craftsmen listings below.

League of New Hampshire Craftsmen Galleries

In the mid-1920s Mary Hill Coolidge, wife of Boston architect J. Randolph Coolidge, became interested in New Hampshire's burgeoning crafts scene, still in its infancy from a marketing perspective. Mrs. Coolidge helped boost the craft economy by sponsoring shows and helping to organize the League of New Hampshire Craftsmen. Today the league has over 1,300 members, with ten crafts shops throughout the state. It sponsors an annual crafts fair, craft classes, networking, public education, and advocacy. It also publishes an annual visual arts map to help visitors locate galleries, museums, craft shops, and studios. Each listing is keyed to the map and provides addresses, hours, and directions. For a copy, send a business-size SASE to: League of New Hampshire Craftsmen Foundation, 205 North Main Street, Concord, NH 03301; 603-224-1471 (or stop by during business hours).

CENTER SANDWICH

Sandwich Home Industries

In the mid-1920s, a declining economy spurred local residents to focus on crafts as an alternative economic base. A hooked rug and braided rug display in early 1926 led to the opening of a crafts shop that summer. Now known as Sandwich Home Industries, the shop provides an outlet for the work of local artisans.

PRICES: $2–$750. Accepts MasterCard, Visa.

OPEN: Memorial Day–mid-Oct., daily, 10 A.M.–5 P.M. Not wheelchair accessible.

LOCATION: East-central New Hampshire. Center Sandwich, NH 03227; 603-284-6831. Take I-93 to Rte. 3 (south of Plymouth), Rte. 3 east to Rte. 113. Go north on Rte. 113 to Center Sandwich.

CONCORD

Concord Arts & Crafts

Founded in 1932, this league shop offers a variety of items from traditional Shaker-style cherry chairs to unusual necklaces that combine modern designs with glass beads made by a technique that dates to 1200 B.C. Also worth seeing is pottery with an Asian flair by Derek and Lina Marshall.

PRICES: $1.50–$5,200. Accepts MasterCard, Visa.

OPEN: Sept.–June, Mon.–Fri., 9:30 A.M.–5:30 P.M.; Sat., 9:30 A.M.–5 P.M. July & Aug., Mon.–Fri., 9:30 A.M.–5:30 P.M.; Sat., 9 A.M.–1 P.M. Closed all national holidays except Martin Luther King Day, George Washington's Birthday, and Columbus Day. Not wheelchair accessible.

LOCATION: Downtown Concord. 36 Main Street, Concord, NH 03301; 603-228-8171. From I-93, take exit 14. Go west on Rte. 4 to Main Street, left on Main.

EXETER

This league shop features area crafts including Norton Latourelle's whimsical wood carvings of birds, fish, and other animals; Jane Kaufman's fanciful raku figures; Martha Wetherbee's Shaker baskets; and David Virtue's 14K gold "Victorian" jewelry.

OPEN: Mon.–Sat., 10 A.M.–5:30 P.M. Closed national holidays.

LOCATION: 12 miles southwest of Portsmouth. 61 Water Street, Exeter, NH 03833; 603-778-8282. From I-95, or Rte. 1, follow signs to Exeter. The shop is in downtown Exeter, across from bandstand, one block from Philips Exeter Academy.

HANOVER

Directly behind Hopkins Center at Dartmouth College, this league shop includes works of many talented local craftspeople.

OPEN: Mon.–Sat., 9:30 A.M.–5 P.M.

LOCATION: West-central New Hampshire. 13 Lebanon Street, Hanover, NH 03755; 603-643-5050. Take I-89 to Rte. 12A. Go north on Rte. 12A to Hanover. The shop is located directly behind Hopkins Center at Dartmouth College.

LINCOLN

The league's northernmost store offers a full spectrum of crafts including American-made ethnic items. Of particular interest is the pottery by Joseph Godwin. The dramatic multistrata surfaces of his work are created by carving through layers of different colored slips. For pure whimsy, buy one of

Dianne Shapiro's "Humane Trophies"—mounted fabric heads of not-very-ferocious hippos, moose, and other unwild mammals.

PRICES: 40¢–$1,000 (average, $10–$50). Accepts American Express, MasterCard, Visa.

OPEN: Daily, 10 A.M.–6 P.M. Closed Thanksgiving, Christmas, and New Year's. Not wheelchair accessible.

LOCATION: North-central New Hampshire. Main Street Marketplace, P.O. Box 1118, Lincoln, NH 03251; 603-745-2166. Take exit 32 from I-93, then Rte. 112 east one-quarter of a mile. Main Street Marketplace is on the left.

MANCHESTER

Specializing in one-of-a-kind home furnishings, this league shop is located in downtown Manchester's Theater District.

OPEN: Mon.–Sat., 10 A.M.–5:30 P.M.

LOCATION: South-central New Hampshire. 36 Hanover Street, Manchester, NH 03101; 603-623-4108. The shop is just off Elm Street, first block on Hanover.

MORE: While in Manchester, see the collection of New Hampshire–made furniture at the Currier Gallery of Art, 192 Orange Street; 603-669-6144.

MEREDITH-LACONIA

Near Lake Winnipesaukee, this league shop has a good selection of pottery and other functional crafts.

OPEN: Mon.–Sat., 10 A.M.–5 P.M.; Sun., noon–5 P.M. Closed Tues. & Wed., Jan.–March.

LOCATION: Central New Hampshire. Rte. 3, Meredith, NH 03253; 603-279-7920. On Rte. 3, half a mile north of intersection with Rte. 104.

NORTH CONWAY

Over 300 craftspeople are represented by this league shop, which opened in 1938. Particularly worth seeing is Linda Gray's paper jewelry, which combines the fragility of handmade paper with collagelike sculptural elements of silver and pearl, with silk and other fibers.

PRICES: 50¢–$3,000 (average $50–$150). Accepts American Express, Discover, MasterCard, Visa.

OPEN: Daily, 9 A.M.–5 P.M. Closed Easter, Thanksgiving, Christmas. Wheelchair accessible.

LOCATION: East-central New Hampshire near Maine border. Route 16, Box 751, North Conway, NH 03860; 603-356-2441. The shop is in a new, large building on Rte. 16, across from the Congregational church.

WOLFEBORO

For fifty years this league shop has been exhibiting work from Wolfeboro area craftspeople. Look for Peter Block's woodworking, Dorothy Conery's weaving, and Donald Blue's pottery.

PRICES: $2–$1,500 (average, $25–$75). Accepts Master-Card, Visa.

OPEN: Mon.–Sat., 9:30 A.M.–5 P.M.; Sun., 11 A.M.–4 P.M. Wheelchair accessible.

LOCATION: East-central New Hampshire. 9 Mill Street, P.O. Box 1570, Wolfeboro, NH 03894; 603-569-4944. Follow Rte 28 to Wolfeboro. In downtown Wolfeboro, Rte. 29 joins Rte. 109 and also becomes Main Street. Take Main Street north, along the shore of Lake Winnipesaukee, through the shopping district, to Mill Street. Turn right onto Mill Street then drive down the hill one block to Hampshire Pewter entrance.

RHODE ISLAND

If you aren't attentive while driving along I-95, you may miss Rhode Island. A mere speck on the map, this state, from offshore Block Island to quiet seacoast towns and Newport's grand mansions, is worth a traveler's time. Craft highlights include contemporary glass and jewelry artisans as well as shops offering folk art, Hmong needlework, and Native American tribal arts. If colonial crafts are your bailiwick, coordinate your trip with Ashaway's Labor Day festival.

ASHAWAY

Hopkinton Colonial Craft Festival

Pretend it's still summer! Visit this very noncommercial craft show, then eat a picnic lunch under the trees. Exhibitors, many in period dress, sell and demonstrate colonial crafts such as basketmaking, quilting, woodworking, stenciling, and making grannie dolls. This event is sponsored by groups who hope interest in the festival will spur local residents to establish a year-round historic village offering permanent craft exhibits and demonstrations.

EVENT: First weekend after Labor Day. Sat. & Sun., 10 A.M.–dusk. Free admission.

LOCATION: Southwestern Rhode Island, near Connecticut border. Crandall Field, Ashaway, RI. Take I-95 to Rhode Island exit 1 (Rte. 3), then go south on Rte. 3 for 2 miles. Just after Rte. 216 goes off to the left, Crandall Field will be on your left. Ample off-street parking.

MORE: Food and musical entertainment are provided by local groups. For more information contact H.O.P.E., Box 32, Hopkinton, RI 02833; 401-377-2054.

AVONDALE

Sun-Up Gallery, Inc.
CONTEMPORARY CRAFTS

Southwestern Rhode Island has a point of land that sticks like a comma into the ocean, then points toward Connecticut. Just inland is Sun-Up Cove, a pretty inlet along the Pawcatuck River. "We share our property," gallery owner Nancy Klotz says, "with swans and ducks." Complementing its setting, the gallery offers a collection of attractive pieces.

Among the craftspeople represented are a fine stable of Rhode Island artisans, including Jullian Barber, who creates colorful earthenware wall masks. In one, above the forehead of a smiling woman is a recessed spot awaiting a purchaser's planting of flowers or foliage, which will then become the mask's living headdress.

The gallery also has a good selection of jewelry, including mythological sterling silver necklaces by Robert and Rose Ann Place and the dramatic gold-on-brass work of Erica Zap. Tired of dressing like everyone else? Stop by the gallery's contemporary clothing area, an entire floor of wonderfully draped dresses, unusual sweaters, and stunning capes.

PRICES: $10–$3,500 (average, $50–$100). Accepts American Express, MasterCard, Visa. The annual fall catalog is free.

OPEN: Mon.–Sat., 10 A.M.–6 P.M.; Sun. (in summer and before Christmas), noon–5 P.M. Closed major holidays.

LOCATION: Far southwestern Rhode Island. 95 Watch Hill Road, Avondale, RI 02891. The gallery is 3 miles south of Westerly on scenic Rte. 1A, halfway between Westerly and Watch Hill.

NEWPORT

Matthew Buechner
Thomas Street Glass House
HAND-BLOWN GLASS

After seeing the ornate excess of Newport's summer palaces, visitors will find it a welcome relief to view the simple, graceful lines of the creations by this glass studio. Co-owner Matthew Buechner comes by his talent naturally—he was virtually raised under glass. With a father who was both president of Steuben Glass and director of the Corning Museum of Glass, it seems logical that Matthew became an artist in this molten medium.

Along with a small crew of workers, Matthew gathers 2,000° liquid glass on the end of a 4.5-foot steel blowpipe, then fashions vases, perfume bottles, paperweights, and other transparent finery. Shaped by hand with water-soaked newspaper and various tools, some vases emerge as gently curved shapes with a brilliant hyacinth-blue or ruby-red core.

Particularly striking are Matthew's "Emerging Form" perfume bottles, which resemble the outline of a stately woman swathed at the bottom in twists of opaque glass. The studio also creates bottles accented with gold leaf, transparent tourmaline-green bowls, and even Christmas ornaments. "Whatever I make," Matthew says, "is a total extension of myself. When someone buys one of my pieces, he is buying a small part of me: my time in making the item, my skill, and my sense of design and color."

PRICES: $6–$800. No commissions.

VISITORS: Mon.–Sat., 10 A.M.–6 P.M.; Sun., noon–5 P.M. The best time to watch glassblowing is 1–5 P.M. There is no catalog/brochure, but serious purchasers can request slides.

LOCATION: 688 Thames Street, Newport, RI 02840; 401-846-0576 (ask for Adrian). From I-95, 8 miles east of the Connecticut border, take Rte. 138 east. Cross Newport Bridge, then take the next exit (immediately after the bridge). Turn right at the bottom of the ramp, proceed to the second stoplight, then turn right onto America's Cup Avenue. Continue until you reach the Ark Restaurant, then turn right onto Lower Thames Street; continue to #688.

MORE: Even though Newport's opulent mansions often trip over the boundary of good taste, it's well worth visiting a couple to see how others once spent their summers. Be aware, however, that summer traffic, especially on weekends, is terrible. Try to visit off-season. For more information contact the Newport Chamber of Commerce; 401-847-1600.

PROVIDENCE

Donald Friedlich
CONTEMPORARY JEWELRY

You really *can* improve on nature, especially if you have Don's fine sense of design. By sandblasting slate, agate, onyx, jasper, and other stone, Don reveals uncommon features of these well-known materials, emphasizing subtleties otherwise missed. "My jewelry are abstract compositions involving tension, balance, and gesture," Don says. "Although Isamu Noguchi's sculpture and the abstract landscape canvasses of Richard Diebenkorn have influenced my designs, my inspiration is drawn primarily from four things: the simplicity and order of a Japanese garden, the stability and refinement of geometric forms, the delicacy and texture of handmade paper, and the monumentality of geological formations."

Don creates sculptural brooches by creating illusions and contradicting what is expected of a specific stone or material. Using a sandblaster to mimic the eroding forces that shaped the Grand Canyon, Don's Erosion Series exposes features rarely glimpsed in a raw chunk of agate or slate. To add even more dramatic accents and subtle commentary, Don sometimes adds a stripe of titanium or the contrasting luster of gold. He also creates a production line of less expensive jewelry that is also based on his unique design aesthetic.

Donald Friedlich: *Interference Series Brooch.* Slate, 18K gold. H. 2″; W. 2″; D. ⅜″. JAMES BEARDS

PRICES: $16–$3,000. Commissions accepted "only if they directly relate to the current work I'm doing." A catalog/brochure is available for the production line only; send an SASE.

VISITORS: By appointment only.

LOCATION: 70 Arbor Drive, Providence, RI 02908; 401-331-0119. Directions will be provided when appointment to visit is made.

PROVIDENCE

Peaceable Kingdom Gallery
Black Crow Gallery
FOLK ART AND NATIVE AMERICAN CRAFTS

When you visit 116 Ives Street, you can explore two fine shops at one location. Stop first at Peaceable Kingdom to see exquisite Pa Ndau needlework made by Hmong women who have been resettled in Providence. This gallery's other work also has an international focus, including textiles from Afghanistan and Latin America, clothing from China and Turkey, and primitive masks and shields. Black Crow, the companion gallery, specializes in Native

American pottery and jewelry, Kachina dolls, textiles, and beadwork. Ask to see the work of Anita Nielson, a Rhode Island Wampanoag Indian, who creates finger-twined bags from hemp.

PRICES: $6–$160 (average, $30–$75). Accepts American Express, MasterCard, Visa.

OPEN: Tues.–Sat., 11 A.M.–6 P.M. Closed major holidays. Not wheelchair accessible.

LOCATION: 116 Ives Street, Providence, RI 02906; 401-351-3472. From the east, take I-195 west to exit 3, follow Gano Street to Wickenden Street. Right on Wickenden, then another right onto Ives. From the west, take I-195 east to exit 2. Left onto Wickenden Street, then left on Ives. Galleries are on left side of street.

PROVIDENCE

Chang Xiong
PA NDAU *(HMONG NEEDLEWORK)*

Like a beautifully illustrated picture book, *Pa Ndau* tells a story without words. Made for centuries by Southeast Asia's Hmong women, this needlework originally recounted fables and recorded history for a culture that had no written language until the 1950s. Made of brilliantly colored fabric with intricate reverse appliqué and embroidery, a single piece can tell an entire fairy tale, or show scores of village scenes. Many traditional Pa Ndau pieces are actually stylized religious patterns meant to banish bad spirits or appease demons.

As a child, Chang Xiong learned this ancient art from her mother, and she now continues the tradition with only a few changes. Although she still hand sews the painstakingly tiny stitches that are a Pa Ndau hallmark, she does use a sewing machine for some work that does not affect the overall look and quality of a piece. Traditional Pa Ndau was also made in brilliant colors that Mrs. Xiong believes Americans find too extreme, so now she works often with more muted colors.

Although Pa Ndau is traditionally made only for one's own family, Mrs. Xiong's work is available to the public. Each one of her bedspreads, blankets, wall hangings, or caps (called *kaomoa*) tells its own story and is also part of the important heritage of the Hmong people.

PRICES: $5–$800. No commissions. No catalog/brochure.

VISITORS: By appointment only.

LOCATION: 69 Gallatin Street, Providence, RI 02907; 401-461-8398. Directions will be provided when appointment to visit is made.

MORE: Mrs. Xiong's work is also available through the Peaceable Kingdom Gallery (see preceding entry).

VERMONT

Country inns and winding back roads, not to mention ski areas and time-share condos, beckon hordes of travelers to Vermont. Overdiscovered in some areas, the state manages to retain much of the charm and gritty independence for which it is so famous. Reflecting the state's schizophrenic identity, Vermont's craftspeople create everything from traditional tin and pewterware to abstract glass spheres and haunting fabric collages. There's also a strong inclination to use local materials: granite for hand-carved tombstones, cedar and hardwoods for baskets or novelties, and soapstone for a variety of functional items.

Classic furniture (including Windsor chairs), violins, and guitars; hand-carved briar pipes; and stoneware fountains are just some of the items Vermont travelers can purchase directly from area craftspeople. Other crafts are available at the State Craft Centers in Middlebury and Windsor or at annual events such as Northfield's quilt extravaganza. Look also for official directional road signs, which feature a white spinning wheel on a blue background, that lead the way to some craft and antique shops.

BARRE

GRANITE TOMBSTONES, MONUMENTS

The world's largest granite quarry is near Barre, and it produces the famous, extremely durable, white and blue-gray stone. For over 100 years this granite has been crafted into some of the country's most beautiful monuments and tombstones, including several of note in Barre.

On the lawn of the former Spaulding High School is a 22-foot granite memorial to poet Robert Burns. Erected in 1899 on the hundredth anniversary of his death, the monument was a joint project of immigrant Scottish and Italian stone carvers. The statue depicts Burns walking home from a day plowing the fields, sleeves rolled up, gazing far away, perhaps captured by his muse. He stands on a pedestal covered with four intricately carved pan-

els depicting his cottage in Ayr, Scotland, and scenes from three of his best-known poems.

In nearby Hope Cemetery visitors can locate the grave of Elia Corti, the Italian stone carver who created the Burns panels. Corti was killed at age thirty-four, during an argument between socialists and anarchists, and his granite monument shows him leaning against a broken column, symbolizing his death in the prime of life. The detail work on this piece is exquisite, with the buttons, buttonholes, and seams of his coat clearly defined. Nearby are granite lambs on children's graves, elaborate crosses, and a mausoleum with granite filigree inserts.

Many of Barre's stonemasons searched for years to find perfect pieces of granite for their own family tombstones. Carved with love, these exquisite memorials dot area graveyards. At Elmwood Cemetery, granite tombstones range from the simple tablets of early colonists to gamboling cherubs, a hand-carved 30-foot spiral column, and an enormous angel. Another, marked simply "Max," shows a curly-headed little boy dressed in an 1890s-style outfit with high-button shoes and a ruffled dress.

ROCK OF AGES QUARRY AND MANUFACTURING PLANT: Tours are given May 1–October 31, 8:30 A.M.–5 P.M. The quarry is located in Graniteville, one mile south on Rte. 14, then follow signs for three miles. Call 802-476-3115 for information.

ROBERT BURNS MONUMENT: Take I-91 to White River Junction, then I-89 north to exit 7 (Barre/Berlin). Follow exit ramp through three lights. At third light bear to left to Barre (there is a sign). Follow road through two lights. At second light take a right onto Rte. 302. Follow Rte. 302 through Barre, bearing left at the park. The monument is on the left.

HOPE CEMETERY: The entrance is off Upper Merchant Street in Barre, Vermont.

ELMWOOD CEMETERY: Located near the intersection of Washington and Hill streets in Barre, Vermont.

BENNINGTON

Bennington Museum
VERMONT POTTERY, SILVER

The museum's 1798 musical tall-case clock, a major Bennington pottery collection (locally produced nineteenth-century salt-glazed stoneware and yellowware), and Vermont-made silver make this museum a worthwhile stop. There are also some oddities here to spark up your visit: a glass walking cane, a salt-glazed water cooler, and a 10-foot pottery "monument" that holds the bust of Christopher Webber Fenton, the founder of U.S. Pottery.

OPEN: March 1–Dec. 22, daily, 9 A.M.–5 P.M.; Jan. & Feb., Sat. & Sun., 9 A.M.–5 P.M. Closed Thanksgiving. Admission is $4 for adults, $3 for seniors and children over 12, children under 12 free. Tours by appointment only. Wheelchair accessible.

LOCATION: Southern Vermont. West Main Street, Bennington, VT 05201; 802-447-1571. The museum is on Rte. 9 (also called West Main Street), west of town center, on the crest of a hill leading to Old Bennington and Bennington Battle Monument.

MORE: While in Bennington, stop by Bennington Potters, a production pottery known for its "trigger"-handled cups. It's located at 324 County, Bennington, VT 05201; 802-447-7531.

BRIDGEWATER

Peter Bramhall
BLOWN-GLASS "INTERIORS"

The interiors of Peter's glass sculptures seethe with activity. Strands of multicolored glass appear to move perpetually inside a clear globe. Forget-me-not-blue filaments seem about to escape their transparent cage. "I'm influenced by nature," Peter says, "the sparkling water of a mountain brook, activity under the surface."

Some of Peter's "Interiors" are over 28 inches in diameter. "Few glass artists today work on such a large scale," he notes. "But I've also made soaring steel sculptures up to 19 feet high, as well as smaller cast bronze pieces and sumi ink drawings. I even write poetry. My work reflects the intermingling of all these different disciplines." In his spare time, Peter teaches glassblowing, drawing, and sculpture; is a volunteer fireman; and has designed and built his own passive solar home/studio.

PRICES: $125–$5,000. Commissions accepted. No catalog/brochure.

VISITORS: By appointment only.

LOCATION: East-central Vermont. P.O. Box 18, Bridgewater Center Road, Bridgewater, VT 05034; 802-672-5141. Directions will be provided when appointment to visit is made.

MORE: Peter's work is also available through Gallery II, 43 Center Street, Woodstock, VT 05091.

BURLINGTON

Vermont Hand Crafters
MEMBERSHIP DIRECTORY
SUMMER AND FALL CRAFT FAIRS

Vermont Hand Crafters is a juried membership organization that helps promote and sell Vermont crafts. Its annual membership directory includes each member's name, address, phone number, and a brief description of his or her work; travelers interested in a particular medium can consult the craft index for names and locations. Special codes indicate if individual artisans welcome visitors or have a catalog/brochure. Crafts include everything from dollhouse furniture to pottery whistles, bobbin lace to quilts, pewter goblets to gold pinecones. Vermont Hand Crafters also sponsors two annual fairs, a summer one in Stowe and a fall one in Burlington.

MEMBERSHIP DIRECTORY: Send $1 to Vermont Hand Crafters, Inc., P.O. Box 9385, South Burlington, VT 05403; 802-453-4240.

FALL CRAFT FAIR: The week before Thanksgiving. Thurs.–Fri., 10 A.M.–8 P.M.; Sat.–Sun., 10 A.M.–5 P.M. Admission is $1 for adults, children under 16 free. Held at the Burlington Memorial Auditorium. Take I-89 to exit 14W; go right at sixth traffic light onto South Union Street. The auditorium is at this intersection. Free parking at Perkins Pier; free shuttle to auditorium.

SUMMER CRAFT FAIR: Third weekend in July. Daily, 10 A.M.–5 P.M. Admission is $1 for adults, children under 14 free when accompanied by an adult. Held at the Stowe High School, Stowe, Vermont. From Stowe, take Rte. 108 west to Barrows Road and bear left (there will be a sign pointing toward Trapp Lodge). Turn left again at Ten Acres Lodge to high school on the left.

CALAIS

Jill Schultz
WOVEN HARDWOOD SNOWFLAKES

Jill guarantees that her snowflakes will never melt. "Living in Vermont with all our snow prompted me to create what I call my 'Shapes of Vermont,' snowflakes and hearts," Jill says. "The snowflakes cheer you; the hearts warm you. That's a good description of Vermont!" Made of maple, cherry, mahogany, or walnut, the woven eight-pointed snowflakes are a traditional Scandinavian craft. "And there's so much you can do with them," Jill points out. "You can hang them in a window or on a wall, pull apart the two four-pointed halves and use them to hold dried flowers, or even set the halves inside each other as the base for a centerpiece. Of course, the snowflakes also look great on top of Christmas trees!"

PRICES: $10–$21 (3′ size, $50–$60). Commissions "perhaps" accepted. There's no catalog/brochure, but Jill accepts mail orders. Write for details.

VISITORS: By appointment only.

LOCATION: About 20 miles northeast of Montpelier. R.R. #1, Calais, VT 05648; 802-229-0640. Directions will be provided when appointment to visit is made.

EAST FAIRFIELD

J.T. and D. Cooke
HAND-CARVED BRIAR PIPES

"Just think of us as elves in the woods," says J.T. "Hardworking elves. My wife and I make over a thousand pipes per year. Some are for the five different pipe labels we supply, a few are custom-made for collectors." Although the Cookes create a variety of classic designs and sculpted freehand pipes, their specialty is portrait pipes.

"In 1974 Deb, my wife, gave me a prebored briar block for my birthday," J.T. explains. "I carved my first pipe of an imaginary swami. Other portrait pipes soon followed, including ones of Albert Einstein and Abe Lincoln. Two years later I started working in the Briar Workshop in Stowe but eventually Deb and I moved to the northern woods and developed our own line of pipes."

Some of their more unusual work includes a Sherlock Holmes portrait pipe and an elaborate Pegasus pipe. "Anything the European pipe makers can do," asserts J.T., "we can do better, cheaper, and faster. Deb and I strive to be part of that famous Vermont Yankee craftsman tradition."

PRICES: $30–$1,000 +. Commissions accepted. Send $2 for photo-mailer.

VISITORS: Yes, by appointment only.

LOCATION: Far northwestern Vermont, about 50 miles north of Burlington. R.D. #2, East Fairfield, VT 05448; 802-849-6272. Directions will be provided when appointment to visit is made, "or we'll come to you—one wrong turn and you end up lost in Canada!"

ENOSBURG FALLS

Alan Stirt
TURNED WOOD VÉSSELS

Carefully turned wood bowls often reveal subtle grain and delightful coloring, but under Al's skillful fluting they also appear to be constantly in motion. By using wide flutes on the exterior, or fine-line carvings on a wide rim, Al's vessels whirl into view, elegant and fluid, static but stirring. "I looked at a lot of Chinese pottery," Al says, "and I was really taken by their fluted porcelain bowls. I've also been influenced by pottery from 'primitive' cultures and lately by African and Polynesian wood carvings, particularly the masks."

Al brings a master's eye and skill to his work but takes advantage of modern conveniences. Carving by hand gave him sore arms, so he now works with an electronically powered gouge. He also uses a microwave oven to dry his roughed-out bowls before carving and finishing them.

"I use local black cherry, butternut, and other woods for my salad bowls," Al says, "and wonderfully figured burls from around the country for my more sculptural work. My pieces reveal not only the wood, but also myself. I see my work as a means of self-expression as well as a way to show people the incredible beauty inherent in wood. Also, by relaxing some of my ideas of what a bowl should be, I've been discovering more of what it can be. The process is tortuous but exhilarating!"

Alan Stirt: Ribbed bowl, turned and carved. Bigleaf maple burl. H. 5¾"; D. 10¼".

PRICES: $100–$3,000. Commissions accepted. No catalog/brochure.

VISITORS: By appointment only.

LOCATION: Far northern Vermont, about 55 miles northeast of Burlington. R.D. #4, Box 1100, Enosburg Falls, VT 05450; 802-933-2125. Directions will be provided when appointment to visit is made.

MORE: Al's work is also available through the Vermont State Craft Center at Frog Hollow, Middlebury (see listing below) and Vermont Artisan Designs (115 Main Street, Brattleboro, VT 05301).

FAIRFAX

Cleland E. Selby
PRIMITIVE HOOKED RUGS

Real men may not eat quiche, but they do hook rugs. From football player Rosie Grier to elementary school principal Cleland Selby, men are succeeding in this predominately female field. "I've been rug hooking for over twenty years," Cleland says. "I think of myself as a painter who uses burlap and wools instead of canvas and paints. I used to watch my grandmother and mother hook, but they used prescribed patterns. I develop my own designs, New England scenes, folksy animals, Adams and Eves, generally with a good dollop of humor mixed in."

Cleland hand cuts strips of 100 percent wool, then hooks them into playful patterns: a frisky blue horse, a somewhat roguish Adam and Eve, or a fox "visiting" four chickens. His New England scenes are detailed and evocative. Sheep and cows sit in their pastures while a deer strolls through a nearby orchard; a complete town is shown, from the water-driven mill to a school and even outlying pumpkin fields.

PRICES: $300–$1,500. Commissions accepted. There is no catalog/brochure, "but I can send pictures of what is available."

VISITORS: Yes. Please call first.

LOCATION: About 25 miles northeast of Burlington. P.O. Box 271, Fairfax, VT 05454; 802-893-2236 (please call after 6 P.M.). Directions will be provided when appointment to visit is made.

Kristine Myrick Andrews: Basket. MARTHA R. PHOTOGRAPHY

MIDDLEBURY

Kristine Myrick Andrews
BASKETS

Kristine's rugged baskets are like Vermonters, self-reliant and practical yet undeniably attractive. Originally trained as a weaver, Kristine believes basketry is a comparable craft—only the materials are different. Instead of textile fibers, she now works with rattan, a Southeast Asian vine whose shiny outer edge is used for caning chairs. "I don't use that part," Kristine says. "Instead I work with the split center of the vine, which has a pleasing rough texture. Then I stain it for an even warmer, weathered look."

Although her designs are unique, they are based on Shaker and Appalachian patterns. "My baskets are aesthetically pleasing," Kristine admits, "but they're meant to be *used*. Take them to the garden to gather vegetables, store your yarn in one, or let a basket hold wood chips next to your fireplace."

PRICES: $10–$90. Commissions accepted. No catalog/brochure.

VISITORS: Yes.

LOCATION: West of Middlebury. Box 4220, R.D. #2, Middlebury, VT 05753; 802-545-2169. From Middlebury, go west on Rte. 125. A couple of miles after leaving town, take the second right, Sampson Road, at the top of a small ridge. Stay on this small paved road down the ridge, across Lemon Fair Valley, and through the crossroads. House is smaller clapboard house on the right just after the four corners.

MORE: Kristine's home is on Snake Mountain, which local lore says is named after its long, low profile in the middle of the Lake Champlain Valley. Others suggest the name derived from the mountain's exposed ledges and rock slides that served as good denning areas for rattlesnakes.

MIDDLEBURY

John Brickels
CLAY CONSTRUCTIONS

Out-trump Trump! Assemble your own clay real estate empire by acquiring reasonably priced Brickels buildings. Granted they may look like "fixer-uppers"; there definitely are some boards missing on one, a deteriorating roof in another, a teetering porch column here, some missing plaster

John Brickels: *Silo Barn*. H. 12″; W. 14″; D. 10″.

there, but think of the charm! Your chance to own a genuine 1950s diner, a Victorian house with a beauty salon in the basement, a genuine (though dilapidated) Vermont barn, or even a cabin with its own RV under the carport. No liens, no mortgages, no upkeep. Interested? See clay architect John Brickels.

"I was raised in a huge Victorian rectory surrounded with cavernous porches and turrets," John recalls. "And I've always been fascinated by architecture. I see it as just really large sculpture. My recent work is based on buildings I've seen along Vermont's back roads from elegant old houses to trailer homes and neglected barns."

"I work with stoneware," John continues, "using clay slabs to construct each piece. During the process, I leave my work uncovered to produce random warping. As it dries, the piece mirrors natural weatherization, the settling and aging that happen to all buildings. I also pile up a lot of emotional baggage inside each structure, like books, moose heads, period decor, or a set table in a totally bombed-out-looking building. It's a riot to watch people trying to figure out some big heavy meaning for my work. Actually, all I'm doing is having fun."

PRICES: $80–$1,200. No commissions. No catalog/brochure.

VISITORS: No.

MORE: John's work is available through the Vermont State Crafts Center at Frog Hollow (see Middlebury entry below); the Vermont State Craft Center at Windsor House (see Windsor entry); and Gallery 11 in Woodstock, Vermont.

MIDDLEBURY

Judi and Fred Danforth
Danforth Pewterers Ltd.
HANDCRAFTED PEWTER

Button, button, who's got the button? The Danforths do! Over sixty styles of buttons are part of the Danforths' "Maiden Vermont" production pewter line. Now you can button up with a scallop, rosebud, or dolphin; even hippos and giraffes will keep your clothes closed. Or you can fasten your coat with a barn or a country cottage. Rather wear them in your ears? You can do that too, since most designs are also made as pierced earrings.

Fred Danforth and his wife, Judi, also offer a line of high-quality pewter hollowware, items for the table, oil lamps, and small boxes. "Fred comes about his skills naturally," Judi says. "His ancestors include Thomas Danforth II of Middletown, Connecticut, who, with his six sons, were all well-known colonial pewtersmiths." "We use many of the processes they developed," Fred says. "We also spin pewter, a centrifugal casting process developed in the nineteenth century but not widely used today. And all our hollowware has an extremely fine satin finish."

PRICES: Buttons, $1.65+ each; hollowware, $8.50–$500. Commissions taken "occasionally, please inquire." There's a catalog/brochure that costs $1.

VISITORS: Yes. Mon.–Fri., 9 A.M.–5 P.M.; Sat. (May–Dec.), 10 A.M.–5 P.M.

LOCATION: West-central Vermont. 52 Seymour Street, Middlebury, VT 05753; 802-388-8666. North of Middlebury on Rte. 7, look for Mobil station on corner of Elm Street. If driving north on Rte. 7, turn left onto Elm. Go down the hill, beneath the railroad underpass, and veer right. Danforth Pewterers is about 100 yards farther, on right in a gray building.

MIDDLEBURY

Gary M. Starr
DUCK DECOYS

"Decoy making is really symbolic expression," Gary says. "An actual duck replica is difficult to create and impractical to use under most gunning conditions. The best decoys suggest a duck through simple lines, color, and attitude."

Gary should know; he carved his first decoy at nine years of age. "My father had a collection of over fifteen hundred decoys," Gary recalls, "so I grew up hearing about decoys and the lore of ducks and hunting. He used to say that decoy making was one of the few folk art forms originating in America. Indians formed crude decoys out of mud, reeds, and skins over one thousand years ago. More modern duck decoys probably were first made sometime before the Revolutionary War."

Gary M. Starr: Atlantic puffin. TED MERRICK

Using Vermont basswood, Gary hand carves and paints a variety of decoys including the Bufflehead drake and hen, a red-breasted merganser, and the sicklebill curlew. He also creates an Atlantic puffin, a common loon, and a 32-inch great blue heron. "Heron decoys," Gary notes, "originally lured herons who were shot for their feathers. Now they're used more as a 'confidence decoy,' set out with other decoys to give the impression of a natural surrounding."

PRICES: $90–$350. Commissions accepted.

VISITORS: Yes. Please call for an appointment.

LOCATION: West-central Vermont. R.D. #1, Route 23, Middlebury, VT 05753; 802-388-6552. Directions will be provided when appointment to visit is made.

MORE: Gary's work is available through the Vermont State Craft Center at Frog Hollow (see next listing for details).

MIDDLEBURY

Vermont State Craft Center at Frog Hollow
CONTEMPORARY AND TRADITIONAL CRAFTS

This is not a gallery where you can put one foot inside, swivel your head, and know instantly if you'll find something for your collection. There's too much here for that: nooks of innovative porcelain and glass, crannies of woodcarving, racks of fiber arts, and showcases of miscellany. With over 2000 square feet of space in this renovated paper mill, the center is a browser's delight of finely crafted items that don't have to (though some can) break your budget. To whet your appetite, here is a sampling of what you will see:

Fibers: Sharon Coleman's contemporary quilts use flowered materials in geometric designs to create a soft tension, like thorns under a fragrant rose. Mary Lynn O'Shea's superb tapestries are reminiscent of Georgia O'Keefe's designs and her stylish shawls occasionally end in a flourish of feathered fringe.

Ceramics: Karen Karnes's internationally acclaimed pottery; pure forms with clean lines and subtle salt-glazed surfaces in muted colors. Irene C. Eilers's earthenware dishes; deep blue, white, and terra-cotta slip designs with a Southwestern kick.

Other: John C. Sollinger's painted wood furniture includes his Holstein Collection of black-and-white stools sporting bright pink udders. Sabra Field's woodcuts are brilliantly colored outdoor scenes, some soothing, some not: Holsteins grazing in the autumn, a field of September corn, or the dark silhouette of a slaughtered deer hanging from a tree.

PRICES: $5–$2,500 (average, $10–$50). Accepts MasterCard, Visa.

OPEN: Mon.–Sat., 9:30 A.M.–5 P.M.; Sun., noon–5 P.M. Closed Sun. in winter. Wheelchair accessible.

LOCATION: Downtown Middlebury. Mill Street, Middlebury, VT 05753; 802-388-3177. Take Rte. 7 to downtown Middlebury, then Main Street across Otter Creek. After the bridge, take an immediate right onto Mill Street.

MONKTON

Peter E. Wendland
PORCELAIN AND STONEWARE FOUNTAINS

Many of Peter's fountains talk, or at least write their own notes. Some are quite chatty: "I am a nice fountain of clay," says one, boastfully. "Some of the minerals used in my glaze came from Lake Champlain, so I give you some of that big water's beauty and history. I make nice noises; I gurgle, shimmer, splash, eddy, and quietly flow. I make glazes shimmer. You can make the water come out of me in different places or tilt me so I make different noises."

Peter's fountains do have personality. The more subtle ones may have a slightly worn lily pad in the center, the more effusive ones are formed more like purple sea cucumbers. Most rest in bowls whose glaze resembles shifting patterns in the sand. There are also hanging fountains that marry slabs of tile with copper, sending streamlets of water to provide subtle background sounds. Although most fountains are about 34 inches by 30 inches, Peter says "You want one ten feet by sixty feet? I'll make it."

In addition to fountains, Peter creates utilitarian stoneware and porcelain pots and is an accomplished silversmith. Visitors will also find it a treat to visit his mountaintop studio/farm with its panoramic view of the Champlain Valley.

PRICES: Fountains, $800–$1,500 +; other items, $7 and up. No catalog/brochure.

VISITORS: Yes.

LOCATION: About 20 miles south of Burlington. Box 14, Monkton, VT 05469; 802-453-2167. Take Rte. 7 south from Burlington for about 15 miles. Turn left at North Ferrisburg and continue to Monkton Borough. In Monkton Borough, cross blacktop and go east on Boro Hill Road for 1 mile. You will see the Wendland sign on your left. Turn left up driveway and continue for seven-tenths of a mile to the house.

NORTHFIELD

Vermont Quilt Festival

Festival director Richard Cleveland has a "Salami Theory of Quilt Shows": "Running a quilt show is like eating salami—if you try to ingest the entire loaf at one gulp, you'll kill yourself, but if you take it a slice at a time, you can eventually swallow the whole thing." What started off in 1977 as just a few slices has become a Guiness-record loaf: one of the top quilt shows in the country, filling an armory with an enormous smorgasbord of design, color, and fabric.

Visitors can see antique quilts on loan from major collections, get their own quilts appraised, attend workshops and lectures, buy a ticket for the quilt raffle, or ask white-gloved "turners" to show them the backs of exhibited quilts. But the highlight is the annual "new quilter" contest. Open only to people submitting their very first quilt project, and limited to only 180 quilts, the pieces run the gamut from reproductions of traditional patterns to innovative abstract designs. All of them, winners and also-rans, are displayed in the armory in a dizzy kaleidoscope of color.

EVENT: Mid-July weekend, Fri. & Sat., 10 A.M.–6 P.M.; Sun., 10 A.M.–5 P.M. Admission is $5 for adults, children free. Additional fees for quilt appraisals, classes, and lectures. For more information contact the Vermont Quilt Festival, Inc., Box 349, Northfield, VT 05663; 802-485-7092.

LOCATION: Central Vermont. Plumley Armory, Norwich University, Northfield, VT. From the south, take I-89 to exit 5, then Rte. 12 north. Continue for 4 miles to the Norwich campus. The armory is on left side of road, just past main entrance. From the north, take I-89 to exit 8 in Montpelier, then follow Rte. 12 south into Northfield. The campus is half a mile past the center of town. The armory will be on the right.

PERKINSVILLE

Vermont Soapstone Co.

It may not be as pure as Ivory, but Vermont's soapstone has a texture that feels just as slippery as the real thing. Easy to carve, it is also known for its ability to retain heat longer than any other stone. Since 1850, Vermont soapstone has been quarried and crafted by this company into useful household products including griddles that cook pancakes to perfection, boot driers that can also keep a sleeping bag cozy, and bed warmers that, wrapped in flannel, can heat winter sheets, then, keep your feet toasty for hours. The company also makes soapstone sinks on request and sells chunks of soapstone to carvers.

PRICES: $14–$90+. Accepts American Express, MasterCard, Visa. Free catalog/brochure.

OPEN: Mill—weekdays, 8 A.M.–4 P.M. Gift shop—summer weekdays, 9 A.M.–5 P.M.; Sat. & holidays, 10 A.M.–4:30 P.M. Winter weekdays, 9:30 A.M.–4:30 P.M.; Sat., 10 A.M.–1 P.M.

LOCATION: About 38 miles southeast of Rutland. P.O. Box 168, Stoughton Pond Road, Perkinsville, VT 05151; 802-263-5404. Take I-91 to Springfield exit, Rte. 11. Continue to North Springfield, then right on Rte. 106 to Perkinsville.

PLAINFIELD

Edmond Menard
CEDAR FANTAILED BIRDS

Edmond didn't seek out his craft; it walked up his front porch steps and knocked on the door. One day in 1975, Chester "Birdman" Nutting stopped at the Menard farm to ask directions to a craft fair. On the backseat of his car was a suitcase full of small white cedar birds, each carved from a single piece of wood. "Chester showed them to me," Edmond recalls, "and I was fascinated. He said he always hoped someone would show an interest in carving the birds, to carry on the tradition. He died six months later, but before then he shared his special talent with me."

Nutting made over 50,000 of the birds, each one carved in about seven minutes. Now Edmond, who calls himself "Birdman II," makes about 3,000 to 5,000 a year. After cutting down a northern cedar, he roughs the wood into 8-inch blanks, wraps the blanks in cloth, and tosses them into his freezer. "They have to be damp when I work them," Edmond explains. When he's ready to carve, he forms the head, splits each of the 30 or more feathers with a knife, fans them out, then interlocks them.

"After I let them dry," Edmond says, "I finish the larger birds with a light coat of shellac, then add wing or tail detail with a wood burner." Some birds also get a daub of color on their wing tips, and tiny ones are given a glossy surface, then made into earrings or pins. Whatever their size, these simple, sweet birds carry with them the best of Yankee ingenuity and warmth. It's impossible to look at one without smiling.

PRICES: $5–$25. No commissions. No catalog/brochure.

VISITORS: Yes. July–Oct., Mon.–Sat., 8 A.M.–5 P.M.; Nov.–June, open by chance or appointment.

LOCATION: Northeast of Montpelier, midway between Plainfield and Marshfield. R.F.D. #1, Box 840, Plainfield, VT 05667; 802-426-3310. Take Rte. 2 north from Montpelier. After Plainfield, look for yard with large painted bird and BIRDMAN sign.

MORE: Edmond's work is also available through the Vermont State Craft Center at Frog Hollow in Middlebury, the Vermont Historical Society Pavilion in Montpelier, and the Trapp Family Lodge Gift Shop in Stowe.

Edmond Menard: Cedar fantailed bird. H. 3½"; W. 4"; D. 4".
SUZANNE CARMICHAEL

PLAINFIELD

Susan Norris and Fred Carlson
Beyond the Trees Musical Instruments
VIOLINS, GUITARS

When Susan was a little girl playing the violin, she always wanted to see what the instrument looked like inside. Now she knows! Susan is the violin maker in this instrument studio, and Fred specializes in steel-string guitars. Both served apprenticeships with established instrument makers before starting their own studio. Everything is custom-made from quality woods. "We try to use local or North American woods whenever we can," Susan says, "out of concern for the endangered tropical rain forests."

They also design violins and guitars that use extra strings. "These sympathetic strings resonate when the others are played," Fred explains. "Susan developed a violin with five bowed strings which combines the range of the violin and viola and has up to eleven sympathetic strings." Fred also creates an asymmetrical guitar with sympathetic strings.

Susan and Fred also offer a repair service and make a range of other instruments, including violas da gamba and violas d'amore, rebecs, dulcimers, and hardanger fiddles. "Most of our inspiration," Susan says, "comes from the beauty of Vermont. We often get new ideas while out walking in the woods and meadows."

PRICES: $500–$5,000. Commissions accepted. Send an SASE for the catalog/brochure.

VISITORS: Yes. By appointment only.

LOCATION: About 10 miles northeast of Montpelier. R.D. #1, Box 2250, Plainfield, VT 05667; 802-479-0862 or 802-467-6097. Directions will be provided when appointment to visit is made.

ST. JOHNSBURY

Stephen Hunek
ANIMAL SCULPTURES, RELIEF CARVINGS, CABINETWORK

Most of us have to wait a lifetime for our fifteen minutes of Warholian fame, but for Stephen Hunek it came early and stayed. An antiques dealer who carved purely for personal pleasure, Stephen was catapulted to fame in 1983 by a quirky occurrence. Returning to his pickup after delivering antiques, Stephen noticed a man rifling through the blankets in the back of the truck. As Stephen approached to wave him off, the man pulled out one of Stephen's carvings, a painted angel, and asked how much it cost. Stephen flippantly answered "one thousand dollars." The man, a Manhattan art dealer, immediately pulled out his wallet and handed Stephen $1,000 cash.

Since then Stephen's whimsical carvings and intricate folk cabinetry have met with phenomenal success, including one-man shows in New York, purchases by major private and public collections, and praise by some of the country's toughest art critics. None of this seems to have gone to Stephen's head. He continues to live in a restored eighteenth-century farmhouse outside of St. Johnsbury, begins carving daily at 4 A.M., and retains the same enthusiasm for his work that he had before his instant fame.

Noted for his life-size folk carvings of dogs and cats, one of Stephen's most popular works is the 6-foot high, 12-foot long *Dog Walker*, which includes a life-size man walking a menagerie of nine dogs. Another favorite is *Cat Doors*, which depicts the front half of a cat emerging onto a checkered floor from a hole in a regular-sized door. There are also carvings of sheep, a flying dalmatian, and even a nun holding a Hershey bar. As versatile as he is talented, Stephen also creates intricately carved and painted cabinetry, including a *State of Vermont* cabinet celebrating the state from cows to apples (see color plate #2).

PRICES: $200–$20,000. No commissions. For the free catalog/brochure, write to Stephen at R.F.D. #1, St. Johnsbury, VT, 05819.

VISITORS: No.

MORE: Stephen's work is also available locally through the Vermont State Craft Center at Frog Hollow (see listing under

Middlebury). Although you won't be able to visit Stephen if you're in the St. Johnsbury area, one stop worth making is the St. Johnsbury Athenaeum Art Gallery. This museum has a superb collection of Hudson River School paintings, including Bierstadt's *The Domes of Yosemite.*

SHOREHAM

Gordon and Christopher Bretschneider
CLASSICAL FURNITURE

This father-son team crafts fine furniture by borrowing from traditional designs and modifying them for modern tastes. A mahogany chest of drawers or headboard may suggest Chippendale but has fewer of the elaborate and expensive details that are unlikely to appeal to modern tastes or budgets. Although the Bretschneiders are acknowledged as master craftsmen, much of their skill is hidden from the casual viewer in perfectly made joints that assure the piece will never come apart. The finish is also an integral part of every design, a rich, warm surface that appears "natural" but is the result of meticulous sanding, staining, and up to eight coats of hand-rubbed oil.

Although the Bretschneiders also make more contemporary furniture, the quality shines best from their more classic pieces: a Chippendale mirror with a carved Phoenix, a Willard-style grandfather clock, or an executive stand-up desk of mahogany and subtle brass fittings.

PRICES: $500–"no limit." Commissions accepted. No catalog/brochure.

VISITORS: Yes.

LOCATION: About 40 miles south of Burlington. Box 12, School Street, Shoreham, VT 05770; 802-897-2621. From Rte. 22A between Fair Haven and Vergennes, take Rte. 74 west one block. Turn left at church, go to first mailbox on right, and drive to a white Federal house with black shutters.

MORE: The Bretschneiders' work is also available through the Vermont State Craft Center at Frog Hollow in Middlebury and the Windsor State Craft Center in Windsor.

SOUTH WOODBURY

David Sawyer
WINDSOR CHAIRS

David Sawyer decided that being a mechanical engineer was too far removed from actually making things, so he started fabricating wooden pitchforks. Later he graduated to crafting ladderback chairs, then creating the Windsor chairs that now mark him as a master woodworker.

Developed in seventeenth-century England as an alternative to Rigid Queen Anne pieces, the Windsor's delicacy belies its strength. Both features are a function of time-tested techniques. "My chairs are made like the Windsors of two hundred years ago," David says. "I use the same materials and most of the same tools, although my lathe has a motor instead of foot power and I occasionally use a bandsaw. But ninety-eight percent of every chair is hand work: careful shaving, carving, turning, bending, fitting, and finishing."

Although he follows the design of traditional Windsor chairs, David has refined their comfort and grace. "I curve the back a bit more to make it more comfortable for sitting," he points out, "and I've designed a Windsor rocker." Preferring to finish the chairs in the original milky greens or browns, he also offers "natural chairs" with oil-finished butternut seats, cherry turnings, and oak backs.

PRICES: $400–$1,000. Commissions accepted. Send an SASE for the catalog/brochure.

VISITORS: Yes (but prefers appointment).

LOCATION: South Woodbury, Vermont, about 25 miles northeast of Montpelier. The mailing address is R.D. #1, Box 107, East Calais, VT 05650; 802-456-8836. From Montpelier, take Rte. 14 north. David's home/shop is located in the center of South Woodbury, just off Rte. 14.

MORE: David's wife, Susan, creates traditional quilts in a range of subtle hues.

STOWE

Vermont Hand Crafts
SUMMER CRAFT FAIR

See listing and description of Vermont Hand Crafters activities under Burlington.

WESTON

David Lee Claggett
TINSMITH

Everyone knows you give silver gifts for a twenty-fifth wedding anniversary, but how many recall you're supposed to give tin on the tenth? During the height of the Tin Age in America (1780–1840) tinsmiths made tenth anniversary gifts by copying items normally made from other materials. David now reproduces these unusual objects for modern celebrants. One popular piece is an 8-foot tin basket with fragile, twisted sides and fluted edges. Even more unusual are the tin top hat and bonnet that couples once wore during anniversary festivities. Crafted to look like the real thing, the bonnet has all the features of the original cloth model: crimped sides, a flared back, frills, curls, and even two brass bows.

But David's real specialties are the items that once lighted American homes. Using the same type of tinplate, tools, and techniques employed over 200 years ago, he crafts mirrored sconces, intricately pierced table lanterns, and elegant two-tiered chandeliers. Over 100 of these items are illustrated in David's outstanding catalog. Befitting the publication of a licensed craftsman for both Colonial Williamsburg and the Winterthur Museum, the catalog includes historical information and detailed descriptions, an introduction to tinsmithing techniques, a glossary, and a bibliography.

Travelers will also enjoy the Old Mill Museum, where David works. Built in 1780 by Ezekiel Pease as a sawmill, it later became a gristmill and its water turbines produced the town's electricity in the early 1900s. Now a museum of old tools and machinery, the building is owned by the community under a deed that requires that there always be a working craftsman on site. Presently David is the museum's only artisan. "But there's room for more to join me," David notes, "just no takers yet."

PRICES: $5–$800. No commissions. The catalog/brochure costs $3.

VISITORS: July–Oct., daily, 10 A.M.–5 P.M.; Nov.–June, "by chance."

LOCATION: South-central Vermont, about 35 miles southeast of Rutland. Old Mill Museum, P.O. Box 41, Weston, VT 05161; no telephone. Take I-91 to Rockingham exit, then Rte. 103 north to Chester. Go west on Rte. 11 to Londonderry, then take Rte. 100 to Weston. The shop is on Rte. 100, just past the town green; look for TINWARE sign.

David Lee Claggett: Tenth wedding anniversary bonnet. Tin. H. 9″; W. 8″.

WILLIAMSVILLE

Deidre Scherer
FABRIC COLLAGE

Although Deidre's palette is composed of printed fabrics and colored threads, her portraits have the shading and subtlety of fine oil paintings. Focusing on the faces of elderly women, Deidre captures their personalities, the effects of passing time, and a glimmer of their youthful beauty (see color plate #3). A piece of red-and-cream fabric accentuates a cheekbone or shadows a forehead, small floral prints form a lady's coiffure, darker ones show the gentle dewlaps on a throat.

Deidre began making fabric collages when she created a patchwork book for her daughters. "Slowly, over time," she says, "I acquired the skills for handling fabric, using scissors and a sewing machine as my 'drawing tools.' It's more than choosing the right color and print; textures also add to each collage." She often composes the portrait in her head, then begins a search for the proper fabric, eyeing clothes a friend may be wearing or scraps from a neighbor's newly upholstered sofa. Using her sewing machine, she adds highlights with contrasting thread or depth and contour with zigzag stitching.

PRICES: $450–$3,500. Commissions "may be" accepted. No catalog/brochure.

VISITORS: By appointment only.

LOCATION: Southern Vermont, northeast of Brattleboro. P.O. Box 156, Williamsville, VT 05362; 802-348-7807 (please call afternoons or evenings only). Directions will be provided when appointment to visit is made.

MORE: Deidre's work is also available through the Woodstock Gallery, Rte. 4E, Woodstock, VT 05091; 802-457-1900.

WINDSOR

Vermont State Craft Center at Windsor House
CONTEMPORARY AND TRADITIONAL CRAFTS

Windsor House, the largest Greek Revival structure ever erected in Vermont, was once the site of a flossy hotel. Now its elegant lobby is home to a crafts center that exhibits the work of over 275 Vermont craftspeople. In addition to work by many of the artisans listed in this chapter, other pieces especially worth seeing include Lydia Corrow's traditional coverlets and table runners, Augie Dworak's carved basswood loons, Sat Kavr Khalsa's luminous blue earthenware, and Frank Peterson's country-style clock cabinets.

PRICES: $1–thousands (average for gift items, $15–$65). Accepts MasterCard, Visa.

OPEN: Mon.–Sat., 9 A.M.–5 P.M.; Sun. (June–Jan. only), noon–5 P.M. Closed Thanksgiving, Christmas, and New Year's Day. Wheelchair accessible.

LOCATION: East-central Vermont along the Connecticut River. Main Street, P.O. Box 1777, Windsor, VT 05089; 802-674-6729. Take I-91 to either exit 8 or 9. The Craft Center is located in between these exits on Rte. 5.

MORE: An adjoining art gallery features rotating exhibits that change every six to eight weeks.

Vermont Craft Shows

There are almost as many craft shows in Vermont as there are cows. In addition to the ones listed previously, Craftproducers Markets, Inc. sponsors four shows that feature a wide assortment of crafts, entertainment, and a "Vermont Gourmet Specialty Food Tent" (which may be reason enough to attend).

Manchester Show: Early Aug., Hildene Meadows, Manchester.
Shelburne Show: Mid-Aug., Shelburne Farms, Shelburne.
Stowe Show: Late Sept., Topnotch Field, Stowe.
West Dover Show: Early Oct., Mount Snow Base Lodge, West Dover.

For more information on any of these shows contact Craftproducers Markets, Inc., P.O. Box 5180, Burlington, VT 05402; 802-864-8178.

MORE

Two excellent books on Vermont crafts provide more information on the state's rich craft heritage: *Vermonters at Their Craft: Vermont Craftspeople Talk about Their Life and Work*, by Catharine Wright and Nancy Means Wright (New England Press, 1987; $19.95), and *Always in Season: Folk Art and Traditional Culture in Vermont*, by Jane C. Beck (Vermont Council on the Arts, 136 State Street, Montpelier, VT 05602; 1982) *Always in Season* is now out of print, but it should be available in many libraries.

NEW YORK

The Empire State offers visitors almost every recreational and leisure-time pursuit from skiing and wilderness hiking to museum hopping and sophisticated nightlife. Mirroring this diversity, the state's crafts range from traditional Indian tribal arts and rustic Adirondack pieces to avant-garde contemporary work found in Manhattan's galleries. The listings in this chapter are only a drop in the state's artistic bucket, meant to introduce dominant craft themes, suggest unique creative work, and entice travelers to branch out on their own aesthetic discoveries.

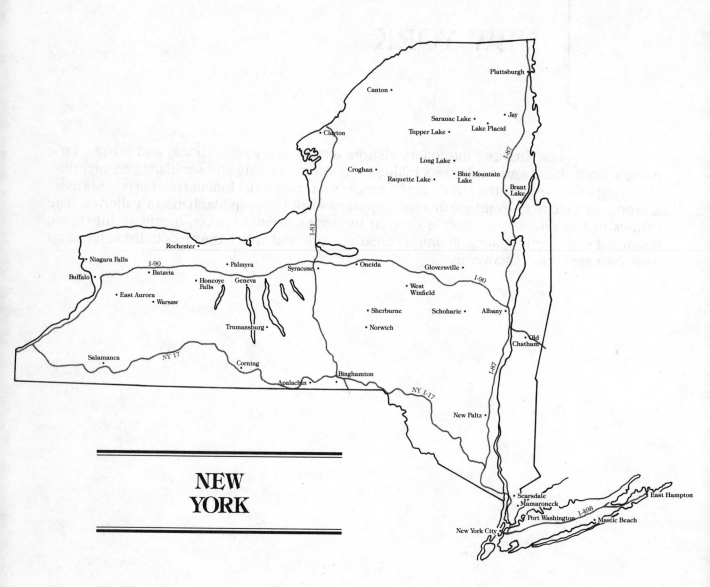

NEW YORK

ADIRONDACK AND NORTH COUNTRY

The mountains, lakes, and deep forests of Adirondack Park cover over six million acres, an area the size of Massachusetts. Home to the Algonquin Indians, called "Ha-De-Ron-Dah" (bark eaters) by the Iroquois, this remote area later became the province of loggers, miners, and guides. Even the wealthy came here in summer, erecting enormous log mansions called "Great Camps." Linked by geography, these Adirondack residents were also known for their distinctive crafts made from native materials: guide boats, pack baskets, and rustic furniture. Today these continuing craft traditions are supplemented by the work of more contemporary artisans. For additional listings of craftspeople, see the map and entries in *Craft Trails in the Adirondack North Country*, published by the Adirondack North Country Craft Center, Box 148, Saranac Avenue, Lake Placid, NY 12946. This publication is free with an SASE.

BLUE MOUNTAIN LAKE

Adirondack Museum
TRADITIONAL ADIRONDACK CRAFTS

The steep admission price is worth it. First, head straight for the Boat Building and the largest public collection of Adirondack guide boats. Developed in the 1830s by Indians who needed a fast rowboat that could carry large loads but be easily portaged, these 16-foot boats weigh only 50 to 70 pounds. Other examples of Adirondack ingenuity are the sturdy and lightweight pack baskets displayed in the Transportation Building and for sale at the gate house. Made of pounded ash splints with a leather shoulder harness, these baskets were the standard way to carry trapping equipment, camping supplies, and even children before the advent of aluminum-frame packs.

In Bull Cottage, visitors can see the rustic furniture that once graced the great camps: sturdy chairs of yellow birch, elegant chests and desks veneered with sheets of birch bark, and elaborate cabinets faced with "twig mosaics." To venture into the realm of the decidedly odd, ask to see the museum's collection of fungus art. Demonstrating that you should never underestimate the ability of tourists to create their own bizarre souvenirs, these strange mementos are pieces of shelf or bracket fungus whose soft, white surface is marked with a blunt tool, then dried and painted. The result is . . . unique.

OPEN: Memorial Day weekend–mid-Oct., daily, 9:30 A.M.–5:30 P.M. There is a museum shop, the best buys are the pack baskets. Admission is $7.25 for adults, $6 for seniors, $4.50 for children. No tours. Wheelchair accessible.

LOCATION: Central Adirondacks. Blue Mountain Lake, NY 12812; 518-352-7311. Take I-90 to Utica, then Rtes. 12 and 28 north to Alder Creek. Go east on Rte. 28 for 52 miles to Blue Mountain Lake. The museum is 1 mile on the left. If on I-87, go to exit 23 (Warrensburg), take a left off the exit ramp to the T intersection. Go right on Rte. 9, left on Rte. 28 to

Indian Lake. Go north on Rte. 30 to Blue Mountain Lake, then right on Rte. 28N/30 for 1 mile. The museum is on the left.

MORE: There are July and August craft demonstrations of rustic furniture, fungus art, wood-canvas canoes, snowshoemaking. Additional regional crafts at the Shop, Adirondack Lakes Center for the Arts, Rte. 28, Blue Mountain Lake, NY 12812; 518-352-7715.

BRANT LAKE

Carl E. Heilman II
SNOWSHOES

With Carl's help you can walk on water, at least in its crystalline form. And if you've never tried snowshoes, Carl will not only make you a pair, he'll show you how to use them. An experienced craftsman, guide, and wilderness photographer, Carl has produced snowshoes since 1974. "Although I make a variety of styles," he says, "most of them are the 'Western bearpaw' type, smaller, streamlined, with a rounded heel. These are great for mountaineering, recreational snowshoeing, and racing." Carl also recommends them for "skishoeing," a term he coined for using snowshoes to climb mountains, then cross-country skis to glide back down.

Carl personally selects each white ash tree he uses, then splits them into small sections for the frame. Following the wood's natural grain, he steams, bends, then cures the frames before applying a waterproofing finish. Next he adds urethane, neoprene, or rawhide laces and reinforces heel sections. "I've also designed 'CatClaw' bindings," Carl adds. "These feature removable, 'retractable' crampons which help on packed snow or icy conditions, yet won't prevent you from a smooth glissade."

PRICES: $155–$315. Exclusively commissions. Free, very informative catalog/brochure.

VISITORS: Yes.

LOCATION: Eastern Adirondacks. Box 213A, Rte. 8, Brant Lake, NY 12815; 518-494-3072. Take I-87 to Brant Lake/

Carl Heilman II: Snowshoes.

Chestertown exit, then go east on Rte. 8 for 4 miles. Look for sign that says CUSTOM BUILT SNOWSHOES.

MORE: Although the catalog tells how to choose and maintain snowshoes and gives detailed descriptions of each variety, if you want to know more, or even want to try to make your own, order Carl's *Crafting Techniques for Handsplit Snowshoes*, $5.50 plus $1 shipping.

CANTON

Upstairs Gallery
CONTEMPORARY CRAFTS

The Upstairs Gallery represents over 100 North Country artisans, but its choicest crafts are local textiles and baskets, including wall hangings by Canton quilter Lucretia Romey. Using fabric instead of bricks and clapboards, and stitches instead of mortar and nails, Lucretia constructs architectural landscapes. Emphasizing the high-rise jumble of New York City or the closely aligned roofs of Provincetown, each quilt distills the essence of a familiar cityscape. In quilts representing more rural landscapes, Lucretia uses rows of stitches as topographic contours or subtle coloring to capture the Adirondacks.

Other local artisans recreate "Old Order" Amish quilts using the bright colors and traditional patterns found in the originals. These boldly colored quilts are a welcome contrast to the pastel knockoffs that too often pass today as "authentic." For top-notch traditional baskets, ask to see those by Charlotte Morey, a Mohawk Indian from Potsdam, New York. Using fragrant sweet grass, she creates tightly woven scissor sheaths and sewing baskets ranging from 1 inch in diameter (for a thimble) to 10 inches.

PRICES: $1–$800 (average, $25–$50). Accepts MasterCard, Visa.

OPEN: Mon.–Sat., 10 A.M.–5 P.M. Closed legal holidays. Not wheelchair accessible.

LOCATION: Far northern New York, 60 miles northeast of Watertown, 105 miles south of Ottawa, Canada. 111 Main Street, Canton, NY 13617; 315-379-9526. Take I-81 to Watertown, then Rte. 11 north to Canton. The gallery is located across from the Village Park.

CLAYTON

Thousand Islands Craft School and Textile Museum

Seventeen hundred islands, not 1,000, dot the St. Lawrence River above and below Clayton, but you won't have time to count them all and in summer the tourists may block the view. If you can't find an island of your own, get off the tourist treadmill by stopping at this small museum.

An offshoot of a successful craft school with a large weaving department, the museum specializes in twentieth-century American handweaving and also displays a number of antique coverlets and unique fabrics. Special exhibits are well curated and one on "The Weaver as Mathematician" is planned for 1990. Of particular interest to weavers are sixty-three three-ring binders of twentieth-century handweaving samples (actual textiles, not photos). Additional samples and a comprehensive textile library are also on the premises.

OPEN: Mon.–Sat., 9 A.M.–3 P.M. Closed all holidays. The museum shop sells handwoven and early American decorative items. The suggested donation for admission is $2. Tours are given, with a prior appointment required. Wheelchair accessible.

LOCATION: 20 miles northwest of Watertown, 7 miles from Canadian border. 314 John Street, Clayton, NY 13624; 315-686-4123. Take I-81 to Rte. 12, go west on Rte. 12 to Clayton. Go straight under the large overhead sign that says WELCOME TO CLAYTON and continue straight to the riverfront. Take a right on Riverside Drive, then go one block to John Street. Turn right on John; the museum is two blocks farther.

CROGHAN

Butch and Pat Bramhall
MINIATURE SILVER/GOLD BASKETS

When is an Adirondack pack basket not meant for carrying camping supplies? When it's 2¾ inches tall and made of sterling silver. Complete with leather harness and working silver buckles, these little jewels are meant to be worn as pendants or sit decoratively on display. The Bramhalls create perfect miniature replicas of traditional baskets, authentic in every detail. The only difference is that silver or solid gold replaces reed and oak splits.

"As antique dealers during the 1960s," Butch says, "we were fascinated by baskets, especially Shaker styles and those made by Northeast Native Americans. We started making some of our own, with natural fibers, and also made a line of jewelry. The jewelry started selling so well we had little time left for basketry. Finally we realized we could use sterling silver wire in place of reed to weave miniature replicas."

Using jewelers' tools and dental picks, Butch and Pat create a range of replicas including exquisite melon-style baskets, Akwesasne Indian curlicue baskets, grapevine egg baskets, and even a tiny fishing creel that comes with its own silver fly rod and fishnet. "Our pieces range in size from three-quarters of an inch to eight inches," Pat says.

Stonehouse Silversmiths, Pat and Butch Bramhall: Miniature Adirondack pack basket. Sterling silver. O.H. 2½"; H. 2¼"; W. 1¾"; D. ¾".

"And we even shape some of them, like the Kitten Basket, around a tiny form of white pine or black walnut, just like the full-scale fiber ones are made."

Butch and Pat also create other work, including sterling silver cordials, necklaces, candle holders, baby rattles with garnets, and even a sterling oil lamp. But the stars of the show are the baskets, which are only big enough to hold memories and love.

PRICES: $300–$4,000. Commissions accepted. Catalog/brochure available.

VISITORS: Yes.

LOCATION: About 35 miles southeast of Watertown. The Stonehouse Silversmiths, R.D. #1, Box 325, Croghan, NY 13327; 315-346-1205. From Utica, take Rte. 12 north to Lowville (about 56 miles). Turn right at the blue Sonoco station and continue for 5 miles. Stonehouse studio will be on the right side. From Watertown, take Rte. 3 northeast to Deferiet, then proceed southeast on Rte. 3 to Carthage. Follow Rte. 26 south to Lowville, turning left at the Sonoco station, and continue 5 miles to the studio.

GLOVERSVILLE

Gene E. Valk
EARLY AMERICAN HANDWEAVING

"When I started weaving in the 1940s there weren't many how-to books, so I used the 'trial and error' method," Gene recalls. "But there wasn't much 'error,' since I have a natural bent for crafts." Specializing in early American techniques and patterns, Gene uses natural fibers to re-create typical household textiles.

"Living in a region so rich in colonial, revolutionary, and early nineteenth-century history, I just naturally became interested in the textiles of those periods," Gene says. She also discovered an eighteenth-century pattern book brought to the area in 1830 by Xavier Gartner of Württemberg. After transcribing his drafts to modern weaving instructions, Gene had the text translated. "It included a family history," she says. "Xavier wasn't a first son, so he didn't inherit his father's business and family Bible. Instead he got the next most valuable possession, his father's book of weaving patterns. This was used as a 'catalog.' Customers would bring in handspun yarns, choose a pattern from the book, then order a coverlet or tablecloth. I now re-create many of his patterns as well as other period designs."

PRICES: $1 (bookmarks)–$500. Commissions are accepted if the appropriate warp is on the loom. There is no catalog/brochure, but Gene will answer inquiries accompanied by an SASE.

VISITORS: Yes.

LOCATION: Southern Adirondacks, 50 miles northwest of Albany. Weefhuis Studio, 402 North Main Street, Gloversville, NY 12078; 518-725-3371. Take I-90 to exit 28 (Fultonville). Go north on Rte. 30A to Gloversville, west on Rte. 29A (East Fulton Street) to North Main Street. Go right onto North Main for 1.1 miles. The studio is between Eleventh and Twelfth avenues.

JAY

Sue Burdick Young
STONEWARE

Want your soup served by a chubby bear? How about keeping a special treasure in another bear's tummy? That's just what you can do with Sue Young's delightful pots. Handbuilt from iron-rich red stoneware, her Ursus series includes a portly sitting bear jar (just remove his head to store candy or other treats), a standing bear casserole, and a soup tureen featuring a patient mother bear letting cubs cavort on her back (the lid). If you're not taken by her terra-cotta teddies, you may want one of

Sue Burdick Young: *Ursus,* soup tureen. Stoneware. H. 14″; L. 16″.

Sue's traditional stoneware platters or bowls. Wheel-thrown using simple forms, each is decorated with patterns inspired by the Adirondacks.

Visitors to Sue's studio will also see the work of ten other Adirondack artisans, including fine intaglio and lithography prints by Sue's husband, Terrance, along with silver jewelry, baskets, weavings, and other textiles.

PRICES: $7–$350 (Ursus series, $50–$450). Commissions accepted. No catalog/brochure.

VISITORS: June–Dec., Mon.–Sat., 10 A.M.–4 P.M.; Jan.–May, Tues.–Sat., 10 A.M.–4 P.M.

LOCATION: Northeastern Adirondacks, 35 miles southwest of Plattsburgh. Handwork Gallery, Rte. 86, Jay, NY 12941; 518-946-7301. From I-87, take Keeseville exit, then Rtes. 9N/86 west to Jay. The gallery is on Rte. 86, on the right, just before Rte. 9N turns south.

LAKE PLACID

Adirondack North Country Crafts Center
TRADITIONAL ADIRONDACK CRAFTS

Lake Placid has avoided the fate of many former Olympic sites whose facilities go unused and buildings are left to deteriorate. Instead, Lake Placid has become a major winter and summer recreational area. As might be expected, it has more than its share of knickknack shops, but high-quality Adirondack crafts can be found at the Crafts Center.

The real gems here are the traditional Adirondack guide boats by Jim Cameron, Tom Phillips's rustic furniture, the subtle but appealing pottery created by Bill Knoble, and the Bramhalls' traditional baskets reproduced as silver and gold miniatures. If you're interested in a particular medium, ask to see the center's extensive slide file of regional craftspeople.

PRICES: $1–$1,000 (average, $30–$100). Accepts American Express, MasterCard, Visa.

OPEN: Mon.–Sat., 10 A.M.–5 P.M.; Sun. (July & Aug. only), 1–5 P.M. Closed on Christmas and New Year's Day. Wheelchair accessible.

LOCATION: Northeastern Adirondacks, 52 miles southwest of Plattsburgh. 93 Saranac Avenue, P.O. Box 148, Lake Placid, NY 12946; 518-523-2062. If traveling north on I-87, take Underwood/Rte. 73 exit. Follow Rte. 73 past junction with Rte. 86 to Lake Placid. If traveling south on I-87, take Keeseville/Rte. 9N/86 exit, then follow Rtes. 9N/86 to Lake Placid. The center is located on Rte. 86 across from the Howard Johnson's restaurant.

LONG LAKE

Mason Smith
ROWBOATS

"**I**'ve had a lifelong interest in wood boats," Mason says. "In fact, I spent years building them part-time, writing for boating magazines, and attending boat-building workshops. What finally convinced me to do this full-time was realizing that the region was so fixated on its famous guide boat that it lacked really good practical alternatives." About the same time, Mason also learned of the "constant camber" construction technique developed to assist third-world countries that need practical, inexpensive rowboats.

"This is a cold-molded method permitting the rapid shaping of veneer using epoxy and atmospheric pressure," Mason explains. "I use local poplar veneer, and for fancy boats I use other woods for the surface plies. My boats, which I call 'Good-boats,' are perfect for inland waters and, since you can add a sail or a motor, they're very versatile."

PRICES: $2,475–$5,500. Commissions accepted. Free descriptions and photos.

VISITORS: Yes.

LOCATION: Central Adirondacks. North Point Road, Box 44, Long Lake, NY 12847; 518-624-6798. Take I-87 to North Hudson exit, then Rte. 28N west 37 miles to Long Lake. The shop is located behind Day's Garage on Rte. 30 in the center of Long Lake village.

RAQUETTE LAKE

Sagamore Lodge Museum
TRADITIONAL ADIRONDACK CRAFTS

The famous Adirondack Great Camps where the wealthy summered in the late nineteenth century were just that: huge, self-sufficient compounds even boasting furniture, boat, and other craft workshops. One of these, Great Camp Sagamore, was built by William Durant in 1897, enlarged by the Vanderbilts in 1901, and is now fully restored. Although the camp operates as a conference center during the week, lodging is available to the public on weekends, and tours are available daily. Visitors will see the massive three-story main lodge, the separate dining hall overlooking mile-long Sagamore Lake, a covered bowling alley, guest cottages, and the craft workshops.

The camp's restored Rustic Furniture Shop, Blacksmith Shop, and Boat Shed offer visitors an opportunity to watch craftsmen create items once made exclusively for use in the Durant/Vanderbilt complex. And, in contrast to some "living museums," these shops allow visitors to take these crafts home. "But if you're worried about getting a piece of rustic furniture to fit in your car," says craftsman Jackson Smith, "I also offer miniature replicas." Visitors may also be interested in Jackson's carved walking sticks, which he fashions from small maple trees pulled up by the roots.

OPEN: By two-hour tour only, last Sat. in June–Columbus Day. Museum shop on premises. Admission is $5 for adults, $2.50 for children. Tours begin at 10 A.M., 1 P.M., and 2 P.M.; at other times by appointment only. Partially wheelchair accessible.

LOCATION: Central Adirondacks. Sagamore Road, Raquette Lake, NY 13436; 315-354-4303. Take I-87 to exit 23 (Warrensburg), then Rte. 9N north. 2 miles north of Warrensburg, turn left on Rte. 28 west to Raquette Lake. At the big crossroads in Raquette Lake, turn left onto Sagamore Road (sign will say SAGAMORE LODGE, 4 MILES). After 3.7 miles there is a fork in the road; take the right fork. After crossing a small bridge and going up a short hill, Sagamore will be on the left, the parking area on the right.

SARANAC LAKE

Carl G. Hathaway
TRADITIONAL ADIRONDACK GUIDE BOATS

"The traditional guide boat was really the pickup truck of the Adirondacks," Carl says. "Instead of highways and railroads, we have lakes and rivers. And these boats are so light, they can be carried by one man." A caretaker for a private camp on Upper Saranac Lake, Carl has been making guide boats for almost thirty years.

"I build them in the traditional way," Carl notes. "Some people think they're expensive, but it takes me three hundred to three-hundred-and-fifty hours to build just one. I use sawed spruce roots for ribs, white pine for planking, black cherry for trim, brass screws, and either brass or copper tacks. And all the seats are hand-caned. I include also a pair of oars, a stern paddle, and a carry yoke."

PRICES: 16' guide boat, $6,500. Commissions accepted.

VISITORS: Yes.

LOCATION: Northeastern Adirondacks, 60 miles southwest of Plattsburgh. 7 Algonquin Avenue, Saranac Lake, NY 12983; 518-891-3961 (shop), 518-359-7643 (home). Take I-87 to Underwood/Rte. 73 exit, then Rte. 73 north to junction with Rte. 86. Continue on Rte. 86 past Lake Placid to Saranac Lake. The shop is on Saranac–Tupper Lake Highway (Rte. 3) just outside of Saranac Lake.

TUPPER LAKE

Thomas Phillips
RUSTIC FURNITURE

Tom is a perfectionist. When he realized his first set of dining room chairs weren't just right, he took a chain saw to them and threw the pieces in the wood stove. He doesn't need to do that anymore. Tom creates top-quality chairs, settees, and even complete entrance gates and arches. Many of his pieces have fine detail work not often associated with rustic furniture: twig rosettes decorate the doors of a pine hutch, complicated twig mosaics cover desk drawers, and the curved braces of a yellow birch settee add strength but also suggest delicacy.

Tom's trademark pieces are diamondback

Carl G. Hathaway: 14' Adirondack guide boat. JUDY PHILLIPS

Thomas Phillips: Headboard and nightstands. JUDY PHILLIPS

chairs: pine chairs with caned seats and a back featuring a twig diamond surrounded by a square. Seemingly fragile, they are both sturdy and comfortable. "In fact," Tom says, "everything I make is designed for comfort. It has to be durable and pleasing to the eye, of course, but if it's not comfortable, you'll never use it and you won't want to buy more."

PRICES: $20–$3,000. Commissions accepted. There is no catalog/brochure, but "pictures will be sent to sincere buyers."

VISITORS: Yes. By appointment only.

LOCATION: North-central Adirondacks, about 75 miles southwest of Plattsburgh. Star Rte. 2, Tupper Lake, NY 12986; 518-359-9648. Directions will be provided when appointment to visit is made.

CENTRAL NEW YORK

Traveling the back roads of central New York, east of Syracuse and Binghamton, visitors will discover gentle valleys, rolling farmland, and towns like Cazenovia, which sits prettily at the end of a small lake. The larger Finger Lakes dominate the western half of central New York, sparkling reminders of the last glacial age. Nearby are some of the state's finest vineyards, the sites of early Abolition and women's rights movements, and towns with boulevards lined with Victorian homes. As befits a region not dominated by contemporary façades and values, many of the area's artisans continue craft traditions handed down through generations or inspired by early settlers. Exceptions are the glass artisans of Corning, the city's major industry since 1868.

APALACHIN

Otsiningo Pow Wow & Indian Craft Fair

The Chenango Valley, where nearby Binghamton is now located, attracted a number of Indian nations in the eighteenth century. Although some were indigenous, others came here to accept the Iroquois pledge of protection and land after being ejected from their homes by white settlers. The valley, called "Otsiningo" by the Indians, was considered the "southern door" of the symbolic Iroquois longhouse. Now "Otsiningo" refers to an annual summer pow wow that attracts Indians from throughout the Northeastern United States and Canada.

The two-day festival includes Indian dancing, singing, food, and the booths of over sixty Native American artisans selling traditional crafts. Visitors can also watch demonstrations of Mohawk basketry; Iroquois woodcarving; stone, bone, and antler carving; beadwork; and other crafts. In addition, each year the pow wow honors one Indian nation by showcasing its artisans, dances, storytelling, and history.

EVENT: First weekend in June (rain or shine). Sat., 10 A.M.–10 P.M.; Sun. 10 A.M.–6 P.M. Admission is $2 for adults, $1 for children.

LOCATION: South-central New York. Fred L. Waterman Conservation Education Center, Hilton Road, Apalachin. Take Rte. 17 west of Binghamton to exit 66. Turn right onto Rte. 434. Continue for 1.3 miles, then turn left onto Hilton Road. The center will be .3 mile on the left.

MORE: For information contact Dolores Elliott, Waterman Conservation Education Center, P.O. Box 288, Apalachin, NY 13732; 607-625-2221.

At other times of the year, the Otsiningo program sponsors occasional craft demonstrations and workshops: Iroquois soapstone carving, porcupine quill jewelry making, Iroquois cornhusk mat making, and others. For details contact Dolores Elliott at the Waterman Conservation Center.

CORNING

Tom Buechner III
CONTEMPORARY BLOWN GLASS

Most vases are enhanced by the flowers they hold, but a few are complete works of art in themselves.

Tom's superb work falls in the latter category. A simple vase in a riveting color, cobalt blue or aquamarine, is dressed with clear glass arcs like fancy sleeves on a cocktail dress or a translucent cape over a simple sheath. In another, the lips of an opaque blue vase pour sidewise in fluid, elongated lines. Visitors can watch Tom and his glassblowers create these unusual vases as well as free-form paperweights, perfume bottles, and a line of hand-blown Christmas ornaments.

Tom's studio, Vitrix, hosts demonstrations and shows by visiting glass artists, and also displays the work of non-glass artists.

Tom Buechner III: Cobalt Multibit perfume bottle. Blown glass with ground-glass stopper. H. 4½″.
RAY ERRETT

PRICES: $10–$1,000. Commissions accepted. Slides of Tom's work are available.

VISITORS: Mon.–Fri., 9:30 A.M.–5:30 P.M.; Sat., 10 A.M.–4 P.M..

LOCATION: South-central New York. Vitrix Hot Glass Studio, 77 West Market Street, Corning, NY 14830; 607-936-8707. Take Rte. 17 to Corning, then go north on Walnut Street, left on Market Street. The studio is half a block down, in the Hawkes Building.

MORE: Two other West Market Street glass studios also welcome visitors: Brand and Greenberg Glass, and Noslo Glass. Ask Vitrix for their locations.

CORNING

Corning Glass Center
STEUBEN GLASS FACTORY, GLASS MUSEUM

If you're in central New York and even minimally interested in glass, then add this as a "must" to your itinerary. While it's possible to spend an entire day touring the center, it makes more sense to choose only the parts that interest you. The Corning Glass Center includes six shops and three touring centers: the Steuben Glass Factory, the Corning Museum of Glass, and a glass science/industry exhibit.

The Steuben Glass Factory: No one is wishy-washy about Steuben glass. Everyone agrees that high degrees of artistry and technical skill are demonstrated in the clear crystal, often intricately engraved, Steuben pieces. But while some collectors find them to be the ultimate artistic use of glass, others protest that Steuben is too conservative and predictable. In either case, this factory of master glassblowers and artisans is worth seeing. From a viewing gallery visitors can watch the glass specialists (gaffers, gatherers, servitors, design cutters, and engravers) transform molten glass into finished works of art.

The Corning Museum of Glass: Claiming to have the world's most extensive collection of glass, the museum introduces visitors to 3,500 years of glassmaking, some of it in a "time tunnel" where examples are arranged chronologically. It is impossible not to be dazzled by this collection, which includes everything from a 2,000-year-old perfume bottle to modern studio art glass. For additional viewing, over 20,000 glass objects can be found in study cases, including a glass trombone, a potato masher, and a walking cane.

The Hall of Science and Industry: Probably more than you care to know about glass, but the hands-on exhibits will fascinate the kids, and even you won't be able to resist looking through a 6-foot-thick piece of clear glass.

The Six Shops: Recommended are the Artists' Gallery Shop, featuring some of America's top studio glass, and the Steuben Shop, where you can purchase the sculptured, decorative, and functional pieces created in the factory. There's also a World Glass Shop, offering functional and decorative European glass; a Museum Shop, with books, slides, and posters; a Gift Shop of T-shirts and glass trinkets; and the Consumer Shop's Corning cookware.

OPEN: Daily, 9 A.M.–5 P.M. Closed Thanksgiving, Christmas Eve and Christmas Day, and New Year's Day. Admission is $4 for adults, $3 for seniors, $2 for children 6–17; the maximum charge for a family is $10. Majority of areas are wheelchair accessible.

LOCATION: South-central New York. Corning Glass Center, Corning, NY 14831; 607-974-8271. Take Rte. 17 to Corning Glass Center exit. Proceed through first traffic light, turn right at second traffic light. Corning Glass Center is on immediate right.

CORNING

Rockwell Museum
CARDER STEUBEN GLASS

Although Steuben is known today for its clear lead crystal, from 1903–1933, under the direction of founder Frederick Carder, it produced a myriad of colorful glass and art nouveau patterns. In later years Carder continued to experiment with color and form. The largest collection of this original Carder-Steuben glass is exhibited at the Rockwell Museum. Of particular note are Carder's stained-glass window, designed as a World War I memorial, and his *Diatreta Vase*, resembling a carved jade vessel covered with opaque blue and green vines.

OPEN: Mon.–Sat., 9 A.M.–5 P.M.; Sun., noon–5 P.M. In July and August., Mon.–Fri. hours are extended to 7 P.M. Closed Thanksgiving, Dec. 24, Dec. 25, and Jan. 1. The museum shop features Southwestern Indian crafts. Admission is $2 for adults, $1.50 for seniors, $1 for children. Tours by appointment. Wheelchair accessible.

LOCATION: South-central New York. Cedar Street at Denison Parkway, Corning, NY 14830; 607-937-5386. Take Rte. 17 to Corning. The museum is in old Corning City Hall, at the corner of Rte. 17 and Cedar Street.

MORE: The Rockwell Museum also specializes in American Western art and has an amusing collection of antique toys.

GENEVA

John H. McGuire
BASKETS AND WOVEN NECKLACES

Chester D. Freeman
TEDDY BEARS

Surrounded by upstate New York's wine country, Geneva is a pretty little town at the tip of Seneca Lake. In the midst of its historic district is number 398, a row house with a distinctive painted-grain doorway. Inside, John McGuire weaves fine reproductions of Shaker, Nantucket, and other New England baskets and some of the most interesting wearable art you're likely to find in New York State. Starting with black ash splints, John weaves intricate collars, then mounts them on arcs of exotic wood to form stunning chokers. Comfortable and lightweight, this unusual jewelry is equally impressive displayed on a wall.

Sharing the studio is Chester Freeman, a former chaplain at Amherst College who is now a full-time teddy bear maker. Made of 100 percent German mohair, all bears are fully jointed and have hand-embroidered faces. His specialty is Freeman Backpacker, a bear wearing a miniature Adirondack pack basket.

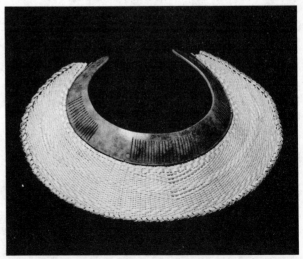

John E. McGuire: *Chevron,* ornamental collar. Black ash, dune grass, calabash. H. 4″; W. 12½″. HENRY E. PEACH

PRICES: John, $100–$1,200; Chester, $50–$150. Commissions accepted by both John and Chester. John has no catalog/brochure, but Chester will send you his if you supply him with a business-size SASE.

VISITORS: Anytime. "But phone ahead to make sure we're in."

LOCATION: 45 miles southeast of Rochester. 398 South Main Street, Geneva, NY 14456; 315-781-1251. Take I-90 to exit 42, then Rte. 14 south to Geneva. Rte. 14 turns up a steep hill and becomes South Main Street. Continue for a few hundred yards to the studio.

NORWICH
Doris M. Graves
CHAIR CANING

Chair caning isn't a craft you can purchase like a glass vase or an Amish quilt, but Doris's work is so exquisite that you'll wish she made framed samples as wall hangings. Even if you don't have a chair or settee that needs recaning, stop by to watch this master craftswoman weave elaborate designs, re-creating antique patterns or creating ones of her own. Caning for over fifty years, Doris learned the craft from her parents, who did seat weaving. Although she works primarily with the bark of rattan cane native to the Far East, Doris also makes natural rush seats from cattail leaves.

PRICES: Depend on size, pattern. Commissions accepted. No catalog/brochure.

VISITORS: Yes. "Visitors welcome anytime they can find me."

LOCATION: 40 miles northeast of Binghamton. R.D. #1, Box 598, Norwich, NY 13815; 607-334-6155 (it's best to call between 7 and 8 A.M. or after 8 P.M.). Directions will be provided when appointment to visit is made.

MORE: Doris canes in Florida during the winter: Blue Parrot Camp, Lady Lake, FL 32659; 904-753-4320.

ONEIDA
Traditional Craft Days

Some attempts to re-create the atmosphere of yesteryear become true embarrassments, but this festival is an exception. Every September, for over twenty-five years, upstate New York artisans have dressed in period costumes to demonstrate and exhibit crafts from the 1680s through the early 1900s. Some crafts, such as quilting, basketweaving, and blacksmithing, are well known, others are rarely seen today: shinglemaking, tatting, eighteenth-century drop-spinning, quilling, and custom fly rod crafting.

Seeking to re-create the flavor of an old-fashioned festival, street mongers peddle flowers, soap, and lace; entertainers present puppet shows; and singing minstrels stroll the grounds. Visitors can also sample traditional foods including apple butter, fry bread, meat pies, and corn soup.

EVENT: Second weekend in Sept., 10 A.M.–5 P.M. Admission is $2.50 for adults, $2 for seniors with ID, children under 16 free.

LOCATION: 23 miles west of Utica, 34 miles east of Syracuse. Grounds of Cottage Lawn, 435 Main Street, Oneida. Take I-90 to exit 33. Go south on Rte. 365 to Rte. 5, right on Rte. 5 to Broad Street, right on Broad to Main Street, right on Main Street.

MORE: For information contact Madison County Historical Society, 435 Main Street, P.O. Box 415, Oneida, NY 13421; 315-363-4136.

SHERBURNE
Dudley H. Frasure
FRASURE ADIRONDACK PACK BASKETS

"My first Adirondack pack baskets sold for five dollars, because," Dudley notes, "unlike the Indians, I made and fitted a comfortable, sturdy harness to my basket. Theirs only cost two dollars." In his late seventies, Dudley is the Grand Old Maker of the famous pack baskets. A genial, energetic man, Dudley welcomes visitors with an enormous smile and tales of his decades of basketmaking.

"In 1945," he says, "I followed Thoreau's advice to go to the woods to see what it had to teach. I

Dudley H. Frasure: Adirondack pack basket.

lived in a log cabin on Hunt's Mountain and had to carry in food, tools, everything. I needed a good pack basket, so I ended up being my own first customer. I basically taught myself, although I did talk to an eighty-five-year-old Indian basket maker who lived nearby."

Five years later Dudley moved back to Maplehurst, the Sherburne farmstead built by his grandfather in 1866. Now, with the help of several apprentices, he continues to make sixty to seventy pack baskets a year. "There are fifty-two steps involved in every one," Dudley points out, "from selecting the right logs to fastening on the last buckle." The baskets range from 16 inches with a one-third bushel capacity to 24 inches capable of carrying one and a half bushels. When they're completed, Dudley uses his flowing calligraphy to sign, date, and note the customer's name on the bottom of each basket.

PRICES: $200–$279 (includes harness, liner, and cover). All work is done by custom order. Free catalog/brochure.

VISITORS: Yes. "Anytime."

LOCATION: 51 miles northeast of Binghamton, 33 miles south of Utica. Maplehurst, R.D. #1, Box 123, Sherburne, NY 13460; 607-674-9785. Take Rte. 12 north from Binghamton or south from Utica. Dudley's home/shop is on Rte. 12, 1 mile south of Sherburne, across from Lok-n-Logs, Inc.

TRUMANSBURG

Joe W. Robson
SHAKER FURNITURE

Though Shaker furniture may appear spare and simple, if you understand the Shakers' desire to create perfect practical objects it becomes clear that beauty can be defined through function. No one understands this better than Joe, whose knowledge of Shaker spirituality is as thorough as his study of their furniture. "I became interested in their pieces after studying Shaker ethics in a college philosophy course," Joe explains. "As a working carpenter at the time, I was drawn to their furniture. By discarding the ornamentation of the classical styles and elevating the work of country cabinetmakers to the level of worship, they created furniture of elegant design; works which contributed to a harmonious environment."

Joe's work captures Shaker history as well as its distinctive designs. An Enfield chest of drawers recreates an original made by Brother Abner Alley. A Shaker counter with drawers and doors is based on work counters found in Shaker kitchens. A blanket chest with arched, cut-out feet is fitted with a lock and brass escutcheon, as in the original.

PRICES: $65–$10,000. Commissions accepted. The catalog/brochure costs $2 (it includes photographs).

VISITORS: Yes.

LOCATION: 11 miles northwest of Ithaca. 14 Prospect Street, Trumansburg, NY 14886; 607-387-9280. Take Rte. 96 north from Ithaca to Trumansburg, then Union Street one block to Cayuga Street, and Cayuga one block to Prospect Street.

WEST WINFIELD

Ida Bouck
CROCHETED RAG RUGS

"**M**y grandmother taught me how to make these," Ida says, "but I got too busy raising a family to make many. When my mother died, she left some unfinished ones. I finished the rugs and people wanted to buy them. I like to keep busy while watching TV in the evenings, so now I'm always making my rugs."

Ida's bright patterns come from the materials she uses: old pieces of clothing, plastic bags, even panty hose. "All it really costs is my time," Ida notes, "and some used materials."

PRICES: Depend on size, but generally are under $25. No commissions. No catalog/brochure.

VISITORS: Yes.

LOCATION: 22 miles south of Utica. RR #2, Box 154, West Winfield, NY 13491-9513; 315-855-4215. From Utica, take Rte. 8 south to Bridgewater. 1 mile east of Bridgewater turn south 2 miles to Unadilla Forks. Turn left; the house is second on the left.

HUDSON RIVER REGION

The lower Hudson River region is a study in contrasts. On its way from the state's seat of government to America's culture capital, the river passes through the resort-dotted Catskills, tranquil river valleys, wealthy Westchester County, and the repetitious mega-suburbs surrounding New York City. Mirroring this cultural mélange are superb craft galleries as well as kitsch curio shops, unusually creative artisans, and hordes of hobbyists. We've identified a few that are worth a detour, but would like to hear of others in the star category.

ALBANY

State Capitol
ALBERT PALEY'S ALBANY GATES

When New York's State Capitol Building underwent restoration in the 1980s, master metalsmith Albert Paley was asked to design and construct two double gates leading from the main floor of the Senate to the antechambers. The result are two 14½-inch symmetrical gates of brass, bronze, and blackened steel whose light grace belies their substantial size. Set under Romanesque arches between 18-inch Corinthian columns, Paley's gates are some of the finest pieces of metalwork created in this century.

OPEN: Daily, 9 A.M.–4 P.M. The Senate chambers are on the fourth floor.

MAMARONECK

Mari Galleries of Westchester
CONTEMPORARY CRAFTS

If you're traveling from Manhattan up Long Island Sound, Mamaroneck, site of the East Coast's largest small boat harbor, makes a pleasant stretch stop. Craft buffs will enjoy exploring Mari's exhibit areas, located throughout a converted 200-year-old barn. Displaying top-notch crafts as well as fine art, the gallery includes a jewelry exhibit and a separate art-to-wear boutique. Two artisans of note are Linda Levine-Madori, whose free-flowing raku vessels resemble iridescent sculpted fiber, and Nanci Brokke, whose whimsical animal and human figures have carved hardwood faces atop soft-sculpture bodies.

PRICES: Vary. No credit cards.

OPEN: Wed.–Sun., noon–5 P.M. Closed Thanksgiving and Christmas. Main and garden levels are wheelchair accessible; upper and lower floors are not.

LOCATION: 25 miles northeast of downtown Manhattan. 133 East Prospect Avenue, Mamaroneck, NY 10543; 914-698-0008. Take I-95 to Mamaroneck Avenue exit, then proceed to center of town, then left at light on Prospect Avenue to gallery.

NEW PALTZ

David C. Freda
CONTEMPORARY METAL JEWELRY. TABLES

Want to become a walking natural history museum, with snakes on your ears or a colorful poison dart frog pinned to your blouse? Master metalsmith David Freda will accommodate you. Integrating the art of taxidermy with traditional metalsmithing techniques, David creates jewelry so realistic you don't know whether to store it in your jewelry box or place it in a cage.

Tiny turtles hatch from delicate cream-colored eggs in one unusual necklace (see color plate #4). In another, a hooked butterfly fish dangles from a fishline necklace, a snap swivel still hanging from its mouth. In addition to jewelry, David creates glass-top tables revealing underwater scenes so realistic it's tempting to ask him how often the fish need to be fed.

"I've always been influenced by the natural history of an area," David says. "In fact, as an active falconer in the 1970s, I took my first metalsmithing class so I could make falcon bells. In my jewelry I try to make totally accurate replicas. I want the animals to look alive. To do this, I make a plaster of paris mold from a reptile or other creature, inject wax into the mold, cast the form in metal, then enamel it. Many of my pieces are created by high-fire enameling on aluminum."

PRICES: $150–$35,000. Commissions accepted. No catalog/brochure.

VISITORS: Yes, by appointment.

LOCATION: 8 miles west of Poughkeepsie. P.O. Box 431, New Paltz, NY 12561; 914-255-3521. Directions will be provided when appointment to visit is made.

MORE: David's work can also be seen at the Tembaran Gallery, Surrey Hotel, 20 East 76th Street, New York, NY 10021; 212-570-0655.

OLD CHATHAM

Shaker Museum
SHAKER CRAFTS

Considered the premier collection of Shaker crafts, this museum's exhibits span over 200 years of Shaker craftsmanship and all nineteen communities. Displayed in appropriate room and shop settings are over 7,500 objects including more than 300 baskets and the pre-1840 molds used to make them; the largest collection of Shaker textiles, including rare silks from the Pleasant Hill community; and an array of tools used in Shaker blacksmithing, carpentry, coopering, and other crafts.

OPEN: May 1–Oct. 31, 10 A.M.–5 P.M., daily including holidays. Museum shop on premises. Admission is $4.50 for adults, $4 for seniors, $3 for children. Tours by prior reservation. Limited wheelchair accessibility.

LOCATION: 23 miles southeast of Albany, 1 mile south of Old Chatham. Shaker Museum Road, Old Chatham, NY 12136; 518-794-9100. Take I-87 to I-90E. Take exit 11E, then go right on Rte. 20 to Rte. 66, located between Nassau and Brainard. Go south on Rte. 66 to Malden Bridge, then left on Shaker Museum Road.

SCARSDALE

The Craftsman's Gallery
CONTEMPORARY CRAFTS

Many of America's most innovative artisans are represented by this classy gallery where the emphasis is on bold creativity and superb craftsmanship. Don't miss Jay Bedient's massive ceramic vessels, William Accorsi's toy sculptures that poke fun at the foibles of human relationships, Ea Jensen's still-life tapestries, quirky glass forms by Robert Levin, and eccentric ceramic architectural cubes by Thomas Lollar.

PRICES: $30–thousands (average, $100–$500). No credit cards.

OPEN: Tues.–Sat., 10:30 A.M.–5:30 P.M. Wheelchair accessible.

LOCATION: 30 miles north of downtown Manhattan. 16 Chase Road, Scarsdale, NY 10583; 914-725-4644. From Manhattan, follow the Bronx River Parkway to Scarsdale. The gallery is two blocks east of the railroad station.

SCHOHARIE

Iroquois Indian Museum
CONTEMPORARY AND TRADITIONAL IROQUOIS CRAFTS

A powerful and influential force in colonial and revolutionary America, the Iroquois confederation includes the Mohawk, Oneida, Onondaga, Cayuga, Seneca, and Tuscarora nations. Emphasizing the contribution of artists and craftspeople to the preservation of their heritage, this excellent museum displays traditional and contemporary Iroquois work. "It's important," notes director Christina Johnson, "that people understand these aren't souvenirs of an exotic people but art objects from nations who have maintained a significant craft tradition."

In addition to archaeological exhibits, there are cornhusk moccasins, containers, mats, and dolls; wood lacrosse sticks, sleds, and musical instruments; intricate beadwork often done in traditional wampum or clan animal designs; and a range of fancy and utilitarian black ash and sweet grass baskets.

OPEN: May 1–Oct. 31, July & Aug., daily except Thurs., 10 A.M.–5 P.M. May, June, Sept., & Oct., Tues. & Wed., Fri. & Sat., 10 A.M.–5 P.M.; Sun., noon–5 P.M. Museum shop on premises. Admission is $1 for adults, children free. Tours for groups by prior arrangement. Not wheelchair accessible.

LOCATION: Old Stone Fort Museum Complex, about 35 miles southwest of Albany. North Main Street, Box 158, Schoharie, NY 12157; 518-295-8553. Take I-88 to Central Bridge/Schoharie exit, then Rte. 30 to Old Stone Fort Museum Complex, 1 mile north of Schoharie. Or take I-87 to exit 21 (Catskill), then Rte. 23 north to Rte. 145. Follow Rte. 145 to Middleburgh, then Rte. 30 north to Schoharie. The museum is 1 mile north in Old Stone Fort Museum Complex.

LONG ISLAND

Looking like the head of a giant alligator about to drink the entire North Atlantic, Long Island includes Brooklyn and Queens at its western end and the famous Hamptons to the east. It's hard to think of eastern Long Island without conjuring up fantasies of F. Scott Fitzgerald's Jay Gatsby and enormous mansions with vast green lawns sweeping down to the sea. Some of that aura remains, but visitors will also find acres of productive farmland, some scenic if overcrowded beaches, and a few craft highlights.

EAST HAMPTON

Pritam & Eames
CONTEMPORARY FURNITURE AND FUNCTIONAL CRAFTS

How appropriate to find a top-notch gallery in the midst of the fashionable Hamptons! Begun as a showplace for America's preeminent furniture makers, P&E now has a second showroom featuring distinctive functional crafts. But first the furniture. Emphasizing quality as well as innovation, the gallery features America's most talented and creative furniture makers. Look especially for Richard Scott Newman's neo-neoclassical furniture, David Ebner's sculptural tables, and Ben Mack's architecturally inspired pieces. Next door, unusual items include metal collars by Eugene and Hiroko Pijanowski and Glasser and Nakayama's marble-glazed stoneware. There are also copper woven baskets, Tiffany-style leaded shell lamp shades, and even bejeweled utensils.

PRICES: $25–$30,000. Accepts American Express, MasterCard, Visa.

OPEN: Memorial Day–Sept. 30, Mon.–Sat., 11 A.M.–6 P.M.; Sun., noon–4 P.M. Oct. 1–late May, Fri., Sat., & Mon., 10 A.M.–5 P.M.; Sun., noon–4 P.M. Closed Thanksgiving, Christmas, New Year's, & Easter. Wheelchair accessible.

LOCATION: Eastern Long Island. 27–29 Race Lane, East Hampton, NY 11937; 516-324-7111. Take the Long Island Expressway (I-495) to exit 70, then Manorville Road south to Rte. 27. Follow Rte. 27, which becomes Main Street in East Hampton. At traffic light intersection, turn left onto Newtown Lane. Continue for three blocks. Just before the railroad tracks, bear left onto Railroad Avenue. Continue past the East Hampton train station, then bear left onto Race Lane. The shop is about 200 yards from the train station.

MASTIC BEACH

Jamie Tawodi Reason
BAS-RELIEF CEDAR BOXES

For Jamie, a Cherokee Indian, it is part of his heritage to create boxes portraying spiritual aspects of his culture. "For centuries, my ancestors carved boxes to hold sacred items such as gourd rattles and fans," Jamie says. "And although my designs come from within me, the themes are common to Indian beliefs."

Each box is carefully carved, then painted in strong colors. Many feature carved eagle feathers. On one, a finely detailed buffalo is bordered by eagle feathers whose quills and barbs are clearly defined. On another, bright red butterflies rest gently on a single feather. "The eagle feather represents the spirit of my people," Jamie says. "It is delicate and soft, yet contains the strength and power to lift the eagle to soar above the earth. Indian people have this same quality of delicate strength."

PRICES: $65–$2,500. Commissions are accepted, "but it must be something that I feel good about doing." Free catalog/brochure.

VISITORS: Yes.

LOCATION: South-central Long Island. Sacred Earth Studio, 197 Longfellow Drive, Mastic Beach, NY 11951; 516 399-4539. Please call for directions.

MORE: Jamie's work can be seen at many galleries, including Yah-Ta-Hey Gallery, 279 Captain's Walk, New London, CT 06320; 203-443-3204.

PORT WASHINGTON

Holt Haus Fiber Art Gallery

If "tapestry" suggests to you the flat, finely woven, pictorial pieces from ancient China and Renaissance Europe, let Holt Haus redefine this medium for you. Its contemporary tapestries include Susan Klebanoff's multilayer open weaves and Mary Kester's shaped sculptures, which defy traditional rectangular shapes by presenting the outline of a gigantic abstract fan or other irregular forms.

"I like to call this work 'haptic art,'" says owner Mary Ann Holthaus, "because 'haptic' is a Greek word meaning tactile. Good fiber art not only pleases visually but it also conveys a sense of how a piece feels to touch. Today texture is more important than ever, a welcome complement to the sleek, formal, and sometimes cold surfaces found in so many of our business and residential interiors." Displaying a range of wall hangings, fabric collages, and rugs, other "haptic art" exhibited at Holt Haus includes the layered and stitched modules of Ruth Geneslaw and the relief effect of Florence Samuels's quadruple linen weaves.

PRICES: $50–$6,000 (average, $1,000–$3,000). No credit cards.

OPEN: Tues., Thurs., Sat., noon–5 P.M., at other times by appointment. Closed major holidays. Not wheelchair accessible.

LOCATION: Western Long Island. 7 Irma Avenue, Port Washington, NY 11050; 516-883-8620. Take I-495 east to exit 36 (Searingtown Road/Port Washington). Go left at light onto Searingtown Road (also Rte. 101N). Continue north on Searingtown (which becomes Port Washington Boulevard) about 3 miles to Main Street, left on Main Street to third light, right on Irma to first house on the right. Park in driveway.

NEW YORK CITY

As might be expected, America's cultural hub offers a smorgasbord of craft galleries and museums. Due to costly overhead, however, many galleries are surprisingly small, and heavy competition means a short life for others. Listed below are the top museums and a few favorite galleries. Our recommendation? Wander around SoHo and Greenwich Village to sample a variety of craft galleries. For a listing of current area exhibits, get a copy of the *New York Gallery Guide,* published by Art Now Inc., P.O. Box 219, Scotch Plains, NJ 07076 ($3 for single copies, free at some New York City galleries, subscriptions also available).

BROOKLYN

New York Experimental Glass Workshop
CONTEMPORARY GLASS STUDIO/GALLERY

Leave behind the chic SoHo galleries, the vast holdings of major museums, and spend an afternoon at the country's most unusual glass studio, where visitors can view the full panoply of glassmaking: blowing, casting, slumping, fusing, lampworking, sandblasting, coldworking, neon, and other techniques. The studio was founded in 1977 to provide emerging glass artists with accessible, affordable studio time. Director Tina Yelle says, "We operate like a Laundromat. Artists don't have to be members, pass a portfolio review, or enroll as students. Anyone who can operate the equipment can pay by the hour to use our studio."

Although the artists have no regular schedule, you may be able to watch John Brekke use a "graal" technique involving glass overlays, Jane Bruce incorporate nontraditional materials in her work, James Harmon combine neon and blown glass, or William Gudenrath expertly blow Venetian-style glass. "Visitors should also stop by our gallery, which is an experimental space for the glass arts,"

Tina suggests. "Some exhibitions are only installation works; others are for sale. We also include glass artists who work outside of our studio, so there's a real variety."

PRICES: $35–$2,000. No credit cards.

OPEN: Mon.–Fri., 10 A.M.–6 P.M.; Sat. & Sun., noon–6 P.M. Wheelchair accessible.

LOCATION: Downtown Brooklyn. 647 Fulton Street, Brooklyn, NY 11217; 718-625-3685.

MORE: The workshop sponsors lectures and demonstrations that are free and open to the public and a full roster of workshops, classes, and seminars.

MANHATTAN

American Craft Museum
CONTEMPORARY CRAFTS

A dominant force in contemporary crafts, America's preeminent craft museum can trace its roots to 1940, when benefactor Aileen Osborn Webb first opened a craft sales outlet in Manhattan. Since 1986 the museum has been housed in its impressive new home opposite the Museum of Modern Art. Focusing on post–World War II crafts, the two major exhibition areas feature special shows and occasional displays from the permanent collection.

Often exhibiting work on the cutting edge of craft innovation, many of the museum's shows add fuel to the is-it-craft-or-is-it-art controversy. What can't be debated, however, is the curatorial excellence, which constantly challenges viewers to see crafts in new contexts. The range of shows is also impressive, from exhibits featuring premier artisans or a particular media to a serious consideration of robots or even the confectioner's art.

The only disappointment, especially to out-of-town visitors, is the inability to view more of the museum's superb permanent collection. On the positive side, however, travelers will always find new exhibits that challenge, inform, and surprise.

OPEN: Tues., 10 A.M.–8 P.M.; Wed.–Sun., 10 A.M.–5 P.M. Closed Christmas and New Year's. There is a small museum shop. Admission is $3.50 for adults, $1.50 for seniors and children 12–18. Admission is free for children under 12, ACC members, and Tues. after 5 P.M. Group tours only, by appointment. Wheelchair accessible.

LOCATION: Central Manhattan, between Fifth and Sixth avenues. 40 West 53rd Street, New York, NY 10019; 212-956-6047.

MORE: The ACC publishes a *Guide to Craft Galleries and Shops USA*, available for $5 plus $1.50 shipping/handling.

James Harmon: *Turquoise bowl with yellow wrap.*

MANHATTAN

James Harmon
CONTEMPORARY GLASS/NEON

Harmon paints with neon, decorates glass with glass. An internationally recognized artist, his work plays on subliminal and symbolic imagery, permitting viewers to delve into their own subconscious for interpretation. Influenced by painter Arshile Gorky's philosophy and Miró's imagery, Harmon's pieces have an aura of playful mystery. A luminous blue vase carries bright hieroglyphics next to squiggles of clear glass that encapsulate white streaks. A neon wall assemblage appears to be a glowing abstract sketch, changing definition with each viewing. Harmon also collaborates with Harry Anderson to create lamps that appear to be supernatural creatures composed of copper and brass tubes, blown and neon glass.

PRICES: $2,000 and up. Commissions accepted. Listed in *The Guild: A Sourcebook of American Craft Artists* (see separate entry in "National Crafts Catalogs and Events" for details).

VISITORS: Yes, by appointment.

LOCATION: 31 Second Avenue, New York, NY 10003; 212-529-8409.

MORE: Harmon's work can also be seen at the Heller Gallery (see next entry) and the Corning Museum of Glass (see Corning entry in Central New York section).

MANHATTAN (SOHO)

Heller Gallery
CONTEMPORARY GLASS

Unless you follow every nuance in the development of glass art, a visit to this gallery will have you constantly exclaiming "I didn't know you could do *that* with glass!" Located in the heart of artsy SoHo, the Heller Gallery has been exhibiting the latest in glass artistry since 1974. Generally exhibiting two glass artists, Heller is a virtual Who's Who of contemporary glass.

PRICES: Expensive. Accepts American Express, MasterCard, Visa.

OPEN: Tues.–Sat., 11 A.M.–6 P.M.; Sun., noon–5 P.M. Wheelchair accessible only with assistance at entrance.

LOCATION: In SoHo between Spring & Broom streets. 71 Greene Street, New York, NY 10012; 212-966-5948.

MANHATTAN

Julie: Artisan's Gallery
WEARABLE FIBER ART

This small shop bursts with innovative textiles: triangular-shaped knitted sweaters with glistening colors gradually shading from one hue to another, a black coat covered with squiggles of colored velvet, and Linda Mendelson's knitted scarves, where conservative centers are bound by a riot of colorful, contrasting edges. There are also fabric sculptures and jewelry, hand-painted silk garments by Julia Hall, and Jean Williams Cacicedo's wild pieced, dyed, and felted clothing.

PRICES: $50–$5,000 (average, $200–$1,500). Accepts American Express, Diners Club, MasterCard, Visa.

OPEN: Mon.–Sat., 11 A.M.–6 P.M. Closed major holidays. Wheelchair accessible.

LOCATION: Between 61st and 62d streets. 687 Madison Avenue, New York, NY 10021; 212-688-2345.

MANHATTAN

Metropolitan Museum of Art
AMERICAN CRAFTS

The perfect place to escape the frenzied hubbub of New York City is the Metropolitan's American Wing, particularly the Charles Englehard Court. Here, in a two-story indoor garden, the loudest sound is the trickle of water from a fountain. Surrounding the area is an array of stunning stained-glass windows by Tiffany, John La Farge, and Frank Lloyd Wright. On the second floor overlooking the garden, is a collection of Pennsylvania redware and other American ceramics, glass, silver, and pewter. Off the courtyard are eighteenth- and nineteenth-century American period rooms, furniture galleries, and a Frank Lloyd Wright living room reconstructed from a residence in Wayzata, Minnesota.

OPEN: Tues., 9:30 A.M.–8:45 P.M.; Wed.–Sun., 9:30 A.M.–5:15 P.M. Closed Thanksgiving, Christmas Day, and Jan. 1. There are several museum shops. Admission is $5 for adults, $2.50 for seniors and students, children under 12 accompanied by adult free. Tours daily. Wheelchair accessible.

LOCATION: On Fifth Avenue between 80th and 84th streets, on the east side of Central Park. Fifth Avenue, New York, NY 10028; 212-879-5500.

MANHATTAN

Museum of American Folk Art

With a collection spanning American folk art from the seventeenth century through the present day, the museum presents a breathtaking array of folk sculpture and painting, weathervanes and decoys, textiles and decorative arts. In its spiffy new home at Lincoln Square, the museum has an atrium and a Garden Court that serve as backdrops for an impressive collection of large-scale folk sculpture, including a 9-foot weathervane, several carousel animals, and cigar store Indians. Selections from the museum's permanent collection are displayed on a rotating basis in the south wing, while the north wing houses special exhibits.

The museum also sponsors an annual "Great American Quilt Festival," regular demonstrations by craftspeople, and a series of lectures and workshops through its Folk Art Institute. Next to the entrance is a large gift shop stocked with one-of-a-kind handcrafted objects created in the folk tradition, including whirligigs of Abraham Lincoln, wrought iron "courting" candles, jacquard coverlets, and ceramics.

OPEN: Every day of the year, 9 A.M.–9 P.M. There are two museum shops: one at the museum site, with books and items relating to special exhibits; the other at 62 West 50th Street (Rockefeller Center), offering some folk art. Free admission. Regularly scheduled tours. Wheelchair accessible.

LOCATION: Columbus Avenue between 65th and 66th streets. 2 Lincoln Square, New York, NY 10023; 212-977-7298.

MANHATTAN

Museum of the American Indian

No visit to New York City is complete without a stop at this comparatively unknown museum. The breadth and depth of this fine collection is astonishing: pottery and masks, textiles and basketry, beadwork and carving, decorative and functional crafts spanning over 10,000 years of native North American habitation. To take it all in requires several visits.

Begin on the first floor, where exhibits are arranged geographically by region and tribe. Among other items you will see: Huron buckskin embroidered with moose hair, Penobscot etched bark panels, elaborate Iroquois beading, Sauk/Fox woven reed mats, Cherokee finger-weaving, and Paiute baskets. The second floor displays crafts predating the arrival of colonists, including charming pottery ducks and owls from 200 B.C., intricately stamped ancient burial urns from the Carolinas, Hohokum and Mimbre pottery, and impressive Kwakiutl, Tlilngit, and Eskimo masks. The third floor includes Central and South American exhibits and paintings by Indian artists.

The object of a ferocious tug-of-war over a new site, the museum does need a modernized building and room to display even more of what is acknowledged as the largest and finest collection of Indian holdings in the world. Current exhibits tend to be crammed into old-fashioned display cases, sometimes inadequately labeled and poorly lighted, but

without question still worth seeing. One caution: Since the museum is not located in the best of areas, take a taxi instead of the subway or bus.

OPEN: Tues.–Sat., 10 A.M.–5 P.M.; Sun., 1–5 P.M. There is a museum shop of moderate variety and quality. Admission is $3 for adults, $2 for seniors and children. Tours by appointment. Not wheelchair accessible.

LOCATION: Harlem. Broadway and 155th Street, New York, NY 10032; 212-283-2420.

MANHATTAN

New York Historical Society
TIFFANY LAMP COLLECTION

Prepare yourself for the most dazzling assemblage of Tiffany lamp shades anywhere in the world. Bristling with color, a Tiffany kaleidoscope greets visitors to this otherwise drab museum. Arranged chronologically, the exhibit begins with simple, one-piece Favrile shades in muted browns and yellows, continues on to colorful but simple geometric shades, then passes into a shade garden blooming with bands, rows, and borders of bright flowers and gloriously colored dragonflies. The display ends with irregularly bordered shades that follow the realistic contours of leaves, flowers, and other natural forms. Although totally overshadowed by the Tiffany display, the adjoining room does have a nice selection of glass paperweights and pressed glass.

OPEN: Tues.–Sat., 10 A.M.–5 P.M.; Sun., 1–5 P.M. There is a museum shop. Admission is $2 for adults, $1.50 for seniors, $1 for children. Docents are available to answer questions. Not wheelchair accessible.

LOCATION: Central Park West between West 76th and West 77th streets. 170 Central Park West, New York, NY 10024; 212-873-3400.

MANHATTAN (SOHO)

Wallengren/USA
CONTEMPORARY CERAMICS

In contrast to every other gallery in the country, when you come to this one you're likely to hear owner Henry Wallengren say "Please touch!" "I've never had anyone break a piece," he says. "And ceramics are so tactile, you just have to feel their texture. It's part of appreciating the work."

You won't find a clash of garish colors or a range of bizarre shapes in this friendly gallery. Instead the emphasis is on highly traditional, classically derived form. Surface decoration is more likely to be texture than bold color, shapes are more often sensuous and flowing than jagged and jarring. "We're definitely anti-trendy," Henry agrees. "What we offer are exquisite objects with very subtle character." Ask him to show you the unusual black-on-black porcelain of Beth Forer; the restrained, oxide-tinged bottles and sake cups by George W. Peterson III; and the playful terra-cotta ewers and urns by Woody Hughes. And remember, touch (but be careful).

PRICES: $100–$2,500 (average, $250–$400). Accepts American Express.

OPEN: Wed.–Sun., noon–6 P.M. Closed federal holidays. Wheelchair accessible.

LOCATION: SoHo, between Spring and Prince streets. 75 Thompson Street, New York, NY 10012; 212-966-2266.

WESTERN NEW YORK

With the exception of Niagara Falls, western New York is rarely a tourist destination. It is known best for industrial Buffalo and Rochester, and travelers are likely to breeze through this region on their way elsewhere. Recommended craft stops, however, will introduce you to excellent Native American crafts, contemporary woodworking, a coverlet cornucopia, and one of America's historic craft communities.

BATAVIA

Donald J. Carmichael
WHIRLIGIGS

Move over, prize-winning roses and perfectly kept lawns, there's a new attraction garnering neighborhood attention: whirligigs that re-create famous American classics, both fact and fiction. Look! Over there! The headless horseman is jumping over a fence, Orville and Wilbur are about to become airborne, and Robert Fulton's steamship *North River* is heading upstream, paddles beating at full power.

"I'm making a series of forty classics," Don says, "from toy soldiers whose arms flap in the breeze to Harry Houdini sawing a woman in half. I've also done Mrs. O'Leary milking her cow and Sally Rand dancing with one leg while her arms twirl the famous fans." One of Don's most popular whirligigs is *Tom Sawyer Painting the Fence.* A realistic piece, this whirligig shows nails in the fence that have rusted and streaked, footprints where Tom has stepped in and tracked the whitewash, and even drips of whitewash that have run through the fence's knotholes. As the wind turns the main paddle, Tom paints the fence at a furious pace.

An artist who works by day preparing advertising copy for cable TV commercials and other promotions, Don is also a talented painter. "I do a little bit of everything," he agrees, "from pen and ink or watercolor renderings of homes, historical landmarks, and wildlife to folk art wood carvings, decoys, and wind toys. But whirligigs are my favorite. They're whimsical, colorful, and elaborate, but they also have to work just right when a breeze passes by."

PRICES: $100 and up. Commissions accepted. No catalog/brochure.

VISITORS: Yes. But "please call first to make sure I'm home."

LOCATION: Between Rochester and Buffalo. 26 Prospect Avenue, Batavia, NY 14020; 716-343-0130. Directions will be provided when you call.

EAST AURORA

Historic Roycroft
UTOPIAN ARTS & CRAFTS COMMUNITY

A successful soap company executive turned author/philosopher, Elbert Hubbard established a late nineteenth-century crafts community committed to "better art, better work, and a better and more

Roycroft Associates: Tall magazine pedestal. H. 63″; base 18″ sq.; top 14½″ sq.

reasonable way of living." Begun as a print shop, Roycroft reached its zenith in the early twentieth century with over 500 "Roycrofters" creating a variety of crafts from furniture and pottery to leather, copper, and blacksmith goods. A prominent force in America's Arts and Crafts movement, the community survived Hubbard's 1915 death only to fail during the Depression.

The fourteen remaining buildings of the Roycroft campus are now a National Historic Landmark and are slowly being restored. A refurbished Roycroft Inn will reopen in 1990, offering accommodations decorated with period crafts. Meanwhile, visitors can tour the other buildings, then stop by the former blacksmith/copper shop, which once served as Hubbard's bank but now houses a Roycroft Renaissance craft gallery.

Once again drawing quality craftspeople to take up residence in the area, the community is still only a shadow of its former self. Kitty Turgeon, however, is dedicated to making Roycroft the Williamsburg of the Arts & Crafts era. "That era," she explains, "was spawned by the Industrial Revolution and its dehumanization of life, much as the computer and technical world of today has created revived interest in the crafts. It's the perfect time for a Roycroft revival."

In addition to contemporary crafts made under the Roycroft Renaissance mark, visitors will find reproduction Roycroft pieces that reprise the community's heyday. With elements sometimes reminiscent of Tiffany lamp shades or Frank Lloyd Wright furniture, most pieces are uniquely Roycroft. Look for somewhat heavy, typically angular furniture like the magazine pedestal, which is shaped like an enclosed ladder, towers 63 inches high, and is fitted with five interior shelves. Also for sale are reproductions of the only companion wallcovering and china offered by anyone other than Limoges. Using a rich terra-cotta and dark, forest green motif, Roycroft Stripe wallpaper mirrors Roycroft dinnerware.

PRICES: Reproduction crafts, $12–$3,300. Accepts American Express, MasterCard.

OPEN: Mon.–Sat., 10 A.M.–5 P.M.; Sun., noon–5 P.M. Wheelchair accessible except for a small loft area.

LOCATION: Roycroft Campus is 20 miles southeast of Buffalo. Take I-90 to exit 54 (Rte. 400 south). Go south on Rte. 400 about 11 miles to Maple Street exit. Right on Maple Street and continue until it ends in East Aurora. Go left on

Main Street for two blocks, right on South Grove. Reproduction crafts are available at Roycroft Associates, 31 South Grove Street, East Aurora, NY 14052; 716-652-3333.

MORE: For information on the Roycroft Inn call or write 41 South Grove Street, East Aurora, NY 14052; 716-652-9030.

HONEOYE FALLS

William Keyser
WOOD FURNITURE AND ECCLESIASTICAL OBJECTS

The old adage "those who can, do; those who can't, teach" certainly doesn't apply to Bill Keyser. Although he *is* Chairman of Crafts at Rochester Institute of Technology's prestigious School for American Craftsmen, he is also an internationally recognized artisan. Working only on commission, Bill designs furniture for corporate and private clients as well as public and religious sites. What all his pieces have in common is a sculptor's interpretation of function. At first glance the eye sees only a graceful arch, a flowing curve, or a leaf form. Later it registers that the object is actually a subway bench, a church baptistery, or a music stand.

Bill's work can be seen at many public sites in upstate New York. Look for his unusual arched bench set between two natural rocks at the Artpark in Lewiston (north of Niagara Falls), the altar and other furnishings at RIT's Interfaith Chapel, or the baptistery at St. Joseph's Church in Penfield (east of Rochester).

PRICES: $500–$50,000. Most pieces are commissioned. Slides and other materials are available for commission clients.

VISITORS: Yes.

LOCATION: About 15 miles southeast of Rochester. 6543 Rush-Lima Road, Honeoye Falls, NY 14472; 716-533-1041. Take I-90 to exit 46, then Rte. 390 south to exit marked "Rush." Go left on Rte. 15, then one block to light and turn left on Rte. 251 to next light. Right at light to Rte. 15A. Bear left at white church; the house is 1 mile farther on the right.

MORE: Send an SASE for a list of other churches and public locations where Bill's work can be seen.

NIAGARA FALLS

Native American Center for the Living Arts

Whether it's your honeymoon or not, you'll want to see the famous falls (they're prettier from the Canadian side), but then what? Forgo the wax museum and other gimcrack offerings and head straight for one of the most unusual buildings you'll ever see, a 63,000-square-foot turtle that is both realistic and symbolic. According to the Iroquois, it was upon the back of a giant turtle that the earth was created.

The building was designed by Arapaho Indian architect Dennis Sun Rhodes, and it's difficult to pry yourself away from the exterior to take a peek inside. The central 160-foot diameter geodesic dome (the turtle's body) represents the Iroquois belief that the sky is a dome separating our world from the Creator's. The eagle, who flies highest toward that dome and is the Creator's messenger, is a sacred bird for all Native Americans and is represented here by a stylized skylight. The turtle's three-story head houses a restaurant, offices, and artist-in-residence quarters, and its appendages encompass a gift shop and a National Indian Art Gallery displaying contemporary work.

A major Indian cultural facility, the center has a permanent collection spanning the crafts and artifacts of almost seventy-five different Native American tribes. The museum's Orientation Hall stresses tribal diversity while highlighting some of the common symbols and philosophies found in Indian art. There is also a museum emphasizing the culture of the six Iroquois nations, a performing arts amphitheater, rotating exhibits in a central display area, and a gift shop offering a variety of Indian crafts.

OPEN: May–Sept., daily, 9 A.M.–6 P.M.; Oct.–Apr., Tues.–Fri., 9 A.M.–5 P.M., and Sat. & Sun., noon–5 P.M. Closed Christmas and New Year's Day. There is a museum shop. Admission is $3 for adults, $2.50 for seniors, $1.50 for students and children 5–12, children under 5 free. Wheelchair accessible.

LOCATION: 25 Rainbow Mall, Niagara Falls, NY 14303; 716-284-2427. Take I-190 to Robert Moses Parkway exit at the

James VanNess: Detail of 1849 double-weave jacquard coverlet. Wool, linen. W. 80″; L. 90″. COURTESY ALLING COVERLET MUSEUM

base of the second Grand Island bridge. Exit is to the right. Stay to the extreme right and follow the parkway downtown. Take the third exit and go straight to a stop sign. Go through this intersection and you will see a huge turtle on your right.

PALMYRA

Alling Coverlet Museum
NINETEENTH- AND TWENTIETH-CENTURY COVERLETS

Known as the birthplace of Mormonism, Palmyra is also home to America's largest coverlet collection. Often called the American Tapestry, coverlets were usually 80 inches by 90 inches and woven of homespun fibers. Although some were made at home by women, men created the more intricate ones on looms with up to twenty-four harnesses.

Using the French jacquard punched card method, elaborate patterns were created, often incorporating the owner's and weaver's names as part of the border design.

The work of James VanNess and Ira Hadsell, two of Palmyra's famous weavers, is part of the museum's collection. There are also double-weave, unusual tied structures, summer and winter, and overshot coverlets on display. The museum shop sells a variety of woven items as well as antique shuttles and bobbins.

OPEN: June–Sept., daily, 1–4 P.M. There is a museum shop. Free admission. Wheelchair accessible on first floor only.

LOCATION: 20 miles east of Rochester. 122 William Street, P.O. Box 96, Palmyra, NY 14522; 315-597-6737. Take I-90 to exit 43, then Rte. 21, 7 miles to the junction with Rte. 31 in Palmyra. Go right on Main Street, left on William. The museum is in a two-story brick building on the right.

MORE: While here, see the remnants of the 1856 Erie Canal Aqueduct located west of town, off Rte. 31.

WESTERN NEW YORK

97

SALAMANCA

Seneca-Iroquois National Museum
SENECA CRAFTS

One of six tribes in the Iroquois confederation, the Seneca nation once owned all of western New York and a portion of Pennsylvania. Now living on three reservations, the Seneca still create many of their traditional crafts, including beadwork, basketry, pottery, and cornhusk items.

Visitors are introduced to Seneca crafts by the building's exterior, which is covered with designs taken from wampum belt beadwork. Inside, the museum displays Seneca crafts from all time periods. Look particularly for the tightly woven cornhusk hat by Mattie Young, finely beaded purses, and wood utensils with carved handles that resemble snakes. In summer the museum's "living exhibits" feature Seneca artisans demonstrating their crafts.

OPEN: May 1–Oct. 1, Mon.–Sat., 10 A.M.–5 P.M.; Sun., noon–5 P.M. Oct. 2–Apr. 30, Tues.–Sat., 10 A.M.–5 P.M.; Sun., noon–5 P.M. There is a museum shop. Free admission. Tours. Wheelchair accessible.

LOCATION: Southwestern New York, about 60 miles south of Buffalo. Broad Street Extension, Box 442, Salamanca, NY 14779; 716-945-1738. Take Rte. 17 to exit 20. Veer right; the museum is on the immediate left.

MORE: Seneca crafts can be found in several local shops and at the annual Seneca Nation Christmas Bazaar; contact the museum for details. The Seneca Nation also operates a number of local businesses, including a campground (716-354-4855).

WARSAW

Steve Loar
TURNED-WOOD VESSELS

What makes Steve's vessels so unusual is their presentation. Resting on a painted root ball on sculpted arms of exotic wood, or balanced tenuously on a rock, the bowls appear to be actively offering themselves to the viewer. "I force my forms away from conventional pedestals and the 'foot'

Steve Loar: *Post-Melvin Bud-bowl, #3.* Ornamental crabapple, persimmon, spalted maple, rock, paint. H. 10″; W. 6″; D. 8″.
FRANK PETRONIO

people are used to seeing," Steve explains. "To give them a different grounding I use all sorts of things, even bricks, plastic, shattered chunks of wood, and found objects."

The heart of each piece, however, is a thin, carefully turned, spalted wood vessel. Sometimes Steve also sandblasts the exterior, or even adds a coat of paint, perhaps stark white or brilliant purple. "I look to ceramics and glass for inspiration," Steve says. "I'm also affected by the contrast between man's mania for rigid order versus the infinitely varied order of nature."

PRICES: $250–$1,000. Commissions accepted. No catalog/brochure.

VISITORS: Yes. Please call first.

LOCATION: 40 miles southwest of Rochester. 6 East Court Street, Warsaw, NY 14569-1302; 716-786-5864. Directions will be provided when appointment to visit is made.

MORE: Steve's work can also be seen at the Dawson Gallery, 349 East Avenue, Rochester, NY 14604; 716-454-6609.

MID-ATLANTIC

The mid-Atlantic region presents a colorful tapestry of traditional and contemporary crafts, found in upscale galleries as well as back road shops, major museums and artists' studios, established festivals and casual craft shows. Travelers can design craft itineraries that will take them from Virginia's colonial crafts to Pennsylvania's predominant German and Amish work; from West Virginia's traditional Appalachian crafts to collector-quality galleries in Baltimore, Washington D.C., Philadelphia, and Pittsburgh. Tantalizing craft side trips can also be made to New Jersey, Delaware, and Maryland.

MID-ATLANTIC

PENNSYLVANIA

Muncy •
Wapwallopen •
Bushkill •
• Layton
• Tenafly

I-80

Northampton County
I-78 **NEW JERSEY**
• Newark

Boalsburg
Lenhartsville •
Stouchsburg •
• Marlboro

• Pittsburgh
• Roaring Spring
Lebanon •
• Robesonia
• Doylestown

I-79

Elizabethtown •
Phoenixville •
Philadelphia •
Lancaster •
Paoli •
Millersville •
• Media
Red Lion •
Intercourse •
Winterthur • Arden
• Lavallette

New Martinsville •
Star City •
• Morgantown
Wilmington •
North East •
• Salem

MARYLAND

Williamstown •
Odessa •
Garden State Parkway
• Atlantic City
Seaville •

• Baltimore

• Weston
Bethesda •
WASHINGTON, D.C.

WEST VIRGINIA

Chloe •
The Plains •
Alexandria •
DELAWARE

Ceredo Milton Scott Depot
Huntington • Hurricane • Charleston
I-81

Beckley •
Charlottesville •
I-64
Lewisburg •
VIRGINIA
I-64

Richmond •
West Point •

• Lynchburg
Williamsburg •
Jamestown •
• Roanoke
Newport News •

Floyd • Ferrum •

I-77
I-95

DELAWARE

There's more to the country's second smallest state than meets the hurried interstate eye: sand and surf pursuits on the southeastern shore; excellent fishing in lakes, streams, and along the Delaware Bay; and one of the eastern seaboard's prime craft experiences—Winterthur Museum's extraordinary collection of period American crafts. A nearby artist's community, an April traditional crafts fair, and a fine contemporary gallery offer a welcome intermission from the highway blues.

ARDEN

Artists' Community

Even if you don't visit Arden in person, it is an oddity worth knowing about. Surrounded by parkland, sprinkled with footpaths and curving roads, the entire village of Arden is listed on the National Register of Historic Places. Founded in 1900 by artists, craftspeople, and others, Arden is a Utopian community that survived.

Arden's founders, followers of philosopher-economist Henry George, believed in a "single tax community," with the sole tax levied on the value of land, irrespective of its improvements. Today the land is still owned by the community; residents receive ninety-nine-year leases and are obligated to pay only "rent," a single local tax that covers community services.

Although Arden is still home to many artisans, there is no longer a local gallery. Visitors may, however, contact several craftspeople who work out of their homes, including: Alan Burslem, a potter (302-475-8763); jewelry makers Naomi Clark (302-475-2608) and Helga Melton (302-475-7667); and Sally Thurston, who, doing business as Glorious Mud, creates costumes and custom tiles (302-475-5604).

LOCATION: North of Wilmington. Take I-95 to the Harvey Road exit. Turn left on Harvey Road. Arden is about half a mile west.

MORE: Since 1907 Arden has held an annual arts and crafts fair. The fair includes over fifty craftspeople and features one booth designated for Arden residents, an antiques flea market, music, and pony rides. It is held on the Sat. of Labor Day weekend, 10 A.M.–6 P.M., on the grounds of Arden Gild Hall. Free admission.

ODESSA

Odessa Spring Festival
TRADITIONAL CRAFTS

Settled by the Dutch in the seventeenth century, Odessa was a major grain-shipping port during the early nineteenth century before settling down to a relatively quiet existence. Its restored district, known as Historic Homes of Odessa, offers a glimpse into early nineteenth-century architecture, furnishings, and decorative arts. It is also the site of an annual festival where craftspeople demonstrate, display, and sell their traditional crafts. A sampling might include everything from beekeeping and tin-smithing to the art of painting floor cloths and making brooms. It's definitely worth a short side trip if you're breezing through Delaware on your way from D.C. to New York.

EVENT: Last Sun. in Apr., noon–5 P.M. Admission is $5 for adults, $4 for seniors and children 12–16, children under 12 free.

LOCATION: 23 miles south of Wilmington. Corbit-Sharp House, Main Street & 2d Street, Odessa. Take I-95 to Newark/Rte. 896, go south on Rte. 896 to Middletown, left on Rte. 299 to Odessa.

MORE: For information contact Historic Homes of Odessa, P.O. Box 507, Odessa, DE 19730; 302-378-4069

WILMINGTON

Blue Streak Gallery
CONTEMPORARY CRAFTS

Most travelers know Wilmington as an urban blur speeding past in the car window on I-95 just south of Philadelphia. If you're not in a hurry, stop and visit Blue Streak, Delaware's only contemporary crafts gallery. Located in a converted row house, Blue Streak provides good browsing, including work by twenty area artisans.

Among the most intriguing items are Mitch Lyons's unusual vessels, which combine stoneware and porcelain. "I start with a slab of stoneware clay," Mitch explains, "which I inlay with colored porcelain. I then wrap the slab around a cardboard tube centered on a slow-moving kick wheel. Later I remove the tube, pinch and paddle the vessel into the shape I want." The result? Colorful vessels with soft abstract designs.

Also worth seeing are quilted wall hangings and wearable art by Arlinka Blair, and sleek sculptural jewelry by Charlie Buck. If you want a bizarre memento of your Wilmington stop, buy one of Ken Loeber's fish pins, real little fish dipped in plastic (buy several and tell your children it's snack time).

PRICES: $11–$900 (average, $20–$80). Accepts MasterCard, Visa.

OPEN: Tues.–Fri., 10 A.M.–5 P.M.; Sat., 10 A.M.–4 P.M.. Closed Thanksgiving, Christmas, and New Year's Day. Not wheelchair accessible.

LOCATION: About eight blocks from I-95. 1723 Delaware Avenue, Wilmington, DE 19806; 302-429-0506. Take I-95 to the Delaware Avenue north exit. Continue on Delaware Avenue about eight blocks to intersection with Scott Street. The gallery is on the right.

MORE: The Delaware Art Museum Craft Fair is a one-day juried event featuring over sixty craftspeople and their work, both contemporary and traditional. It is held on the first Sat. in June, 10 A.M.–5 P.M. at Kentmere Parkway & the museum grounds. Free admission. For more information contact the Delaware Art Museum, 2301 Kentmere Parkway, Wilmington, DE 19806; 302-571-9594.

WINTERTHUR

Winterthur Museum and Gardens
EARLY AMERICAN DECORATIVE ARTS

A 1737 Pennsylvania-made chest was the first of over 89,000 American craft objects collected by the late Henry Francis du Pont. After purchasing the

Pennsylvania walnut dresser, 1750–1825, filled with sgraffitoware. COURTESY WINTERTHUR MUSEUM AND GARDENS

chest in 1923, du Pont began collecting other American furniture. Later his interest expanded to encompass all decorative arts made or used in America between 1640 and 1840, including textiles, needlework, ceramics, glassware, and metalwork as well as paintings, prints, books, and newspapers.

Developing a personal collecting philosophy, du Pont was interested in what distinguished the work of American artisans from their European counterparts—how foreign forms were adapted to the needs of a new country. Although he recognized that the items were objects of beauty, he was more interested in their ability to tell America's story.

Displaying this many objects would boggle the minds of most curators, but this museum has succeeded superbly. Rather than rows of dreary showcases, objects are displayed in 196 period room settings spread throughout Winterthur, the former du Pont estate. Unfortunately, but understandably, visitors can't wander the halls on their own. Instead, you must choose a general tour called "Two Centuries," one of three topical tours, or, with advance reservations, a tour tailored to your own particular interests.

Designed by du Pont himself, "Two Centuries" provides a survey of the collection, leading visitors chronologically through 200 years of American interiors. Topical tours offered include "American Craftsmanship," which traces the design history of American decorative arts; "American Interiors," which emphasizes furniture styles and regional differences in domestic furnishings; and "A Diverse Nation," which focuses on ethnic and regional crafts made by the New York Dutch, the Pennyslvania Germans, the Shakers, and the English.

No matter which tour you choose, you will be confronted with a craft feast, from Chippendale furniture by Newport cabinetmakers and Paul Revere's silver tankards to cabinets filled with chalkware figures or sgraffito. A final bonus are the gardens, 200 acres of naturalized planting surrounding the museum, intended to be an interpretation of an eighteenth-century English landscape park.

OPEN: Tues.–Sat., 9 A.M.–5 P.M. The museum shop offers reproduction furniture, textiles, accessories. Free catalog with color illustrations, some of museum reproductions. Admission for "Two Centuries" tour and gardens is $8 for adults, $6.50 for seniors, children under 12 free. Admission for one-hour topical tours is $8 for adults, $4 for children 12–16. Admission for two-hour topical tours is $12.50 for adults, $6 for children 12–16. Advance reservations are suggested for topical tours. Wheelchair accessible.

LOCATION: 6 miles northwest of Wilmington. Route 52, Winterthur, DE 19735; 800-448-3883 or 302-888-4400. Take I-95 to exit 7 (Rte. 52). Follow Rte. 52 north for 6 miles to museum entrance.

MARYLAND

Baltimore's renaissance has transformed the state's urban center from a dilapidated naval town to a sparkling cultural center with a lively arts scene. Fine galleries, ceramic studios, and the outstanding winter ACC Craft Fair are some of the city's craft highlights. The crowning jewels, however, are East Baltimore's painted window screens, a unique tradition revived by artisan Dee Herget.

To explore beyond the Washington, D.C.–Baltimore urban corridor, visit the upper Potomac River and Appalachian Mountain regions, which offer a scenic, peaceful contrast. Equally appealing but even more remote are the small bays and islands that dot Maryland's Chesapeake Bay shoreline. Please let us know about craftspeople you meet in these areas: decoy makers, traditional boat buildings, and others.

BALTIMORE

ACC Craft Fair
CONTEMPORARY CRAFTS

Zip up your parka, pull on those galoshes, and DON'T forget your wallet. It's time to brave February storms to see the largest of the American Craft Council's incomparable craft fairs. In 1976, the Baltimore winter fair was the first indoor craft show in the country. Before then, craft events were considered mere offshoots of flea markets or summer carnivals. Putting a roof overhead showed that craftspeople meant business, and business is just what these exhibitors do, almost $10 million worth a year just in Baltimore.

The fair is open the first two days only to the "trade" (wholesalers); the public then has three days to explore the work of over 500 craftspeople. Chosen from almost 2,000 applicants, exhibitors cover the artistic gamut. The one consistent factor in every piece is fine workmanship. Although specific items may not be your collectible cup of tea, it's impossible not to admire their quality. One piece of advice: For the best selection show up a few minutes before the opening on the first day of the public show.

EVENT: Third week of Feb., Fri., 11 A.M.–8 P.M.; Sat. 11 A.M.–6 P.M.; Sun. 11 A.M.–5 P.M. Admission is $5 for adults, children under 12 free.

LOCATION: Baltimore Convention Center, corner of Pratt and Sharp streets, Baltimore. From Washington, D.C., take I-295 (Baltimore-Washington Parkway) north. I-295 becomes Russell Street in Baltimore. Continue through several lights to Pratt Street. Turn right on Pratt; the Convention Center is two blocks farther. From the north, take I-95 to I-695, I-695 (toward Towson) to I-83, I-83 south to the Maryland Avenue exit. Left on Maryland (which becomes Cathedral Street, then Hopkins Place) for about sixteen blocks to Pratt Street; the Convention Center is on the corner of Pratt and Sharp.

MORE: For information contact American Craft Enterprises, Inc., P.O. Box 10, New Paltz, NY 12561; 914-255-0039.

BALTIMORE

Baltimore Clayworks
CONTEMPORARY CERAMICS

"**A**rtists really *can* plot out their own destiny," Deborah Bedwell says, "and that realization is the cornerstone of Baltimore Clayworks." Bedwell, executive director of Clayworks, was one of nine founding members. "We wanted," she says, "a building we owned, a space we controlled, a center for quality programming in the ceramic arts." Since 1978 Clayworks has offered classes and workshops, a sales gallery, and, its core, fifteen studios for ceramic artists. "Visitors are welcome to drop by the studios any time we're open," she adds.

Linked only by their common interest in ceramics, Clayworks's studio artists include founding member Ronni Aronin. Ronni specializes in straightforward porcelain forms decorated with sparse wisps of color that occasionally sprout exuberant bursts of colored raffia. In another studio, David Yocum's wall pieces combine ceramics and neon. Although these two media are seemingly incompatible, neon lights otherwise hidden recesses in the sculpted forms and infuses them with an almost palpable color. Some pieces are an essay in color and form, others appear to offer viewers a peek at the internal organs of a mystical creature. Interested in the bizarre? Look for Volker Schoenfliess's sculpted diners for dogs or his "Pim-

ple mobile," a miniature VW covered with ceramic zits.

PRICES: $15–$300. Accepts MasterCard, Visa.

OPEN: Mon.–Sat., 10 A.M.–5 P.M. Not wheelchair accessible.

LOCATION: Northwestern Baltimore. 5706 Smith Avenue, Baltimore, MD 21209; 301-578-1919. Take I-695 (Baltimore Beltway) to exit 22 (Greenspring Avenue). Follow Greenspring south to the second light. Turn left on Smith Avenue and proceed for 1.75 miles to a DO NOT ENTER sign. Clayworks is immediately on the right.

BALTIMORE

Dee Herget
PAINTED WINDOW SCREENS

Don't confuse Baltimore's painted window screens with the tasteless copies found in the back windows of pickup trucks and campers. In stark contrast, Baltimore's trademark screens are created by professional artists such as Dee Herget and are part of the city's craft history.

"They originated during the hot summer of 1913," Dee says. "Produce store owner William Anton Oktavec wanted to advertise what he sold, but didn't want his wares wilting outside in the heat. He solved the problem by painting fruits and vegetable on his window screens. Shortly thereafter, a neighborhood woman complained to him about local bar patrons peering in her living room window. His suggestion? A painted screen to protect her privacy, yet allow her to see out. Soon Oktavec was filling almost as many orders for screens as for apples and oranges."

Popular from the 1920s through the 1950s, painted screens were most common in East Baltimore, where they graced the windows of the famous marble-stooped row houses. When air-conditioning became more common, however, the need for screens decreased and the art almost died out. Today Dee Herget is one of the few practitioners of this unusual and appealing craft.

"I learned from another screen painter, Ben Richardson," Dee says. "But the designs are very much my own." Dee's colorful screens may depict

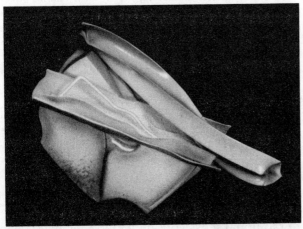

Dave Yocum: *Wave-cut.* Clay, neon. H. 20″; W. 28″; D. 8″. PHIL LAMBDIN PHOTOGRAPHY

Dee Herget: Painted screen door.

a country cottage with swans in a nearby pond, a lighthouse perched on a rocky shore, a Rocky Mountain forest, or a Swiss chalet. "Or I can paint any scene you'd like," she adds. "And, if you have screens on your front door and several nearby windows, I can continue the motif across all of them."

PRICES: $25–$150. Commissions accepted. No catalog/brochure.

VISITORS: Yes.

LOCATION: Off Rtes. 695 and 40. 910 Sue Grove Road, Baltimore, MD 21221; 301-391-1750. Directions will be provided when appointment to visit is made.

BALTIMORE

Tomlinson Craft Collection
CONTEMPORARY CRAFTS

With an emphasis on functional crafts, Tomlinson's two Baltimore galleries offer a good variety of reasonably priced jewelry, ceramics, and glass. The Chester Street gallery is located in the hub of Baltimore's cultural district, while Tomlinson's Rotunda shop is housed in a former insurance building reincarnated as a mini-mall. Although most artisans' work is carried in both galleries, changing exhibits are featured only at the Chester Street location.

Need a wedding gift? Consider Peter Saenger's black-and-white porcelain tea sets or Nol Putnam's standing wrought iron candelabra. Want a treat for yourself? Then take home one of Thomas Kluss's birds. Up to 3 inches tall, these perky sculptures are guaranteed to entertain without requiring messy cage cleanups.

PRICES: $5–$5,000 (average, $50–$100). Accepts American Express, MasterCard, Visa.

OPEN: Charles Street shop—Mon.–Sat., 10 A.M.–5:30 P.M.; Sun., 1–5 P.M. Rotunda shop—Mon.–Sat., 10 A.M.–9 P.M.; Sun., noon–5 P.M. Closed major holidays. Both locations wheelchair accessible.

LOCATION: Charles Street shop—516 North Charles Street, Baltimore, MD 21201; 301-539-6585. Charles Street is the main north/south street in the city. The shop is located one block from Walters Art Museum and Peabody Institute. Rotunda shop—711 West 40th Street, Baltimore, MD 21211; 301-338-1572. Take I-83 to the Cold Spring Lane exit. Proceed to Falls Road. Go left on Falls to 41st Street, then left on 41st, which becomes 40th.

BETHESDA

Glass Gallery
CONTEMPORARY GLASS

Traditional glassworking techniques have been left in the dust by this gallery's artisans. One example is Richard Royal's deeply ribbed, ruffled vessels, which are fashioned by a unique process. After blowing the initial bubble with three to five overlays, he cuts them on a bandsaw, then reblows, enlarges, and shapes them further.

The gallery also exhibits Kent F. Ipsen's massive sculptures, which are cast using the lost wax method and fired in a computerized kiln of his own design. Also worth noting are the sand-etched bowls of Patrick Wadley, Vincent Olmstead's cast abstract sculptures, and scuba diver David Leppla's inspired sea forms. If you're visiting in January, don't miss the gallery's annual Capitol Glass Invitational. Open only to glass artists working professionally for less than five years, the show permits a glimpse at the next generation of glass masters.

PRICES: $10–$7,000 (average, $150–$2,000). Accepts Discover, MasterCard, Visa.

OPEN: Tues.–Sat., 11 A.M.–5 P.M. Closed major holidays. Wheelchair accessible.

LOCATION: 20 minutes from downtown Washington, D.C. 4931 Elm Street, Bethesda, MD 20814; 301-657-3478. Take I-495 (Capital Beltway) to the Wisconsin Avenue exit, then Wisconsin Avenue south about 2.5 miles to Elm Street. Go right on Elm. The gallery is one and one half blocks down, on the right.

MORE: For a peaceful break from metropolitan D.C., picnic at nearby Great Falls on the Potomac River. From the gallery, go south two blocks on Arlington Road, then right on Bradley Boulevard for three blocks to Goldsboro Road, left on Goldsboro to MacArthur Boulevard, right on MacArthur to Great Falls.

NORTH EAST

Day Basket Co.
TRADITIONAL WHITE OAK BASKETS

After the Civil War, brothers Edward and Samuel Day began supplying Southern farmers with cotton picking baskets. Seeking cheaper transportation costs and closer proximity to Maryland's fine white oak forests, they relocated their company from Massachusetts to North East in 1876. By the start of World War I, they employed thirty-five people and made 2,000 baskets a week.

When the company was for sale a few years ago, Ross Gibson bought it. Still producing each basket by hand using the same 1876 techniques, the company offers ten different varieties from a berry picking basket to a large laundry basket. "They can be used," Ross points out, "in the home or, better yet, outside. They weather beautifully. The only care I recommend is washing them with water once or twice a year to keep them from getting too dry."

PRICES: $16.50–$71. No commissions. Send a business-size SASE for the catalog/brochure.

VISITORS: Mon.–Fri., 7 A.M.–4 P.M.; Sat., 10 A.M.–4 P.M.

LOCATION: About 30 miles southwest of Wilmington, Delaware. 110 West High Street, North East, MD 21901; 301-287-6100. Take I-95 to exit 100, then Rte. 272 south. Continue past the red light, then take the first right. Look for the sign with a basket on top.

NEW JERSEY

New Jersey isn't just Atlantic City gambling, Miss America contests, and sprawling suburbia. It's also a geologically fascinating state from the Delaware Water Gap region in the north to the marshes and forest of the Pine Barrens and the outer bank's barrier beaches. Crafts inspired by the sea (decoys, shorebird carvings, traditional wooden boats, and abstract ceramic vessels) vie for attention with a variety of contemporary crafts.

LAVALLETTE

Charles Hankins
WOODEN BOATS

Narrow barrier islands shadow New Jersey's coast for over forty miles, mimicking the mainland shore, providing lush wildlife habitat and protected bays. Although the islands have the usual summer tourist hoopla, it's still easy to grasp what the area was like in the early eighteenth century, when whalers and other fishermen were the only inhabitants. One way to evoke those memories is a visit with Charles Hankins, one of the last craftsmen still building

Jersey sea skiffs. "I learned boatbuilding from my father," Charles says. "For over seventy-five years, the firm has built the surf boats native to this coast."

Outside Charles's workshop, visitors will find rows of boats waiting for final finishing or pickup by their new owners. Inside, the shop is filled with partially built hulls, wood scraps, a pile of back orders, and the smell of paint. "I make the Sea Bright Dory Surf Boat," Charles says. "It's an ideal general utility boat designed for rugged ocean use by sport fishermen, lifesavers, and commercial users. It's easily handled, easily maintained, and built for surf launching." Available also as power or sailing skiffs, the boats are 16 to 18 feet in length

Charles Hankins: 16′ Jersey sea skiff.

108

with a 5'3"-to-6'3" beam. Stem and stern are made from white oak, planking from white cedar lapstrake, and all fastenings are copper-riveted bronze and brass.

PRICES: $3,400–$35,000. Free one-page descriptive sheet.

VISITORS: Yes. Mon.–Sat., 8 A.M.–4 P.M.

LOCATION: Mid-coast, about 60 miles northeast of Atlantic City. 504 Grand Central Avenue, Lavallette, NJ 08735; 201-793-7443. Take I-195 east, past Howell, to the Garden State Parkway, Garden State Parkway south to the Rte. 37 exit (just north of Tom's River). Take Rte. 37 east to the ocean, then Rte. 35 north to Lavallette. The shop is right on Rte. 35.

LAYTON

Peters Valley Crafts Center
ARTISAN STUDIOS, GALLERY

Smack dab in the middle of the gorgeous Delaware Water Gap National Recreation Area is a year-round residential crafts community where selected artisans are invited to work on their projects for up to three years. Located in buildings that once formed the now defunct town of Bevans, Peters Valley offers studio space and living quarters for up to ten resident craftspeople. In addition, the former general store/post office is the center for a summer crafts school that attracts students and well-known instructors from throughout the world.

Travelers can drop by studios to watch work in progress, peek into a workshop, attend lectures by visiting craft notables, or stop by the gallery to purchase completed creations. Limiting its media to blacksmithing, ceramics, jewelry, photography, textiles, and woodworking, Peters Valley often explores unusual approaches to contemporary crafts. Depending upon who is in residence, visitors may find decorative marine carvings, marbled fabrics, repoussé jewelry, Korean inlay ceramics, or even Damascus steel bladesmithing.

Of particular interest to pottery devotees is the site's *anagama* kiln. Stretching for 50 feet up on a nearby hill, large enough to stand in at one point, this is one of the only single-chambered "climbing kilns" outside of Japan. Fired for four days with wood, *anagama* ceramics reflect the distribution of ash in the kiln with results both unpredictable and unique.

PRICES: $2–$1,000 (the gallery sells work by center residents, visiting instructors, and over 450 other artisans). Accepts MasterCard, Visa.

OPEN: Year-round, daily, 10 A.M.–5 P.M. Closed Easter, Christmas, New Year's Day. The lower level is wheelchair accessible; the upper level is not.

LOCATION: Northwestern New Jersey, along the Delaware River. Peters Valley Craftsmen, Inc., Route 615, Layton, NJ 07851; 201-948-5200; 201-948-5202 (gallery). Take I-80 to exit 34B (Rte. 15, Dover). Take Rte. 15 north to Rte. 206. Continue on Rte. 206 north past the main entrance to Stokes State Forest. One mile farther, turn left onto County Road #560. Continue to center of Layton. At the blinking light, bear left onto Rte. 640. Proceed about 1.5 miles to stop sign. Turn right onto Rte. 615 and go 1 mile. The gallery and studios are on the right (look for the Peters Valley sign).

MORE: Annually, during the last weekend in July, Peters Valley sponsors a crafts fair featuring over 150 juried artisans. Contact the center for details.

DELAWARE WATER GAP: This presents spectacular geologic definitions. The "gap" was created over millions of years as the Delaware River cut through the Appalachian mountains. Wooded mountains and waterfalls, scenic valleys and riverbanks provide outstanding canoeing, horseback riding, hiking, and cross-country skiing. Biannual hawk migrations and July rhododendron displays are among the seasonal attractions.

MARLBORO

Scherer Gallery
CONTEMPORARY CRAFTS

Made from inlaid woods or nicely turned pieces of bird's-eye maple, kaleidoscopes abound in gift shops and galleries. Generally, seeing and playing with one for five minutes is the extent of their allure. Not so with the slew of eyepieces offered at Scherer. Boasting one of the largest collections on the East Coast, this gallery even sells kaleidoscopes made from goose eggs.

But there's more. Look for Myrna Goodman's ceramic "quilts" made from stoneware squares sewn on linen, and her contemporary wood tables, which display abstract ceramic constructions in a glass-topped well. Also made of wood, and arguably more fine art than craft, are R. H. Karol's female sculptures formed with layered slabs of hardwood. Working from a photograph, Karol divides a female form into forty or more horizontal planes, then re-creates each plane from ¼-inch to ½-inch hardwood. Reconstructing the figure, Karol relayers the slices in a slightly offset manner to create the illusion of movement.

PRICES: $50–$5,000 (average, $100–$500). No credit cards.

OPEN: Wed.–Sun., 10 A.M.–5 P.M. Closed Father's Day, Thanksgiving, Christmas, and New Year's Day. Not wheelchair accessible.

LOCATION: South of Perth Amboy. 93 School Road West, Marlboro, NJ 07746; 201-536-9465. Take the Garden State Parkway to exit 123 (Rte. 9), Rte. 9 south 7 miles to Rte. 18. Turn left on Rte. 18 and go 4 miles to Rte. 79. Go left on Rte. 79 to School Road West, right on School Road. The gallery is 1 mile farther, on the left.

SALEM

Malcolm Jones
ENGRAVED SLATE, BRASS MOULDED THIMBLES, MEDALS, AND BUTTONS

"For thirty-nine years, I was a mould maker in the glass industry," Malcolm says. "I made hand-cut iron bottle moulds. But in 1950 machines started to replace hand cutting and I just stopped enjoying my work. I decided to strike out on my own and now I create a full line of engraved and moulded items."

"For a lot of my work I use black Pennsylvania or green Vermont slate," Malcolm continues. "Then, using just my hammer and chisels, I make belt buckles and nameplates for homes or boats. I do the same thing in brass. I can make them as fancy as you like with dogs, bear, birds, or just some nice lettering. They've been pretty popular. Made a belt buckle for Tom Jones and one for his manager. Even made three for Walter Cronkite which showed a Massachusetts yacht club pennant."

Malcolm also custom designs commemorative medals, hand engraving the moulds, then casting them from fine pewter. Personal favorites for many collectors, however, are Malcolm's ornate pewter thimbles. Offered in grape, forget-me-not, "goose chase," and other patterns, each thimble is a miniature work of art.

PRICES: $6–$75; thimbles, $5–6; large slate signs, $200–$500; custom medals, $450 and up. Commissions accepted. Send an SASE for the catalog/brochure.

VISITORS: Yes.

LOCATION: Southwestern New Jersey, about 24 miles from Wilmington, Delaware, and 10 minutes from the Delaware Memorial Bridge. R.D. #1, Box 157, Bassett Road, Salem, NJ 08079; 609-935-4159. Please call for directions.

Malcolm Jones: Moulded thimbles.

SEAVILLE

Harry V. Shourds
DUCK DECOYS, CARVED BIRDS

Although Harry is a third-generation master carver whose works are sometimes sold by Sotheby's, he still makes what he terms "working" decoys, meant for a good day's duck hunting, not a museum shelf. "I make them the same way my grandfather did," Harry says. "I use white cedar and hand tools. I hollow each one out and weight them for balance, carve them carefully, then paint in the details."

Whatever type of duck or bird you desire, for hunting or display, Harry's special touch will create them within a breath of being alive: swans, mallards, quail, sandpipers, even a goldfinch or the dramatic hooded merganser. "I've been fascinated with decoys ever since I watched my dad carve them when I was a young boy," Harry continues. "I've never gotten over it. I like to work and create with my hands, capture the beauty of birds. All of my decoys and birds, by the way, are "happy"—I don't ever show them angry or frightened."

PRICES: $40–$600. Commissions accepted. Free catalog/brochure.

VISITORS: Yes.

LOCATION: Southern New Jersey, upper Cape May area. Ducks Nest, 2025 South Shore Road, Oceanview, NJ 08230; 609-390-0427. (Note: mailing address is in nearby Oceanview.) From Atlantic City and points north, take Garden State Parkway south to exit 25. Turn right to Rte. 9 and continue south on Rte. 9 for 4.5 miles. Ducks Nest is on the left side of the road.

TENAFLY

America House Gallery of Contemporary Crafts

Located across the Hudson River from Yonkers, Tenafly is a busy suburban town. If you're nearby, plan a visit to this delightfully eclectic gallery.

For blooms that won't fade, consider Cam Langly's blown glass flowers, single fluted blossoms 8 inches in diameter. Other blown glass items include Richard Marquis's "Wizard teapots," made using the "murrini" technique. Richard creates glass canes ¼ inch in diameter with miniature designs in their centers. After slicing the canes, he applies them to the surface of a teapot to create a work steeped in sparkling designs.

The gallery's pottery offerings include Sara Mott's ceramic birdhouses; Madeline Kaczmarczyk's gaudy, cockeyed teapots; and elegant sculptured raku vessels by David Norton. For something even more unusual, look for Eve Kaplin's high-tech clocks, Gail Rapoport's luminous cloisonné jewelry, and Steve Malavolta's multilevel wood puzzles, which combine exotic woods and stone inlay.

PRICES: $11–$3,000 (average, $75–$150). Accepts MasterCard, Visa.

OPEN: Mon.–Sat., 10 A.M.–5:30 P.M. Closed July 4th, Labor Day, and Christmas. Wheelchair accessible.

LOCATION: New York City metropolitan area. 24 Washington Street, Tenafly, NJ 07670; 201-569-2526. Take I-85/I-90 to Rte. 9W, Rte. 9W north to East Clinton Avenue. Turn left onto Clinton for about three-quarters of a mile to Railroad Avenue. Turn right on Railroad and go one block to Washington Street. Turn left on Washington. The gallery will be on your left.

TENAFLY

Coco Schoenberg
CONTEMPORARY STONEWARE VESSELS

Coco's vessels are sea-shaped from sand forms, shoreline close-ups. Brown and charcoal surfaces resemble beach ripples, washed by the tide, hardened by the sun. Some vessels look as if a small creature just moved out, others suggest the ruffled curves and colors of an elaborate oyster shell. Illustrating the effect of the sea on other items, a vessel may resemble an abandoned basket now draped with strands of seaweed; a hollowed, surf-sworled rock; or a gourd whose fibrous shell has begun to deteriorate and droop.

"I create my organic shapes and unusual textures," Coco says, "with slab and coiled stoneware, which I color directly with oxides and slips. I rarely use any glazes. I'm interested in the interplay between positive and negative space, in minimalism. And, of course, I've been very influenced by the landscape of water, beaches, and dunes."

PRICES: $12–$2,300. Commissions accepted. No catalog/brochure.

VISITORS: Yes. By appointment only.

LOCATION: New York City metropolitan area. 119 Erledon Road, Tenafly, NJ 07670; 201-569-5414. Directions will be provided when appointment to visit is made.

PENNSYLVANIA

Dominating this state's craft tradition are the "plain" and "fancy" Pennsylvania Dutch of southeastern Pennsylvania. The "fancy" folks are worldly descendants of German immigrants (primarily Lutheran), known today for their folk art, hex signs, redware pottery, and other crafts that often include heart, tulip, and bird motifs. The "plain" offshoots of this tradition are the Mennonites and Amish. Distinguished by their simple clothing and rigorously plain life-styles (the more conservative Amish use no electricity or automobiles), Mennonite and Amish artisans create quilts, rag rugs, furniture, and faceless dolls.

Visitors will find a variety of other traditional crafts exhibited at annual festivals and sold by artisans who re-create rare Leni-Lenape Indian arts, eighteenth-century firearms, Jacquard coverlets, primitive carvings, and Appalachian musical instruments. For more contemporary work, visit galleries in Pittsburgh and Philadelphia or stop by to see work by some of the state's most unusual early twentieth-century artisans: Wharton Esherick's unique woodwork is preserved in his Paoli home/studio, and Henry Chapman Mercer's intricate tiles can be found installed in his former Bucks County home and reproduced at the nearby Moravian Tile Works.

BOALSBURG

Bob Moore
NATIVE AMERICAN CRAFTS

Bob's Cherokee name, Unita, means "He who knows how," an appropriate name for this talented craftsman. As a small boy, Bob watched his father make deerhide clothing and other crafts. Although Bob tried a few himself, it wasn't until after a successful thirty-year career as a professional engineer that he became a full-time craftsman.

Now working in Boalsburg, a quaint town at the foot of Tussey Mountain, Bob re-creates the crafts of Eastern Woodland tribes: intricate beaded clothing and jewelry, ceremonial pipes and scabbards, baskets and cradle boards. Among other items, he reproduces traditional crafts of the Leni-Lenape. This Indian nation inhabited the beautiful Pennsylvania/Delaware River region until it was cheated out of its lands by the heirs of William Penn in the notorious "walking purchase." Bob reproduces Leni-Lenape designs on brain-tanned deerhide moccasins decorated with porcupine quills, and in elaborate ceremonial bandoliers that incorporate over 140,000 beads.

"Everything I make," Bob says, "is authentic." In fact, Bob's work is so highly regarded that the Pennsylvania Folklife Art Program funds Native Americans who want to apprentice with him.

PRICES: $2–$500. Commissions accepted. Accepts Discover, MasterCard, Visa. No catalog/brochure.

VISITORS: Mon.–Sat., 10 A.M.–6 P.M. Closed national holidays.

LOCATION: Central Pennsylvania, about 80 miles northwest of Harrisburg. Native American Craft Shop, 137 West Main Street, Boalsburg, PA 16827; 814-466-6833. (The mailing address is 530 West Main Street, Boalsburg, PA 16827). Take I-80 to State College/Rte. 26 exit, Rte. 26 to State College, then go east on Rte. 322 to Boalsburg. The shop is one block west of the village square.

BUSHKILL

Darryl and Karen Arawjo
TRADITIONAL BASKETS

Although the Arawjos' repertoire includes fine Appalachian, Nantucket, and Shaker baskets, some of their most interesting work is based on Darryl's own designs. His finely split white oak fishing creels make the nicest coffin a fish ever had. Sometimes Darryl adds a leather strap, transforming the creel into a stylish shoulder bag.

Karen specializes in traditional ribbed baskets. In addition, the Arawjos weave large hampers, a 5½-inch wood-lidded "dresser box," and a baby cradle with a wood bottom sporting an inlaid teddy bear. Darryl also makes finely woven miniatures (to scale) in most styles.

PRICES: $100–$1,500+. Commissions accepted. The catalog/brochure costs $1.

VISITORS: By appointment only.

LOCATION: Northeastern Pennsylvania, about 55 miles southeast of Scranton. P.O. Box 477, Bushkill, PA 18324; 717-588-6957. Directions will be provided when appointment to visit is made.

MORE: Located on the Pennsylvania shore of the Delaware Water Gap National Recreation Area, the Bushkill area abounds in spectacular scenery, boating, fishing, and hiking opportunities. Don't miss Bushkill Falls, two miles north of town, where eight falls drop 300 feet.

DOYLESTOWN

Fonthill Museum
Moravian Pottery & Tile Works
Mercer Museum

Henry Chapman Mercer (1856–1930) left a legacy of fine tiles and eccentric cast-concrete architecture. Born in Doylestown, educated at Harvard, and a recognized archaeologist, Mercer was forty-one when a visit to a junk dealer refocused his interests. Seeing spinning wheels, plows, and other discarded objects, Mercer realized that these would be the items future archaeologists would want to study. He decided to help.

Darryl and Karen Arawjo: Fishing creels, H. 10″; W. 5½″; D. 7½″. Creel handbag, H. 8½″; W. 4½″; D. 6½″. MICHAEL BRYGIDER.

Moravian Pottery and Tile Works: *Norumbega,* relief panel illustrating fabled city ancient geographers said was the capital of a populous region in unknown forests of England and Canada. 9½" sq.

As he began accumulating the material remains of preindustrial America, Mercer stumbled on what would become his second lifelong passion, ceramics. Captivated by Pennsylvania German redware, he was distressed to learn that it, like much handmade pottery, was rarely produced. Determined to revive the craft, Mercer studied ceramics and quickly became a master, specializing in colorful architectural tiles. Mercer's tiles were used in buildings ranging from Grauman's Chinese Theater in Hollywood to the floors of Pennsylvania's capitol rotunda to John D. Rockefeller's bowling alley. Visitors can explore the Mercer legend by visiting his home, his tile works, and the museum he designed to house his craft and tool collection.

Fonthill Museum

As a bachelor, Mercer certainly had enough living space. Included in Fonthill, the medieval castle he designed, are thirty rooms, twelve baths, and countless corridors, archways, and staircases. Embedded in every conceivable location are samples from Mercer's own tile works as well as his collection of ancient Babylonian tablets, Chinese roof tiles, and intricately patterned European tiles.

OPEN: Mon.–Sat., 10 A.M.–5 P.M. Closed Thanksgiving, Christmas, New Year's. Admission is $5 for adults, $2.50 for seniors, $1.50 for students. Guided tours only, reservations suggested; the last tour leaves at 4 P.M. Wheelchair accessible on first floor only.

LOCATION: East Court Street, Doylestown, PA 18901; 215-348-9461. Take I-76 to the Willow Grove/Rte. 611 exit, north of Philadelphia, Rte. 611 north to Doylestown, where it becomes Main Street, left on East Court Street. Fonthill is on the left, at the junction of East Court and Swamp Road.

Moravian Pottery & Tile Works

Choosing California Spanish mission-style architecture for his tile factory, Mercer included towers, cornices, and an interior courtyard. Opened in 1912, the factory specialized in decorative tiles and mosaics before closing in the 1950s. Revived in 1974, it is now a living museum where visitors can watch craftspeople reproduce over 300 Mercer patterns. Tiles range from simple floral designs to intricate pictorials, many in high relief.

OPEN: Mon.–Sun., 10 A.M.–5 P.M. Closed Thanksgiving, Christmas, New Year's, and Easter. Retail shop on premises. Excellent mail-order catalog available for $3.50. Admission is $2 for adults, $1.50 for seniors, $1 for students, $4.50 for families. Wheelchair accessible on ground floor only.

LOCATION: 130 Swamp Road, Doylestown, PA 18901; 215-345-6722. Same directions as for Fonthill, except proceed to Swamp Road, then turn left. The tile works is on the left. (NOTE: Swamp Road is also Rte. 313).

Mercer Museum

The museum is actually a six-story concrete fortress Mercer designed to house the 40,000 items he collected for future archaeologists. There's a little bit of everything here from tools used to make musical instruments and hats to those employed in tortoiseshell work and animal husbandry. An odd place.

OPEN: Mon.–Sat., 10 A.M.–5 P.M.; Sun., 1–5 P.M. Closed Thanksgiving, Christmas, and New Year's. Admission is $3 for adults, $2.50 for seniors, $1.50 for students. Self-guided tours. The shop sells traditional mid-Atlantic crafts. Limited wheelchair accessibility.

LOCATION: Pine Street, Doylestown, PA 18901; 215-345-0210. Same directions as for Fonthill to Doylestown. From Main Street, turn right on Ashland, then take an immediate right on Green, left on Pine.

MORE: Doylestown is located in the heart of Bucks County, well-known for its winding roads, covered bridges, and pastoral beauty. New Hope, 12 miles northeast, is a somewhat touristy artists' colony with many small galleries, antique shops, and cafés.

ELIZABETHTOWN

Pat Hornafius
PRIMITIVE HOOKED RUGS

The Bicentennial not only celebrated our country's heritage, it encouraged some folks to re-create it. "I'd never seen rug hooking demonstrated," Pat says, "until I attended a Bicentennial fair. Since then, I've cataloged hundreds of rugs in museums, studied under an instructor from Old Sturbridge Village, and started writing my master's thesis on rug hooking."

Obviously not one to do anything halfway, Pat has identified design characteristics, tools, and techniques used to create traditional Pennsylvania German rugs. "I do everything the old, labor-intensive way," she points out. "I hand dye, hand cut the quarter-inch wool flannel strips, and hand hook." Pat's traditional motifs include farm animals, flowers, and pictorials.

PRICES: $60/sq ft.; design fee charged for exclusive, original patterns. Commissions accepted. Send an SASE for photo, prices, résumé.

VISITORS: By appointment only.

LOCATION: Southern Pennsylvania, 18 miles southeast of Harrisburg. 113 Meadowbrook Lane, Elizabethtown, PA 17022; 717-367-7706. Directions will be provided when appointment to visit is made.

MORE: Pat also sells instructional videos on dyeing and rug hooking; prices range from $28 to $30 per tape.

INTERCOURSE

The People's Place
AMISH MUSEUM, CRAFTS

Because they're different, and located not far from major East Coast population centers, the Amish have long been a tourist draw. Unfortunately, this results in a zoolike atmosphere as visitors gawk at and impose themselves on a population trying only to live its own life-style. In an attempt to educate travelers about this unique American community, the People's Place offers films, a museum, and several top-notch crafts outlets.

Begin by viewing the center's excellent film *Who Are the Amish?*, which provides an introduction to Amish beliefs, diversity, and traditions. Next, stop by the Quilt Museum to see the country's only permanent display of antique Amish quilts, over seventy-five of them dating back to the 1890s. You may be surprised that many of the quilts are filled with bright, strong colors. Ready to purchase your own? Amish quilts, faceless dolls, rag rugs, and reproduction Amish furniture, as well as Mennonite baskets, wheat-weavings, and pottery are for sale in five shops operated by the People's Place. If you're interested in a particular craft, ask the museum staff which shop to visit. Shops include the Old Country Store, Old Road Specialties, the People's Place Gallery, and the Village Pottery.

OPEN: Mon.–Sat., 9 A.M.–5 P.M. Admission to museum (includes film) is $3 for adults, $1.50 for children. Not wheelchair accessible.

LOCATION: Southeastern Pennsylvania. The People's Place and shops are situated along Main Street (Rte. 340). The People's Place, Main Street, Intercourse, PA 17534; 717-768-7171. Take I-76 (the Pennsylvania Turnpike) to the Morgantown (Rte. 10) exit. Go south on Rte. 10 to Compass, west on Rte. 340 to Intercourse.

LANCASTER

Heritage Center
LANCASTER COUNTY CRAFTS (1700–1950)

Escape Lancaster's perennial kitsch fest with a visit to this finely curated museum that provides an excellent introduction to *quality* crafts produced by county residents for over 250 years. Housed in three late eighteenth-century buildings (the Old City Hall, State Capitol, and Masonic Lodge), the museum displays both "town" and "country" works, elegant pieces as well as simple utilitarian crafts.

Elaborate Lancaster-Chippendale-style furniture and gaily decorated Pennsylvania Dutch pieces are displayed in roomlike settings. There are also Lancaster-crafted clocks, metalwork, and the famous Pennsylvania long rifle. Among the folk art displays are wood carvings, ceramics, textiles, and fraktur.

OPEN: Late Apr.–Nov., Tues.–Sat., 10 A.M.–4 P.M. Closed major holidays. The museum shop sells books and cards only. Free admission ($1 donation is suggested). Self-guided tours. Wheelchair accessible.

LOCATION: Southeastern Pennsylvania, 69 miles west of Philadelphia. Penn Square, P.O. Box 997, Lancaster, PA 17603; 717-299-6440. Take I-76 (the Pennsylvania Turnpike) to exit 21 (Lancaster). Go south into the center of town. The museum is at Penn Square (King and Queen streets).

LEBANON

Jeff R. White
TRADITIONAL PENNSYLVANIA REDWARE

Redware was produced throughout New England and the mid-Atlantic states from early colonial times until 1850. Pennsylvania Germans added their own distinctive touch with colorful slip trailing and sgraffito decoration. "In the first," Jeff explains, "yellow slip, essentially liquified clay, is painted or dripped in trails over the red clay. With sgraffito, the surface, or a portion of it, is completely covered with yellow slip, then carved through to expose the red clay underneath. Sometimes black and green are added for highlights, then all pieces are covered with a clear glaze."

Jeff re-creates original redware pieces using the same red clay, decorative colors, and techniques. "There are two exceptions," Jeff points out. "Mine contain no lead and are fired at a hotter temperature to make them more durable." Offering sturdy pitchers, crocks, and jugs, Jeff also creates delightful plates and platters (see color plate #5).

PRICES: $3–$250. Commissions accepted. Send $3 for the catalog/brochure; color photos are included.

VISITORS: Yes.

LOCATION: 22 miles east of Harrisburg. Jeff R. White, Hephaestus* Pottery, 2012 Penn Street, Lebanon, PA 17042-5771; 717-272-0806. From Harrisburg, take Rte. 422 east. Turn right at light in front of Lebanon Valley Mall. At the T, turn left, then take the first right. Go three blocks to another T, then take a right onto Penn Street. The house is the last one on the left.

*Hephaestus was the Greek god of potters. There was also a minor god, Ceramicus, who had his own room in the Hephaestum in Athens.

LENHARTSVILLE

Johnny Claypoole
HEX SIGNS

House haunted? Having fertility problems? Need help to bring in a good crop? Johnny Claypoole won't guarantee that his hex signs will make a difference, but some of his customers insist they do.

Considered an outgrowth of *fraktur,* the ornate, decorated German calligraphy used in special certificates, hex signs have adorned Pennsylvania Dutch country barns for over 200 years. "The first hex signs were probably painted by the farmers themselves," Johnny says. "Later, itinerant artists wandered from farm to farm painting them, often in exchange for bed and board."

A student of legendary hex sign painter John Ott, Johnny painted signs in his spare time until the Smithsonian called. "They asked me for an order I couldn't refuse. But I also couldn't fill it working only nights and weekends," Johnny recalls, "so I quit my job. I've been painting signs full-time ever since."

Johnny's richly symbolic signs include the Unicorn Hex, representing virtue and plenty, and the Mighty Oak Hex, with oak leaves and acorns symbolizing strength and an ocean border to assure smooth sailing in the autumn of life. Others celebrate love and happiness or attempt to ward off famine, plague, and other evils.

PRICES: Hex signs, $15–$200; decorated milk cans, furniture, and other items, to $500. Commissions accepted.

Johnny Claypoole: Hex sign. TOM GRAVES

Send $1.60 for a book on Claypoole and the history of hex signs.

VISITORS: Yes.

LOCATION: Eastern Pennsylvania, about 18 miles west of Allentown. Box 746, R.D. #1, Lenhartsville, PA 19534; 215-562-8696. Take I-78 to the Lenhartsville (Rte. 143) exit. Bear right on the off-ramp to the stop sign. Turn right onto Rte. 143; go to the intersection with Rte. 22 (a hotel will be on the left). Turn left onto Rte. 22 and go about three blocks over a bridge. Turn right at the first road (Drivillviss Road). Continue about 1 mile (a creek will be on your right). Take the second left (Shock Road). Johnny's driveway is about two blocks farther, on the left.

MEDIA

Traditional Craft Show
AMERICAN CRAFTS (1650–1850)

You may feel out of place driving up to this show in an automobile instead of a buggy, but that's part of the point. Held at the Colonial Pennsylvania Plantation, a "living museum" set in the period 1760–1790, this is a show that emphasizes traditional crafts without jarring distractions.

Juried to assure authenticity, exhibited crafts vary from year to year but may include redware, eighteenth-century clothing, English smocking, handcrafted brooms, fraktur, bandboxes, and wood dolls. For diversion, listen to the resident itinerant storyteller, who relates "tales, fongs, and goffip from the American Colonies Interfperfed with Obferved Incidents."

EVENT: Third weekend in May. Sat. & Sun., 10 A.M.–5 P.M. Admission is $2.50 for adults, $1.50 for seniors and children.

LOCATION: 16 miles southwest of Philadelphia. Colonial Pennsylvania Plantation, Ridley Creek State Park, Media, PA 19063; 215-566-1725. Take I-76 to Rte. 1 south, Rte. 1 to Rte. 252 west, Rte. 252 past Rose Tree Park. Go left on Providence Road to Gradyville Road, left on Gradyville. Follow RIDLEY CREEK STATE PARK—COLONIAL PLANTATION signs.

MILLERSVILLE

Phyllis A. Giberson
AMERICAN PRIMITIVE FIGURES

A permanently startled cat, with a bird on his back, waits for a child to pull him home. Two pigs board Noah's ark while bunnies wait their turn. And Uncle Sam, atop a bunted stand, permanently waves the flag. Re-creations of American primitive carving, Phyllis's pieces all seem about to say something either terribly profound or profoundly silly; it's hard to tell which.

"I try to carry on the themes and ideas of the early primitive artists," Phyllis says. "They were untutored, so there was often a naive exaggeration of details and disproportionate human figures. Also, the relation of different forms was determined more by decorative considerations than perspective." Although all of Phyllis's carvings are original, they are based on traditional primitive themes: patriotic symbols, nursery rhymes, nature, and biblical subjects.

PRICES: $5–$200. Commissions accepted. The catalog/brochure costs $1.

VISITORS: By appointment only.

LOCATION: Southeastern Pennsylvania, about 1 mile west of Lancaster. 332 Manor Avenue, Millersville, PA 17551;

1. Judith Larzelere (Dedham, Mass.): *Stop Action.* H. 61″; W. 71″. JAN BINDAS STUDIOS.

2. Stephen Huneck (St. Johnsbury, Vt.): *State of Vermont Cupboard.* Handcarved, hand-painted basswood. H. 42″; W. 20″; D. 14″.

3. Deidre Scherer (Williamsville, Vt.): *Glimpse.* Fabric collage. H. 9″; W. 7½″.

4. David C. Freda (New Paltz, N.Y.): *Fresh water painted turtle neckpiece.* Sterling silver, fine silver, transparent enamels. WHITE LIGHT.

5. Jeff R. White (Lebanon, Pa.): Slip-trailed redware plate. Diam. 11″.

6. Ivan E. Hoyt (Wapwallopen, Pa.): *Tree of Life,* hex sign. Diam. 36″.

7. Ed Moulthrop (Atlanta, Ga.): Rolled-edge bowl. Georgia pine. D. 18″.

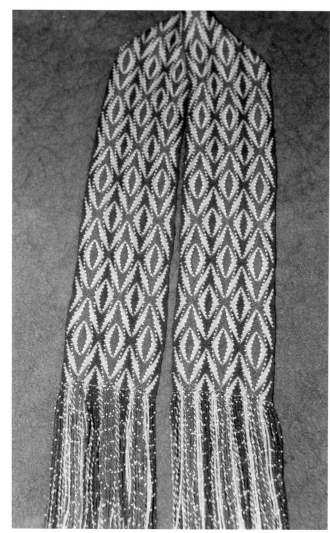

8. Dick Carney (Doyline, La.): *Powhatan,* finger-weaving. Original design adopted by all seven Powhatan tribes as their official sash design. Naturally dyed, 4-ply knitting wool, 0-size pony beads. W. 7″; L. 65″ plus fringe.

9. Irvan J. Perez (St. Bernard, La.): Decoy of green-wing teal hen and drake. Life-size.

10. Ethel Wright Mohamed (Belzoni, Miss.): *4th of July Picnic,* embroidered pictorial. H. 18″; L. 26″.

11. Sarah Mary Taylor (Yazoo City, Miss.): *Everybody,* quilt. H. 86″; W. 76″. SUZANNE CARMICHAEL.

12. Dona Look (Chicago, Ill.): Lidded basket. White birch bark, silk thread. H. 10¾″; W. 6¼″; D. 6¼″. JIM THREADGILL.

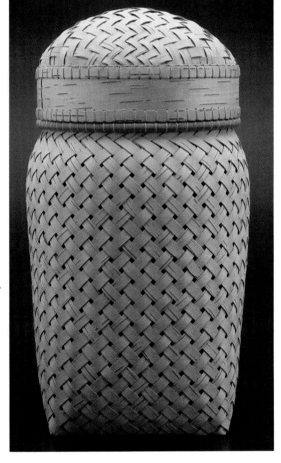

13. Steven M. Lalioff (Deming, Ind.):
Reproduction c. 1790–1830 trunk with grain-painted interior. Poplar, calfskin, brass tacks, paint.

14. Shirley M. Brauker (Coldwater, Mich.):
Mountain Sheep, pot.

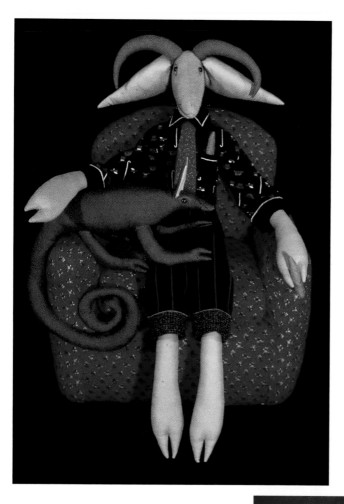

15. Deborah Banyas (Oberlin, Ohio): *Goat at Home,* fabric sculpture.

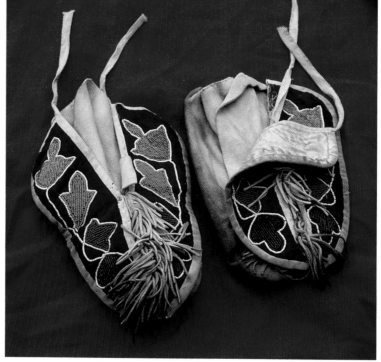

16. Gerald F. Hawpetoss (Oshkosh, Wis.): Beaded moccasins.
RICHARD MARSH.

Phyllis A. Giberson: *Cat with bird on back.* Wood, cast iron, paint. H. 9″; L. 13″. MICHAEL E. GOCKLEY

717-872-7139. Take I-83 to York/Rte. 30 exit, Rte. 30 to Millersville exit. Proceed to traffic light, turn right onto Manor Avenue. The house is on the left before the shopping center.

MUNCY

William W. Kennedy
EIGHTEENTH-CENTURY FIREARMS

Firearms played a decisive role in early America's survival, and William Kennedy now re-creates these historical weapons for collectors. "I can make custom firearms of any regional school design produced during the muzzle-loading era,"

William W. Kennedy: Kentucky rifle.

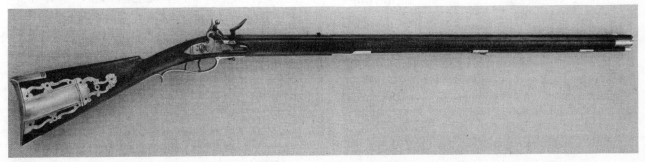

William says. "This includes everything from the matchlock period through percussion. I meticulously research each firearm to assure that construction and decoration are authentic. In fact, most of my work is done using the same tools and techniques that were used to make the originals."

William's American Revolutionary War officer's pistol is a working replica that comes with a variety of options: type of wood, size, finish, carving, and engraving. Another speciality is the Kentucky rifle, developed by Lancaster County's Swiss and German immigrants. Its use spread throughout the eastern colonies and traveled westward with the pioneers. This rifle combined great range and accuracy for its era, and was of equal efficacy in dispatching "bar," deer, and Redcoats.

PRICES: $500 + . Commissions accepted.

VISITORS: Yes. Please call first.

LOCATION: North-central Pennsylvania, about 90 miles southwest of Scranton. 10 North Market Street, Muncy, PA 17756; 717-546-6695. Take I-80 to I-180N (exit 32B). Go north on I-180 to exit for Main Street. Take a left off the ramp and go to the second traffic light. Turn left onto Water Street to the third house on the left. The shop is in the building at back of the property.

NORTHAMPTON COUNTY

Pennsylvania German Tombstones

Bordered by the Delaware River on the east and the Lehigh River on the west, Northampton County is best known for its steel and industrial center,

Bethlehem. To careful observers of Pennsylvania German crafts, however, the county is known for the unique folk art found in some of the tiny towns scattered across the countryside. Clustered in Lutheran and Reformed church cemeteries are Pennsylvania German tombstones that share the same motifs found on hex signs, fraktur, ceramics, and textiles. Many of these gravestones have no dates or inscriptions, only stylized decoration: a lone heart, a sun, tulips, or two six-pointed compass stars encased in a circle.

LOCATIONS: Various cemeteries, including those at St. Paul's Union Church near Cherryville, Christ Union Church in Lower Saucon Township, and Dryland Trinity Union Church near Hecktown. Also look for Bern Church in Berks County and Muddy Creek Cemetery in Lancaster County. (NOTE: Please show respect for these family gravesites. To obtain specific addresses/directions, ask locally.)

PAOLI

Wharton Esherick Museum
ESHERICK FURNITURE, INTERIORS

Step inside the studio and livng quarters of Wharton Esherick (1887–1970) and you will immediately understand why he is considered the dean of American craftsmen. "The studio was built over a period of forty years," museum director Mansfield Bascom notes. "It includes the 1926 stone portion with tapered walls flaring out at the base like a tree trunk, the 1941 cubist addition, and a 1966 free-form tower. Inside, no detail escaped Esherick's attention. He carved the doors, forged the hinges, shaped the copper sinks, sculpted the andirons and heater grills, inlaid the floors and walls. He even made a set of coat pegs caricaturing the workmen who helped him."

Known for his wood sculptures, furniture, and interiors, Esherick started his career as a painter. His fifty-year romance with wood began when he started carving decorative frames for his paintings. Soon he was experimenting with woodcuts, working on sculptures, and creating his own furniture. "Many clients who came to his studio intending to buy a painting," Bascom notes, "left with a chair or table, or commissioned him to create entire interiors."

"Esherick is considered the spiritual godfather of contemporary woodworking," Bascom continues, "for having pioneered the way for individual design in furniture. He started with organic forms, passed through the sharp angles of cubism, and evolved a swirling, lyrical style." Visitors will see over 200 examples of Esherick's work, including his famous flared staircase. The only drawback? None of the pieces are for sale—postcards and a catalog will have to suffice.

OPEN: One-hour guided tours by reservation only. March 1– Dec. 21, Sat., 10 A.M.–5 P.M.; Sun., 1–5 P.M. Closed major holidays. The shop sells no crafts. Admission is $3 for adults, $2 for children under 12. Two floors out of three are wheelchair accessible.

LOCATION: 20 miles west of Philadelphia, 3 miles west of Valley Forge Park. Horseshoe Trail, P.O. Box 595, Paoli, PA 19301; 215-644-5822. Directions will be provided when reservation for tour is made.

PHILADELPHIA

The Works Gallery
CONTEMPORARY CRAFTS

Located in a renovated artists' district adjacent to the Society Hill section of historic Philadelphia, this well-known gallery really does offer "the works." "In every medium we carry a tremendous range of items," says owner Ruth Snyderman, "in size, design, and price. In ceramics we have everything from mugs to giant columns. Glass items range from paperweights and goblets to large sculptures. Our fiber work includes small wall-hangings as well as elaborate large quilts and tapestries. The wood pieces vary from boxes to rocking chairs, and our metalwork includes fine jewelry as well as sturdy weathervanes." Take note of jewelry by Eileen Sutton and Susan Jo Klein, Bob Ingram's redefinition of traditional furniture, and the three-dimensional wool tapestries by Adela Akers.

PRICES: $25–$15,000 (average, $50–$2,400). Accepts American Express, MasterCard, Visa.

OPEN: Mon.–Fri., 11 A.M.–7 P.M.; Sat., 11 A.M.–11 P.M.; Sun., noon–6 P.M. Closed major holidays. Wheelchair accessible.

LOCATION: 319 South Street, Philadelphia, PA 19147; 215-922-7775. Take I-95 to Historic Area/Vine Street exit. Go west on Vine Street to 6th Street, left on 6th Street to South Street, left on South Street. The gallery is between 3rd and 4th streets on the south side of the street.

PHOENIXVILLE

Long Family Potters
EARLY AMERICAN REDWARE

Anticipating a renewed interest in early American pottery during the Bicentennial, established potters Dorothy and Alton Long researched colonial redware materials and techniques. "At the same time," Alton says, "we unearthed information describing the potters' lives. Red clay was easily accessible; all you had to do was dig in the ground, so many farmers spent the winters potting. It wasn't uncommon for one of these 'country potters' to make over a thousand pieces."

"These folks were also known as 'bluebird potters,'" Dorothy adds. "As soon as roads were passable they were out peddling their pots. They signified the coming of spring about as accurately as bluebirds. Back then a mug sold for one cent, a large crock for eight cents. But around 1800 people started to realize that the redware glazes caused lead poisoning. The alternative salt-glaze was just too complicated for most farmers to bother with, so production of handmade pottery rapidly declined."

Using lead-free glazes, the Longs re-created the famous redware pottery. Customers can choose from over 100 different patterns in a choice of six glazes, including a black one known as "Poor Man's Pewter." There are also twenty-nine sayings that can be added to plates, including "This dish is made of earth and when it breaks the potter laughs."

PRICES: $3.50–$200. Commissions accepted. The catalog/brochure costs $2.50.

OPEN: Weekdays, 10 A.M.–5 P.M.

LOCATION: Southeastern Pennsylvania, about 15 miles from Philadelphia. Old Eagle Studios, 237 Bridge Street, Phoenixville, PA 19460; 215-933-3080. Take I-76 to the Valley Forge exit, then Rte. 23N through Valley Forge to Phoenixville. Go right at the second light in Phoenixville. At dead end, turn left onto Bridge Street. The pottery is on the right, just after the movie theater.

Long Family Potters: Redware with sgraffito decoration. Clockwise from upper left: *Bird in Tulips,* Diam. 10"; *Welcome to our Home,* Diam. 8½"; wedding platter, Diam. 12"; *Flowers in Urn,* Diam. 10".

PITTSBURGH

The Clay Place
CONTEMPORARY CRAFTS

Many of this gallery's pieces prefer to provoke and challenge viewers rather than present a pretty face. A work by Jerry Caplan stands on end like the sides of a mismatched red suitcase and is surrounded by nails and bisected by a textured metal-like strip. Linda Shusterman and Alan Willoughby's terracotta plate has a reverse image design that creates a three-dimensional puzzle. Kirk Mangus's *Ocean Front Jar* resembles children's sand scribblings preserved on an attractively odd three-footed jar.

But there *are* pretty faces here too, including Karen Howell's winsome plates, with their night portraits of rabbits, and Donn Hedman's functional stoneware, with slip-trailed flora and fauna.

PRICES: $5–$2,000 (average, $20–$100). Accepts Master-Card, Visa.

OPEN: Mon.–Sat., 10 A.M.–5 P.M.; Wed. evenings, 7–9 P.M. Closed major holidays. Wheelchair accessible; elevator available.

LOCATION: Between Aiken and Copeland near Carnegie Museum in Shadyside section of Pittsburgh. 5416 Walnut Street (Mineo Building, second floor), Pittsburgh, PA 15232; 412-682-3737. Take I-376W to exit 8 (Squirrel Hill). Continue on Forward Avenue to Shady Avenue. Go left on Shady to Fifth Avenue, left on Fifth to Aiken Avenue, right on Aiken to Walnut Street.

PITTSBURGH

Society for Art in Crafts
CONTEMPORARY CRAFTS

Dedicated to advancing crafts as a major contemporary art form, this multipurpose center includes an exhibition gallery for major one-person or thematic shows, a permanent collection display area, a resource facility, and the Shop, featuring affordable contemporary crafts. It is possible to see a Dale Chihuly glass sculpture worth thousands of dollars in the gallery, then visit the Shop to purchase art glass for under $100. A welcome contrast!

Among the more interesting crafts in the Shop are the highly decorative, but totally functional, cast aluminum cookware by Don Drumm and Judith Zieve's sculptural, slab-built teapots and tableware.

PRICES: $5–$300 (average, $20–$70). Prices are higher when exhibition works are available for sale. Accepts MasterCard, Visa.

OPEN: Tues.–Sat., 10 A.M.–5 P.M.; Sun., 1–4 P.M. Closed Christmas, New Year's. Wheelchair accessible.

LOCATION: 2100 Smallman Street, Pittsburgh, PA 15222; 412-261-7003. Take I-376 to the Grant Street exit. Follow Grant Street (which becomes Liberty Avenue) into Strip District. Turn left onto 22nd Street and go through one light. At the next stop sign, turn left onto Smallman Street. Proceed to the corner of Smallman and 21st Street.

MORE: Located in the heart of Pittsburgh's Strip District, the society is only steps away from a bustling riverside market offering exotic food from around the world.

PITTSBURGH

Ukrainian Festival
TRADITIONAL UKRAINIAN CRAFTS

If you're already planning to be in Pittsburgh at the end of September, reserve an hour to drop by this popular festival. Although crafts are only one of this event's many offerings, they're worth seeing. Included are Ukrainian beadwork, free thrown pottery, loom weaving, counted-thread embroidery, leathercraft, greenware glazing, and egg batiking. Don't miss demonstrations by masters from the Ukrainian Heritage Studies Center at Manor Junior College (Jenkintown, Pennsylvania). One suggestion: Go near mealtime so you can sample the superb Ukrainian food.

EVENT: Last weekend in Sept., Sat. & Sun., noon–6 P.M. Free admission.

LOCATION: Cathedral of Learning, University of Pittsburgh. On quadrangle bordered by Bigelow Boulevard and 5th, Bellefield, and Forbes avenues.

MORE: For information contact the Pittsburgh Ukrainian Festival, 46 Lexington Court, Carnegie, PA 15106; 412-279-3458.

RED LION

David and Carole Kline
JACQUARD COVERLETS
INGRAIN CARPETS

After losing their jobs when a textile mill closed, David and Carole Kline decided to be their own bosses. "We knew the 'country look' in decorating was popular," David says, "and that jacquard coverlets fit that style well. When we realized that no one was making authentic reproductions, we decided to fill the void."

The coverlets are named for Joseph-Marie Jacquard, who, in the nineteenth-century, developed a rotating punched-card system permitting hand-loom weavers to create intricate pictorial designs both easily and rapidly. "Our coverlets are based on traditional patterns and techniques," Carole says. "We use cotton warps and wool wefts. Each coverlet is woven in one long 38-inch-wide strip, cut in half, then sewn together by hand to double the width. But we do use engines instead of feet to operate the looms. We can also make queen- and king-size coverlets."

After researching nineteenth-century Pennsylvania Dutch patterns, the Klines settled on two designs: "four roses with bird and bush border," from an 1838 coverlet; and "house border with picket fence and animals," from an 1848 original. "Each coverlet is personalized along the border with the owner's name, our name, and the date," David adds. "And we give the customer the punch cards used to create that part."

The Klines also weave jacquard ingrain carpets, which were popular in nineteenth-century middle-class homes. "Ingrain" refers to the fact that the yarn is dyed before it is spun into yarn. One characteristic of these carpets is that the patterns and colors are reversed on the back.

PRICES: Coverlets, $45 (child's)–$525; table runners, $30–$60; 36"-width carpets, $97–$125/yd. Commissions accepted. The catalog/brochure costs $2 and includes a yarn chart.

VISITORS: Yes. Weekdays, 9 A.M.–4:30 P.M.; Sat. "by chance."

LOCATION: Southern Pennsylvania, between Baltimore and Harrisburg. Family Heir-Loom Weavers, Meadow View Drive, R.D. #3, Box 59E, Red Lion, PA 17356; 717-246-2431. Take I-83 to exit 6E; proceed for 5 miles to Dallastown. Turn right onto South Duke Street. After 1.5 miles, turn right onto Meadowview Drive. Heir-Loom Weavers is in the tan building on the left.

ROARING SPRING

Mike and Walt Martin
APPALACHIAN DULCIMERS
FRETLESS BANJOS

The Appalachian mountains of central Pennsylvania are an appropriate setting for a shop that makes dulcimers and banjos, but this shop definitely has one foot in the twentieth century. "Contemporary musicians often want to create both traditional and modern music," says Mike. "To accommodate them, we combine traditional craft techniques and aesthetically pleasing designs with new technologies to assure correctness of scale, voicing, volume, and ease of tuning."

The Martins' Appalachian dulcimer models include a teardrop design that produces a range of treble sounds, an hourglass shape offering a fuller tone with more volume, and the Lorraine Lee model developed for the famous dulcimer player who wanted an instrument appropriate for both mountain ballads and modern jazz. Also available are hammered dulcimers and custom instruments such as the Tommy Thompson gourd-back slave banjo.

PRICES: $210–$1,275+. Commissions accepted. Free catalog/brochure.

VISITORS: Yes. Please call first.

LOCATION: South-central Pennsylvania, between Pittsburgh and Harrisburg. Sunhearth, Box 74, R.D. #1, Roaring Spring, PA 16673; 814-224-2890. Take I-76 to the Rte. 220 exit, Rte. 220 north to East Freedom. Go right on Rte. 164 to Roaring Spring, then south on Rte. 867. Sunhearth is located on the west side of Rte. 867, 1 mile south of Roaring Springs.

MORE: The Martins also operate a bed and breakfast. Large bedrooms are decorated with crafts and antiques; enormous breakfasts include eggs from the Martins' chickens and homemade breads. There's also a practice casting (fishing) pond, four acres of lawns for family games/picnics, baby-sitting service, and nearby fishing, hunting, and skiing. Rates are $50 for a double room; children 3–12 cost $5 extra.

ROBESONIA

Lester Breininger
TRADITIONAL REDWARE

A ninth-generation Pennsylvania German, Lester has two full-time jobs, one as a biology teacher at the local high school and one as a recognized master craftsman. "I was an avid collector of redware," Lester says, "and I wanted to know how it was made. So I took a ceramics course, talked to a few old potters, and practiced a lot. That's how all this got started." "All this" includes a 1986 Pennsylvania Governor's Award for excellence in the arts, the first awarded to a craftsperson.

Lester relies on his extensive collection of redware for inspiration, and on antique molds to shape his plates. The plates, from 4 to 22 inches in diameter, are gaily decorated with traditional slip-trail and sgraffito patterns. Visitors will also find crocks, animal figures, collanders, and even Christmas ornaments (see cover illustration). "And each year," Lester says, "I produce one new design based on a piece I own or one I've seen. I make a limited edition, then I don't use the pattern again."

A special treat is the Breiningers' annual August show, held on the porch of their Taylor Mansion. Collectors from throughout the country can be seen sipping mint tea, nibbling on cookies, viewing Lester's latest designs, or watching demonstrations by his assistants.

PRICES: $3–$245 (average, $10–$35). Commissions accepted. Send a business-size SASE for Lester's catalog/brochure.

VISITORS: Yes.

LOCATION: 10 miles west of Reading. 476 South Church Street, Robesonia, PA 19551; 215-693-5344. From Reading, take Rte. 422, which becomes Main Street in Robesonia. Two blocks past the only traffic light, at the William Penn Station, turn left on Church. The house is on the right.

MORE: The annual porch show is held the third or fourth weekend in August. Park in the field across the street from the Breiningers' home.

STOUCHSBURG

Pennsylvania Traditional Crafts and Folk Art Sale

One day each October, eleven top Pennsylvania German artisans sell their work at one of the best traditional craft shows in the country. This show is stringently juried, and new craftspersons are added only when a current one drops out. All exhibitors are well known in the folk art world, sell their work through museum shops (often to the Museum of American Folk Art), and many are regularly featured in national magazines.

The most recent lists of exhibitors includes:

Lester Breininger, redware; Jeffrey M. Fiant, Windsor chairs; Claudia and Carroll Hopf, Scherenschnitte (fancy scissor cuttings); Pat Hornafius, hooked rugs; Susan Leed, miniature houses; Thomas Loose, tinsmith and blacksmith items; Barbara Bonfanti and Brenda Reedy, baskets; Patricia Siegrist, fraktur and American primitives; Jay Thomas Stauffer, pewter; Daniel Strawser, woodcarvings; and David and Carole Kline, jacquard coverlets and ingrain carpets.

EVENTS: Last Sat. in Oct., 10 A.M.–4 P.M. Free admission.

LOCATION: Eastern Pennsylvania, between Reading and Lebanon, 2.5 miles east of Myerstown. Old School House, Water Street, Stouchsburg, PA. Take Rte. 422 to Stouchsburg and old Rte. 422 (Main Street). Continue to Water Street, in the center of town; the show is held opposite the fire hall.

MORE: For information contact the Hopfs, 13 Mechanic Street, Kennebunk, ME 04043; 207-985-4654. (The Hopfs were curators at the Pennsylvania Farm Museum in Landis Valley, have deep roots in Pennsylvania, and only recently moved to Maine.) (WARNING: This show is *mobbed*. Plan to come as early as possible—before 10 A.M. for best selection.)

STRASBURG

Lancaster Towne Quilts
LANCASTER COUNTY AMISH QUILTS

The availability of authentic, high-quality Amish quilts has declined rapidly in recent years, almost in proportion to their popularity. Now a small, family-run, mail-order business provides fine quilts and personal service.

Lancaster Towne's two catalogs are quilt cornucopias of pieced and appliquéd quilts in styles ranging from the optical illusions of *Tumbling Blocks* to the delicate *Tree of Life*. "Each quilt is made by a single Amish lady," owner Austin Helsel says. "And all are completely handstitched, even the appliqué work. But you have to be patient; quilts are made to order and some have over three thousand pieces."

Quilts can be ordered in any color, size, or pattern. It's also possible to have a quilt made from your own design or have a wall hanging made from a favorite color photo. You can even save $20 by providing your own fabric (Austin will tell you how much of each color is needed).

PRICES: $159 (wall hanging)–$985 (king-size quilt). Ask for quotes on special orders. For a catalog, contact Lancaster Towne Quilts, Box 277, Strasburg, PA 17579; 717-687-8600. The price is $5 for two full-color catalogs.

WAPWALLOPEN

Ivan E. Hoyt
HEX SIGNS

Everyone agrees that hex signs originated in southeastern Pennsylvania, but no one knows why they were painted on farmers' barns. "Some folks suggest they were strictly decorative or merely a show of vanity, to make your barn look better than your neighbor's," Ivan explains. "Others say the farmers believed in their symbolic meaning."

There are even competing stories about Ivan's favorite design, the colorful Distlefink. "There are two legends about its origin," Ivan says. "One story says a farmer saw a goldfinch pull fuzz from a thistle to line its nest. The farmer began to call it a 'thistlefinch,' and, with his German accent, it was misunderstood as 'distlefink.' The Distlefink was considered good luck because it helped eliminate weeds in the farmers' fields. The other legend says that God made the Distlefink with all the colors he had left after making the other species."

Reflecting the variety of patterns found in Pennsylvania Dutch frakturs (illuminated manuscripts), Scherenschnitte (paper cuttings), and springles (cookie and butter molds), Ivan creates unique designs (see color plate #6) ranging from elaborate geometric patterns to the belsnickle, a special Christmas hex.

PRICES: $20–$150+. Commissions accepted "if they're within my style." The catalog/brochure costs $2.50.

VISITORS: Yes. Please call first if possible.

LOCATION: Eastern Pennsylvania, about 45 miles southwest of Scranton, 6.5 miles from I-81. R.D. #2, Box 49-D, Bell Drive, Wapwallopen, PA 18660-9625; 717-379-3533. Take I-81 to exit 42 (Dorrance). Proceed west 1.6 miles to stop sign that says RIGHT TURN KEEP MOVING. Turn right, then go 1.7 miles to the Rustic Tavern, a white building on your left. Turn left and go .2 mile, then bear right on Creek Road. Continue for 2.4 miles to stop sign. Continue straight for .1 mile, then take a sharp right on Eroh Road. In about .3 mile, at the top of a hill, there is a T; turn left and go .1 mile. The house is on the right side of the road.

VIRGINIA

Virginia offers the perfect opportunity for time travel: adventures in historical crafts that reach back to traditional Mattaponi Indian pottery. There's also a substantial dollop of colonial crafts: artisans who reproduce seventeenth-century Jamestown glassware and Williamsburg's authentically garbed craftspeople who create everything from wooden wheels to bonnets. For other traditional crafts, visit festivals in Charlottesville and Ferrum, order your own historical footwear and clothing, or steep yourself in shipshape crafts at Newport News' Mariners' Museum. Collectors of contemporary crafts can visit artisans who work in a variety of media or drop by Alexandria's three-story maxi-gallery, the Torpedo Factory.

ALEXANDRIA

Connie Wyatt
HANDWOVEN SILK ITEMS
FINE EMBROIDERY

"For as long as I can remember," Connie says, "I have carefully unraveled the edges of cloth to see how a weaving was created. Now, I go the other direction and weave my own cloth. I work primarily with silk because it provides an incomparable play of color and light as well as draping better than wool or cotton." Often weaving with more than fifty threads to the inch, Connie creates scarves, shawls, and, on commission, yardage.

"The silks I most often choose for scarves are the filament yarns," Connie explains. "These are threads drawn from as many as sixteen cocoons at a time, which are then spun very loosely, if at all. Filament silks usually have fluffy slubs which take dye at a gentler rate than the rest of the thread. This adds to the texture and color of the finished piece. For heavier items, I use plied silks or blend silk with cashmere, alpaca, or mohair. I also do most of the dyeing myself so I have total control over my color palette."

Working with silk as her canvas, Connie also creates abstract paintings with embroidery. Incorporating metal and silk threads as well as small glass bead highlights, the embroideries seem to be constantly moving, repositioning themselves to catch a different light.

PRICES: Scarves, $70–$100; shawls, $150–$300; embroideries, $150+. Commissions accepted. No catalog/brochure.

VISITORS: By appointment only.

LOCATION: South of I-95. 4406 Cheatham Court, Alexandria, VA 22310; 703-960-2682. Directions will be provided when appointment to visit is made.

MORE: Connie's work is also available through the Potomac Craftsman Gallery, 105 North Union Street, Alexandria, VA 22314; and Sylvia Designs, 103 South Columbus Street, Alexandria, VA 22314.

ALEXANDRIA

Torpedo Factory
CONTEMPORARY CRAFTS GALLERIES AND STUDIOS

"**D**amn the critics, full speed ahead" could be the motto of this former torpedo factory. Reincarnated in 1974 as an art center with eighty-three studios and five galleries, the Torpedo Factory offers three floors of crafts and fine art. Light and airy, with colorful corrugated aluminum dividers, the heavy cast cement building seethes with creative activity. Visitors can view artisans making everything from contemporary jewelry to wood sculptures, watch them spin wool, or oil paint.

The most interesting stop is on the first floor at Studio 9. Here Donald Cohen makes bows for some of the world's finest musicians, including Rostropovich and Yehudi Menuhin. Using fine woods and time-honored methods, he creates each bow from scratch, even fashioning his own gold fittings. Also on the first floor is the Potomac Craftsmen Gallery (Studio 18) specializing in handwoven clothing and fabric wall hangings.

The second floor houses printmakers as well as stained-glass and etched-crystal artists. At #201, Metallum displays contemporary metalwork, including a good selection of anodized aluminum jewelry. Fiber craftspeople, painters, printmakers, and even a computer artist share space with sculptors and glass artists on the third floor. Look particularly for Ann Di Placido's vividly colored wall hangings (Studio 320) and Mark Anderson's striking contemporary art glass (Studio 316).

OPEN: Daily, 10 A.M.–5 P.M. Closed on Thanksgiving, Christmas, and New Year's Day. Wheelchair accessible.

LOCATION: Old Town Alexandria, one block from the Potomac River. 105 North Union Street, Alexandria, VA 22314; 703-838-4565. From Washington, D.C., cross the Potomac River to George Washington Parkway. Follow the parkway south, past the airport, to Alexandria. Turn left on Queen Street to river, then go right on Union Street. The Torpedo Factory is one and a half blocks farther on the left. From Maryland/Virginia, take I-95/I-495 (Beltway) to exit 1 north (Rte. 1). Go six blocks, then turn right on King Street to the river. Turn left on Union Street. The Torpedo Factory is half a block farther on the right. There is ample parking directly across the street.

CHARLOTTESVILLE

Colonial Crafts Weekend
TRADITIONAL CRAFTS (1760–1830)

James Monroe, the fifth president of the United States, cordially invites you to celebrate the 4th of July weekend by visiting the late eighteenth and early nineteenth centuries at his home, Ash Lawn. Guests accepting this invitation will be entertained by craft demonstrations of the period.

Although President Monroe will be unable to attend the event, that shouldn't keep you from becoming acquainted with the crafts, costumes, and manners of the Monroe Era. Emphasizing authenticity and education rather than hype and sales, this annual two-day event features thirty craftspeople fashioning period cabinetry, shoes, bobbin lace, pewter, and other items. Demonstrating popular pastimes of the era, artisans also make handcut silhouettes and create decorative wheat weaving.

EVENT: First full weekend in July, Sat. & Sun., 10 A.M.–6 P.M. Admission is $6 for adults, $4.50 for seniors, $2 for children.

LOCATION: Southeast of Charlottesville, on the grounds of Ash Lawn–Highlands estate. Take I-64 to the Charlottesville/Rte. 20 exit, then Rte. 20 south to Rte. 53. Go left on Rte. 53 past Monticello to Rte. 795, right on Rte. 795 to Ash Lawn.

MORE: For information contact Ash Lawn–Highland, Rte. 6, Box 37, Charlottesville, VA 22901; 804-293-9539.

MORE: If you notice piercing shrieks and squawks while you're here, it's just the peacocks in the boxwood garden. During Monroe's time, these colorful birds were considered estate "ornaments."

FERRUM

Blue Ridge Folklife Festival
TRADITIONAL FOLK CRAFTS

Sponsored by the Blue Ridge Institute at Ferrum College, this annual festival celebrates the folkways of the area. If you're interested in a "crafts only" event, then pass this one by. But if you want to experience the full gamut of Blue Ridge Mountain culture from folk music to fried chitterlings, crafts to coon dog contests, add this to your itinerary.

The festival's craft component exhibits Blue Ridge Mountain items once made from necessity but now tradition bearers, passing a rich cultural heritage to modern Americans. Using many of the same materials and techniques as the original settlers, today's craftspeople offer dough trays and wooden rakes, brooms, tobacco twists, quilts, and rag dolls. Don't miss Audrey Hash Miller's fiddles and teardrop-shape dulcimers, or the carved canes by Norman Amos and Emory Robinson.

EVENT: Fourth Sat. in Oct., 10 A.M.–5 A.M. Admission is $3 for adults, $2 for seniors and children.

LOCATION: Ferrum College campus, Ferrum, VA. Take I-81 to I-581/Rte. 220 exit (Roanoke) or the Blue Ridge Parkway to Roanoke/Rte. 220 exit. Take Rte. 220 south to Rte. 40, Rte. 40 southwest 10 miles to Ferrum College.

MORE: For information contact the Blue Ridge Institute, Ferrum College, Ferrum, VA 24088; 703-365-4415.

FLOYD

Glendon Boyd
TRADITIONAL DOUGH TRAYS

Even if you let your food processor do the kneading, dough trays are still the perfect place to let your dough rise. They're also attractive for holding fresh fruit, chips, and any number of other items. "The Boyd family has been making these trays for four generations," Glendon says. "As a tiny tot I watched my father work with wood. In addition to these bowls, he made ax handles, baskets, wood rakes, and split-bottom chairs. Now I'm teaching my son these same skills.

"To make the dough trays really durable, I make them out of wood from the cucumber tree. That's what we call our magnolia trees, since their fruit looks like a small cucumber. It's the same tree favored by moonshiners for their stills. When I can't get any cucumber wood, I use black walnut or wild cherry." Glendon also makes other wood

crafts, including carved figures and historical scenes.

PRICES: Dough trays, $4–$50+; other crafts, $3–$45; wood sculptures, $60–$1,200. No commissions. No catalog/brochure.

VISITORS: Yes.

LOCATION: About 40 miles southwest of Roanoke, 6 miles north of the Blue Ridge Parkway. Rte. 1, Box 791, Floyd, VA 24091; 703-745-2556. Take I-81 to Christiansburg/Rte. 8 exit. Follow Rte. 8 south past Floyd about .3 mile to Rte. 710. Turn left on Rte. 710 and continue for 1.5 miles to Rte. 637. Turn left on Rte. 637 for .2 mile. House is first one on the left.

JAMESTOWN

Jamestown National Historic Site
REPRODUCTION SEVENTEENTH-CENTURY GLASS/ POTTERY

The first glass made in America was blown in 1608 at the Jamestown settlement. Then, from 1608 to 1609 and, after six Italian glassmakers arrived, from 1621 to 1624, glass production is thought to have included windowpanes, small bottles and vials, and simple drinking glasses. Although no complete pieces have survived, small fragments and drippings found during a 1948 excavation provided clues as to the color (green) and composition of the glass. Today visitors can view the ruins of the original glasshouse, then visit its open-sided,

Glendon Boyd: Black walnut dough tray. Diam. 12″:D.3″.

timber-and-shake reconstruction. Inside, only a few yards from where America's first glass was formed, artisans produce glassware in much the same manner as seventeenth-century craftsmen.

Re-creations of Jamestown's early pottery can be found at the Dale House. Based on ware found in the site's artifact collection, crocks and other items are formed using authentic methods and materials but not the lead glazes colonists employed. Continuing a seventeenth-century practice, many of these reproduction pieces bear the potter's fingerprint on the bottom.

GLASSHOUSE: open daily (except Christmas), 8:30 A.M.–5 P.M., with extended hours in summer and fall. Wheelchair accessible except the approach, which is paved with oyster shells.

DALE HOUSE: Open March–Dec., daily (except Christmas), 9 A.M.–4:30 P.M. Not wheelchair accessible.

LOCATION: Southeastern Virginia, about 13 miles from Williamsburg, on Jamestown Island. Take I-64 to Williamsburg exit, then follow Colonial Parkway to Jamestown.

MORE: Glass and pottery are for sale at demonstration sites. Admission to the Jamestown historic site is $5 per car. For more information contact the Colonial National Historical Park, P.O. Box 210, Yorktown, VA 23690; 804-898-3400.

LYNCHBURG

Michael Creed
CONTEMPORARY FURNITURE

Crank a cat's tail or punch him in the nose and you can generally expect to get your face rearranged. Except for Michael's cats, disguised as desks, who actually *beg* you to do it. In *Kattmose II*, a gaily colored box sits atop four claw legs, a curlicued tail on the left. Lift the lid, crank the tail, and a cat's face slowly emerges. The stripes on its face are cubbyholes, its outstretched tongue a writing surface. Now, punch the nose. Out pop two eyes, secret drawers for hidden messages or your store of catnip.

Michael is equally adept at creating imaginative, outlandish furniture or crafting a conservatively elegant sideboard. His hallmark is definitely fine workmanship, but humor is his muse. In addition to furniture, Michael unleashes his wit in fantasy musical instruments and wallpieces such as *Twocan Tango,* where a crank of a carved banana touches off a frenzy of sympathetic motion.

So, whether you want a hippopotamus nightstand or a classic mahogany cabinet, Michael can probably make it for you, suggest a better alternative, or volunteer to interpret your furniture fantasies through his own singular vision.

PRICES: $150–$15,000. Most work is done by commission only. Send an SASE for information.

VISITORS: By appointment only.

LOCATION: South-central Virginia. 2129 Broadway Street, Lynchburg, VA 24501; 804-845-6452. Directions will be provided when appointment to visit is made.

Michael Creed; *Kattmose II,* desk. Maple, curly maple, steel, brass. H. 32″ (46″ when opened); L. 30″; D. 14″.

NEWPORT NEWS

Mariners' Museum
MARINER CRAFTS

On the shore of America's largest natural port is a museum dedicated to men who were not only masters of the sea but also master craftsmen. From a one-and-a-half-ton, gilded, eagle figurehead to a miniature replica of Columbus's *Pinta,* the museum traces over 3,000 years of mariner craftsmanship. Visitors can also watch demonstrations of mariner woodcarving, Chesapeake Bay boatbuilding, and marlinespike seamanship (knot tying and rope work).

The museum's figurehead collection, the largest in the United States, displays nineteenth-century carvings that once decorated and identified sailing vessels. Another exhibit shows scrimshaw and whalebone carvings, including a pastry crimper made from a whale's tooth. Also on view are over fifty traditional small crafts as well as hand-carved trailboards, rudder heads, and paddleboxes. A new gallery, opened in the fall of 1989, is devoted to traditional Chesapeake Bay boats and decoys.

The museum's most popular exhibit is its display of sixteen miniature sailing vessels built by Oregon craftsman August Crabtree. Created over a twenty-five-year period, the ships range from an Egyptian seagoing vessel to the nineteenth-century *Britannia.* The most elaborate ones include a Venetian galleass (c. 1650) lavishly decorated with 395 carved figures, an English warship (c. 1687) adorned with gilded carvings from figurehead to stern, and a Venetian gondola (c. 1692) that weighs just over half an ounce, is less than 8 inches long, and yet includes sixty carved figures, some so small they are barely visible.

OPEN: Mon.–Sat., 9 A.M.–5 P.M.; Sun., noon–5 P.M. Closed Christmas. The museum shop features carved waterfowl. Admission fee is subject to change. Tours daily at 11 A.M.; at other times when docents are available. Wheelchair accessible.

LOCATION: Southeastern Virginia. 100 Museum Drive, Newport News, VA 23606; 804-595-0368. Take I-64 to exit 62A,

August Crabtree: Miniature English 50-gun warship, stern detail. COURTESY MARINERS' MUSEUM

then follow museum signs to the intersection of Warwick Boulevard (Rte. 60) and J. Clyde Morris Boulevard.

MORE: Every five years, the museum sponsors a ship model competition. The next one is planned for late 1991; call for details.

RICHMOND

"Butch" J. R. Myers, Jr.
HISTORICAL FOOTWEAR AND EQUIPAGE

"Making historical footwear may seem like an unusual line of work," Butch says, "but there is a real market for it. I sell a lot of shoes to interpreters at American museums. They like my work because I don't take any shortcuts. I custom-build each item with original methods, tools, and materials. The leather is tanned using historical techniques, and I even try to duplicate the old finishes."

Butch's work, made on commission only, includes styles of men's and women's footwear from the seventeenth through the nineteenth century, and leather equipage such as replica cartridge boxes, period luggage, and Civil War Smith & Wesson gun holders. "I also receive some unusual commissions," Butch says. "Once I made a pair of 1860s carpet slippers used by Sam Waterston when he portrayed Lincoln in a television miniseries."

Butch's plans for the future include expanding to offer "one-stop historical purchasing." In addition to footwear and leather products, Butch and two partners will offer period clothing, ironware, tin items, treenware, and other authentic historic crafts. "I also offer conservation services," he adds, "for the restoration and protection of valuable historic leather items."

PRICES: $25–$1,500. Commissions accepted. Free list of most requested items.

VISITORS: Yes. Mon.–Sat., 9 A.M.–5 P.M., and by appointment.

LOCATION: Western end of Henrico County. J. R. Myers Co., 6507 Horsepen Road, Richmond, VA 23226; 804-288-9380. Take I-95 to the Parham Road exit, Parham Road to Rte. 250. Turn left on Rte. 250 and continue for about 4.5 miles to Horsepen Road. Go right on Horsepen. The shop is two and a half blocks farther, on the left.

MORE: Butch also demonstrates cordwaining during Colonial Crafts Weekend (see the Charlottesville entry above).

ROANOKE

Gallery 3
CONTEMPORARY CRAFTS

Most jewelry boxes don't lead double lives, unless they're made by Jane Campbell. Jane's silver boxes disassemble to become . . . jewelry. The lid turns into a pendant set with precious stones, the hinges are stickpins and tie tacs, other parts transform themselves into bracelets and earrings. This is a gift for a person who has everything!

Located in Roanoke's historic Farmer's Market area, Gallery 3 is actually 2 in 1. The first floor is a fine arts gallery offering original oils, watercolors, graphics, and art posters; the second floor features

American crafts. Sleek display areas set off the crafts, including handwoven wooly coats by Linda Phillips, crackled-glaze vases by Mary Lou Deal, and delicate hand-painted porcelain flower jewelry by Linda van der Linde.

PRICES: $10–$2,500 (average, $30–$300). Accepts Choice, MasterCard, Visa.

OPEN: Tues.–Sat., 9:30 A.M.–5 P.M.; also open Mon., 9:30 A.M.–5 P.M., Thanksgiving–Christmas. Closed Thanksgiving, Christmas week, July 4th. Wheelchair accessible on first floor only.

LOCATION: Southeastern Virginia. 213 Market Street, Roanoke, VA 24011; 703-343-9698. Take I-81 to I-581, I-581 south to the Elm Avenue exit. Turn right on Jefferson Street, then right again on Campbell Avenue. The first right off Campbell is Market Street. The gallery is in the first block on the right side of the street.

THE PLAINS

Nol Putnam
HOT-FORGED DECORATIVE IRONWORK

"Hot, hard, dirty, and beautiful" is the way Nol describes his work. A self-taught artist-blacksmith, Nol creates architectural ironwork that is both decorative and functional. A garden gate not only leads to a garden but is one itself, blooming with iron tulips and daylilies. Other gates either contradict their sturdy purpose with wispy leaves or reinforce it with shafted arrows. In addition to gates, Nol creates striking fireplace tools, ornate porch and stair railings, and does restoration work for historic sites.

Private residences aren't the only ones to be graced by Putnam gates. Visitors to Washington, D.C., can find his work at the National Cathedral. Located to the rear of the Chapel of St. Joseph of Aramathea, Nol's Gothic gate is filled with rich repeating details that soar to an arch of boughed leaves symbolic of eternal life.

PRICES: $5–$50,000. Commissions accepted. Send $10 for his portfolio.

VISITORS: Yes. By appointment only.

Nol Putnam: Flower gate.

LOCATION: Northern Virginia, about 35 miles west of the D.C. metropolitan area. White Oak Forge, Ltd., P.O. Box 341, The Plains, VA 22171; 703-253-5269. Directions will be provided when appointment to visit is made.

WEST POINT

Margaret A. Allmond
Christine Rippling Water Custalow
MATTAPONI INDIAN POTTERY

Although pottery is a traditional craft of the Mattaponi Indians, in modern times it became a lost art. Then, in 1978, an archaeologist familiar with the historic methods of Mattaponi pottery revived interest in the craft by offering classes. Margaret and Christine took the course and both now produce prize-winning, traditional vessels and sculpture.

"I'm very proud to be able to bring back the forgotten craft of my ancestors," Christine says. "The methods I use are the ones woodland Indians have followed for three thousand years. The black and smoky-white colors are a result of wood firing; the intensity of the heat and smoke determines the final outcome and color pattern. The smooth, shiny appearance comes from burnishing with either a smooth stone or a wood tool." Christine creates ceramic masks, bowls, and sculptures, but some of her most charming pieces combine the latter two. A diving whale, a sitting deer, and a preening duck sit on the lids of smoky brown bowls that resemble giant, shiny buckeye seeds.

Margaret, a member of the Upper Mattaponi tribe thought by some to be the remnant of the Indian tribe of John Smith's time, also creates fine bowls, sculptures, and ceramic masks. The interesting texture on some of her bowls is created by wrapping stripped yucca around a wood paddle, then pressing the paddle against the clay. Margaret

Christine Rippling Water Custalow: Traditional wood-fired bowl with four Indian faces. H. 4″; Cir. 10″ PATRICIA S. ADAMS

Margaret A. Allmond: Traditional coiled clay bowl with rippling water, wave design. H. 9″; Cir. 24″. PATRICIA S. ADAMS

also hand forms small sculptures of women and animals.

Both women's work is sold at the River of High Bank Craft Shop on the reservation.

MARGARET A. ALLMOND: Mattaponi Indian Reservation, Rte. 2, Box 235, West Point, VA 23181; 804-769-2257. Prices range from $5 to $300. Commissions are accepted. No catalog/brochure.

CHRISTINE RIPPLING WATER CUSTALOW: River of High Bank Craft Shop, Mattaponi Indian Reservation, Rte. 2, Box 270, West Point, VA 23181; 804-769-4711. Prices range from $3 to $400. Commissions are accepted. No catalog/brochure.

LOCATION: 27 miles northeast of Richmond. Take I-295 to Rte. 360. Go north on Rte. 360 for 17 miles to Rte. 30. Go right (southeast) on Rte. 30 for 12 miles to Rte. 640, then turn left on Rte. 640 for 1 mile to Rte. 625. Turn left on Rte. 625. The reservation is 1.3 miles farther. The reservation is small and the road goes in a circle. The shop is in the old school building (red roof, white sides).

WILLIAMSBURG

Abby Aldrich Rockefeller Folk Art Center
(Closed for renovation/expansion until Jan. 1991)

In the late 1920s, Abby Aldrich Rockefeller, wife of John D. Jr., began collecting folk art that few people recognized as collectible, much less art. The Rockefeller collection grew over the years; it now numbers over 2,600 objects and is soon to have a revamped home in the heart of Colonial Williamsburg. When the center reopens, visitors will be able to see decorated furniture and other functional crafts, toys and sculptures, oil paintings and watercolors, calligraphic drawings and fraktur.

LOCATION: Across the street from Williamsburg Lodge and Conference Center. Approaching the Historic Area of Williamsburg from the east on Rte. 60, turn left (west) on York Street, which, after one block, becomes Francis Street. Continue to South England Street, go left on South England. The center is one block down on the left.

MORE: For hours, admission charges, and other information contact the Abby Aldrich Rockefeller Folk Art Center, 307 South England Street, P.O. Box C, Williamsburg, VA 23185; 804-220-7670.

WILLIAMSBURG

Colonial Williamsburg

The granddaddy of "living museums," Williamsburg has lured visitors back to the eighteenth century for over sixty years. The best way to experience the town's historical visage is to avoid the tourist rushes of summer and Christmas; rent accommodations in one of the small, restored colonial homes; and leisurely explore the meticulous re-creations of colonial life.

Spread across the 173-acre Historic Area are a variety of authentic trade shops whose priority is education, not production. Some crafts can be purchased, others only photographed. In small shops, at forges and workbenches, appropriately costumed artisans ply their trades, creating the essentials of eighteenth-century life from books, boots, and guns to hats, harnesses, and wigs. Tinsmiths, silversmiths, gunsmiths, wheelwrights, carpenters, and coopers painstakingly fashion their wares in seemingly total ignorance of modern methods or materials.

Williamsburg is wonderful, especially for older children, but it can be both expensive and crowded. Don't try to see it all in one visit.

LOCATION: Tidewater Virginia, about 10 miles northwest of Newport News, about 45 miles southeast of Richmond. Take I-64 to Colonial Parkway, Colonial Parkway to Williamsburg.

MORE: There is a variety of admission charges to visit the various sites. Prices vary from "package admissions" of $15.50–$24.50 per adult ($8.25–$12.25 for children 6–12) to individual admission charges. The best bet is to call Colonial Williamsburg at 1-800-HISTORY and request the "Vacation Planner" packet.

WASHINGTON, D.C.

Spice up a capitol sight-seeing spree with an occasional craft respite. After dropping in on the president, cross the street to the Smithsonian's Renwick Museum, the Department of Interior's excellent Indian Craft Shop, or walk several blocks to see the latest in contemporary jewelry at Jewelerswerk. Just popped in to see your favorite congressman? Reward yourself with a Capitol Hill jaunt to Moon, Blossoms & Snow, a gallery specializing in wearable art.

For glass, ceramics, and other top-notch crafts, visit D.C. galleries as well as those in Bethesda, Maryland, and Alexandria, Virginia. In spring or summer, plan on devoting at least half a day to attend some of the country's finest craft festivals and sales shows. For an extra little treat, take the children to the Washington Dolls' House and Toy Museum.

CAPITOL HILL

Beth Minear
CONTEMPORARY WOOL RUGS

Viewing one of Beth's rugs is like watching a tennis match. Your eyes move from side to side, following the action. On one rug, wide black and white stripes form the body with a narrow border of bright stripes on the left. On the right is an even narrower border of colorful stripes, in a different order. Back on the left, some of the border invades the stolid center. And on the right . . .

"I'm influenced by a long-standing interest in architecture," Beth says, "which explains in part why the inherent discipline, geometry, and solidity of a rug appeal to me. I use two weave structures: the 'Summer and Winter Weave' found in early American coverlets and 'Krokbragd,' seen in traditional Scandinavian textiles. I use a wool weft and an Irish linen warp to make the rugs sturdy, although generally my pieces are hung on walls." To achieve subtle color gradations, Beth twists several strands of closely related colors to obtain what appears to be a third hue.

In contrast to some artisans who prefer to work only on their own designs, this award-winning weaver actually enjoys doing commissions. "I love the challenge," she says, "of understanding what clients want in color and design and collaborating with them on the final work."

PRICES: $60–$70/sq. ft. Sizes available are 3′ × 5′, 4′ × 6′, runners, and some larger pieces. No catalog/brochure.

VISITORS: Yes. By appointment only.

LOCATION: Capitol Hill. 1115 East Capitol Street SE, Washington, DC 20003; 202-544-1714. Directions will be provided when appointment to visit is made.

CAPITOL HILL

Moon, Blossoms & Snow
WEARABLE ART, CONTEMPORARY CRAFTS

The Japanese believe the three most beautiful things in the world are the moon, cherry blossoms, and snow. You can become the fourth by wearing this gallery's innovative fashions. Whether you're a professional tired of generic suits with predictable fabrics and lackluster design or want to create a stir at the next cocktail party, this gallery has just what you need.

For office or boardroom, try on Judith Bird's handwoven, hand-painted garments. Their classic shapes in subtle but unusual patterns look great in any season and travel well. For nightlife, choose something more daring, perhaps a piece by Tim Harding. Tim's one-of-a-kind apparel has complex surface textures achieved by dyeing, layering, quilting, slashing, and fraying woven cottons. Before you go, accessorize with jewelry by Jane Martin.

If you're on your way to a party, the gallery also offers perfect hostess gifts: functional ceramics and glass, baskets and kaleidoscopes, even whimsical wooden toys by Dona Dalton.

PRICES: $6–$1,500 (average, $25–$250). Accepts American Express, MasterCard, Visa.

OPEN: Mon.–Fri., 11 A.M.–6 P.M.; Sat., 10 A.M.–5 P.M. Closed major holidays. Not wheelchair accessible.

LOCATION: Two blocks east of the Capitol Building. 225 Pennsylvania Avenue SE, Washington, DC 20003; 202-543-8181. Take orange or blue-line Metro (subway) to the Capitol South station.

GEORGETOWN

American Hand—Plus
CONTEMPORARY CERAMICS

Georgetown, with its narrow streets and expensive brick row houses, used to be the height of fashionable Washington shopping. It still has some outstanding galleries and a few good boutiques, but they've been joined by many forgettable shops and yuppie chains. One quality gallery still worth exploring, however, is American Hand.

With a range of ceramics from Sylvie Granatelli's bright barium-glazed mugs to large, smoke-fired vessels, this gallery emphasizes fine design and tantalizing surfaces. Look for Andrew Baird's burnished pots, including those that are purposely broken and then reassembled and refired. The gallery's front room has modestly priced functional work, and the back room offers more unusual, sometimes sculptural, pieces. In addition to ceramics, see Linda Hesh's unusual sterling earrings in the form of tiny straightback chairs, window frames, or people reclining on sofas.

PRICES: $10–$7,500 +. No credit cards; personal checks are accepted with ID.

OPEN: Mon.–Sat., 11 A.M.–6 P.M.; Sun., 1–5 P.M. Closed July 4th, Thanksgiving, Christmas, and New Year's Day. Wheelchair accessible.

LOCATION: Georgetown between 29th and 30th. 2906 M St. NW, Washington, D.C. 20007; 202-965-3273.

GEORGETOWN

Maurine Littleton Gallery
CONTEMPORARY GLASS

From its quality announcements and exhibit catalogs to a stable of America's most renowed glass artisans, this gallery is among America's most elite showrooms. Almost every piece is of museum quality, created by artists who exert a major influence in their media. In addition to work by Harvey Littleton and Dale Chihuly, look for ornate filigree designs in Fritz Dreisbach's vessels, Jay Musler's "Ugly Bowl" series, cast glass forms by Colin Reid that resemble carved geode sections, and the bold colors of Concetta Mason's broken and reformed vessels.

Although the emphasis is on glass, the gallery also offers some outstanding ceramic art, including pieces by Dan Gunderson, Norman Schulman, and James Tanner. Tanner, a former studio glass artist, creates three-dimensional ceramic paintings by juxtaposing layers of color to add depth and intensity. Often using a mask form as the starting point, Tanner's work reflects not only his Afro-American heritage and his spiritual explorations but also the fluid lines of a master glass artist.

PRICES: $95–$25,000 (average, $2,000–$10,000). Accepts American Express, MasterCard, Visa.

OPEN: Tues.–Sat., noon–6 P.M. Closed all major holidays. Wheelchair accessible.

LOCATION: Georgetown, half a block off Wisconsin Avenue. 3222 N Street NW, Washington, DC 20007; 202-333-9307.

GEORGETOWN AND WHITE HOUSE AREA

Indian Craft Shops

Washington, D.C., may seem an unlikely site for an Indian craft shop, but since 1938 it has been the location of one of the finest on the East Coast. Situated in the otherwise drab Department of the Interior building two blocks from the White House, the shop celebrated its fiftieth anniversary by opening a new gallery in Georgetown. If you're interested in Indian crafts, visit *both* locations.

Gloomy government corridors, somewhat brightened by WPA murals, lead the way to the original shop. Offering crafts from almost every Native American group in the country, the shop's two rooms are crammed with baskets and rugs, pottery and sandpaintings, jewelry and soapstone carvings. There are even antique baskets and Navajo rugs for sale. Down the hall, in the museum, is a small collection of Indian crafts, including a wonderful Acoma ceramic turkey.

The Georgetown shop, specializing in Southwestern Indian crafts, is in a restored nineteenth-century town house along the B&O Canal. As you enter, and turn to the left for a fine selection of contemporary Indian jewelry and a whole case of Indian pawn. Upstairs, one room displays Indian rugs and the other has pottery and a major selection of top-quality Kachina dolls. The overall quality and variety of the merchandise are as close as what you'll get in Gallup or Santa Fe without making the trip.

PRICES: Both shops, $3–$5,000 (average, $35–$200). Accepts American Express, Choice, MasterCard, Visa.

OPEN: Georgetown shop—Mon.–Sat., 10 A.M.–7 P.M.; Sun., noon–6 P.M. Closed Easter, Thanksgiving, and Christmas. Not wheelchair accessible. Department of Interior shop—Mon.–Fri., 8:30 A.M.–4:30 P.M. Closed holidays. Wheelchair accessible from E Street entrance.

LOCATION: Georgetown shop—1050 Wisconsin Avenue NW, Washington, DC 20007; 202-342-3918. Department of Interior shop—1800 C Street NW, Washington, DC 20240; 202-343-4056. (NOTE: Due to increased security at govern-ment buildings, expect to be greeted by a Pinkerton guard, asked for ID, then handed a limited visitor's pass.)

NATIONAL MALL AREA

Festival of the Building Arts

Often forgotten in today's craft scene is the rich and varied world of America's architectural crafts. Perhaps because they are primarily adornment, generally not portable, and rarely collected, these crafts get little exposure. Seeking to right that imbalance is the National Building Museum's annual Festival of the Building Arts.

Established to celebrate the growth, evolution, and diversity of the country's building trades and their heritage of craftsmanship, this one-day festival offers a variety of craft demonstrations, including comparisons of old and new building crafts and materials. Visitors can watch decorative bricklaying, wrought ironwork, plaster and sheet metal ornamentation, stenciling, gilding, application of faux finishes such as marbleizing and graining, window glazing, stonecarving, terra-cotta design, and others.

Also offered are walking tours to explore specific architectural crafts on new and old buildings, architectural craft activities for children, and performances presenting music related to the American worker.

EVENT: Held in conjunction with National Historic Preservation Week. Mid-May, Sat., 11 A.M.–5 P.M. Free admission.

LOCATION: Eleven blocks east of the White House, four blocks north of the National Mall and National Gallery of Art. National Building Museum, F Street NW between 4th and 5th, Washington, DC 20001; 202-272-2448.

NATIONAL MALL AREA SMITHSONIAN

Festival of American Folklife
ANNUAL FOLK CULTURE EVENT

Summer is probably the worst time to visit Washington. It's hot, humid, and packed with tourists from all over the world. But it's worth all the discomfort if your goal is the annual Festival of American Folklife, sponsored by the Smithsonian Institution.

Based on scholarly research, with the lofty goal of preserving the rich diversity of American folk culture, the festival is a heady celebration of traditional American crafts, music, dance, food, and storytelling. Like a multi-ring circus, it has so many things going on that it's hard to take them all in.

Among other themes, the festival often honors the folk culture of a specific state. In the past this has included craft demonstrations of Louisiana boat building, Massachusetts netmaking, Native American quillwork, Finnish-American rag rug weaving, Tennessee white oak basketry, and East Indian floor painting. All are presented by contemporary craftspeople either carrying on America's oldest craft traditions or introducing ones brought by more recent immigrants.

EVENT: Ten days, last week of June–July 4th weekend. Daily, 11 A.M.–5:30 P.M. Free admission.

LOCATION: National Mall between 10th and 14th streets, near Smithsonian museums. (NOTE: Parking is extremely limited. Take the Metrobus or Metro (subway), to either the Smithsonian Station (mall exit) or Federal Triangle Station.)

MORE: Sign language interpreters, oral interpreters (by advance request only), and services for visually impaired and handicapped visitors are provided. For more information contact the Office of Folklife Programs, Smithsonian Institution, 2600 L'Enfant Plaza, Washington, DC 20560; 202-287-3424 (the TDD number for the hearing impaired is 202-357-1729). During the festival, call 202-357-4574 for a daily event recording.

SMITHSONIAN

Washington Craft Show
CONTEMPORARY CRAFTS

The Smithsonian seems to leave its imprint on every craft endeavor in the D.C. metropolitan area, including the city's only national, juried craft show. Hosted by the Women's Committee of the Smithsonian Associates, this event draws crowds of collectors, as well as museum and gallery directors.

The show accepts only 100 artisans from over 1,100 applicants, and crafts are judged on the basis of originality, quality of workmanship, and artistic conception. The result is a cross section of contemporary American crafts, from bottles, vessels, and necklaces of glass to leather purses and sculptural masks. Furniture of exotic woods, aluminum, and clay is displayed next to wearable art of silk, wool, and fur. Also vying for attention are baskets, ceramics, metalwork, and mixed media.

Be forewarned. The quality and prices are high, and things go in a flash. Come early, wear your tennis shoes, and bring your checkbook!

EVENT: Four days in mid-to-late Apr. Daily, from 10 A.M. (Closing time varies; call for information.) Admission is $5 for adults, $4 for seniors and children.

LOCATION: Smithsonian Departmental Auditorium, 1301 Constitution Avenue NW, across from the National Museum of American History. (Note: Parking is very limited; use public transportation.)

MORE: For information contact the Women's Committee, Smithsonian Associates, A&I Building, Room 1465, Smithsonian Institution, Washington, DC 20560; 202-357-4000.

WHITE HOUSE AREA

Jewelerswerk
CONTEMPORARY JEWELRY

Every jewelry lover knows that good things come in small packages, so they'll feel right at home in this tiny gallery. Located in a tasteful indoor mall entered through a row of attached Victorian houses, Jewelerswerk features both American and international designers offering innovative pieces from accordion-folded paper necklaces to unusual gold earrings.

Don't be concerned when you first walk in and see only two small showcases—there are drawers and drawers of other jewelry that the staff encourages you to open and explore. Avant-garde designs, sometimes outrageously clever, and the use of nontraditional materials link these otherwise disparate works. Be sure to see Rebekah Laskin's enameled copper pin "constructions" and Birgit Laken's steel-and-gold-foil necklaces.

PRICES: $4–$10,000 (average, $100–$500). Accepts American Express, MasterCard, Visa.

OPEN: Mon.–Fri., 10 A.M.–7 P.M.; Sat., 10 A.M.–6 P.M. Closed major holidays. Wheelchair accessible.

LOCATION: Four blocks from the White House. 2000 Pennsylvania Avenue NW, Washington, DC 20006; 202-293-0249.

WHITE HOUSE AREA

Renwick Gallery
CONTEMPORARY AMERICAN CRAFTS

According to its brochure, the Renwick is charged with exhibiting the "creative achievements of designers and craftspeople in the United States, past and present." Specializing in crafts from 1900 to the present, this arm of the venerable Smithsonian Institution is housed in the former Corcoran Gallery of Art. An architectural exhibit itself, the French Second-Empire building was designed by James Renwick, Jr.

On the main floor, dominated by an ascending grand staircase, are temporary exhibit rooms. Focusing on design elements, individual craftspeople, or particular themes, displays have included everything from Western saddles to Amish quilts, Tiffany glass to children's toys.

Up the carpeted stairway, bordered by velvet-covered railings, is a second-floor exhibit area including small rooms displaying part of the museum's permanent collection, a gallery for special exhibits, and the dominant nineteenth-century Grand Salon. Although a fine room, the Salon devotes too much of the museum's limited space to one period, contains almost no crafts, and seems strangely out of place with the other exhibits.

The museum's permanent collection is small (250 to 300 pieces) but exemplary, especially Albert Paley's *Portal Gates.* You may also be able to see Katherine Westphal's art quilt *Seven Camels Find Buried Treasures,* Mary Lee Hu's silver-and-gold woven necklace, and Rudy Autio's stoneware *Listening to the East,* as well as Voulkos ceramics and Chihuly glass.

OPEN: Daily, 10 A.M.–5:30 P.M. Closed Christmas. The museum shop has an excellent selection of craft books. Free admission. Tours by appointment only; call 202-357-3095. Wheelchair accessible.

LOCATION: One block from the White House. Pennsylvania Avenue at 17th Street NW, Washington, DC 20560; 202-357-2531.

FRIENDSHIP HEIGHTS CHEVY CHASE

Washington Dolls' House and Toy Museum

Before your children complain about all the historic landmarks they've been forced to see in the nation's capital, promise them a trip to this fantasy world displaying wall-to-wall dolls' houses. Visitors can see miniature Victorian mansions, five Baltimore row houses, a six-story 1903 New Jersey seaside hotel, and even a tiny 1800 Swiss toy shop.

Established in 1975 by dolls' house historian Flora Gill Jacobs, the museum is dedicated to the (adult) proposition that dolls' houses of the past comprise a study of architecture and the decorative arts in miniature and that children's toys reflect social history.

While you're contemplating the veracity of that assertion, your children will be running from room to room lost in a Lilliputian dream of dolls' houses, toys, and "set-pieces" such as the 1910 *Teddy Roosevelt on Safari.* Be forewarned: The museum's two shops sell completed dolls' houses as well as building and wiring supplies and a full selection of miniature furniture, accessories, and dolls.

OPEN: Tues.–Sat., 10 A.M.–5 P.M.; Sun., noon–5 P.M. There is a museum shop. Admission is $2 for adults, $1 for children under 14. Tours are available. Wheelchair accessible for only one wheelchair at a time.

LOCATION: One block from the corner of Wisconsin and Western avenues, near Lord & Taylor and Neiman-Marcus. 5236 44th Street NW, Washington, DC 20015; 202-244-0024. Take the red-line Metro (subway) to the Friendship Heights station.

WEST VIRGINIA

West Virginia is a state of contradictions: hills and "hollers," pristine Appalachian mountain beauty and dingy coal mine towns, isolated cabins and the luxurious Greenbrier Hotel. The consistent thread that links these characteristics, however, is a very open, friendly populace. Travelers will find traditional Appalachian crafts available in shops or from individual artisans: quilts and folk art wood carvings, handmade toys and sturdy baskets. Glass factories also dot the state, including those that create paperweights as well as ones that specialize in large, architectural, stained-glass work. A smattering of contemporary crafts is also available, primarily in Charleston.

BECKLEY

Annual Appalachian Arts & Crafts Festival

Stop by this Labor Day show to see the quilts. Over 100 of them ring the inside of the armory, providing a backdrop for arts and crafts booths. Each quilt has been prejudged before hanging, and most are for sale. The other items at this show vary tremendously but include some fine traditional Appalachian crafts.

EVENT: Labor Day Weekend. Fri. & Sat., 10 A.M.–10 P.M.; Sun., 10 A.M.–6 P.M. Admission is $2 for adults, $1.50 for seniors, $1 for children.

LOCATION: 63 miles southeast of Charleston. Raleigh County Armory–Civic Center, 19–21 Bypass, Beckley, WV. Take I-64 to the Eisenhower Drive exit. Turn north onto Eisenhower Drive; the armory is located about a quarter of a mile farther on the right.

MORE: For information contact Mr. William A. Wilbur, Beckley-Raleigh County Chamber of Commerce, P.O. Box 1798, Beckley, WV 25802-1798; 304-252-7328. For a pretty side trip, drive through Bluestone Canyon, on Rte. 19 south of Beckley.

CHARLESTON

Cabin Creek Quilts Cooperative
HANDMADE QUILTS AND PATCHWORK

Quilting originated in China and was brought to the West during the eleventh and twelfth centuries by the Crusaders. Now this cooperative helps to preserve the Appalachian version of this ancient art. Founded in 1970 through the efforts of VISTA, the cooperative includes over eighty low-income, rural women ranging in age from sixteen to ninety-two.

Working at home with fabrics provided by the co-op, the women work in a variety of traditional patterns such as Lone Star, Log Cabin, and Double Wedding Ring. One of the most appealing is Trip Around the World, where coordinating colors "travel" outward in concentric rectangles from the center of the quilt, ending in a bound, sawtooth edge.

Through the Charleston store and a color catalog, the co-op offers quilts from crib-size to king-size, wall hangings, quilted Christmas stockings, purses, and even an apron with a quilted house on the bib. Consistent high-quality work has resulted

139

in sales to collectors including John Denver, Mel Tillis, and Jackie Onassis. But reasonable prices mean you don't have to be a Rockefeller to have your own Appalachian quilt.

PRICES: $1.40–$1,000. Accepts MasterCard, Visa. Send $2 to Cabin Creek Quilts Cooperative, Box 383, Cabin Creek, WV 25035, for a catalog.

OPEN: Tues.–Fri., 10 A.M.–5 P.M.; Sat., 10 A.M.–3:30 P.M. Closed Easter, Labor Day, Christmas, and New Year's. Not wheelchair accessible.

LOCATION: Downtown Charleston. 200 Broad Street, Charleston, WV 25301; 304-342-0326. Take I-64, exit 100, onto Broad Street. The shop is on the left at the third stoplight.

CHARLESTON

The Cultural Center Shop
TRADITIONAL AND CONTEMPORARY WEST VIRGINIA CRAFTS

Some government programs actually work! West Virginia has a state division that aggressively and effectively helps craftspeople find marketing outlets throughout the country. As a result, the work of these artisans can be found in national mail-order catalogs, department stores, major craft exhibits, and locally at this excellent state-sponsored shop.

Exhibiting the work of over 500 craftspeople, the shop includes an equal mix of traditional and contemporary crafts, from folk toys and patchwork pillows to blown glass and jewelry. Look for well-made white oak baskets, folk art wood carvings, furniture, and Appalachian quilts.

PRICES: $1.50–$750 (average, $10–$40). Accepts American Express, MasterCard, Visa.

OPEN: Mon.–Fri., 9 A.M.–5 P.M.; Sat. & Sun., 1–5 P.M. Closed Thanksgiving, Christmas, Easter, New Year's. Wheelchair accessible.

LOCATION: Cultural Complex Center, Capital Complex, Charleston, WV 25305; 304-348-0690. Follow signs to the State Capitol from I-77. Also located at the Shop, West Virginia Independence Hall, 1528 Market Street, Wheeling, WV 26003; 304-233-1333.

MORE: Special events include the Vandalia Gathering—an annual festival featuring the traditional arts of West Virginia including crafts, music, dance and storytelling. The Gathering is held on Memorial Day Weekend at the State Capitol Complex. For more information contact Billie Wiant; 304-348-0220.

CHLOE

Connie and Tom McColley
TRADITIONAL AND CONTEMPORARY BASKETS

Connie and Tom made their first basket in a neighbor's living room. "We just wanted to make a basket for our own use," Connie says. "And then we made another, and another and . . ." Five years later their work was exhibited at the Renwick Gallery in Washington, D.C.

Each of their baskets has a dramatic focus. In some, colorful elliptical swirls pull the eye away from the basket's natural shape. In others, the sides culminate in delicately carved wood rims, or a rib emerges as a naturally shaped branch handle. The McColleys have also made unusual sea shapes: a woven snail shell that begins from a smooth wood center, or a fat whelk that ends in a spiral, carved-wood tip.

Each basket is a shared effort. "Tom and I work together, but there are parts of the process which each of us excels in," Connie notes. She does the dyeing and most of the weaving, but wood is the center of Tom's work. He gathers and splits white

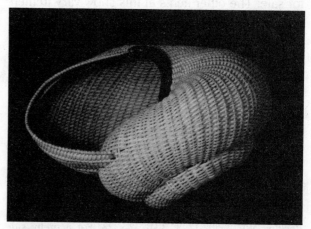

Connie and Tom McColley: White oak basket with walnut. H. 10"; W. 15"; D. 14".

oak and carves the baskets' wood accents. "My life revolves around wood," Tom says. "It heats our home, cooks our food, and provides our income. Our house was even built from the trees that grow here."

And for serious collectors only, Connie and Tom have another treat: bed and breakfast in cabins they built to house their basketry workshop students.

PRICES: $65–$1,200. Commissions accepted. No catalog/brochure, but photos available on request.

VISITORS: Yes. But please call first.

LOCATION: 50 miles northeast of Charleston. Rte. 3, Box 325, Chloe, WV 25235; 304-655-7429. From I-79, take Rte. 16

to Chloe. Half a mile north of Chloe, turn left on Oka Road. Go 2 miles; look for sign/mailbox on right that says McCOLLEY BASKETRY SCHOOL. Turn left on the gravel driveway and follow it to top of hill.

MORE: Bed and breakfast, $35/double, small rooms with bath.

HURRICANE

Rev. Herman Lee Hayes
FOLK ART WOOD CARVINGS

"As a child," Reverend Hayes recalls, "I made wood whistles and deadfall traps. Later I carved a woman out of redwood, found it would sell, been

Rev. Herman L. Hayes: Hand-carved miniature stadium with interchangeable centers: church service (pictured), baseball game, and boxing match. Michael Keller. COURTESY WEST VIRGINIA DEPARTMENT OF CULTURE AND HISTORY

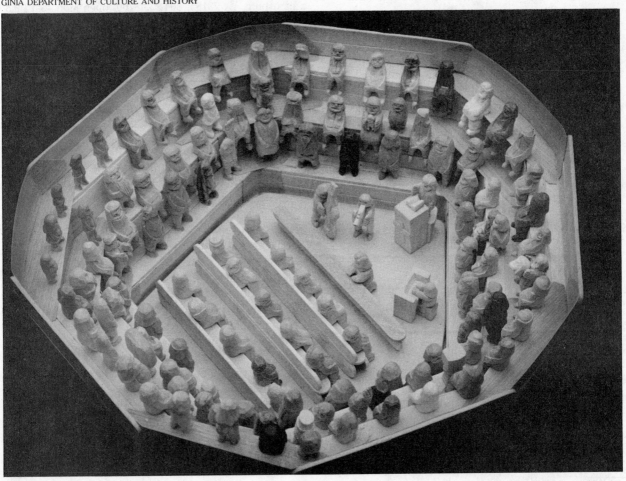

at carving ever since. In the Appalachian region," he continues, "people are shut off from each other by mountains and rivers. Each group does his own thing, the way he wants. There's lots of strong individualism, many trees, and quite a few wood carvers. But the things I make, you've never seen before."

He's right! This retired Methodist minister can carve everything from a man out of a toothpick to 6-foot-high farmers. The figures are primitive, detailed, and unusual. In *Ballgame,* which is only 7 by 10 by 7 inches, over 150 wood figures stand in the stadium or play baseball on the field. Recognized as a wood carver of national stature, he has seen his work exhibited at the Renwick Gallery and Smithsonian Museum in Washington, D.C., and at New York City's Museum of American Folk Art.

PRICES: $3–$850. Commissions accepted. No catalog/brochure.

VISITORS: Mon.–Sat., 10 A.M.–10 P.M.

LOCATION: Between Huntington and Charleston, West Virginia. 2630 Montana Avenue, Hurricane, WV 25526; 304-562-6411. Take I-64 to exit 34. Turn left and go half a mile. Turn right and go to the stoplight. Go right again on Lynn Street. One block later turn left on Virginia Avenue. In two blocks, turn right on Reynolds, go one block, then left on Montana. The house is the third on the right.

MORE: Reverend Hayes's work is also available through the Smithsonian Institution's museum shops in Washington, D.C.

LEWISBURG

Quilts Unlimited
TRADITIONAL QUILTS, NEW AND ANTIQUE

Quilts Unlimited is located in a restored antebellum home not far from the famous Greenbrier Resort. In this gracious setting visitors can find a great variety of quilts, new and old, three-quarters of them from Appalachia. For armchair travelers, an equal treat is the catalog of antique quilts supplemented by color snapsnots that illustrate many of the pieces. Catalog descriptions include color, pattern, condition, estimated date of origin,

number of stitches per inch, and comments such as "washed once" or, for an 1890 quilt, "Mint condition, but needs a bath, as there are some stains which we should be able to get out." A catalog of new quilts is planned for the future; ask if it is available.

PRICES: Average, $550. The catalog costs $5. Accepts MasterCard, Visa.

OPEN: Mon.–Sat., 9:30 A.M.–5:30 P.M. Not wheelchair accessible.

LOCATION: Southeastern West Virginia. 203 East Washington Street, Box 1210, Lewisburg, WV 24902; 304-647-4208. Take I-64 to the Lewisburg exit. Head toward Lewisburg to the first light. Take a left at the light onto Washington Street. The shop is two blocks ahead, on the right.

Other locations are at Quilts Unlimited Cottage Row (the Homestead Resort, Hot Springs, VA 24445; 703-839-5955; open Mon.–Sat., 9:30 A.M.–5:30 P.M.; Sun., 10 A.M.–5 P.M.) and Quilts Unlimited (Merchants Square, Williamsburg, VA 23185; 804-253-8700; open Mon.–Sat., 9:30 A.M.–6 P.M.; Sun., 10 A.M.–5 P.M.).

NEW MARTINSVILLE

Mountain Craft Shop
TRADITIONAL AMERICAN FOLK TOYS

Tell your children it's okay to play with their whimmydiddle. Unless, of course, you get to it first.

Whimmydiddles, described as genuine "gee-haw lie detectors," can be found at the Mountain Craft Shop, one of the largest sources of authentic American folk toys. Its owner, Dick Schnacke, began carving simple wooden toys in 1963. He still designs them, but now employs over forty local craftspeople to make them. The toy business has been a boon for these artisans, many of whom live in isolated mountain communities where poverty is the rule. Working out of their homes, they can earn a good income crafting hundreds of puzzles, fine doll furniture, or toys like those their parents once made.

Visitors will find this shop set on a wooded mountaintop at the southern end of West Virginia's panhandle. Inside are puzzles and games, puppets and dolls, and toys called flipperdingers, Jacob's ladder, and the do-nothing machine. Made primarily of native hardwoods, these inventive items are inexpensive and make perfect stocking stuffers.

PRICES: $1–$27 (average, $3–$8). Free catalog. No credit cards.

OPEN: Tues.–Sat., 9 A.M.–5 P.M. Not wheelchair accessible.

LOCATION: Near the Ohio River, between Wheeling and Parkersburg. American Ridge Road, Rte. 1, New Martinsville, WV 26155; 304-455-3570. From Newman's Exxon on Rte. 2 in New Martinsville, go east on Doolin Run Road 5.5 miles to the top of the hill. Take a sharp left onto American Ridge Road, go .25 mile to parking lot on left. (NOTE: Ignore sign 1 mile from Rte. 2 that says AMERICAN RIDGE ROAD; it is not a shortcut.)

West Virginia Glass Factories

Although arguably not a producing "handcraft" in the traditional use of that word, a number of glass factories that dot West Virginia may be of interest to American glass collectors. Generally large production facilities, most offer tours and have an outlet shop.

Ceredo: Pilgrim Glass Corporation, P.O. Box 395, Walker Branch Road, Ceredo, WV 25507; 304-453-3553. Located just west of Huntington, south of I-64, off SR 52, .25 mile from airport. Visitors can see glassmaking from observation area only.

Milton: Blenko Glass Co., P.O. Box 67, Henry Road, Milton, WV 25541; 304-743-9081. Producer since 1921 of fine stained glass used in famous buildings such as the Washington National Cathedral and the Air Force Academy. Also makes a variety of vases, pitchers, bowls, and the Country Music awards. Features a museum, tours, and a shop.

Milton: Gibson Glass, Rte. 1, Box 102A, Milton, WV 25541; 304-743-5232. Smaller glass operation that produces decorative pieces. Call for details/catalog.

New Martinsville: Viking Glass Co., 802 Parksway, New Martinsville, WV 26115; 304-455-2900. Specializes in ornamental glassware.

Scott Depot: Hamon Glass, 102 Hamon Drive, Scott Depot, WV 25560; 304-757-9067. Small operation making decorative glass. Call for details/visitor information.

Star City: Gentile Glass Co., 425 Industrial Avenue, Star City, WV 26505; 304-599-2750. Glass paperweights, hand-cut crystal tableware, and shades. Features a Showroom and plant tours.

Weston: West Virginia Glass Specialty Co., Rte. 19, Weston, WV 26452; 304-269-2842. Produces hand-blown glassware. Features an outlet and tours.

Williamstown: Fenton Art Glass Factory/Museum, 420 Caroline Avenue, Williamstown, WV 26187; 304-375-7772. Has made hand-blown and hand-pressed glassware for over eighty years. Features tours, a shop, and a museum collection of work from over thirteen Ohio Valley glass companies.

THE SOUTH

Although the American South is not as homogeneous as many outsiders believe, there *are* major craft traditions that cross state borders. Kentucky, Tennessee, and North Carolina are centers for traditional Appalachian crafts created from native materials and almost indistinguishable from turn-of-the-century prototypes. For a thorough discussion of this American craft tradition, see the Foxfire series of books published by Anchor/Doubleday.

Travelers along the back roads of Georgia, North Carolina, and Alabama will discover multigenerational potteries that produce everything from simple flowerpots and birdbaths to unusually glazed vases and grotesque "face jugs." For an in-depth introduction to this substantial ceramic legacy, see *Raised in Clay: The Southern Pottery Tradition,* by Nancy Sweezy (Smithsonian Institution Press, 1984).

The South's ethnic diversity is reflected in its Afro-American crafts (found throughout the region but most notably in South Carolina and Mississippi); Native American tribal arts (Mississippi, North Carolina, Florida, and Louisiana); Florida's multiethnic crafts, including those of recent immigrants; and Louisiana's glorious mixture of crafts from European, Cajun and Acadian, to African-American, and a multitude of other ethnic heritages.

Less well known (but definitely worth exploring) are the region's contemporary crafts, showcased in sophisticated galleries from Louisville to Atlanta to Palm Beach or offered through artists' studios. Inspired by the South's legendary beauty, craftspeople transform and concentrate its essential colors and outlines into a variety of work from massive tapestries and free-form pine needle vessels to abstract ceramic pieces.

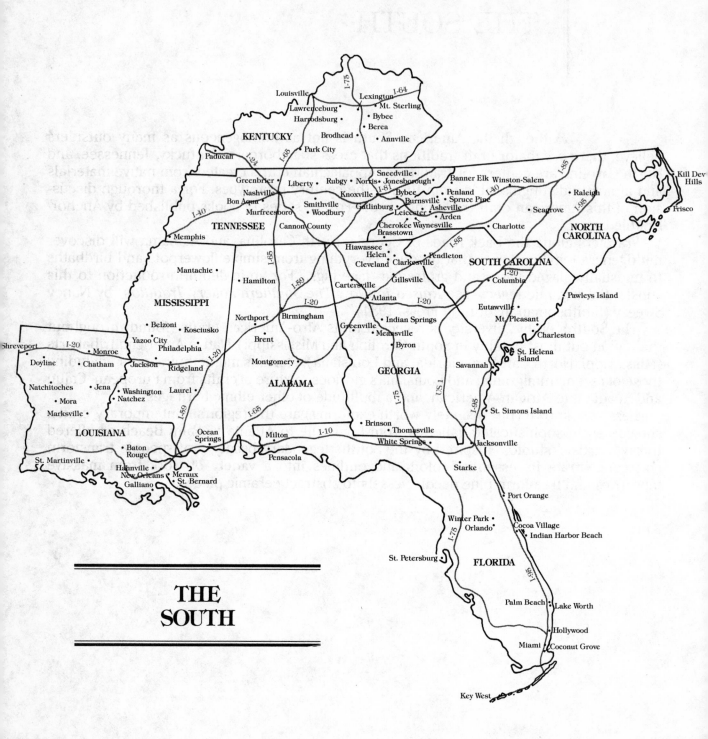

THE
SOUTH

ALABAMA

Alabama artisans tend to create items for their own use, for friends, and for church auctions, so it's relatively difficult for travelers to find quality crafts. The exceptions are the simple, functional, production potteries that can be found in a few small towns and Northport's increasingly lively contemporary craft scene, which revolves around the popular Kentuck Art Center. Please let us know about any other Alabama artisans you discover—especially those continuing multigenerational crafts.

BRENT

Miller's Pottery
TRADITIONAL, FUNCTIONAL POTTERY

Miller's Pottery is for the birds, literally. Its unglazed feeders, baths, and houses meet every bird's basic needs. In fact, "basic" and "traditional" are the keys to all of Miller's work. Started in 1865 by Abraham Miller, this no-nonsense pottery is now run by his great-great-grandson, Eric.

"We have two specialties," Eric says, "unglazed gardenware and very practical, glazed kitchenware." The unglazed gardenware includes strawberry pots and planters, many with the pottery's signature blue or red stripes circling the buff-colored clay. The kitchenware often sports fluted rims, is glazed a simple brown or blue, and comes in a variety of forms: five-gallon churns, pitchers, bean pots, mugs, and even holders for steel wool pads.

PRICES: $2–$25. Commissions accepted. Free catalog/brochure.

VISITORS: Yes.

LOCATION: Central Alabama, about 30 miles south of Tuscaloosa. Rte. 1, Box 107, Brent, AL 35034; 205-926-4420.

Take I-20/I-59 to the Rte. 82 (Tuscaloosa) exit, then Rte. 82 south to Rte. 5. The pottery is on Rte. 5 about 8 miles south of Brent.

HAMILTON

Brown's Pottery
TRADITIONAL POTTERY

Jerry Brown is probably the only potter in the country whose star employee is a mule. Jerry's mule-driven "pug" mill may be the last of its kind and is certainly the highlight of most customers' visits. The process begins five miles away, where Jerry hand digs his clay. Up to 1,500 pounds of it is then dumped into the mill's trough, water is added, and the mule begins its circular route, turning a shaft set with spiraling steel blades. Several mule hours later, the clay is the right consistency for Jerry to start turning it into kitchenware.

"I'm a ninth-generation potter," Jerry says, "and I enjoy doing things the old-timey way. I've experimented with more modern equipment, but the old processes always seem to work better. I had an electric kiln once, but the pieces just didn't turn out well. Now I use a modified, wood-fired groundhog kiln. I fire it with slabs of oak and also add some dry pine. The pine resin makes a slicker

Brown's Pottery: (clockwise from top) 5-gallon churn with dasher, H. 18″; mixing bowl, H. 7″; covered bean pot, H. 10″; 1-gallon milk pitcher, H. 10″. LES WALTERS

glaze." Items are either glazed with Albany-slip or salt-glazed with decorative cobalt blue hearts and stripes.

Claiming to be the only potter still making six-gallon churns, Jerry also turns out a variety of glazed jugs and jars, pitchers and plates. A few unglazed items are also part of his regular line, including fluted birdbaths that sit on pedestals incised with wavy lines.

PRICES: $5–75. No commissions. No catalog/brochure.

VISITORS: Yes.

LOCATION: Northwest Alabama, about 75 miles northwest of Birmingham. Rte. 4, Box 66, Hamilton, AL 35570;

205-921-9483. Signs on either Rte. 17 or Rte. 78 will lead you directly to the pottery.

NORTHPORT

Kentuck Art Center, Museum & Festival
REGIONAL CRAFTS

In a state that is surprisingly quiet about crafts promotion and marketing, Northport is gaining a reputation as Alabama's craft center. Home to a growing number of good-quality studios and galleries, it is also the location of the Kentuck complex. The heart of Kentuck, which uses the town's original name, is its art center. Here visitors can pop into seven different studios to watch a variety of artisans at work, including a fine woodworker, harpischord maker, jewelry designer, potter, glassblowers, and a portrait artist. After hobnobbing with the craftspeople, walk one block to the Kentuck Museum to see an exhibit of Alabama basket makers and potters, both traditional and contemporary. The museum shop carries a variety of crafts, half of which are made by regional artisans.

For an even larger array of local crafts, attend the annual Kentuck Festival, a whirlwind two-day event with craft booths, demonstrations, children's art activities, and regional music. Both traditional and contemporary items are featured, including representative Afro-American and Japanese crafts. Tummies will be pleased too, with such regional specialties as fried chicken, sausage and biscuits, barbecue, jambalaya, funnel cakes, spiral fries, and pork skins.

ART CENTER: Studio hours vary but are generally Tues.–Sat., 10 A.M.–4 P.M. Not wheelchair accessible. Located in west-central Alabama, just across the river from Tuscaloosa, at 503 Main Avenue, Northport, AL 35476 (no central telephone). Take I-59 to I-359, then I-359 north across the bridge to the first exit (on right). Go left from the exit ramp. The gallery is located at the first intersection, Main and 5th, in the Kentuck Art Center.

MUSEUM: Open Mon.–Fri., 9 A.M.–5 P.M.; Sat., 11:30 A.M.–4:30 P.M. Closed major holidays. Free admission. Wheelchair accessible. Located at the corner of Rte. 82 and Main Street; 3500 Highway 82, P.O. Box 127, Northport, AL 35476; 205-333-1252.

KENTUCK FESTIVAL: Three days in early fall. For specific dates/hours, contact the Kentuck Museum. Admission is $3 for adults, $1 for seniors and children 6–12. Children under

6 free. The festival is held in Kentuck Park, on the corner of 30th Avenue and 5th Street, Northport, AL. Take Rte. 82 to Northport, go south on Main Avenue, then right on 5th Avenue to 30th Avenue.

NORTHPORT

Main Avenue Gallery
CONTEMPORARY CRAFTS

Located in Northport's Kentuck Art Center, this gallery exhibits the work of regional craftspeople and serves as a showcase for owner Timothy Weber's wheel-thrown stoneware. Combining crisp symmetry with well-balanced forms, Timothy creates functional pieces whose surfaces may be pierced, colored from vibrant blue to muted neutral, or covered with expert sgraffito.

Look also for the inlaid porcelain of Sunyoung Chung, with its bright colors and animal images, and Craig Nutt's supremely odd flying vegetables (see the next entry). For pure silliness, purchase one of Tim Reed's whirligigs. "Come," Tim says, "the wondrous Caliph of Windsculptures welcomes you to his imaginative world of enchantment, whimsy, and stupidity, a world where old and new techniques combine to make tomorrow seem like yesterday . . . with that extra added touch of menthol."

PRICES: $10–8,000 (average, $50–$100). Accepts Master-Card, Visa.

OPEN: Tues.–Sat., 10 A.M.–5 P.M. Closed July 4th, Thanksgiving, and Christmas. Wheelchair accessible.

LOCATION: West-central Alabama, just across the river from Tuscaloosa. 503 North Main Avenue, Northport, AL 35476; 205-758-5002. Take I-59 to I-359, then I-359 north across the bridge to the first exit (on right). Go left from the exit ramp. The Gallery is located at the first intersection, Main and 5th, in the Kentuck Art Center.

NORTHPORT

Craig Nutt
CONTEMPORARY FURNITURE AND SCULPTURE

If Craig Nutt were asked where he gets the inspiration for his striking furniture and sculpture, he

Craig Nutt; *Deinonychus Desk.* Mahogany, ebony. H. 35″; W. 30″; L. 84″. RICKEY YANAURA

would undoubtedly credit antiques and avant-garde music, dinosaurs and vegetables. "After college I got a job restoring antiques," Craig explains. "I became fascinated with furniture. The experience of taking apart old pieces, learning about construction, what worked and what did not, proved invaluable. After a while I began reproducing antique furniture but found it too confining. I longed for the creative freedom in wood that I'd found playing experimental music in college."

Enter the dinosaurs. As a child, one of Craig's favorite toys was a set of dinosaurs. Translating their graceful mass and innate power into wood, Craig drew on this childhood fantasy to create "Art Dino." In one piece, a striking mahogany desk suggests the skeleton and massive legs of a Deinonychus, a bipedal dinosaur whose name means "terrible claw." In this case, the claws are ebony and guaranteed nonlethal.

In the hands of a less capable woodworker, these striking details could overwhelm a piece of furniture or contradict its function. In Craig's, they only add intriguing detail to finely crafted furniture. In other pieces dinosaur imagery gives way to ele-

gant function. Craig's graceful mahogany rockers are pleasing to the eye and depend solely on design for comfort—no pillows or padding are necessary.

And now . . . the vegetables. A frustrated gardener, Craig used to pour over seed catalogs. "The claims they make! The pictures they show!" Craig exclaims. "The vegetables look so large and luscious, they should be able to fly!" Now they do. Craig sculpts giant wood corn and squash, mounts them on carved rocket bases or basting bulbs, then adds bright paint and a propeller. Perfect whirligigs to grace your porch and confuse the birds.

PRICES: $1,000–$40,000. Commissions accepted. The catalog/brochure costs $1.

VISITORS: Yes.

LOCATION: West-central Alabama, across the river from Tuscaloosa. 2014 5th Street, Northport, AL 35476; 205-752-6535. Take I-59 to I-359, then I-359 north across the bridge to the first exit (on right). Go left from the exit ramp. Continue to the first intersection, Main and 5th. The studio is in the Kentuck Art Center complex.

MORE: Craig's work is also available through the Kentuck Museum Shop, 3500 Hwy. 82, Northport and Main Avenue Gallery, 503 Main Avenue, Northport.

FLORIDA

If you want to get behind the tourist gloss that envelops so much of Florida's natural beauty, explore some of the state's traditional crafts. Native woods and vegetation provide the raw materials for cypress furniture, walking canes, palm frond weaving, and even cigars. Florida's multiethnic legacy and generations of craftsmanship are reflected in Seminole patchwork, Yuchi Indian carving, Venezuelan masks, Arabic cross-stitch, and Hungarian embroidery. For an extensive, one-stop introduction to the dazzling array of Florida's traditional and immigrant crafts, plan your trip to coincide with the Florida Folk Festival, held in White Springs each Memorial Day weekend.

Contemporary crafts aren't slighted in Florida either. For a special treat visit with one of the state's finest contemporary basket makers in Starke, a stained-glass artisan in Indian Harbor Beach, or drop by first-rate galleries in Palm Beach and St. Petersburg.

COCOA VILLAGE

This n' That Shop
NATIVE AMERICAN CRAFTS

Skip Joan McCarthy's other miscellany and head directly for her high-quality Native American crafts, which sell for 20 percent less than you'd pay in Sante Fe or Phoenix. A Blackfoot Indian and third-generation trader, Joan offers the full array, from Navajo rugs and Zuni inlay work to less well known Penobscot quill jewelry, Apache cradle boards, and Ute pottery.

Look for authentic kachinas hand-carved from a single piece of cottonwood by traditional Hopi artisans, Taos tomahawks made from aspen and local creek rocks, authentic Santo Domingo beadwork by the Montoya and Moquino families, and award-winning jewelry. If you collect Native American crafts you will delight in the selection. If you're new to this work, Joan will provide a superb and knowledgeable introduction.

PRICES: $2.95–$20,000 (average, $25–$100). Accepts American Express, MasterCard, Visa.

OPEN: Mon.–Fri., 10 A.M.–6 P.M.; Sat., 10 A.M.–5 P.M. Closed Christmas. Wheelchair accessible.

LOCATION: Near Cape Canaveral, about 38 miles southeast of Orlando. 204 Brevard Avenue, Cocoa Village, FL 32922 (no phone). Take I-95 or Rte. 1 to Rte. 520 east. Go right at Cocoa Village. Brevard Avenue is the main street. Additional locations are This n' That, Merritt Square Mall, Merritt Island, FL; 407-453-2415; and Rags to Riches, 18 Minuteman Causeway, Cocoa Beach, FL (no phone).

COCONUT GROVE

Edward R. Kowall
COCONUT PALM FROND WEAVING

Edward, a part-time magician who goes by the name of Peter Jack Rabbit, lives at anchor, working out of his sailboat and houseboat. Visitors, however, can find him weaving his unusual baskets and hats at a Coconut Grove restaurant or on the docks nearby. "I first learned palm frond weaving when I was twelve," Peter says. "Back then there were hundreds of palm weavers in Florida from the Caloosahatchee River south to Key West, but now I'm one of only nine. We're all pretty territorial, too, since you have to maintain your own trees in the area you work. We use only the fronds of the coconut palm that is found exclusively in Florida.

"I select each frond myself, climbing up the tree using only my hands and feet, no spikes or ladders. I can harvest the trees all year round, but only take fronds from each tree once every three months. I weave, braid, hitch, and plait the fronds into a variety of items including several different styles of hats, baskets, planters, and wall pieces. I also make three-dimensional pieces: grasshoppers, butterflies, lizards, shrimp, and even spiders."

PRICES: $2–$300. No commissions. No catalog/brochure.

VISITORS: Yes.

LOCATION: "You can find me any day at Monty Trainer's Bayshore Restaurant, 2560 South Bayshore, Coconut Grove, FL; 305-858-1431."

HOLLYWOOD

Betty Mae Jumper
SEMINOLE PATCHWORK

An eighteenth-century schism within the Creek Indian Nation forced a dissenting group to establish a new nation in Florida. The Seminoles (their name means "separatist") remained in Florida until their removal in 1842 after a bitter and costly war with the United States. Although most Seminoles were exiled to Oklahoma, a few remained hidden in the Everglades, and their descendants now populate three small reservations in southern Florida.

Betty Mae, from the Ft. Lauderdale–area reservation, is one of a handful of Seminole Indians who continue the nation's craft tradition. Although she is skilled in sweet grass basketmaking, woodcarving, and beadwork, her specialty is traditional patchwork clothing. Using vivid reds, blues, and other bright colors, Betty Mae creates complex patchwork designs. Resembling the finest hand-made quilts, some skirts incorporate rows of four or five different patterns interspersed with brilliant stripes. Betty Mae also makes patchwork shirts, jackets, aprons, hats, and children's clothing, and even dresses small dolls in typical Seminole apparel.

PRICES: 50¢ and up. Commissions accepted. There is no catalog/brochure, but you can call the reservation office for mail-order information.

VISITORS: Yes. Call the Seminole Okalee Indian Village Reservation office for an appointment; 305-583-7112, ext. 348.

LOCATION: About 7 miles from downtown Ft. Lauderdale, 3 miles west of I-95. Directions will be provided when appointment to visit is made.

MORE: For other authentic Seminole crafts, visit the reservation's Indian Arts & Crafts Center at the junction of Rtes. 441 and 848 (SW 60th Street).

INDIAN HARBOR BEACH

Angelika Traylor
STAINED GLASS

One measure of an artisan's skill is the extent to which the medium itself is invisible, dominated by subject matter and artistic presentation. Using this gauge, Angelika is a master of her craft. Asked quickly to name her medium, people might well guess oil painting, tile mosaic, or color photography as often as stained glass.

Angelika's subjects are diverse. Some are complex wall hangings of tightly grouped flower blossoms or sparse but riveting portraits of posing parrots. Others portray small villages or quiet domestic scenes. Angelika also has a flair for minute details that reveal themselves only after many viewings: stray parrot feathers along a border, a tiny hex sign on a barn, a decorative gold medallion on a classic side table.

Angelika's pieces can be installed as windows or as wall hangings encased in her custom-made metal frames. No matter how they're used, they seem to meet her stated goal of "using beautiful colors, design, and going beyond the limits."

PRICES: $500–$5,000. Commissions accepted. Send an SASE for the catalog/brochure.

VISITORS: By appointment only.

Angelika Traylor: *Make It Mine*. 851 individual pieces of glass, copperfoiled and soldered. H. 21¼"; W. 38¼".

LOCATION: About 17 miles south of Cape Canaveral. 100 Poinciana Drive, Indian Harbor Beach, FL 32937; 407-773-7640. Directions will be provided when appointment to visit is made.

JACKSONVILLE

Nadia A. Michael
ARABIC CROSS-STITCH

"**I** was born in Ramallah in Palestine," Nadia says, "where my mother taught me to cross-stitch (we call it *tatreez*) at a very young age. Cross-stitch dates to the time of the Crusaders. Back then the only dyes available were black and red, and these are still the only colors we use. The patterns are all very symbolic; every design has a meaning. In fact, each village has its own patterns. In Ramallah we use designs from nature such as palm trees, feathers, horses, and the moon. Traditionally a woman would apply cross-stitch designs to her entire wardrobe. Today I use these patterns on smaller items from bookmarks and pincushions to place mats, runners, and tablecloths."

In addition to seeing Nadia's exquisite cross-stitch pieces, visitors may also want to visit her at Mussallem Oriental Rugs. "I reweave Oriental rugs," Nadia explains. "These rugs take years and years to make and they're quite durable. But people don't take care of them. I cut out the rotten parts, put in a new foundation, and reweave them."

PRICES: "It depends on how much cross-stich work is in the piece." Commissions accepted. No catalog/brochure "but people can contact me by mail if they're interested."

VISITORS: Yes. Please call for an appointment.

LOCATION: Northeast Florida. 7832 Stephenson Drive, Jacksonville, FL 32208; 904-765-4780 (evenings). Directions will be provided when appointment to visit is made.

MORE: To make an appointment to watch Nadia reweave Oriental rugs contact Mussallem Oriental Rugs, 1922 Phoenix Avenue, Jacksonville, FL; 904-356-7117. Take I-95 north to the 20th Street exit east. Continue to the Phoenix Street exit. The store is five blocks farther on the right side (green building).

KEY WEST

Eleanor Walsh
KEY WEST CIGAR FACTORY

Key West is at the tip of the Florida Keys, a series of small tropical islands that curve into the Gulf of Mexico like a long fishing line held by a Miami giant. Linked by the last 100 miles of famous U.S. Route 1, which begins in Van Buren, Maine, the islands are postcard assemblages of coral reefs, palm trees, and ocean horizons.

Key West seems like a romance novel's fanciful setting, perfect for tropical liaisons and dangerous intrigue. At various times a center for commercial fishing, turtle hunting, and antipiracy efforts, Key

West was also once an artists' haven for luminaries such as Ernest Hemingway and Tennessee Williams.

Cigar lovers, however, know that Key West was the hub of nineteenth-century American cigarmaking. After Cuba's 1868 revolt against Spain, many Cubans fled for their lives, successfully making the ninety-mile trip from Havana to Key West. Almost overnight this sleepy fishing village was transformed into a major industrial city anchored in cigars. Producing a high-quality product that sold for two-thirds the price of imported Cuban cigars, the industry flourished, at one point employing over 20,000 cigar makers.

Toward the end of the nineteenth century, however, labor unrest convinced many of the larger companies to switch their operations to Tampa and Ybor City. The Spanish-American War, difficulty in importing Cuban tobacco, major hurricane disasters, and competitive machine-made cigars forced the closing of more factories. Done in finally by the Great Depression and an increasing preference for cigarettes, Key West's dependence on cigars faded, and the city turned to tourism for economic sustenance.

A few small-scale cigar factories remain, however, including Eleanor Walsh's Key West Cigars. "I wanted to bring back this fine craft of cigarmaking," says Eleanor. "It was a dying art until I revived it." Although some might argue that cigar making is not a craft, it is difficult to do so after watching Eleanor's six employees painstakingly fill binder leaves with filler leaves, then carefully cover them with spirally applied wrapping leaves. "All of my workers served an apprentice term," Eleanor says. "It takes a great deal of skill to make a top-quality cigar."

PRICES: 80¢–$2.50 per cigar, usually sold by the box. The price list is free.

VISITORS: View the entire cigarmaking process Mon.–Fri., 9 A.M.–closing.

LOCATION: Mallory Square in the Old Town area of Key West. Pirates Alley at Front Street, Key West, FL 33040; 305-294-3470.

LAKE WORTH

Robert Rudd
CYPRESS FURNITURE

Every four to six weeks, Robert and his wife, Betty, head to a swamp west of Gainesville to harvest cypress, avoid water moccasins, and duck yellowjackets. "My father also made cypress furniture," Robert says, "but there was a swamp right near his house that provided all the material he needed. That swamp's now a landfill, and I have to drive two hundred and seventy miles north to get my supplies."

"There just aren't many cypress groves left," Betty adds. "Cypress need constant moisture, but a lot of the swamps where they once grew have been drained to control mosquitoes or provide land for subdivisions. In other areas timber companies have bulldozed cypress to get to the more valuable pines. Even on the land we lease up north, Robert has to walk for miles and miles in order to find enough small, straight cypress."

The fifty or sixty trees they bring home on each trip are quickly made into chairs and settees, chaise lounges, tables, and headboards. Robert strips the bark off with a knife, then bends small saplings to form the framework and graceful curves of his distinctive furniture. The larger "poles" are used as legs and support pieces. "The color of the furniture depends on what time of year we harvest the cypress," Betty adds. "Summer cypress dries to a creamy white, while winter wood is warm brown. We don't add any finish to them, just leave them plain so the wood can breathe."

PRICES: $75–$1,500. No commissions. No catalog/brochure.

VISITORS: "If you're passing by, stop in. If you're making a special trip, call first to see if we're out hunting cypress."

LOCATION: Just south of Palm Beach. 9199 Lake Worth Road, Lake Worth, FL 33467; 407-964-0039. Take the Florida Turnpike to exit 65 (Lake Worth), then go west for about 1.25 miles. The home is on the north side of Lake Worth Road. Look for the RUDD'S CYPRESS FURNITURE sign.

MIAMI

Manuel Albalate
VENEZUELAN YARE DANCE MASKS

Florida may be a calliope of differing cultures and artistic expression, but not all of the traditions are equally well known. One that has drawn little attention is the making of Venezuelan dance masks (see illustration on cover). "In the part of Venezuela where I grew up," Manuel explains, "the dancers' masks of Yare have been made for more than three hundred years. They represent a fusion of three different cultures: native, African, and Spanish."

"For centuries," Manuel continues, "natives and Africans used a variety of masks in their festivities, spiritual acts, and healings, but early missionaries took a dim view of this practice and prohibited their continued use. Rather than abandon the masks altogether, their owners wore them during Spanish 'Carnival' street celebrations. This way they avoided persecution but maintained some of their traditions."

Over the years the masks took on common characteristics. Made of painted papier-mâché, most masks are bull's heads with human qualities. Fanciful and humorous, these colorful masks may sport horns of yellow or red, green curled mustaches, calico-colored "ears," and star-centered eyes. Green masks symbolize the female; blue the male. Many also have leaves, flowers, and other references to nature.

"Today these masks are worn by the devil dancers of Saint Frances of Yare," Manuel explains. "The dances are supposed to chase away bad spirits. Here in Florida, the dancers perform every year in Corpus Christi during the second week of June. Except for the masks, each participant is covered totally in red. The dancers begin with a blessing from the church, then lead a crowd to a public square where they perform throughout the afternoon."

PRICES: $175–$1,000. Commissions accepted. No catalog/brochure.

VISITORS: Yes.

LOCATION: 10738 NE 2d Place, Miami, FL 33161; 305-759-9060. Take I-95 to the 103 Street exit. Go east on 103 Street to 2d Avenue. Go left on 2d Avenue, right on 107 Street, left on NE 2d Place, to the third house on the left.

MIAMI

Historical Museum of Southern Florida
TRADITIONAL FLORIDA CRAFTS

Although only 20 percent of this museum's holdings are crafts, if you've overdosed on plastic flamingos and miniature, made-in-Taiwan palm trees, these exhibits will provide a pleasant respite. On display are Spanish colonial crafts including pottery and weaponry, Key West spongefishing crafts (hooks, trawls, and other items) unique to the Florida Keys, and historic Seminole Indian costumes and artifacts from south and central Florida.

Located in a Spanish-mission-style building, in the country's only historically designated art deco district, the museum's mission is to exhibit the region's 10,000-year history. It does this admirably using jazzy twentieth-century technology that may even keep your children awake. There are also occasional demonstrations by local ethnic artisans and a gift shop offering Seminole patchwork jackets and other (not necessarily American-made) items.

OPEN: Mon.–Sat., 10 A.M.–5 P.M.; Sun., noon–5 P.M. Closed Christmas, and New Year's Day. Museum shop on the premises. Admission is $3.50 for adults, $2 for children. Free admission Mon. (contribution requested). Self-guided tours. Wheelchair accessible.

LOCATION: Part of the Metro-Dade Cultural Center. 101 West Flagler Street, Miami, FL 33130; 305-375-1492. Discounted parking is available at three nearby garages (Cultural Center Parking, Miami Government Garage, and Dade County Garage). Validate your parking stub at the museum admissions desk.

MILTON

Bill Cooey
TRADITIONAL YUCHI INDIAN WOOD CARVING

"All I need is a pocketknife, a chisel, and a piece of wood," Bill says, "to reveal my Indian heritage, its superstitions and spiritual side, its attitude toward wildlife and ecology. Once I start to work, it's

Bill Cooey: *Indian trader and two Indians,* detail from three hiking staffs. H. 57″.

ment, Bill carves anything he can get his hands on, even pencils. But his most charming pieces are hiking sticks topped with carved folk characters. Using persimmon, magnolia, and sweet gum wood, Bill creates craggy Indian faces surrounded by hair and capped with a wolf or eagle headmask, eighteenth-century woodsmen, Southern Civil War officers, or even an occasional wizard.

"One of the nicest things that ever happened to me," Bill says, "was watching a blind person enjoy my work by feeling it. I'm so happy that after my thirty-year career at Monsanto, my 'true love' career is just beginning. If I were the last person on earth, I would still carve."

PRICES: $2 and up. Commissions accepted "on a limited basis only." No catalog/brochure.

VISITORS: Yes. By appointment only.

LOCATION: Northwestern Florida, about 15 miles northeast of Pensacola. 248 Van Horn Road, Milton, FL 32570; 904-623-5255. Directions will be provided when appointment to visit is made.

MORE: Bill's work is also available through Casas de Cosas (210 East Garden Street, Pensacola, FL; 904-433-5921), Indian Temple Mound Museum (Ft. Walton Beach, FL), and Florida State Museum (Tallahassee, FL).

PALM BEACH

Holsten Galleries
CONTEMPORARY GLASS

Palm Beach is the southern location for this top-notch gallery exhibiting America's glass luminaries. See the Stockbridge, Massachusetts entry for a detailed introduction to one of this country's finest glass galleries.

PRICES: $1,000–$35,000 (average, $3,000–$8,000). Accepts American Express, MasterCard, Visa.

OPEN: Nov.–May, Mon.–Sat., 10 A.M.–5:30 P.M.; June–Oct., daily, 11 A.M.–5:30 P.M. Closed month of Aug. and all major holidays. Wheelchair accessible.

LOCATION: One block from ocean. 206 Worth Avenue, Palm Beach, FL 33480; 407-833-3403.

amazing to me how swamp wildlife just seems to grow out of a large cypress or juniper slab." Grow and continue to move. Many of Bill's deep-relief panels quiver with tension: a rabbit just escapes an eagle's grasping talons, a bass leaps from lily pads toward a dragonfly, a wickedly benign alligator waits for dinner to swim by.

"When I was growing up, we lived quite primitively in the Choctaw Hatchee Swamp in northwest Florida," Bill recalls. "My mother entertained me by teaching me to carve with a pocketknife. She taught me to make all the swamp animals and reptiles."

Since his retirement in 1982 from Monsanto's engineering research and development depart-

PORT ORANGE

Margaret P. Horvath
HUNGARIAN EMBROIDERY

"**H**ungarian embroidery has evolved over thousands of years," Margaret explains. "There is evidence that it is based on Sumerian work from as far back as 2000 B.C., and documents from medieval times mention that the women's ornate woolen dresses and veils were embroidered. For three seasons a year the peasants labor in the fields, then during the winter months the women busy themselves with embroidery and other needlework while the men do woodcarving, leatherwork, and pottery."

Knowledgeable in all aspects of Hungarian embroidery, Margaret passes on this traditional craft through classes as well as formal apprenticeships. Visitors to her shop will find examples of a variety of Hungarian embroidery styles, all of them extremely colorful and complex. "There are very distinct differences in embroidery and peasant costumes depending upon which of the four main regions in Hungary you visit: Transdanubia, the Great Hungarian Plain, the Northern Highland, or Transylvania. In Transdanubia the women's brocade-and-velvet skirts are lavishly decorated and their shifts have embroidered sleeves set with spangles. Transylvania is known for its complex cut-and-drawn threadwork embellished with satin-stitch.

"In the Great Hungarian Plain, Kalocsa embroidery is done by 'writing women' who draw the designs freehand on white or pastel fabrics. The motifs are often daisies, marigolds, poppies, and tulips intertwined with leafy scrolls. The designs are so popular that they're even applied to the walls in a house for decoration."

PRICES: $5–$50. Commissions accepted. Free catalog/brochure explains the history and background of Hungarian embroidery and other folk art.

VISITORS: Yes.

LOCATION: Atlantic coast of Florida, just south of Daytona Beach. Debakkery Shop, 4036-D South Nova Road, Port Orange, FL 32074; 904-756-0181. Take I-95 to the Port Orange exit. Follow Rte. 415 east for 2 miles. Turn south on Nova Road, continue past two lights. The shop is on the right.

ST. PETERSBURG

Florida Craftsmen Gallery
CONTEMPORARY FLORIDA CRAFTS

Don't worry about weeding through a slew of ho-hum crafts to find the one or two items right for your collection. This gallery has done the work for you by displaying the work of over 120 of Florida's best contemporary craftspeople, including several with national reputations and others poised on the edge of craft fame.

Offering pieces in every medium, the gallery's fiber wearables and wall hangings are particularly notable, especially fiber constructions by Ray Azcuy. Looking for a wedding gift? Consider one of Cecile Lorenzen's sleek brass serving sets. Doting grandparents should ask to see Bob Kopec's furniture, including his gracefully curving *Close to My Heart* walnut cradle.

For less functional crafts, see Michael Davis's work, which begins with large, superbly executed baskets. Using these as his canvas, Michael adds paint and other surface decoration, transforming them into abstract pieces such as *Sheneeka,* which resembles a reed-fringed African drum. St. Petersburg's own Russ Gustafson-Hilton creates colorful raku vessels with flashes of blazing reds, purples, and blues that mellow over time as the surface chemicals oxidize.

PRICES: $10–$2,000 (average, $25–$200). Accepts MasterCard, Visa.

OPEN: Tues.–Sat., 10 A.M.–4 P.M. Wheelchair accessible.

LOCATION: A renovated firehouse in downtown St. Petersburg. 235 Third Street South, St. Petersburg, FL 33701; 813-821-7391. Take I-275 to downtown. Take South Bay exit to Third Street. Continue for two blocks, then go left to gallery on the left in the "3rd & 3rd" Building.

STARKE

A. G. Horton
CONTEMPORARY AND TRADITIONAL BASKETS

Each of A.G.'s baskets is so totally different from the next that his pieces could be the work of twenty different craftsmen. Sometimes he begins with a superbly woven traditional basket, then accentuates one characteristic or embellishes it with a row of curlicues. Other baskets resemble an accordion fan or ornate seashell, a base for dried tide pool creatures, or a vessel filled with confetti string. Another looks as if it were woven above and below a bird's nest.

"Baskets have always fascinated me," A.G. says. "As far back as I can remember, they've always been associated with special and pleasant times: picnics, Easter, flowers. I begin each one with a basic, functional form, then incorporate atypical materials to express an idea or emotion, adding an extra dimension to an already three-dimensional form. I work with all types of organic and inorganic materials, from locally grown fibers to wicker, wool, plastics, even videotape."

PRICES: $3–$5,000. Commissions accepted. No catalog/brochure.

VISITORS: Yes. Please call or write for an appointment.

A. G. Horton: *Alluvial Fan.* Natural and smoked wicker, bamboo, and bone beads. H. 14″; W. 30″, D. 12″.

LOCATION: Northeast Florida, about 35 miles southwest of Jacksonville. Rte. 5, Box 7451, Starke, FL 32091; 904-964-7523. The studio is located outside of Starke off Rte. 301. Specific directions will be provided when appointment to visit is made.

STARKE

Patrick E. Pattillo
WALKING CANES AND RELATED PRODUCTS

Need an excuse to become a long-distance hiker or a mycologist? Purchase one of Patrick's eminently practical, sparsely aesthetic staffs. Following nature's unadorned mastery of form, Patrick selects each stick personally, then alters it as little as possible to create hiking staffs, mushroom sticks, quarterstaffs, thumbsticks, and walking canes. Big or little, straight or twisted, smooth or gnarled, each piece is coaxed to become a natural extension of your arm, perfectly synchronized with your pace and purpose.

"I harvest saplings and limbs as they grow," Patrick says. "I never use precut blanks or carving gimmicks. Most staffs are made from native Florida woods such as maple, dogwood, pecan, and bamboo." A frugal craftsman, Patrick uses his scraps to make flutes, whistles, and folk toys.

PRICES: $12–$75 (average, $20). Commissions accepted. There is no catalog/brochure, "but anyone needing information should write to me."

VISITORS: By appointment only.

LOCATION: Northeast Florida, about 35 miles southwest of Jacksonville. Rte. 5, Box 7451, Starke, FL 32091; 904-964-7523. Directions will be provided when appointment to visit is made.

MORE: Patrick's work is also available through the Sydney Hauser Gallery, 9 Filmore Drive, Sarasota, FL 33577.

WHITE SPRINGS

Florida Folk Festival

One of the oldest and best folk events in the nation, the Florida Folk Festival has a list of participants that reads like a cultural atlas of the world: Anglo- and African-American; Hispanic and Thai; Jewish, Minorcan, Greek, and Hungarian.

In the "craft demonstration area," you may see Cracker whip braiding, African-American quilting, Norwegian Hardanger embroidery, Seminole wood carving, or even Thai fruit and vegetable carving. Crafts for sale include many items rarely seen outside of Florida, including bamboo flutes, nets, shell cameos, coconut palm weaving, and Guatemalan backstrap weaving.

An annual highlight is the Folk Arts Apprenticeship section. Each year the Florida Folklife Program awards year-long grants to master folk artisans who train apprentices in their craft or musical traditions. During the festival their work is displayed and demonstrated. In addition to those in the better-known crafts, apprenticeships have included piñatamaking; crafting of spun copper deep-sea-diving helmets; performing Irish stepdancing; creating Japanese *temari* (balls decorated with elaborately wound and laced colored thread); and playing Greek *tsabouna* instruments made of goatskin, wood, string, beeswax, and onion skin.

Need to rest your feet? Take a break by listening to a fiddle contest or a performance by traditional singers, tale tellers, and musicians. Tummy gurgling? Saunter over to the Regional and Ethnic Foodways Pavilion to sample apple and cheese strudels, Seminole fry bread, Greek gyros, barbecue, or gumbo.

EVENT: Memorial Day Weekend, Fri.–Sun., 10 A.M.–11 P.M. Admission per day is $7 for adults, $1.50 for children. For more information contact the Bureau of Florida Folklife Programs, P.O. Box 265, White Springs, FL 32096; 904-397-2192.

LOCATION: Northern Florida, about 60 miles west of Jacksonville. Stephen Foster State Folk Culture Center, White Springs. Take I-10 to the White Springs exit. Follow Rte. 41 to the Center.

MORE: The Florida Folklife Program also has a superb folklife archive open to the public Mon.–Fri., 8:30 A.M.–5 P.M. Containing tapes, photos and slides, field notes, and a reference library, the collection is invaluable to anyone wanting to learn more about Florida's diverse traditions.

WINTER PARK

Morse Museum of American Art
TIFFANY GLASS

Although the museum does not have all of its Tiffany holdings on display, it houses an impressive Tiffany collection including leaded windows, jewelry, lamps, rugs, pottery, furniture, and mosaics, as well as photographs and various memorabilia. Many of the items were designed by Tiffany for his own use and are surviving parts of his Long Island estate, Daffodil Terrace.

In the main gallery, look for rare Tiffany windows backlighted as he himself often displayed them. A skylight, cast-iron benches, and Favrile glass panels from Daffodil Terrace are displayed in the west garden gallery, and other work is scattered throughout the museum. The museum also exhibits Rookwood pottery and a variety of other American crafts and fine arts.

OPEN: Tues.–Sat., 9:30 A.M.–4 P.M.; Sun., 1–4 P.M. Closed major holidays. The museum shop sells genuine Tiffany and other art glass (shop is closed Sun.). Admission is $2.50 for adults, $1 for students, children under 6 free. Wheelchair accessible.

LOCATION: East-central Florida, just east of Orlando. 133 East Welbourne Avenue, Winter Park, FL 32789; 407-644-3686. Take I-4 to exit 45. Continue down Fairbanks to the seventh light. Turn left on Park Avenue. Continue through three lights to Welbourne Avenue. Turn right on Welbourne to museum on the left.

GEORGIA

Whether you plan to visit Atlanta on business, relax on St. Simons Island, or fish for record-breaking bass, you can combine your Georgia trip with a variety of craft forays. Scattered across central and northeastern Georgia are pockets of folk potters who continue to create functional ceramics similar to those originally produced by their relatives over 100 years ago. Other local artisans use tulipwood, gourds, and even rattlesnakes to create everything from vessels to baskets, bird cages to stylish belts.

Georgia's craft fairs provide an added incentive to visit the state's Blue Ridge Mountains or explore mineral springs once frequented by local Indians. Throughout the year, a sprinkling of Appalachian mountain crafts can be found in far northeastern Georgia, while sophisticated contemporary jewelry, quilts, and ceramics are the crafts of choice in both Atlanta and coastal resort communities. Beginning in 1990, Atlanta will host one of the famous ACC Craft Fairs. Called Salute to American Crafts, the fair will attract over 150 exhibitors to the Atlanta Apparel Mart in early May. For information contact the American Craft Enterprises, P.O. Box 10, New Paltz, NY 12561; 914-255-0039.

Georgia Folk Pottery

Georgia's most significant craft heritage is in the family potteries that dot the countryside. Most began in the early nineteenth century when Carolinians moved south to settle near creeks in the Piedmont Plateau. Farmers during most of the year, they took advantage of the rich clay deposits to produce practical stoneware during the off-season. Necessity, rather than creativity, led these potters to craft utilitarian vessels for churning butter or storing preserved foods and whiskey.

Eight pottery communities, known as "jugtowns," were scattered throughout Georgia's Piedmont, each with dominant families who passed skills, shapes, and glazes to succeeding generations. Through the years many potteries closed as manufactured goods became popular, refrigeration decreased the need for copious storage vessels, and Prohibition dried up the market for legal whiskey jugs. Some families clung on by switching production to inexpensive flowerpots or by producing "art" pottery for tourists. A few, however, persisted in their original production line and are still in business today.

Listed below are some of Georgia's most traditional potteries, which visitors will find clustered in the northeastern and central portions of the state. Don't expect innovative shapes or bold surface designs. Instead, the simple forms and limited glazes offer true shards of America's ceramic history. A few hints: Prices are extremely reasonable (generally $5 to $50), but bring cash—credit cards and checks are rarely accepted. Potteries are usually open Monday through Saturday, but hours vary. Most potteries are situated along local highways. For specific directions, inquire at the local gas station or post office. One dividend: often on the way to one pottery, you'll discover others.

Northeastern Georgia Pottery

CARTERSVILLE: W. J. Gordy Pottery.

Glazed stoneware has always been this pottery's specialty, most often sporting the dark, Albany-slip glaze. Current owner Bill Gordy, however, has experimented through the years with everything from brightly colored glazes to ones with a metallic luster. Visitors will find a variety of cooking vessels and tableware from teapots and mugs to butter plates and red-eye gravy dishes.

Cartersville is about 45 miles northwest of Atlanta. From Atlanta, follow I-75 to the Cartersville exit.

CLEVELAND: Edwin Meaders Pottery, Lanier Meaders Pottery.

The Meaderses came to Georgia in 1848 to farm cotton, then became potters in the 1890s. Brothers Lanier and Edwin now continue the family tradition. Lanier runs the ancestral pottery; Edwin has his own shop and kiln nearby. Although both brothers produce similarly shaped vessels, Lanier prefers an alkaline glaze, Edwin uses Albany-slip. In addition to the jugs and vases, churns and crocks that both brothers produce, Edwin creates unglazed clay roosters and pitchers decorated with raised grapes.

To reach Cleveland, take I-85/985 about 45 miles northeast of Atlanta to the junction with Rte. 129. Cleveland is 28 miles north on Rte. 129.

GILLSVILLE: Craven Pottery.

Born into one of the oldest pottery families in the entire region, Joe Craven operates a large and very successful pottery. Although his business is primarily wholesale, visitors can sometimes purchase one of his unglazed earthenware strawberry pots, planters, birdhouses, feeders, or decorative urns.

GILLSVILLE: Hewell Pottery.

Another large production pottery, Hewell still uses the time-tested techniques of its owner's ancestors. Creating unglazed planters in sizes up to ten gallons, Hewell also makes strawberry planters, kettle pots, and planters decorated with thumbprints.

Gillsville is about 25 miles southeast of Cleveland. From Atlanta, take I-85/985 about 45 miles northeast of Atlanta to New Holland. Go north on Rte. 53 about 5 miles to Rte. 52, then right on Rte. 52 to Gillsville.

If you're in the Gillsville area, drop by Wilson Pottery in nearby Alto, about 15 miles north. Wilson produces fluted earthenware planters as well as strawberry jars, birdhouses, feeders, and jack-o'-lanterns.

Central Georgia Pottery

BYRON: Cleater Meaders Pottery.

A cousin of Edwin and Lanier Meaders of Cleveland, Cleater became a full-time potter after his retirement in 1978. Before then, he spent his days in aircraft construction while potting at home during his free time. Cleater uses several different glazes, including darkened Albany-slip or an off-white feldspar glaze for jugs and churns, and a white glaze with cobalt blue designs for tableware.

Byron is just off I-75 about 10 miles south of downtown Macon.

GREENVILLE: D. X. Gordy Pottery.

Look for a large log house with a sign on one end proclaiming D X GORDY POTTERY. D.X. will be busily turning a jug or out back chain-sawing some wood for his next kiln firing. Visitors are likely to hear a spate of tales from this affable man, including how he helped his grandfather make bricks for the still operating kiln. One of the more decorative of Georgia's traditional potters, D.X. paints charming country scenes on the sides of pitchers and other tableware. Many of the materials he uses to make glazes and paints are found on his property: local clays, mica, ash from his kiln, and even cattle bones.

Greenville is about 50 miles south of Atlanta. From Atlanta, take I-85 south to the East Newnan exit, then Rte. 27 south to Greenville.

MEANSVILLE: Marie Rogers Pottery.

Pottery was traditionally the province of men. Marie Rogers, however, learned from her husband and, since his death, has continued the family business. She produces small churns, pitchers, and bowls, as well as clay pigs and Santa Clauses. But her specialty is face jugs—grotesque, menacing vessels originally produced to hold "spirits." "Some people," Marie says, "like the face jugs to have the appearance of tobacco spit on them. Others want me to include a snake on the jug. The snake was the custom before the skull and cross, to keep children out of whiskey and harmful things."

Meansville is about 50 miles south of Atlanta. From Atlanta, take Rte. 19 south to Zebulon. Continue for 4 miles to the junction with Rte. 109. Go left (east) on Rte. 109 to Meansville.

ATLANTA

Atlanta Historical Society Museum Gift Shop
TRADITIONAL SOUTHERN CRAFTS

Atlanta's political, artistic, and cultural history is portrayed through this museum's rotating exhibits. Also on the grounds is a restored pioneer home, the Tullie Smith House, which offers demonstrations of mid-nineteenth century crafts including weaving, quilting, and blacksmithing. The museum's gift shop mirrors this collection, carrying an array of traditional Southern crafts: baskets, textiles, forged iron, and the appealingly weird face jugs.

PRICES: $5–$300. Accepts American Express, MasterCard, Visa.

OPEN: Mon.–Sat., 9 A.M.–5:30 P.M. Closed major holidays. Admission is $4.50 for adults, $4 for seniors and students, $2 for children 6–12, $10 for families.

LOCATION: 9 miles north of downtown Atlanta. 3101 Andrews Drive. NW, Atlanta, GA 30305; 404-261-1837. From downtown Atlanta, take I-75 to the Mill Road exit. Go northeast on Mill Road to West Paces Ferry Road, right on West Paces Ferry Road to Andrew Drive NW, right on Andrews Drive NW one block to the museum.

ATLANTA

Great American Gallery
CONTEMPORARY CRAFTS

This gallery's galaxy of top-notch American artisans epitomizes Atlanta's sophisticated, cosmopolitan tastes. Two thousand square feet of exhibition space continuously exhibits work by over seventy-five craftspeople: blown and cast glass, wood, clay, furniture, jewelry, and contemporary quilts.

Look particularly for turned wood pieces by David Ellsworth, who has made a unique contribution to this 3,000-year-old-craft. Pushing the technique of lathe-turned items beyond its traditional limits, David developed a method of creating extremely thin, narrow-necked wooden vessels by hollowing them out through their neck opening using specially bent tools. Another innovator, Earl

Pardon, fashions jewelry that combines hard-edged, sculptured metalwork with Zen abstractions. One of his recurring motifs is surprise. Rings may have black pearls on the underside, moving pearls, or gold stems that sway as the wearer moves.

Therese May, Susan Shie, and Pamela Studstill give traditional quilts a modern twist through their choice of materials and subject matter. Therese combines household references with erotic animals and floating ghosts, and Susan's quilts sport stuffed dolls, bead garnishes, and written messages. Inspired by Impressionist painters, Pamela hand-paints fabric, then pieces it to create abstract gridwork quilts with embellished stripes and pointillistic dots of color.

PRICES: $100–$15,000 (average, $1,000–$2,500). No credit cards.

OPEN: Mon.–Fri., 10 A.M.–5 P.M.; Sat., noon–5 P.M. Open at other times by appointment. Closed major holidays. Wheelchair accessible.

LOCATION: 1925 Peachtree Road NE, Atlanta, GA 30309; 404-351-8210. From downtown Atlanta, take I-75 to the Northside Drive exit. Take Northside Drive north to Collier Road. Turn right on Collier to Peachtree Road, then left on Peachtree. The gallery is immediately on the right.

ATLANTA

Ed Moulthrop
Philip Moulthrop
TURNED WOOD VESSELS

Unveiling nature is a tricky task. It requires keen eyes, steady hands, and the ability to recognize the difference between revelation and alteration. Both Ed and his son Philip are gifted with the special touch needed to do just that.

Ed uses his lathe to shape tree sections into bowls, coaxing them to reveal their painterly grain patterns and splashes of color (see color plate #7). An architect who designed Atlanta's civic center, Ed has been turning wood full-time since 1976. Although he works with a variety of local woods, he prefers tulip wood, especially when it has been struck by lightning. Lightning destroys part of the wood, leaving it prey to bacteria, which in turn mottles the grain with varying brown tones and dashes of red and purple. Ed is a master wood

Philip Moulthrop: Ash leaf maple bowl. H. 9″; W. 11½″.

turner, and his work has been exhibited internationally and is part of major public and private collections.

Although Philip's work is similar to his father's in quality, he is more likely to create vertical forms rather than his father's flattened spheres and "donut" shapes. Juggling a career as an attorney with his turning avocation, Philip still has found time to build his own lathe and forge his own tools. "I also use many of the same techniques as my father," Philip says. "Like him, I only use local woods which are highly figured or exhibit a particularly strong grain pattern or color. I also always turn in green wood, curing the vessel afterwards for several months before adding a very light finish."

PRICES: Ed, $750–$3,000; Philip, $450–$2,000. Commissions accepted.

MORE: Ed's and Philip's work is available through the Signature Shop and Gallery in Atlanta. See the gallery's listing below for details.

ATLANTA

Signature Shop & Gallery
CONTEMPORARY CRAFTS

If the word "pewter" brings to mind staid colonial dinnerware, revise your preconceptions by seeing Joseph Brandom's work. Starting with a flat sheet of pewter, Joseph uses textured hammerheads to shape sleek vessels that resemble flying saucers. Prefer gawky birds to outer space? Then purchase one of Marjorie Claybrook's quilted wall hangings. You might choose *Smiles,* which invites you to peek between the gangly legs of a flamingo to see the rest of the flock in the background.

Signature also offers other one-of-a-kind crafts in ceramics, glass, wood, fiber, and metal, including Ed and Philip Moulthrop's wood vessels and lighthearted majolica earthenware by Stanley Mace Anderson.

PRICES: $10–$5,000 (average, $75–$150). Accepts Master-Card, Visa.

OPEN: Mon.–Sat., 9:30 A.M.–5 P.M. Closed major holidays. Wheelchair accessible.

LOCATION: Buckhead section of Atlanta, north of downtown. 3267 Roswell Road, Atlanta, GA 30305; 404-237-4426. Take I-85 to I-285. Take Roswell Road exit from I-285 and continue on Roswell Road for 4 miles. Look for the YMCA on the right. The shop is just beyond, on the left, in a small, unmarked shopping center. If you pass the traffic light, you've gone too far.

BRINSON

Spring Creek Pottery and Fish Camp

If you crave posh accommodations and like to rub elbows with the wealthy when you shop, head directly for Atlanta. But if you'd like a leisurely stop where you can chat with local potters, then fish for your supper, you may want to visit Brinson and this unprepossessing family business.

Stop first at the studio and sales room to see Sharon Foulk's elegantly simple raku vessels and primitive, darkly glazed work by Ralph Weaver. Outside, facing pretty Spring Creek, you'll find simple rustic rooms that rent for $25 per double. From February through April, match your wits with the bass in the creek or nearby Lake Seminole; during the rest of the year, do a little cane pole fishing for pan fish.

PRICES: $2.50–$1,000. Commissions accepted. No catalog/brochure.

VISITORS: Yes. But please call first.

LOCATION: Far southwestern tip of Georgia, about 65 miles southwest of Albany. Rte. #1, Box 1475, Brinson, GA 31725; 912-246-6045. Take I-75 to the Rte. 84 (Valdosta) exit. Go west on Rte. 84 to Brinson, south on County Road 310 for about 7 miles to Rte. 253, right on Rte. 253 for about 2 miles. After you cross Spring Creek, the pottery is the first building on the right (it's blue-gray with a rust-red roof).

CLARKESVILLE

Co-op Craft Store
TRADITIONAL GEORGIA MOUNTAIN CRAFTS

For twenty years this mountain co-op has sold local folks' eminently practical and comfortably decorative work: pottery, tatting, soft sculpture dolls, wood toys and letter openers, cloth place mats and casserole carriers, mountain jellies, grapevine wreaths, baby and Christmas items. However, it's the stock of over 100 quilts that makes this store a worthwhile stop if you're in the area.

PRICES: 50¢–$100; quilts, $175–$550. Accepts American Express, MasterCard, Visa.

OPEN: Daily, 10 A.M.–5 P.M. Closed Easter, Thanksgiving, and Christmas.

LOCATION: Northeastern Georgia. P.O. Box 214, Clarkesville, GA 30523; 404-754-2244. Take I-85 to the Rte. 441 (Commerce) exit, then Rte. 441 north to Clarkesville. The shop is located in the center of town.

MORE: The co-op also has a store housed in an old railroad station in Tallulah Falls (P.O. Box 67, Tallulah Falls, GA 30573; 404-754-6810).

CLEVELAND

Priscilla Wilson
Janice Lymburner
GOURD CRAFT

"This all began as a lark," Priscilla laughs. "We bought a few gourds at a roadside stand in 1976 and decided to carve them. At the time we thought we were inventing a whole new craft! We later learned that gourds have been used for both practical and ornamental purposes by many different cultures for centuries. In fact, we've put together our own gourd museum to show visitors the vari-

Priscilla Wilson and Janice Lymburner: Gourd basket. H. 12″; W. 20″; l. 20″.

ety. We display gourds used as vessels, funnels, and dippers by early Americans, as well as ones fashioned into musical instruments, dolls, poison dart holders, and even (from New Guinea) a penis sheath."

"We grow most of the gourds we carve," adds Janice. "We harvest them in January, let them dry for several months, then clean, dye, varnish, cut, and carve them into over one hundred different items. Some gourds are elaborately carved, others are decorated, then cut into puzzles. We also cut and incise some gourds to resemble woven baskets or fashion them into bird cages, planters, or rolling toys."

For pure silliness, buy a gourdhead. To create these bizarre masks, Janice and Priscilla cut the bottom off a very large gourd, carefully clean the inside, then cut two round holes for eyes. The gourd is left looking like the misshapen head of an alien being, with the bulbous stem end as an enormous nose. Perfect for scaring the bejeebers out of your neighbors next Halloween.

PRICES: $3–$200. No commissions. No catalog/brochure.

VISITORS: June–Oct., Mon.–Sat., 10 A.M.–5 P.M.; Sun., 1–5 P.M. Nov–May, Sat., 10 A.M.–5 P.M.

LOCATION: North Georgia, about 75 miles northeast of Atlanta. Blue Creek Road, P.O. Box 412, Cleveland, GA 30528; 404-865-4048. From Atlanta, take I-85, then I-985 north to the Gainesville exit. Proceed on Rte. 129W north through Gainesville to Cleveland, go right on Rte. 115E, and travel 3 miles to Rte. 255. Go left on Rte. 255 for 2 miles to Blue Creek Valley. Gourdcraft Originals will be on your left.

HELEN

Tekakwitha Indian Arts & Crafts

A dying lumber mill town has to come up with *something* to revive the local economy. Helen's solution? Instant Bavaria. Alpine façades were applied, alleys were cobblestoned, an eighteen-bell glockenspiel was installed. As far as the town's boosters are concerned, the motif works well.

Let your children join the tourist throngs to discover Bavariana or ride the miniature Chattahochee Choo-Choo (in the Alps?) while you stop by Tekakwitha, a surprisingly good shop offering crafts from sixty different Indian nations. Baskets (both old and new) from over twenty nations run the gamut from miniature containers to large, elaborately woven mats. There are also pottery from ten different tribes, Southwestern jewelry and rugs, bone weapons and rattles, and rare loomed quillwork.

Even Northwestern tribes are represented by masks, bent-wood boxes, and exquisite eagles carved from horn. Striking Native American clothing is also available, including brightly woven Navajo dresses and, from the Plains Indians, luxurious white elkskin dresses.

PRICES: 50¢–$6,000 (average, $20–$200). Accepts Master-Card, Visa.

OPEN: Mon., Tues., & Thur.–Sat., 11 A.M.–5 P.M.; Sun., 1–6 P.M. Closed Christmas Day and Easter. Wheelchair accessible.

LOCATION: North Georgia, about 82 miles north of Atlanta. South Main Street, P.O. Box 338, Helen, GA 30545; 404-878-2938. From Atlanta, take I-85, then I-985 north. When the interstate ends, continue on Rte. 23 to Clarkesville (26 miles). Go left (north) on Rte. 17 to downtown Helen.

MORE: For superb mountain views, take the Richard B. Russell Scenic Highway (Rte. 348) from Helen to its junction with Rte. 129, then continue on Rte. 129 to Blairsville.

HIAWASSEE

Georgia Mountain Fair
MOUNTAIN CRAFTS

Every August little Hiawassee is transformed for twelve days into a giant mountain festival. Situated in the Blue Ridge Mountains, along the shore of Lake Chatuge, this summer festival offers visitors a chance to sample mountain crafts, dancing, and singing. It's a bit commercial, but the traditional crafts are often quite good, and over sixty-five artisans demonstrate skills from quilting to knifemaking. The fair also presents bluegrass, country, and gospel music programs interspersed with clogging, a flower show, and the Miss Georgia Mountain Fair contest.

EVENT: Early Aug., generally first Wed.–second weekend. Mon.–Thurs., 10 A.M.–9 P.M.; Fri. & Sat., 10 A.M.–10 P.M.; Sun., 10 A.M.–6 P.M. Admission is $5 for adults, children under 12 free.

LOCATION: Far northern Georgia near the North Carolina border. Georgia Mountain Fairgrounds, Rte. 76 West, Hiawassee, GA. Take I-85 to the Rte. 441 (Commerce/Athens exit). Go north on Rte. 441 about 50 miles to Clayton, then left on Rte. 76 to Hiawassee.

MORE: For information call the Towns County Lions Club, P.O. Box 444, Hiawassee, GA 30546; 404-896-4191.

INDIAN SPRINGS

Crafts of the 1800s
ANNUAL CRAFT SHOW

Creek Indians visited the local mineral springs long before white settlers entered the area. In the early 1800s, their enterprising half Creek, half Scottish chief, William McIntosh, constructed an elegant two-story hotel to accommodate white visitors. In 1825 McIntosh sealed his own doom by signing a treaty ceding all Creek lands to the whites. Three months later he was dead.

His ambitious Indian Spring Hotel, however, survived and prospered, becoming a fashionable resort and meeting site. In 1900 the hotel closed, was later briefly opened as a museum, then fell into disuse. Now restored by the local historical society, the hotel is the site for this small but authentic annual craft show. Period crafts such as weaving, basketmaking, chair caning, blacksmithing, and furniture making are both demonstrated and for sale. Well worth a visit if you're in the area.

EVENT: Memorial Day weekend. Sat., 10 A.M.–5 P.M.; Sun., 1–5 P.M. Admission is $1 for adults, 50¢ for children 6–12.

LOCATION: Central Georgia, about 55 miles southeast of Atlanta. Indian Spring Hotel, Indian Springs, GA. Take I-75 to the Rte. 16 (Jackson) exit, then Rte. 16 east to Jackson. Go right on Rte. 87, then follow signs to Indian Springs State Park. The hotel is across the highway from the park.

MORE: For more information contact the Butts County Historical Society, P.O. Box 215, Jackson, GA 30233; 404-775-6734. In addition to the mineral springs, Indian Springs State Park offers camping, hiking, and other recreational opportunities.

ST. SIMONS ISLAND

Glass Act
CONTEMPORARY CRAFTS

A popular tourist destination off Georgia's coast, St. Simons Island is a year-round vacation spot that has somehow managed to avoid wall-to-wall condos and unbroken chains of hotels. Continuously occupied, first by the Creek Indians, then by Spanish and English colonists, the island has often been the site of historic events, including the founding of the Methodist Church.

If you want a break between tennis games or rounds of golf, stop by this new gallery, the only one on the island featuring handcrafted items. Offering a little bit of everything, the shop's jewelry includes fluid, understated pieces by Patty Daunis; larger metalwork is represented by Jack Brubaker's hand-forged candle sculptures and wall sconces.

PRICES: $12–$895 (average, $25–$60). Accepts MasterCard, Visa.

OPEN: Mon.–Sat., 10 A.M.–5 P.M. Closed major holidays. Wheelchair accessible.

LOCATION: One of Georgia's barrier islands, St. Simons is just east of Brunswick. 10 Sylvan Drive, #12, St. Simons Island, GA 31522; 912-634-1228. Take I-95 to exit 8N (North

Golden Isles Parkway). Take Spur 25 to Rte. 17, then St. Simons Island Causeway. Once on the island, take a left at the first light, left again at the next light, and left on Sylvan Drive.

THOMASVILLE

Spencer Jarnagin
SNAKESKIN AND CUSTOM LEATHERWORK

Thomasville is in the heart of Georgia's plantation country where grand old mansions (many built by Northerners) sit in luxurious gardens surrounded by Spanish moss, crepe myrtle, and dogwood. "A lot of the plantations offer quail hunting from November to March," Spencer says. "Folks hunt from horseback and mule-drawn hunting buggies. I do the custom leatherwork for the plantations, building the harnesses and other leather tack and doing repairs.

"In addition to quail, we have a lot of diamondback rattlesnakes in the area. During the mid-seventies some of my friends brought poorly processed snakeskins to me and wanted them made into belts and other items. But the skins didn't last very long; the quality of the belts was poor. That forced me to seek better ways to preserve the skins, and I developed some chemicals that do that nicely. Now I make snakeskin belts, hatbands, suspenders, checkbook covers, and gun straps."

PRICES: $15–$150. Commissions accepted. No catalog/brochure at present.

VISITORS: Yes.

LOCATION: South Georgia, about 29 miles northeast of Tallahassee, Florida. Rte. 3, Box 900, Thomasville, GA 31792; 912-377-2038. From Florida's I-10, take the Rte. 19 (Thomasville) exit. Go north on Rte. 19 for 17 miles to Rte. 93, north on Rte. 93 to Beachton. Turn left at crossroads onto Meridian Road. The shop is .6 mile farther, on the left.

GEORGIA CRAFTS DIRECTORY

To locate additional Georgia craftspeople see *Georgia Crafts: Coastal Plains,* published by the Georgia Council for the Arts & Humanities' Craft Project. This 167-page book lists hundreds of craftspeople (indexed by both media and county) as well as fairs, festivals, and retail outlets. The book was published in 1981, so the information is out of date, but it's still worth the $3 price. Write to Georgia Council for the Arts, Suite 100, 2082 East Exchange Place, Tucker, GA 30084; or call 404-493-5783.

Now out of print, the council's *Georgia Crafts: Appalachia* is also informative. Get a copy through your local interlibrary loan program or stop by the council's office to peek at their copy.

KENTUCKY

Kentucky is a craft hound's bonanza. Vigorous marketing by the state government and the pivotal influence of Berea College's craft programs have made Kentucky one of the country's most well known and diversified craft marketplaces. Rag rugs, door harps, and functional pottery share the traditional craft limelight with Shaker and willow furniture, weaving, quilts, and even handmade pitchforks. For contemporary crafts, head to Louisville's galleries and its gala February Crafts Market.

To see a cross section of Kentucky crafts, begin at Lexington's Guild Gallery, then fan out south, east, and west to meet individual craftspeople. Make Berea your headquarters for a weekend to visit the college's craft industries and numerous local artisan's studios. Pencil in a stop at Pleasant Hill's restored Shaker village near Harrodsburg to see the distinctive architecture and crafts.

ANNVILLE

Dorothy Brockman
HANDWOVEN RAG RUGS AND PILLOWS

"I first learned to weave at Berea High School in 1930," Dorothy says. "Then for thirty years, I was manager of the weaving department at Annville Institute, a boarding high school where students worked to help pay their expenses. When it closed in 1978, I bought all the looms and now work with sixteen local women in our shop. We get together to share plants, vegetables, news about our friends, and talk about weaving techniques, colors, and designs."

The rag rugs Dorothy and her friends weave use a variety of materials, from wool, cotton, and corduroy strips to old neckties and nylon hose. The colorful results are made into rugs, place mats, coasters, and even bookmarks. "We've made rugs for a lot of folks," Dorothy notes, "including Efrem Zimbalist, Jr.; former governor Brown; and even a bedroom rug for the mansion in Bardstown known as 'My Old Kentucky Home.'"

PRICES: $2–$37, sometimes higher for large rugs. Commissions accepted "sometimes." Free flyer with map.

VISITORS: Yes. The weaving shop is open Mon.–Fri., 7 A.M.–3:30 P.M. Rugs are sold next door through Annville Crafts, open Mon.–Sat., 9 A.M.–4 P.M.

LOCATION: Eastern Kentucky, about 65 miles southeast of Lexington, 40 miles southeast of Berea. Rte. 1, Box 64, Annville, KY 40402; 606-364-5457. Take I-75 to the Berea exit, then Rte. 21 east to Rte. 421. Go right (south) on Rte. 421 to McKee, right on Rte. 290 to end, left on Rte. 30 to campus and Annville Crafts (less than half a mile).

BEREA

Berea College Student Crafts
TRADITIONAL AND CONTEMPORARY CRAFTS

Preserving Appalachia's craft heritage while providing higher education for disadvantaged students may seem incompatible goals, but not for Berea College. For over 130 years this unusual institution has offered a liberal arts program for needy students with good academic records. Once

168

accepted, students pay no tuition but must participate in a work program, which helps offset college administrative costs, and through which they earn between $400 and $3,000 a year.

Since 1859, Berea's labor departments have offered students jobs in fields from secretarial and building maintenance to tutoring and community work. In 1893 a craft component was added offering employment in six craft areas: broomcraft, ceramics, needlecraft, weaving, woodcraft, and wrought iron. Now over 140 students apprentice with twelve to fifteen master craftspeople creating everything from $6 beanbags to finely crafted furniture costing up to $12,000.

Studios, open to visitors, provide glimpses of the variety of crafts: sturdy brooms from natural broomcorn, wrought iron candelabra and fireplace tools, handwoven shawls called "ruanas," and the famous Berea skittles game.

Many of the woodcraft products are based on designs developed by Wallace Nutting, known for his antique furniture reproductions. During the 1930s, Nutting served as a consultant to Berea's woodcraft program, urging the students to produce more aesthetic work. Using his original blueprints as well as other designs, students now create tables and dressers, elegant secretaries, and even a "Jenny Lind" cradle. A collection of Nutting's own work can be seen at the Log House Sales Room.

PRICES: Log House Sales Room—$2–$12,000 (average, $20–$50). Accepts American Express, MasterCard, Visa. Send $2 for a 24-page color catalog to Berea College Crafts, CPO 2347, Berea, KY 40404.

OPEN: Log House Sales Room—Mon.–Sat., 8 A.M.–5 P.M.; Sun. (Apr.–Oct.), 1–5 P.M. Closed Thanksgiving, Christmas, New Year's Day. Wheelchair accessible. Studios—daily, 8 A.M.–5 P.M.; summers, 7 A.M.–4 P.M. A studio map is available from Berea College Crafts, CPO 1247, Berea, KY 40404; 606-986-9341, ext. 5220.

LOCATION: Central Kentucky, 40 miles south of Lexington. Rte. 25 (Center Street) at North Estill. The mailing address is CPO 778, Berea, KY 40404; 606-986-9341, ext. 5225. Take I-75 to exit 76 (Rte. 21). Follow Rte. 21 east to Berea College campus and sales room.

MORE: Dubbed "The Folk Arts & Crafts Capital of Kentucky" by the state legislature, Berea also has a variety of off-campus craft shops and studios. Ask for a map and directory at the Log House Sales Room or Boone Tavern Hotel. The hotel is operated by Berea students, and most of its guest room furniture is student-made. It also has a restau-

rant serving regional dishes including spoon bread, and a gift shop of student crafts.

BEREA

Brian Boggs
WOODEN CHAIRS

What kind of chair do you fancy? A rocker with arms or without, ladderback armchairs, mule-ear or fanback side chairs, footstools, sitting stools, or bar stools? If you want top-quality, traditional Appalachian wood chairs, then Brian Boggs can fill your order.

"When I started making chairs I'd never taken any classes or even watched a woodworker," Brian

Brian Boggs: Rocking chair. H. 48″. ALBERT R. MOONEY

says. "I mainly learned by reading *Make a Chair from a Tree,* published by Taunton Press. I did apprentice with David Sawyer, the Vermont Windsor chair maker, but I decided to specialize in Appalachian chairs."

Using primarily red oak logs 14 to 20 inches in diameter, Brian starts from scratch. "I rive all posts, rungs, and slats from choice logs," he explains. "I do use power tools to rough out the pieces, but all the shaping and smoothing is done by hand with a drawknife and spokeshave. I also weave the seats and backs myself from hickory bark or oak splints. And, to make the seats really comfortable and wear well, I add a pillow of wool shavings between the woven layers."

PRICES: $200–$1,500. Works on commission exclusively. No catalog/brochure.

VISITORS: Yes. Please call first.

LOCATION: Central Kentucky. 114 Elm Street, Berea, KY 40403; 606-986-9188 (home). From Berea, take Rte. 25N for half a mile to Rte. 1016. Turn right and follow Rte. 1016 for three quarters of a mile. The shop is on the left.

BEREA

Churchill Weavers
HANDWOVEN THROWS, BLANKETS

Churchill Weavers make the most ordinary item seem special. In their capable hands, typically lackluster baby blankets become softly textured cotton wraps of warm pastel plaids. Made for instant snuggling on a cold winter's night, Churchill's handwoven throws range from classic beige to mauve houndstooth, Tartan plaids to colorful blocks of peach and pink with natural cords. They also offer stoles, scarves, ponchos, and men's ties in the same softly woven designs of wool, mohair, cotton, acrylic, and even cashmere wools.

"We're carrying on a tradition begun in 1921 by founders Carroll and Eleanor Churchill," say current owners Richard and Lila Bellando. "The Churchills were missionaries to India before coming to Berea. Once here they were encouraged by local weaving talent but dismayed at the lack of employment opportunities. They decided to help by opening the town's first noncollege industry. Carroll built and perfected the looms while Eleanor designed and marketed the products. After Carroll's death, Eleanor chose us to continue their work."

A self-guided tour of the Churchill loomhouse shows visitors how raw fibers are converted to stylish woven products. Stay as long as you like watching master weavers at work, then visit the gift shop, which sells not only Churchill creations (and bargain discontinued items) but also designer jewelry, pottery, baskets, crystal, and other crafts.

PRICES: $18–$300. Commissions accepted "rarely." No catalog/brochure.

OPEN: Loomhouse—Mon.–Fri., 9 A.M.–4 P.M. (closed for lunch, noon–1 P.M.). Gift shop—Mon.–Sat., 9 A.M.–6 P.M.; Sun., noon–6 P.M.

LOCATION: Central Kentucky. Box 30, Lorraine Court, Berea, KY 40403; 606-986-3126. Take I-75 to exit 76 (Rte. 25N), then Rte. 25N through town until you pass Berea Hospital on the left. Bear right on Rte. 1016 and follow the signs.

BEREA

Charles Harvey
SHAKER WOODCRAFTS, FURNITURE

Charles's specialty is making Shaker oval boxes in seven sizes from 3¼ inches to 9¾ inches wide. "My work is very accurate," Charles says. "I don't use any veneer, plywood, or glue. Instead I use the materials and techniques preferred by the Shakers themselves. The bands are hard maple, which I steam, bend, and secure with solid copper tacks. The tops and bottoms are white pine held by sixteen wooden pegs. I finish the boxes in either oil or old-fashioned milk paint." Charles also re-creates other Shaker pieces, including an ingenious lap desk, a cherry blanket chest, rockers, and other fine furniture.

PRICES: Oval boxes, $25–$64; chairs, $275–$650; other furniture, "expensive." Commissions accepted. Send a business-size SASE for the catalog/brochure.

VISITORS: Mon.–Sat., 9 A.M.–6 P.M. Closed Christmas and New Year's.

LOCATION: Old Town Berea. Simple Gifts, 128 North Broadway, Berea, KY 40403; 606-986-1653. Take I-75 to exit 76 (Rte. 21). Go east on Rte. 21 for 1 mile, then left on Broadway. The shop is on the right.

BEREA

Rude Osolnik
TURNED WOOD VESSELS

"**I**'ve been a woodworker for over sixty years now," says Rude. "I first worked with wood when I was in high school in Illinois. I'm mostly self-taught, although I've read a lot of design books and I've been influenced by early Greek vases and pottery. I work with simple forms because that brings out the individuality of each piece of wood, highlighting its diversity of color, grain, and texture."

From 1937 to 1977, Rude taught at Berea College's woodcraft program. He is credited with improving productivity, insisting on high quality, and sharpening its design aesthetics. But throughout the years, Rude's personal focus has been on creating fine wood vessels with natural, free-form edges. The results are fundamental shapes emphasizing complex natural colors and grain. Many of Rude's pieces are part of major museum and private collections, including one item chosen by Mrs. Eleanor Roosevelt as a wedding gift to Queen Elizabeth.

PRICES: $125–$4,000. Commissions accepted. No catalog/brochure.

VISITORS: No.

MORE: Rude's work is available through the Benchmark Gallery, Jane Street, Box 503, Berea, KY 40403; 606-986-9413. The gallery's summer hours are Mon.–Sat., 8 A.M.–6 P.M.; Sun, 1–5 P.M. Winter hours are Mon.–Sat., 8 A.M.–5 P.M. Take I-75 to exit 76. Heading toward Berea, turn right at the first stoplight following the road past the Holiday Motel. The gallery will be on your right.

BRODHEAD

Phillip and Kathy Payne
WILLOW FURNITURE

Some people think the only use for willow saplings is as switches to use on misbehaving children. Phillip, however, knows that their pliable nature makes them the perfect material for shaping graceful chairs, headboards, and tables. Reminiscent of Adirondack rustic furniture, but more delicate in appearance, willow furniture is a traditional Appalachian craft.

Using saplings from ½ inch to 2 inches in diameter, Phillip bends six or more to form sweeping circular contours for chair backs and arms. Larger pieces provide sturdy legs and braces. Other saplings are used as arched table supports or to form "mosaic" table tops. All you need to complete this summer porch furniture are large, soft pillows for the chairs.

PRICES: $20–$500. Commissions accepted. No catalog/brochure.

VISITORS: Yes.

LOCATION: About 20 miles southwest of Berea, 60 miles south of Lexington. Rustic Willow Furniture Co., 2970 Negro Creek Road, Brodhead, KY 40409; 606-758-8587. Take I-75 to exit 59 (Mt. Vernon/Rte. 150). Take Rte. 150 to Mt. Vernon, then continue straight to Brodhead. About 10 miles out of Mt. Vernon look for Negro Creek Road sign on the left. Follow Negro Creek 3 miles to the sign.

BYBEE

Bybee Pottery
TRADITIONAL POTTERY

Very little has changed since 1809, when Walter Cornelison's great-great-great-grandfather, James Eli, started Bybee Pottery. Even the building is the same, a ramshackle log structure with solid walnut beams. Of course, clay dust has raised the floor several inches over the years, but that's only to be expected. And, since Walter's children are already involved with the pottery, both the tradition and the dust will continue to build.

"We use clay from the original deposit about three miles away," Walter says. "We heard it was used by the first settlers in Kentucky, taken up to old Fort Boonesborough and made into crude dishes. It's real good clay. Doesn't need to be blended with any other clay or chemicals before it's used. We mix it with water, grind it in the old pug mill, then store it in an ancient vault to keep it moist and pliable until we're ready for it. James Eli did things the same way."

The pieces produced by Bybee haven't changed much over the years either. The pottery still offers simple, functional items from a small bear-shape piggy bank to a cuspidor, a flowerpot to a relish dish. Customers can choose from over 130 items, with a choice of seven different plain glazes or fine spongewear patterns.

Famous for its longevity and adherence to tradition, Bybee Pottery is also known for its amazingly low prices. A coffee mug is $1.50, an 8-inch serving bowl is $3 ($4 if fluted), and a 3-quart covered soup tureen is $15. Prices are slightly higher for spongewear glazes. There's no charge for mailing, because Bybee won't ship. Since the local post office closed in 1978, customers have to pick up their orders personally. Though this may seem inconvenient, it's the perfect excuse to visit this quiet rural town, watch the potters pot, and browse for additional Bybee bargains.

PRICES: 50¢–$50. No commissions. Send an SASE for the price list.

OPEN: Mon.–Fri., 8 A.M.–noon, 12:30–4:30 P.M. (closed for lunch, noon–12:30 P.M.); Sat., 9 A.M.–noon. Closed all holidays.

LOCATION: Central Kentucky, about 30 miles southeast of Lexington. P.O. Box 192, Waco, KY 40385; 606-369-5350. Take I-75 to the Richmond/Rte. 52 exit. Continue east on Rte. 52 for 8 miles to the pottery.

HARRODSBURG

Shaker Village of Pleasant Hill
SHAKER CRAFTS

Nestled amidst rolling bluegrass farmland are the restored remnants of a Shaker village that once spread over 7,000 acres and included over 270 buildings. Now thirty structures form the heart of a "living museum" that includes craft exhibits, overnight lodging, and dining facilities.

The Shakers were the originators of the "form follows function" concept, and Shaker architecture, furnishings, and life itself were stripped of superfluities. Believing that work was worship and any task completed to the best of one's ability was a

prayer, the Shakers developed a reputation for fine craftsmanship. Displayed here are examples of their furniture, textiles, tools, and unusual items including a woven straw bonnet with an attached silk skirt.

Pleasant Hill offers daily demonstrations of Shaker spinning, weaving, coopering, broommaking, and quilting. Occasionally visitors can also watch oval box making, wooden rake and pitchfork making, and chair seat listing (weaving). To experience the simple Shaker life, stay here overnight. Savor the exquisite simplicity of the buildings (some of the finest in the nation), walk the almost deserted streets, then drop by the Trustee's House for a slice of Shaker lemon pie.

OPEN: Daily, 9 A.M.–5 P.M. Closed Christmas Eve and Christmas Day. The museum shop sells Shaker and other Kentucky crafts. Admission is $5.50 for adults, $2.50 for students, $1 for children. Self-guided tours. There are interpreters or craftspeople present in the buildings to answer questions. Not wheelchair accessible.

LOCATION: 25 miles southwest of Lexington. 3500 Lexington Road, Harrodsburg, KY 40330; 606-734-5411. Take I-64 to the Frankfort/Rte. 127 exit, then Rte. 127 south 30 miles to Harrodsburg. Go left (northeast) on Rte. 68 7 miles to village.

MORE: Overnight lodging is available in fifteen restored Shaker buildings. Advance reservations for accommodations and dining are essential.

LAWRENCEBURG

Connie Carlton
WOODEN PITCHFORKS, RAKES, AND WALKING STICKS

Although an increasing number of people insist on handmade furniture, clothing, and tableware, they often purchase mass-produced garden tools that fail to last a single season. While there seem to be few alternatives, notable exceptions are Connie's pleasing but practical pitchforks and rakes. The Shakers would have approved.

"It's rewarding," Connie says, "to make something useful and beautiful with simple tools like a drawknife, spokeshave, mallet, and froe. I use only Kentucky woods, the choice depending upon the tool I'm making. For example, in my three-pronged pitchfork, a Pennsylvania Dutch design, I choose

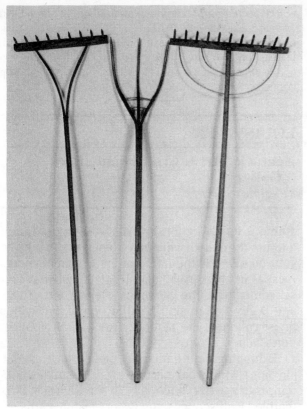

Connie Carlton: (left to right) Split-stale rake, L. 68"; W. 20"; three-pronged pitchfork, L. 68"; W. 11"; bow-rake, L. 68"; W. 25".

hardwoods such as hickory, ash, or oak. For my traditional leaf rakes, I make the heads of sassafrass, the teeth and supporting bows from hickory, and the long handles of either oak or ash."

Connie's carved walking sticks are perfect for a stroll in the woods or completing a jaunty tweed outfit. Made from hickory, ash, oak, walnut, or sassafrass, each stick contains Connie's trademark "cage." "Just below the handle," he explains, "is an openwork container I fill with either marbles or hickory nuts. It makes the sticks different, real conversation pieces."

PRICES: $15–$60. Commissions accepted "sometimes." Send an SASE for the catalog/brochure.

VISITORS: Yes.

LOCATION: Central Kentucky, about 23 miles west of Lexington. Shaving Horse Crafts, 1049 Rice Road, Lawrenceburg, KY 40342; 502-839-6478. Take I-64 to the Lawrenceburg/Graefenburg exit (Rte. 151). Follow Rte. 151 south to Rte. 62. Go right on Rte. 62 to Rice Road, left on Rice Road to the first house on the left.

MORE: Connie's work is also available through the Shakertown Gift Shop, Pleasant Hill, Harrodsburg, KY (see listing above); and the Kentucky Arts and Crafts Foundation, 609 West Main Street, Louisville, KY 40202 (see listing below).

LEXINGTON

The Guild Gallery
KENTUCKY CRAFTS

The world's chewing tobacco and snuff headquarters, Lexington is also known as Kentucky's bluegrass and thoroughbred horse center. If you're a horse fancier you'll probably want to visit the International Museum of the Horse. Better yet, drive around the nearby horse farms, especially in the spring, when flowers are in bloom and the foals are still figuring out how those wobbly legs work. When you've tired of the area's equine offerings, visit the Guild Gallery for an introduction to high-quality Kentucky crafts.

Run by the Kentucky Guild of Artists and Craftsmen, an organization devoted to preserving and developing Kentucky's craft and art traditions, this gallery offers well-crafted, reasonably priced items. Strict jurying assures top-quality work, including Bybee's famous pottery, honeysuckle egg baskets woven at Red Bird, cornshuck dolls made in Viper, and tin lamps by a Lexington craftswoman. There are also mountain dulcimers by Warren May, subtle vessels by nationally known ceramist Sarah Frederick, and multimedia weavings by Arthuro Sandoval, an art professor at the University of Kentucky.

PRICES: $1–$650 (average, $10–$35). Accepts MasterCard, Visa.

OPEN: Jan.–Nov., Mon.–Sat., 10 A.M.–5 P.M. Dec., Mon.–Sat., 10 A.M.–6 P.M.; Sun., noon–6 P.M. Closed major holidays.

LOCATION: Central Kentucky. 811 Euclid Avenue, Lexington, KY 40502; 606-266-2215. Take I-64 to the Broadway exit.

Continue to Main Street. Turn right on Main, then make an immediate left (U turn) onto Vine Street. Follow Vine about three-quarters of a mile to Rose Street, go right on Rose to the second stoplight, left on Euclid Avenue. Continue for about 1 mile. The gallery will be on the left just after Ashland Avenue.

LOUISVILLE

Craig Kaviar
CONTEMPORARY METAL TABLE BASES

Craig's iron and bronze table bases evoke a variety of images, including the curves of ancient Mycenaean metalwork and the encrusted surfaces of weathered iron. All are graceful and unexpected, with leafy branches floating over a highly texturized bronze framework or supports pulling gently on the sides of a lyre-shaped accent. Although the addition of a sheet of tempered glass or a slab of marble will turn Craig's work into an unusual coffee or dining table, some pieces could actually stand on their own as intriguing sculptures.

PRICES: $400–$8,000. Commissions accepted. No catalog/brochure.

VISITORS: Yes.

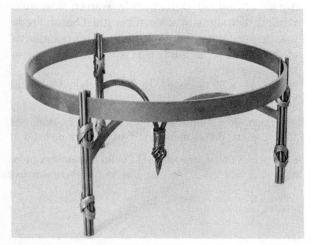

Craig Kaviar; Iron coffee table base with brass wraps. H. 17″; Diam. 30″.

LOCATION: Eastern Louisville. Kaviar Forge, 147 Stevenson Avenue, Louisville, KY 40206; 502-561-0377. Traveling west on I-64, take the Melwood exit. Go right on Melwood. Traveling east on I-64, take the Story Avenue exit. Turn left onto Spring Street, then left onto Melwood. From Melwood, turn right onto Stevenson Avenue. The forge is on the left.

LOUISVILLE

Kentucky Art & Craft Foundation Gallery
KENTUCKY CRAFTS

Famous for Churchill Downs, the Kentucky Derby, and bourbon, Louisville may be of more interest to your children as the home of the Colonel Sanders (yes, as in chicken) Museum. No matter what your schedule, avoid the gift shops offering horse mugs and Derby T-shirts and head to one of Louisville's finest galleries, the Kentucky Art & Craft Foundation Gallery.

Exhibiting both traditional pieces such as Marvin Finn's whimsical folk carvings and striking contemporary work such as David Keator's faux marbled wall sconces, the gallery features artisans who could be in a Who's Who of Kentucky crafts. Drop by to see Sarah Frederick's latest ceramics, which might include terra-cotta fruit or a tea set covered with intricate embroidery patterns. Examine contemporary quilts and traditional baskets, the dazzling glasswork of Stephen Rolfe Powell, or unusual intricately painted gourds.

PRICES: $2.50–$18,000 (average, $25–$75). Accepts MasterCard, Visa.

OPEN: Mon.–Sat., 10 A.M.–4 P.M. Closed national holidays. Wheelchair accessible.

LOCATION: Historic Main Street, near the Kentucky Center for the Arts. 609 West Main Street, Louisville, KY 40202; 502-589-0102. Take I-64/I-71 to the Downtown–3rd Street exit. Turn right on River Road for two blocks. Turn left onto 6th Street. Go one block to Main Street; the gallery will be on the right.

MORE: While in town, visit the Hadley Pottery Co., known for its charming hand-painted mugs and dinnerware originally designed by Mary Alice Hadley. 1570 Story Avenue, Louisville, KY 40206; 502-584-2171.

LOUISVILLE

Kentucky Crafts Market
TRADITIONAL /CONTEMPORARY CRAFTS

Ever since Kentucky's First Lady, Phyllis George Brown, began vigorously promoting Kentucky crafts during her tenure (1979–1983), state resources have been used to support craftspeople and market their work. This all-out effort includes a Governor's Crafts Council, a state Crafts and Visual Arts Marketing Division, a crafts business development loan program, and the annual Crafts Market. There are even offices in London, Tokyo, and New York City that promote Kentucky products, including crafts.

Some people suggest that this aggressive marketing risks turning every craftsperson into an industry and encourages work that can be easily reproduced rather than more time-consuming, one-of-a-kind items. Others say the programs permit craftspeople to earn a decent living and encourage the continuation of traditional crafts that would otherwise die out.

Even if you don't choose sides in this controversy, you'll agree that the state's annual Crafts Market offers very high-quality, sophisticated crafts. Tilted toward the wholesale industry, the first half of the show is set aside for "the trade." The second half provides "walking money" for the craftspeople and gives the general public an opportunity to purchase items before they show up in some tony mail-order catalogs. It is compared by some to a big sale at your favorite department store, so expect crowds and jostling. For the best selection, be there when the doors open to the public.

EVENT: Public show first weekend in Feb., Sat., 1–6 P.M.; Sun., noon–6 P.M. Dates vary, so confirm in advance. Admission is $2 for adults, seniors over 60 and children under 12 free. Parking is $2 per car.

LOCATION: West Hall, Kentucky Fair and Exposition Center, Louisville. Take I-65, I-71, or I-64 to I-264, I-264 to Fairgrounds exit.

MORE: For information contact Fran Redmon, Kentucky Department of the Arts, Berry Hill Mansion, Louisville Road, Frankfort, KY 40601; 502-564-8076.

MT. STERLING

Douglas and Jeannie Naselroad
APPALACHIAN DOOR HARPS,
FOLK AND BLUEGRASS INSTRUMENTS

Want to hear the soft, sweet sound of a mountain dulcimer every time you enter the kitchen? Like to greet guests at the front door with lyre's lilting song? No time for lessons? Tone deaf? Don't worry,

Douglas and Jeannie Naselroad: (left) Mountain Dulcimer door harp, H. 15″; W. 4½″; (right) Davita's door harp, H. 12″; W. 9″.

one of Doug's Appalachian door harps will fill in for you. Made from quarter-sawn Appalachian cherry, each door harp has three to four hardwood balls that strike against tempered steel strings every time the door moves.

Offered in ten different styles, Doug's door harps include his unique Mountain Dulcimer model as well as Davita's Harp, named after the Chaim Potok novel. "I loved musical instruments as a child," Doug says, "but my family could never afford them. We did, however, have tools! Although I'm primarily self-taught, I've been influenced by the famous dulcimer maker Homer Ledford and I'm always folding in Kentucky influences, from bluegrass music to hummingbirds."

Doug and Jeannie also make acoustic guitars and mandolins with custom finishes and pearl inlays. Guitars are made using sitka spruce tops and ebony fingerboards with bodies available in a variety of woods such as black walnut, koa, and rosewood. Mandolins are made to order, each one hand-voiced to meet the needs of the individual musician. Made from choice curly maple, each mandolin has a carbon-graphite bar embedded in the neck to eliminate warpage and enhance sustaining qualities.

PRICES: $22–$5,000. Commissions accepted. Free catalog/brochure.

VISITORS: "Yes, we always enjoy talking to people!"

LOCATION: About 30 miles east of Louisville. 2736 Howell-Drennen Road, Mt. Sterling, KY 40353; 606-498-3724. Take I-64 to exit 110 (Mt. Sterling). Head toward town. Turn right at the first traffic light onto the bypass (Indian Mound Drive). Turn right again at a flashing yellow light onto Grassy Lick Road. Go 3 miles until you see the Fellowship Christian Church on the right. Just past it, but before the I-64 overpass, is Howell-Drennan Road. Turn left. The driveway is the first one on the left, next to a small white house. The shop is a quarter of a mile behind the house.

MORE: Naselroad door harps also are available through the Promenade Gallery, 204 Center Street, Berea, KY 40403; 606-986-1609.

PADUCAH

American Quilter's Society Quilt Show & Contest

If you make a beeline for every major quilting show in the country, here's another to piece into your itinerary. Boasting that it offers more cash awards than any other quilt event, this four-day show includes work by over 400 quilters from throughout the country. When you've seen so many quilts that you feel the only way to see more is to appliqué your eyes open, it's time to attend one of the myriad lectures, workshops, and seminars where you can learn everything from how to photograph quilts to what it takes to become a quilt judge.

EVENT: Third weekend in Apr., Thurs., 10 A.M.–5 P.M.; Fri., 9 A.M.–5 P.M.; Sat., 9 A.M.–8 P.M.; Sun., 10 A.M.–5 P.M. Admission is $4 for adults, children under 12 free.

LOCATION: Executive Inn Riverfront Convention Center, 1 Executive Boulevard, Paducah. The I-24 "Downtown Loop" runs into the hotel.

MORE: For information contact the American Quilter's Society, P.O. Box 3290, Paducah, KY 42001; 502-898-7903.

PARK CITY

Ollie and Lestel Childress
TRADITIONAL WHITE OAK BASKETS

"We were just borned into it," says Ollie. "I can't even remember when I wasn't making baskets." "I remember," Lestel chimes in. "I made my first one when I was eight years old." The fifth generation of the Childress family to make white oak baskets, Ollie and Lestel are now passing on the tradition to their children and grandchildren.

"We've worked on this together all our lives," Lestel says. "I'm proud of my work, really proud of it. When I'm dyeing my splits I just love to mix the colors to see how they'll come out. It's like being an artist."

Although they continue to make the traditional styles they learned from their parents, they also make their own designs. "We offer over fifty styles to our customers," Lestel adds. "But all of them are very characteristic south-central Kentucky baskets.

Ollie and Lestel Childress: White oak peck basket.

You can see it in their shape, the way we lay the ribs and tie the eye."

Every basket starts in the woods with a young white oak tree that is straight and without knots. "We split it until it can be worked with a regular pocketknife," Lestel says. "Then we use the heartwood for handles and ribs, the sapwood for splits."

PRICES: $20–$300. Commissions accepted. No catalog/brochure.

VISITORS: Yes.

LOCATION: South-central Kentucky, near Mammoth Cave. 22390 Louisville Road, Park City, KY 42160; 502-749-5041. Take I-65 to exit 48 (Brownsville/Park City). Turn right and go a quarter of a mile to Rte. 31W. Turn right on Rte. 31W (also called Louisville Road). The house is 1 mile on the right, tenth house from the entrance to Mammoth Cave National Park.

MORE: Inhabited by humans over 4,000 years ago, Mammoth Cave is the longest cave system in the world, with 300 miles of mapped passageways. If you're in an eccentric mood, sign up for the tour, which includes a meal 267 feet underground.

LOUISIANA

Like a menu that offers so many appealing entrées it is impossible to choose just one, Louisiana brims with exotic cultures too numerous to sample in a single visit. The southern part of the state is like a complex jambalaya, with distinct morsels from eleven traditions bound together in a complex cross-cultural broth: Cajun, Spanish, Afro-French, Anglo, Native American, German, Italian, Irish, Slavonian, Isleño, and, more recently, Asian. In contrast, northern Louisiana offers a minimalist menu with three fairly distinct cultural traditions: Native American, English-Scotch, and Afro-American.

Louisiana's craftspeople reflect these wonderfully diverse cultural traditions, creating a range and variety of work both unique and captivating. The entries below will take you from heady New Orleans past leisurely bayous and down back country roads.

For an even more diverse introduction to Louisiana's crafts, order *Fait à la Main* (Made by Hand), an illustrated source book listing over 200 artisans who create everything from Mardi Gras masks to 68-foot shrimp trawlers. Published by the Louisiana Crafts Program, *Fait à la Main* includes excellent introductory materials, essays on major Louisiana craft traditions, seven glossaries, and lists of artisans, festivals, and craft shops. Folk artisans are listed by specific traditions such as "ritual and festive crafts" or "folk instruments," and contemporary and revivalist craftspeople are ordered by media. Although it's not a mail-order catalog, addresses, prices, and other purchasing information are provided. For a copy, send $5 to Louisiana Crafts Program, Division of the Arts, P.O. Box 44247, Baton Rouge, LA 70804; 504-342-8180. By appointment, the Program permits collectors to review slides, see samples of work, and access other information concerning directory artisans.

BATON ROUGE

Pentagon Barracks Museum Shop
Shop at the Top
TRADITIONAL LOUISIANA CRAFTS

Baton Rouge ("red staff") gained its name during the seventeenth century from a cypress tree draped with fresh animal carcasses that divided two Indian hunting grounds. Now a major port and the state's capital, Baton Rouge combines major industrial activities with an Old South gloss of stately mansions and fragrant magnolias.

Two shops that sell heritage crafts are a relatively new addition to the state capitol complex. Offering relatively inexpensive, souvenir-type pieces, the Pentagon Barracks Museum Shop is located in a renovated 1819 army barracks on the grounds of the Louisiana state capitol. Of more interest to collectors is the shop on the twenty-seventh floor of the Capitol Building (the tallest in the United States). Featuring high-quality traditional crafts, the Shop at the Top is a pastiche of cultural expression. Look for Azzie Roland's Afro-American coiled sedge grass baskets or her hand-split oak baskets that incorporate blackened strips discolored in a stain brewed from rusty nails. Visitors will also find double-weave, split river cane Chitimacha Indian baskets; bas-relief Southern scenes carved on aged cypress; traditional brown-and-white Acadian woven textiles; and Coushatta pine straw effigy baskets.

PRICES: $2–$200 (average, $6–$40). Accepts MasterCard, Visa.

OPEN: Barracks Shop—Tues.–Sat., 10 A.M.–4 P.M.; Sun., 1–4 P.M. Shop at the Top—daily, 10 A.M.–4 P.M. Both shops closed Easter, Thanksgiving, Christmas, and New Year's Day. Both shops wheelchair accessible.

LOCATION: Both shops are located at the Louisiana State Capitol Complex, along the Mississippi River. The Barracks Museum is on North Riverside; Shop at the Top is on the 27th floor of the Capitol. The mailing address for both is 900 North Boulevard, Baton Rouge, LA 70802; 504-342-1866 (Barracks), 504-342-5914 (Shop at the Top). Take I-110 to the Louisiana State Capitol/Governor's Mansion exit.

BATON ROUGE

Shiva Ki
HAND-FORGED KNIVES, SWORDS

Adding to Louisiana's cultural kaleidoscope are Shiva Ki's samurai-tradition blades. "Thirty years of devotion to mastering and teaching martial arts got me interested in Japanese bladesmithing," Shiva says. "This is a six-hundred-year tradition, which has produced the best blades in history. Only after many years of work can I understand how samurai swords cut through marine rifle barrels in the South Pacific. Well-worked steel becomes purely magical. There is definitely a living spirit that protects the owner of these blades."

A master bladesmith, Shiva creates 285-layer, fighting folder knives as well as bowie-style knives, gator hunters, guthook skinners, Ninja darts, and other traditional blades. Most of his finest work, done in Damascus steel, is hand-forged multilayer blades of incredible strength and durability with wavy-lined surfaces.

"The number of layers and the pattern in my Damascus knives make a difference in their cost," Shiva says. "I am partial to high numbers of layers.

Shiva Ki: Tanto-Samurai short blade. 1,550-layer Damascus steel (laminated) blade. L. 8½".

I just love to sit and study fine layers in a blade. Fewer layers, however, are much more visible and the average person won't appreciate the fineness of 1,250 layers. I also do a lot of composites, blending up to seven different patterns in one blade. That makes them exciting, unpredictable, beautiful, and expensive."

The handles of Shiva's knives are fashioned as carefully as the blades, some elaborately carved or etched, others finished with silver or gold fittings. "I search all over the world for the most exotic materials," Shiva says. "I use the rarest of fossil ivories, pipe-quality burls and briars, even rare African horn."

PRICES: $150–$3,500. Commissions accepted. The catalog/brochure costs $3.

VISITORS: Yes.

LOCATION: 5222 Ritterman, Baton Rouge, LA 70805; 504-356-7274. Take I-10 to the College Drive exit. Go north on College Drive, which curves to the left and becomes Foster. Continue on Foster across Choctaw. Turn right on Ritterman (a church is on the corner). The house is on the right.

CHATHAM

Clara Combs
QUILTS

Continuing the African-American tradition of fine quiltmaking, Clara creates colorful, meticulously crafted quilts. Particularly appealing are patterns called Grandmother's Basket of Flowers and Grandmother's Flower Garden. Vibrating with color, these pieced quilts incorporate hundreds of five-sided snippets of cloth.

A self-taught quilter, Clara creates other patterns, from the simpler Nine Patch design and the popular Log Cabin to the more complex Missouri Dahlia. "I sell my quilts two ways," Clara says. "People can buy just the finished top and complete it by adding filling and a back, or they can buy a finished quilt. Some folks like to save money by just purchasing the tops."

PRICES: Quilt tops, $40–$400; finished quilts, $125–$500. Commissions accepted. No catalog/brochure

VISITORS: By appointment only.

LOCATION: Northern Louisiana, about 35 miles southwest of Monroe. P.O. Box 201, Chatham, LA 71226; 318-249-2212. Directions will be provided when appointment to visit is made.

DOYLINE

Dick Carney
NATIVE AMERICAN FINGER-WEAVING

Sashes, garters, straps, and bags with colorful diagonal slashes, chevrons, and lightning zigzags (see color plate #8) are the essence of traditional Native American finger-weaving. Originally these items were woven from strands of native hemp, milkweed, or nettle fiber; the inner bark of basswood or mulberry trees; and buffalo or opossum hair yarn. Soon after contact with Europeans, however, the Native Americans adopted wool as the material of choice, with weavers often unraveling trade blankets to obtain yarn.

Like these early weavers, Dick Carney, a Pamankey Powhatan (Algonquin) Indian, creates his work without a loom. As the yarns hang freely from a pole or branch he lifts up alternate yarns, passing an outside edge strand through to the other side. While the yarns hang, they are warps; while passing through they are wefts.

"I use naturally dyed wool yarn," Dick says, "and tightly weave both traditional designs and some I have created myself. Like many of the early sashes, I sometimes decorate them with beads which are directly interwoven into the work and also dot the free-hanging fringe. In other interpretations, I may use silk instead of wool, or braid the fringe with porcupine quills."

PRICES: $50–$4,000. Commissions accepted. There is no catalog/brochure, but write for information on available pieces.

VISITORS: Yes. By appointment only.

LOCATION: Northwestern Louisiana, about 25 miles east of Shreveport. Rte. #1, Box 372, Doyline, LA 71023; 318-987-3724. Directions will be provided when appointment to visit is made.

MORE: For a more detailed explanation of finger-weaving, see *Threads* magazine, no. 12, Aug./Sept. 1987, pp. 46–49.

GALLIANO

Johnny J. Cheramie
CAJUN COUNTRY BOAT MODELS

Travel south from New Orleans across the Intracoastal Waterway, a 300-mile liquid interstate that parallels Louisiana's coastline from Mississippi to Texas. Continue down Lafourche Bayou to the small town of Galliano. Now you're in marshy, picturesque Cajun country.

If Galliano is a typical bayou town, then Johnny Cheramie is the epitome of its water-based traditions. "I come from a fishing family," he says, "and I still run a boat myself. I work seven days on, seven days off. When I'm not out on the water, I create scale models of all the traditional Cajun fishing boats from early sailing schooners to modern work boats. I make these models so people will understand the Cajuns' place in history, what our forefathers went through to carve out a living in this vast and beautiful place."

Johnny's workshop proudly displays over fifty

Johnny J. Cheramie: Model of Cajun lugger, c. 1920–1980. L. 36″.

models, each authentic to the smallest detail and backed with his own verbal history of its construction and purpose. "The sailing schooner I make," he says, "was used from 1898 to 1925 to haul seafood and farm produce to New Orleans. Later it was converted to traditional shrimp boats and oyster draggers. None of these boats are built anymore." A more modern boat is reflected by Johnny's model of a southern Louisiana shallow-draft shrimp boat. "This was first built about 1940," Johnny notes, "and I include all its details from an American flag to floats and shrimp nets."

PRICES: $50–$1,000. Commissions accepted. Send an SASE for the catalog/brochure.

VISITORS: Yes. "Please call first to make sure I'm home."

LOCATION: Far southeastern Louisiana, about 70 miles south of New Orleans. P.O. Box 62, Galliano, LA 70354; 504-632-2313. From New Orleans, follow Rte. 90 southwest about 43 miles to Rte. 308. Go south on Rte. 308 to Galliano. Specific directions to Johnny's home will be provided when appointment to visit is made.

MORE: "Acadians" are the direct descendants of the French Canadians who migrated to Louisiana. "Cajuns" are Acadians who intermarried with the local French population.

HAHNVILLE

Lorraine Gendron
MUD SCULPTURES

There's more to mud than children's pies, splashed nylons, and tracks across the kitchen floor. Lorraine shows it can even turn a profit. "I create a variety of dolls and sculpture from ordinary Mississippi River mud," Lorraine explains. "I dig it up from the riverbank a few blocks from my house, haul it home in tubs, and clean out the grass, rocks, and debris. Then I sculpt it into dolls, Cajun scenes, alligators, frogs, crawfish, anything with a Louisiana flavor to it."

After letting the figures dry for a week, Lorraine fires them in a kiln. Emerging a reddish color, the dolls are then decorated with acrylic paints and dressed in appropriate costumes. Some of her most popular groupings include a six-member Preservation Hall Jazz Band complete with instruments, a group of break dancers, five black girls at a roller-skating party, and a realistically tubby Paul Prudhomme.

Lorraine Gendron: *Cajun Chef,* mud sculpture.

PRICES: $3–$1,000. Commissions accepted. Send an SASE for the catalog/brochure.

VISITORS: Yes.

LOCATION: About 20 miles west of New Orleans. P.O. Box 282, Hahnville, LA 70057; 504-783-2173. From Rte. 18, turn onto Elm Street (between Time Saver store and Daddy's Fried Chicken). The house is the fourth on the left.

JENA

Curtis E. Running Bear Lees
CHEROKEE WEAPONS

It wasn't until after World War II that Curtis became interested in creating traditional Cherokee weaponry. "After returning from the war," Curtis recalls, "I realized that my mother's family had almost died out. I knew then that it was up to me to keep the various traditions alive. My mother and her brother taught me the skills, ones I had seen demonstrated as I was growing up but had never really learned myself. Now I specialize in the weapons that my family used in their everyday living. And, like them, I make all the tools I use."

For over forty years Curtis has fashioned bows and arrows, blowguns, paddle spears, gun darts, and throw spears. "I make my bows from the yellow locust tree," Curtis says, "the one always used by Cherokees. The arrows are made from native switch cane and I feather them with wild turkey wing feathers. I am honored to say that my bows and arrows are in various museums, includ-

Curtis E. Running Bear Lees: Cherokee bows, arrows, blow guns, war bonnet, wristband, dance rattle, flute, prayer feather, and other ceremonial items. CHARLES BOYD

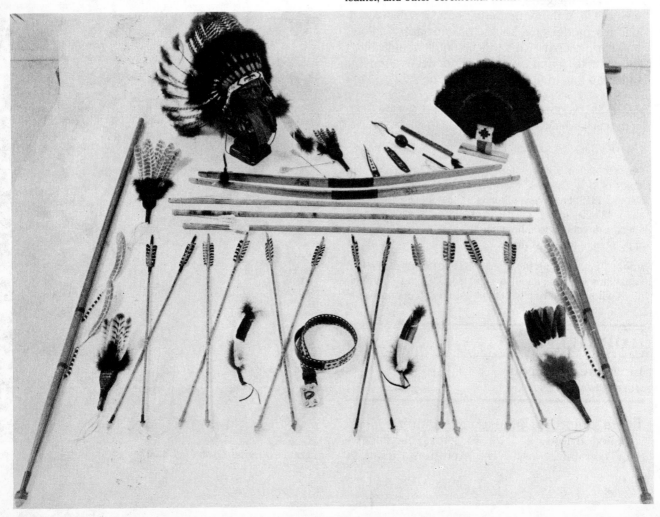

ing the Smithsonian." Curtis also makes ceremonial rattles and turkey feather fan headdresses, flutes, and beaded armbands.

PRICES: $3–$500. Commissions accepted. No catalog/brochure.

VISITORS: Yes. Please call first.

LOCATION: Central Louisiana, about 38 miles northeast of Alexandria. P.O. Box 163, Jena, LA 71342; 318-992-4570. Directions will be provided when appointment to visit is made.

MARKSVILLE

Anna Juneau
PINE NEEDLE BASKETS

If you're in the Alexandria area you may want to see Anna's well-crafted baskets. A member of the Tunica-Biloxi Indian Nation, Anna learned pine needle basketry from her parents. "I grew up on the reservation," she says, "and this was a good way to earn extra income and do something I enjoy. I use long-leaf pine needles found in northern Louisiana and raffia ribbon." In contrast to some makers, Anna uses both natural and dyed raffia, alternating them in pleasing designs.

PRICES: $10–$100+. Commissions accepted. No catalog/brochure.

VISITORS: Yes. 9 A.M.–4 P.M.

LOCATION: Central Louisiana, about 33 miles southeast of Alexandria. 111 Volsin Drive, Marksville, LA 71351; 318-253-9767. From Alexandria, take Rte. 1 south to Marksville. Anna's home is off Rte. 1, south of Marksville on the Tunica-Biloxi Indian Reservation (behind the Charter Food Store).

MERAUX

John Roger
DIATONIC CAJUN ACCORDIONS

When Germans emigrated to Louisiana in the mid-nineteenth century, they brought their diatonic accordions with them. Called "diatonic" because they only have full notes, not sharps and flats, these instruments soon displaced violins as the Cajun instrument of choice. Less damaged than violins by Louisiana's humid climate, the accor-

John Roger: Cajun accordion.

dions were also popular for their great volume and strong bass/chord accompaniment.

Until World War I, Louisiana's musicians imported their accordions directly from Germany. During the war, however, the supply was cut off and the instrument's popularity declined. When interest revived during the 1940s, Cajuns found that the German product had changed considerably in the interval. Preferring the traditional accordions, more suited to their music, Cajuns began fashioning their own. Now a handful of instrument makers continue this tradition.

John Roger creates diatonic accordions that look as pretty as they sound. Using bird's-eye and curly maple, walnut, and mahogany, John creates an elaborate case, often inlaid with exotic woods or abalone. Hand-engraved scrolls and chrome-plated copper buttons are also parts of John's unique instruments, which are popular with folk musicians in Quebec, Canada, as well as in Louisiana.

PRICES: $800–$1,500. Commissions accepted. No catalog/brochure.

VISITORS: Yes.

LOCATION: A few miles east of New Orleans. 2517 Lawrence Drive, Meraux, LA 70075; 504-279-7554. Take I-10 to Rte. 39 (Judge Perez Drive). Go east on Rte. 39 to the Cypress Gardens subdivision. The house is half a block from Rte. 39.

MONROE

Harry J. Willsher
BIRD AND FISH CARVINGS

"Three things got me interested in carving," Harry says, "hunting, bird-watching, and working with the curator at the University of Michigan's Exhibit Museum. First, I started whittling birds on my own, then later I took classes and talked with some of the best American carvers." Retired as Director of Technical Illustrations at the University of Michigan, Harry brings a technician's precision to each carving. In fact, his wood ducks and great blue herons are so lifelike you can almost see their bodies move and preen.

"I do try to imitate nature," Harry says. "Before I start to carve a bird, I research it thoroughly. I want to portray each one in a natural way, a setting and attitude unique to each species. That way I not only know the shape and coloring of the bird but also details such as the correct placement of different feather groups. I bring my carvings to life by defining each individual feather and applying many washes of paint."

PRICES: $15–$1,200. Commissions accepted. No catalog/brochure.

VISITORS: Yes.

LOCATION: Northeastern Louisiana. 22 Martha Drive, Monroe, LA 71203; 318-323-4279. Please call for directions.

MORA

Clifton-Choctaw Indian Crafts

If you're passing through Alexandria, you may want to visit the cottage industries on the Clifton-Choctaw reservation. Encouraged by their leaders to supplement their income and continue tribal craft traditions, several reservation artisans offer good-quality work.

Kathleen Thomas creates coiled long-leaf pine baskets most notable for their varying shapes, from simple round baskets to wide-lipped vases. "This craft has been in my family for a very long time," Kathleen says. "I learned it from an elderly aunt who was taught by her father. To continue the tradition, I'm now teaching my daughter the skills." Kathleen's mother, Ruth Tyler, is also a craftswoman. "She makes wonderful quilts," Kathleen says. "Her specialty is the 'pieces and patches' pattern, which she does with a very fine fan stitch."

PRICES: Baskets, $3–75; quilts, "Depends on size and detail work." Commissions accepted. No catalog/brochure.

VISITORS: Yes. Please call first.

LOCATION: Clifton-Choctaw Indian Reservation, central Louisiana, about 40 miles northwest of Alexandria. Kathleen Thomas and Ruth Tyler, HC-84, Bx 72, Mora, LA 71455; 318-793-8607. Directions will be provided when appointment to visit is made.

NATCHITOCHES

Natchitoches-Northwestern Folk Festival

This festival will test your financial and dietary willpower. Be prepared for defeat. You'll want to take home one of every craft displayed and sample each delectable Louisiana culinary treat. Established in 1979 to help identify, document, and present Louisiana's culture, the festival is a superb conglomeration of crafts, food, music, and dance. In addition, each year the festival has a specific focus, such as "Southwest Louisiana Cajun" with demonstrations of Spanish moss blanket weaving, or "Wildlife and Fisheries" with taxidermy and gunsmithing displays.

Visitors will find Acadian, Native American, Cajun, and a sprinkling of other cultures represented by the more than fifty exhibiting artisans. Look for Catahoula Lake fishnets and gar scale jewelry, Kosati Indian blowguns and carved decoys, flint-knapping, and fiddlemaking. Before your wallet is empty, wander over to the food stands to sample crawfish bisque, Cajun goulash, red beans and rice, pecan pie, and pralines. Too sleepy to drive after such a feast? Take a seat for a concert of bluegrass and gospel, jazz and country music presented by groups with names such as Collard Greens and Loggy Bayou Misfits.

EVENT: Third weekend in July. Fri. (music only), Sat., & Sun., 9:30 A.M.–5:30 P.M. Admission for adults is $5 (daytime), $4 (evenings); $3 for children 3–12.

LOCATION: Between Shreveport and Alexandria. Prather Coliseum, Northwestern State University campus, Natchitoches. From Rte. 1 south, take bypass at Natchitoches city limits and follow to Rte. 6/College Avenue. Turn right onto College Avenue (from Rte. 1 north, continue past Sibley Lake on the right, then turn left onto Rte. 6/College Avenue). Continue on College Avenue to South Jefferson. Turn right onto the Northwestern State University campus. Follow Chaplain's Lake on the left to Prather Coliseum.

MORE: For information contact the Louisiana Folklife Center, Box 3663, NSU, Natchitoches, LA 71497; 318-357-4332.

NEW ORLEANS

The Crabnet
LOUISIANA WOOD CARVINGS

Start off your New Orleans visit right by heading straight for the French Quarter, the heart of this exotic city. As you stroll past iron-bedecked buildings and pop into the numerous stores and antique galleries, take a moment to visit the Crabnet. Here you'll find waterfowl, songbirds, and other carvings created by award-winning Louisiana artisans. Other items range from quaint to beyond bizarre: cypress root sculptures and scale replicas of native Louisiana boats, decorative floral pieces made from gar scales, and preserved crawfish dressed to depict lawyers, fishermen, and other professions.

PRICES: $8–$5,000. Accepts MasterCard, Visa.

OPEN: Daily, 10 A.M.–6 P.M. Closed Mardi Gras, Easter, Thanksgiving, and Christmas. Wheelchair accessible.

LOCATION: 929 Decatur Street, New Orleans, LA 70116; 504-522-3478. The gallery is located in the French Quarter, three blocks from Jackson Square.

NEW ORLEANS

Lois Simbach
"JU-JU" VOODOO DOLLS

Want to whammy your mother-in-law? Be sure you get that promotion? Influence the next election? Perhaps Lois's dolls can help. Based on African fetishes and Caribbean voodoo dolls, the odd little people that Lois creates just may make a difference. "The positive 'gris-gris' spiritual power sewn into these Ju-Ju dolls really works," says Lois.

A well-known New Orleans fashion and costume designer who once created stylish dresses from Spanish moss, Lois began making Ju-Ju dolls in 1983. "I wanted to make something very 'New Orleans,'" Lois explains. "I looked over this wonderful swamp-Afro–Mardi Gras city and saw that no

Lois Simbach: *Ju-Ju of the Vieux Carre.* Mixed media. RICK
OLIVIER

one was making contemporary crafts that were
obviously a part of New Orleans. The touristy
voodoo dolls for sale were likely to be stamped
'Made in Taiwan,' so I decided to create a more
authentic version. I plunged into the history of it
all, studying Caribbean folklore, African fetishism,
Louisiana metaphysical writings."

Used to gain power over someone, voodoo
dolls are generally made from the subject's hair
and clothing. Lois's dolls, however, are more symbolic. Using scraps of cloth, as well as buttons,
beads, and various trinkets, she creates strange
little dolls whose elongated dark heads sprout
wisps of human hair or feathers. Although some of
the dolls are 12 inches tall, most are about 9½
inches high. Covered with charms from plastic
crosses to purple elephants, some Ju-Jus have glit-
tery eyes, others red plastic hearts or keychain
necklaces.

PRICES: $33–$750. Commissions accepted. No catalog/bro-
chure.

VISITORS: Yes. For commissions. The best selection of
Lois's work, however, is at the galleries listed below.

LOCATION: French Quarter. 225 North Peters Street, fifth
floor, New Orleans, LA 70130; 504-566-1067. Call for directions.

MORE: Lois's work is also available through the Rhino Contemporary Craft Co. at both its locations: Canal Place, 333
Canal, second floor, New Orleans, LA 70130; 504-525-1955.
Place St. Charles, 201 St. Charles Avenue, New Orleans, LA
70130; 504-582-1173.

NEW ORLEANS

Wildfowl Carvers and Collectors Festival

"The art of the decoy has come a long, long way,"
says festival chairman Charles W. Frank, "from the
reed lures of the Thule Indians to the acceptance of
wildfowl art in prestigious museums. We've
watched a working artifact become a popular and
collectible art form. In fact, you can say that Louisiana is the home of two truly native art forms, jazz
and duck decoys."

Every September jazz takes a backseat as carvers from throughout the country descend on New
Orleans to compete for prizes in life-size and miniature divisions, decoy painting, feather carving,
and head whittling. Visitors will find shorebirds,
upland game birds, birds of prey, seabirds, and
songbirds set wing to wing. In addition, marsh
ducks, diving ducks, geese, and confidence decoys
all compete for awards and attention. Many of the
works are for sale, so bring your wallet.

EVENT: Last weekend in Sept. Sat., 8 A.M.–6 P.M.; Sun., 9
A.M.–5 P.M. Admission is $3 for adults, $1 for children.

LOCATION: Health and Physical Education Building, University of New Orleans, corner of Elysian Fields Avenue and
Leon C. Simon Boulevard. Take I-10 east from downtown
New Orleans to the Elysian Fields exit. Go left to the intersection with Leon C. Simon Boulevard.

MORE: For information contact the Louisiana Wildfowl
Carvers and Collectors Guild, c/o 615 Baronne Street, New
Orleans, LA 70113; 504-588-9143.

NEW ORLEANS

Dirk Wormhoudt
REPRODUCTION EIGHTEENTH-CENTURY CREOLE FURNITURE

"Creole-style furniture isn't very well known," Dirk explains. "This is probably because the lower Mississippi Valley region wasn't part of the original thirteen colonies and was considered 'foreign territory' until at least 1803. Since the area was also less populous than the rest of the country, fewer pieces were produced, most never left the area, and only a small number still exist.

"Although Creole furniture is really part of French Provincial style, it has some Spanish elements too. And there's much more emphasis on the various woods, since they were available in greater profusion here than in France." Using walnut, cherry, mahogany, and exotic tropical woods, Dirk transforms them into authentic reproduction armoires, "melon" headboards, sideboards, and cabriole-leg tables. He also makes unusual "boutac" and "campeche" chairs unique to Creole furniture.

PRICES: $600–$7,500. Commissions accepted.

VISITORS: Yes.

LOCATION: Magazine Street area, about 39 blocks west of French Quarter. 901 Austerlitz Street, New Orleans, LA 70115; 504-895-0201. The gallery is located on the corner of Magazine Street and Austerlitz. (NOTE: The Magazine Street area of New Orleans is a 6-mile-long strip of antique shops, art galleries, restaurants, and specialty shops. A free shopper's guide with map is available from the Magazine Street Merchants Association, P.O. Box 15028, New Orleans, LA 70175.)

MORE: A documentary on early furniture of the Deep South is available on VHS videocassette. The tape features leading authorities, who discuss the styles and show major collections. For a copy, send $24.95 to Dirk Wormhoudt.

ST. BERNARD

Irvan J. Perez
DECORATIVE AND HUNTING DECOYS

Necessity gave birth to Irvan's fine decoys. Experience and a fine artistic eye now make them master-pieces. "At the age of ten I started carving hunting decoys," Irvan says. "They were sold to earn extra money for the family. My father was a market hunter, trapper, and hunting guide, and every penny we earned was needed to make ends meet. We also made duck callers, which we demonstrated and sold to New Orleans department stores.

"I had other jobs as a child too," Irvan recalls. "At that time it was still legal to use live decoys, so I took care of them for my father. Every day I handled, fed, and trained them. I got to know every detail about their form, coloring, habits, and personality. That probably has made a difference in my carving.

"When I grew up," Irvan continues, "I became a trapper, trawler, and fisherman in my hometown on Delacroix Island. Now that I'm retired I have more time to carve. It takes over forty hours to make a decoy, (see color plate #9) and that doesn't include preparation of the materials. I use the root of the cypress tree. This can't be bought, so I harvest it myself, then place it at a certain angle so all the water and sap drains out one end. In nine to ten months the root becomes light as a feather and is ready to use."

In addition to carving, Irvan is an accomplished Isleño storyteller and *decima* singer. "Isleños," Irvan explains, "came to Louisiana from the Canary Islands, and *decimas* are part of our oral history. They're songs composed by the singers themselves and sung at gatherings such as weddings and dances. They usually poke fun at mistakes made by someone in the community. Some of the *decimas* and stories are over two hundred years old and date back to the Canary Islands."

PRICES: $25–$500, "but most are about $200." No commissions. No catalog/brochure.

VISITORS: Yes.

LOCATION: Southeast of New Orleans. 609 Bayou Road, St. Bernard, LA 70085; 504-682-3181. "Please call from New Orleans for directions."

ST. MARTINVILLE

Acadian Craft Shop
TRADITIONAL LOUISIANA CRAFTS

During the eighteenth century the British drove the French out of Nova Scotia, and the refugees, known as Acadians, settled in Louisiana's bayou country. Their distinctive culture and crafts permeate the St. Martinville area and can be sampled at the Longfellow-Evangeline State Commemorative Area. Amidst trees dripping with Spanish moss, visitors can tour the Acadian House Museum, located in a typical nineteenth-century plantation home.

Crafts are sold in a reproduction early Acadian cottage featuring the traditional staircase that leads directly from the small front porch to the *garconniere*, an attic area where young boys slept. Inside are a variety of Acadian crafts, including miniature Acadian houses and pirogues (dugout canoes) by Hampton Boudreaux and Gladys Clark's Acadian weaving. Representing other area cultures are Coushatta Indian baskets by Mr. and Mrs. John, and white oak baskets by Geraldine Robertson.

PRICES: $1–$100. No credit cards.

OPEN: Wed.–Sun., 9 A.M.–5 P.M. Closed major holidays. Not wheelchair accessible.

LOCATION: Southern Louisiana, about 18 miles south of Lafayette, 72 miles southwest of Baton Rouge. Longfellow-Evangeline State Commemorative Area, 1200 North Main Street, Martinville, LA 70582; 318-394-3754. Take I-10 to the Lafayette/Rte. 90 exit. Take Rte. 90 south 11 miles to Rte. 96. Go east on Rte. 96 to St. Martinville, then north on Rte. 31 to the Commemorative Area. (NOTE: The area is named after Longfellow's famous poem *Evangeline*, which told the (true) story of two Acadian lovers separated during their flight from Canada. Reunited beneath a famous oak (still standing), Evangeline found her lover had already married another. Driven to insanity by the news, she soon died and is supposedly buried in the local Catholic church cemetery.)

MISSISSIPPI

The whiff of magnolias, the grandeur of antebellum homes, and the twists of the mighty Mississippi River all attract travelers' attention. Less well known are some of the indigenous craft traditions: Choctaw Indian basketry; art and folk pottery; and African-American work, including white oak baskets, cypress shingles, and quilts. Other craft treats include excellent shops along the Natchez Trace north of Jackson, stitchery pictures by a Belzoni artisan, and one of the country's largest exhibits of Native American baskets.

BELZONI

Ethel Wright Mohamed
STITCHERY PICTURES

Passed on through dim photos and yellowed letters, family memories rarely survive more than three generations. Ethel Mohamed, however, records her family history in a more colorful and permanent way—by creating intricately stitched "memory pictures."

"My mother taught me embroidery as a little girl," Ethel recalls. "But most of my life I was too busy with my husband, eight children, and our dry goods store to do any needlework." After her husband, Hassan, a Lebanese immigrant, died in 1965, Ethel found that running the store didn't fill enough of her time. Looking for a way to record and relive her happy life, she first tried painting, then returned to embroidery.

Compiling a pictorial diary of her life, Ethel, known to her friends as Mama Mohamed, creates elaborate textile stories from random scraps of material and colorful threads. One picture portrays a family wedding. Others sketch Lebanese legends, a summer outing (see color plate #10), or whimsical recollections of her children. From border to border, each picture is filled with detail. *Reflection on Spring Creek* shows cows and other animals peering at their reflections while background hills are filled with grazing sheep, an apple picker and a farmer, a log cabin, and a Connestoga wagon. Revealing a delightful sense of humor, Mama created one of the hills from a scrap of material depicting jungle animals.

Mama's work is meant for her own family, so she doesn't sell it, not even when the Smithsonian asks. For the Smithsonian, however, she did create a special embroidery titled *Me at the Renwick*, completed after attending a reception there in her honor. And once a year she donates a picture to a local auction. If you want to consider paying the $12,000-plus price, Mama will tell you the date of the next auction.

Although you can't purchase or commission Mama's work, you can visit her in-home museum, dubbed "Mama's Dream" by her children. In addition to viewing all of Mama's completed memory pictures, you may also be able to watch her working on a new one. Although you'll be frustrated that the pieces aren't for sale, Mama has arranged a compromise: notecards and limited-edition prints of two of her works, *Reflection on Spring Creek* and *Harp Singing*.

PRICES: Prints, $150 (size about 2′×3′). No commissions. No catalog/brochure.

VISITORS: By appointment.

LOCATION: West-central Mississippi, about 70 miles northwest of Jackson. 307 Central Street, Belzoni, MS 39038; 601-247-1433. Directions will be provided when appointment to visit is made.

MORE: Mama Mohamed demonstrates her stitchery annually at the Chimneyville Crafts Festival. See the following entry.

JACKSON

Chimneyville Crafts Festival
TRADITIONAL AND CONTEMPORARY CRAFTS

One of two crafts festivals sponsored annually by the Craftsmen's Guild of Mississippi, the Chimneyville event takes its name from the city's incendiary nickname, earned after General Sherman burned Jackson to the ground in 1863. The only thing burning at this quality festival, however, will be the hole in your wallet.

Over 100 craftspeople, all members of the guild, sell their work at this major pre-Christmas festival. Knifemaking, traditional and contemporary pottery, broommaking, weaving, dollmaking, and Choctaw Indian basketry are just some of the crafts displayed. There are also demonstrations, performing artists, and lectures by prominent craft authorities.

EVENT: First weekend in Dec. Preview party, Fri., 7–10 P.M. Festival, Sat., 10 A.M.–6 P.M.; Sun., noon–6 P.M. Admission for the preview party is $7.50; general admission is $3 for adults, children under 12 free.

LOCATION: Mississippi Trade Mart, State Fairgrounds, Jefferson and High streets, Jackson. Take I-55 to the High Street exit. Turn left at the first traffic light. The Trade Mart is a big, low, white building.

MORE: For more information contact the Craftsmen's Guild of Mississippi, Agriculture and Forestry Museum, 1150 Lakeland Drive, Jackson, MS 39216; 601-981-0019. For information on the other guild festival, see the entry under Ridgeland, Mississippi. For a respite from Christmas shopping or travel, explore Mynelle Gardens, a 6-acre botanical extravaganza with almost 1,000 varieties of plants; 4736 Clinton Boulevard, Jackson; 601-960-1894.

KOSCIUSKO

Old Trace Gallery
CONTEMPORARY AND TRADITIONAL CRAFTS

If you're driving north of Jackson along the Natchez Trace Parkway, plan a stop at Kosciusko, named after a Polish officer who aided in the Revolutionary War. The local gallery carries a variety of traditional crafts, Indian baskets, folk art pottery, and contemporary Mississippi crafts, highlighted by Irene Yoder's quilts. Using infinitesimal stitches, traditional patterns, and unusual color combinations, Irene creates instant heirlooms. The gallery's other quilters also offer a fine selection, from fanciful Noah's ark crib quilts to wall hangings. Don't see your dream quilt? The gallery's quilters will make one to your specifications.

PRICES: $10–$850. Accepts MasterCard, Visa.

OPEN: Tues–Sun., 11 A.M.–5 P.M. Closed all legal holidays. Wheelchair accessible.

LOCATION: Central Mississippi, about 50 miles northeast of Jackson. 120 East Jefferson Street, P.O. Box 307, Kosciusko, MS 39090: 601-289-9170. From I-55, travel north from Jackson 56 miles to the Durant/Rte. 12 exit. Go east on Rte. 12 to Kosciusko, then right on Natchez Street (Rte. 43). Continue to Jefferson Street; the gallery is half a block west. From Natchez Trace Parkway, turn off parkway at Milepost 160 (Rte. 14). Follow Rte. 14 to Jefferson Street; the gallery is one and a half blocks west.

MORE: The Natchez Trace Parkway roughly follows the famous Natchez Trace, originally an Indian trail. In the 1780s, as farmers began floating their products down the Mississippi River to Natchez and New Orleans markets, they "traced" their way home along this trail as far north as Nashville. In the early 1800s, this well-trod forest path became the major link between the nation's capital and Natchez, capital of the Mississippi Territory. Once other roads improved and steamships made their way up the Mississippi, the trace fell into disuse. The parkway resembles a long green belt, pleasant but not as scenic as the Blue Ridge Parkway. History buffs will appreciate the numerous explanatory markers and the occasional opportunities to view the flattened depressions that mark the original Trace.

LAUREL

Lauren Rogers Museum of Art
NATIVE AMERICAN BASKETS

Normally this book would not list a museum with a craft collection that represents only 10 percent of its total holdings. But this museum has one of the largest collections of Native American baskets in the country.

The Catherine Marshall Gardiner Collection contains over 650 baskets from more than sixty North American tribes, including many now extinct. Gardiner, who began purchasing baskets in the late 1800s, wanted to preserve an art form she believed was disappearing. Explaining her passion, she wrote, "I read one day that the work would become scarce [because] younger squaws with opportunities for education and purchase of domestic utensils would no longer make the necessary sacrifices in gathering materials or use their time for laborious weaving; nor would they disfigure themselves in the dyeing, sometimes accomplished by chewing, the saliva acting as a mordant for the dyes and discoloring their teeth."

Thanks to Mrs. Gardiner's determination, visitors can see an array of baskets from relatively unknown tribes such as the Yavapai, Chitimacha, and Coushatta, as well as the more well known Navajo, Apache, and Cherokee. Among other items on display are unusual Pomo feather baskets, a woven Pueblo water bottle (c. 1150), and the (reputedly) second smallest basket in the world, made by Pomo Indians and requiring a magnifying glass for viewing.

OPEN: Tues.–Sun., 10 A.M.–5 P.M. Closed major holidays. The museum shop sells locally made Choctaw Indian and pine needle baskets. Free admission. Tours are given twice daily, of the entire museum collection, at 10:30 A.M. and 1:45 P.M. Wheelchair accessible.

LOCATION: Southeastern Mississippi. 5th Avenue at 7th Street, P.O. Box 1108, Laurel, MS 39440; 601-649-6374. Take I-59 to Laurel, then follow directional markers to the museum.

MANTACHIE

Euple & Titus Riley
Peppertown Pottery
FOLK POTTERY AND SCULPTURE

The Rileys' pottery is positively schizophrenic. On the one hand, visitors will find a white face with

Euple and Titus Riley: *King Arthur and His Round Table.* Clay figures, H. 12″–15″. Table, H. 5″; Diam. 14″.
RICK WEBB

swollen eyes and bared teeth looking menacingly out from the side of a jug. On the other, they'll see a gaily decorated seahorse and shelves of functional pottery with pretty raised grape motifs or glazes imprinted with live ferns. In between these extremes are primitive, smokey, foot-tall sculptures of King Arthur, Guinevere, Merlin, and the knights standing next to the proverbial round table.

Using primarily native ball clay and glazes from local minerals, Euple and Titus do everything by hand. "A true potter does not use any type of forms," Euple says. "Everything we do is hand crafted. I like to do sculpture and wheel forming, while Titus does most of his creations using the lump on a wheel. He also made a lot of our own equipment, including the furnaces, clay grinder, mixer, and pug mill."

PRICES: $2–$150. Commissions accepted. Free catalog/brochure.

VISITORS: Tues.–Sat., 9 A.M.–4:30 P.M.

LOCATION: Northeastern corner of Mississippi. Rte. 1, Box 445, Mantachie, MS 38855; 601-862-9861. Take I-55 to the Batesville exit (Rte. 6), Rte. 6 east to Tupelo, then Rte. 78 east 16 miles to the Rte. 363 exit. Turn north onto Rte. 363. Peppertown Pottery is on Rte. 363, half a mile from Rte. 78.

MORE: Peppertown is a small community just south of Mantachie that got its name during World War II. Black pepper was scarce throughout the region, but a local store managed to get a big supply. Soon everyone knew where to get their favorite spice and the area gained its name.

NATCHEZ

Grand Village of the Natchez Indians Gift Shop
SOUTHEASTERN INDIAN CRAFTS

Natchez is like a gentile Southern lady, sitting along the Mississippi, showing only her prettiest side to the camera. Natchez's original inhabitants, however, may be its most fascinating. The Natchez culture reached its height during the mid-sixteenth century but was exterminated by the French in 1729. Central to the Natchez culture were large mounds where the chiefs lived. Upon his death a chief, his family, and his home were burned, the mound was raised, and a new home built on top for his successor.

After touring this unusual archaeological site, stop by the gift shop, which has an excellent selection of Southeastern Indian crafts, including Cherokee, Coushatta, Choctaw, and Chitimacha baskets, and Seminole patchwork. Of particular note are the Choctaw "elbow" baskets. Formed in a V shape, these baskets are used to store and dry herbs and to mix liquid herb medicines. When each medicine is mixed, the point of the V is placed in a pot and the two separate liquids are poured down either side. The basket strains out unwanted particles and the liquid filters into the pot.

PRICES: $1–$250. Accepts MasterCard, Visa.

OPEN: Mon.–Sat., 9 A.M.–5 P.M.; Sun., 1:30–5 P.M. Closed Labor Day, Thanksgiving, Christmas, and New Year's Day. Wheelchair accessible.

LOCATION: East side of Natchez. 400 Jefferson Davis Boulevard, Natchez, MS 39120; 601-446-6502. Take Rte. 61 to Natchez, then go east .6 mile on Jefferson Davis Boulevard. Turn right into Grand Village; the gift shop is next to the parking area.

OCEAN SPRINGS

Shearwater Pottery
ART POTTERY

Deriving its name from the two types of water found in the area, Ocean Springs is a coastal village of curving seashore drives, moss-draped oaks, and streets dotted with artists' studios. Down a winding path not far from the harbor is the Anderson family craft compound known as Shearwater Pottery. Started in 1928, Shearwater specializes in art pottery from mellow green pitchers to gaily decorated candlesticks and pots. It also produces folk pottery figurines of farmers and baseball players, women in beach attire, and stereotypical African-Americans dancing and playing the fiddle.

PRICES: $3–$500. No commissions. No catalog/brochure.

VISITORS: Mon.–Sat., 9 A.M.–5:30 P.M.; Sun., 1–5:30 P.M.

LOCATION: Mississippi Gulf coast. P.O. Box 737, Ocean Springs, MS 39564; 601-875-7320. Take I-10 to the Rte. 90

(Ocean Springs) exit, the Rte. 90 to Ocean Springs. At the stoplight, turn right onto Washington Avenue. Turn left on Calhoun, then right on Pershing/Shearwater. The compound is on the right after the harbor.

PHILADELPHIA

Choctaw Museum of the Southern Indian
CHOCTAW CRAFTS

The Mississippi Band of Choctaw Indians operates six industrial plants on its reservation, making the band one of the largest employers in the state. Producing automotive parts for General Motors, Ford, and Chrysler, it has succeeded at its goal of self-determination after losing its aboriginal homelands through a series of early nineteenth-century "treaties."

The Choctaw Museum celebrates this nation's rich heritage, exhibits and sells traditional crafts. Look for distinctive Choctaw baskets, white oak ones made by men, ones of swamp cane created by women. Of particular interest are the double-woven swamp cane baskets, which incorporate traditional diamond patterns and, when wet, hold water.

Don't miss the dark pottery bowls shaped like fish, mammals, and birds, made by the last remaining Choctaw potter, Grady John. Equally unusual are pieces used in the traditional Choctaw game of *ishtaboli* (stickball). Although the game is related to lacrosse, Choctaw stickball players use two sticks *(kabucha)* per player, a ball of hide *(towa)* about the size of a golf ball, and play to the rhythmic beat of a drum.

Grady John: Choctaw pottery bowls. JULIE KELSEY

OPEN: Mon.–Fri., 8 A.M.–4:30 P.M. Closed holidays. The museum shop sells all crafts described above. Free admission. Wheelchair accessible.

LOCATION: East-central Mississippi, about 40 miles northwest of Meridian. Route 7, Box 21, Philadelphia, MS 39350; 601-656-5251 (ask for the "museum department"). Take I-20 to the Newton exit (Rte. 15). Follow Rte. 15 north for 32 miles to Williamsville. Turn left on Rte. 16 to the Choctaw Indian Reservation. Signs at the reservation entrance direct visitors to the museum.

MORE: Mon.–Fri., 8 A.M.–noon, museum visitors can watch Effie Tubby make traditional Choctaw clothing, including men's shirts and women's long dresses in bright solid colors decorated with diamond patterns and topped by white aprons.

The annual Choctaw Indian Fair is generally held the Wed.–Sat. of the first week after July 4th. The event includes craft demonstrations and sales, the Choctaw Stickball World Series, and traditional dances, music, and pageantry (and country music headliners).

RIDGELAND

Indian & Pioneer Heritage Fair
HISTORIC MISSISSIPPI CRAFTS

Your nose will tell you you're approaching this annual fall event even before your eyes do. The smell of bread being baked in an outdoor oven mixes with smoke from a log cabin fireplace, setting the scene for a fair that tantalizes all your senses. Presenting Indian, African-American, and white folk crafts, this festival entertains and subtly educates.

Begin with the crafts. Over thirty artisans demonstrate their traditional skills, from flintnapping and Choctaw cane basketry to dulcimer making, quilting, and blacksmithing. Grab a piece of that freshly baked bread or gnaw on a stick of sugarcane while you watch a Choctaw stickball match, sway with the melody of gospel singing, or clap your hands at a square dance exhibit.

EVENT: Third Sat. in Oct., 10 A.M.–5 P.M. Free Admission.

LOCATION: Mississippi Crafts Center, on the Natchez Trace Parkway, Ridgeland. See the following entry for address, phone, and directions.

RIDGELAND

Mississippi Crafts Center
TRADITIONAL AND CONTEMPORARY MISSISSIPPI CRAFTS

Behind a split rail fence, in a shady grove near a meadow of wildflowers, sits a reproduction dogtrot log cabin housing Mississippi's finest crafts gallery. "Our building is a good example of local folk architecture," explains executive director Martha Garrott. "The two large rooms of the cabin are linked by a roofed breezeway called a dogtrot." The center is even more interesting inside, displaying work by members of the Craftsmen's Guild of Mississippi from traditional blacksmithing and the famous Mississippi oak porch rockers to contemporary blown glass.

Functional pottery is a specialty here, including work by Jan Carter and Springwood Pottery. Jan's pots unpretentiously perform their functions. Straightforward pitchers are glazed in warm colors, and a covered baking dish may have flowers and butterflies resting on a mottled gray surface. Equally utilitarian, but more highly decorated, Springwood Pottery's work includes angular shapes, pastel surfaces, and soft, abstract patterns.

If you have an eye for design and quality, you will leave the center a basket collector whether you entered as one or not. "We have the world's best selection of Choctaw swamp cane basketry," Martha says. "Their unbroken tradition produces work today no different from that in museums throughout the country. Most of the best Choctaw basket makers are elderly, but there are about five young women who equal their elders in skill and diversity. In fact, most of these artisans are descended from the deceased master, Rosie Denson, including nine of her daughters and four granddaughters."

Visitors will find baskets with red-and-black designs, often in elaborate diamond patterns or subtle stripes. Following traditional shapes, baskets may be hampers (see cover illustration), single-handle egg carriers, V-shape "elbow" baskets, or wall-hanging storage pockets known as "bullnose" baskets.

PRICES: $1–$900 (average, $10–$50); Choctaw baskets, $10–$400. Accepts American Express, MasterCard, Visa. Free price list/brochure on Choctaw baskets.

OPEN: Daily, 9 A.M.–5 P.M. Closed Thanksgiving and Christmas. Wheelchair accessible.

LOCATION: Along the Natchez Trace Parkway, just north of Jackson. P.O. Box 69, Ridgeland, MS 39158; 601-856-7546. Take I-55 to the Natchez Trace Parkway exit at Ridgeland. Proceed north on the parkway for 1 mile.

MORE: On Sat. and Sun. from March through the third week of Oct., artisans demonstrate crafts such as Choctaw basketry and beadwork, dulcimermaking, chair caning, quilting, and folk pottery.

WASHINGTON

Nathan Bennett
SPLIT-OAK BASKETS AND CYPRESS SHINGLES

If you're already in the Natchez area, plan to drive five miles east to watch a living legend demon-

Nathan Bennett creating a split-oak basket. CHRISSY WILSON

strate his crafts. Born in 1900, Nathan Bennett spent most of his life working in logging and lumbering operations throughout the South as well as serving stints as a cook, farmer, and barber. Since the mid-1970s he has been the resident craftsman at this Washington historic site. For over eighty years, Nathan has made white oak baskets and cypress shingles, first for home use and trade, now for his own pleasure and that of visitors. Starting with logs and using a froe and drawknife for most of the work, Nathan creates items almost identical to those his grandfather once made.

Five days a week, visitors can find Nathan creating his baskets and shingles at Historic Jefferson College, the first educational institution in Mississippi. Although the college was closed in 1964, the buildings are being restored for use as a historic landmark and museum. Bring your lunch! The pretty, parklike setting provides a perfect backdrop for a family picnic.

PRICES: $15–$500 (at the museum sales shop). No commissions. No catalog/brochure.

VISITORS: Mon.–Fri., 10 A.M.–4 P.M.

LOCATION: 5 miles east of Jackson, Mississippi. Nathan Bennett, % Historic Jefferson College, P.O. Box 100, Washington, MS 39120; 601-442-2901. Take I-55 to Hazelhurst, then Rte. 28 west to where it intersects with Rte. 61 at Fayette. Follow Rte. 61 to Washington; the college is on the left side of the road.

YAZOO CITY

Sarah Mary Taylor
AFRICAN-AMERICAN QUILTS

African-American quilts may not be as well known as Amish ones, but they derive from an equally strong tradition. In fact, since the tradition is relatively unpublicized, collectors are more likely to find authentic examples, such as those by Sarah Mary Taylor.

Sarah learned to quilt when she was a little girl, piecing Nine-Patch and Four-Patch quilts. "I also used to make string quilts," Sarah says. "They were made of little bitty strips of material no bigger than your finger. But they take a long time to make, so I don't do those anymore."

Still quilting even though she admits to being well into her seventies, Sarah makes brilliantly colored pieces in a variety of themes, sometimes depicting hands or even old-fashioned "mammies." One motif she calls the "everybody" quilt consists of nine large patches, each covered with appliquéd animal forms from dogs and kangaroos to moose and fanciful creatures (see color plate #11). Sarah's innate sense of color creates images that appear to move: brilliant blue animals set on red seem ready to leap off the quilt. In true folk tradition, she uses whatever materials are at hand, not worrying if there isn't enough of one particular fabric to complete a portion of the quilt.

PRICES: Crib quilt, $60–$100; double quilt, $150 ("I can't make them bigger, because I don't have a big enough room"). There is no catalog/brochure; but you can call Sarah to discuss what quilt you would like to purchase, then send her payment and a mailing label.

VISITORS: Yes. Please call first.

LOCATION: West-central Mississippi, about 40 miles northwest of Jackson. 325 Hamilton Street, Yazoo City, MS 39194; 601-746-6411. Directions will be provided by phone.

NORTH CAROLINA

If you're traveling south from Virginia, your introduction to North Carolina crafts begins right at the border in the I-77 Welcome Center. Pass by the rows of tourist brochures and maps to see a display of North Carolina crafts from dulcimers, quilts, and pottery to furniture, rugs, and clocks. Although items are not for sale here, if you see something particularly appealing, the staff can provide the artisan's name and address.

The Welcome Center's tantalizing view of traditional Appalachian crafts is a testament to decades of work by the John C. Campbell and Penland crafts schools as well as the Southern Highland Handicraft Guild. Begun during the 1920s and 1930s, these organizations have encouraged, assisted, and promoted artisans working in a variety of crafts from primitive wood carving and quilting to folk instruments, brooms, weaving, and furnituremaking. Each of these revered institutions offers visitors an opportunity to watch demonstrations as well as browse through well-stocked gift shops. To meet individual artisans, sketch a path through the winding back roads of western North Carolina or visit traditional potters in Seagrove, south of Greensboro.

In the southwestern corner of the state, Cherokee tribal arts are highlighted in shops, a museum, and the outstanding Oconaluftee Indian village, where visitors can watch crafts-people creating traditional items in authentic outdoor settings. Contemporary crafts are spotlighted in galleries throughout the state (including two along the state's famous Outer Banks islands) and in the work of individuals such as tapestry artist Barbara Grenell of Burnsville.

ARDEN

Brown's Pottery
FUNCTIONAL. GLAZED EARTHENWARE

It's possible to say that Charles and Robert Brown have feet of clay without implying a fatal familial flaw. At the very least, some clay must have slipped into the bloodstream of this seven-generation potter clan whose ceramic roots date back to late eighteenth-century Virginia. Since then, Brown potteries have flourished in at least eight Southern states, most recently in Arden, North Carolina.

Once a year, for over fifty years, the Arden Browns have filled their bin with clay dug four miles away. Emerging from the ground a blue-gray, the clay turns buff after firing. Visitors can watch the entire process, from preparation of the clay to removing finished products from the kiln. The work is a real family affair, with each member having his or her own specialty. For some it's mixing powdered clay and water in the mill. For others the work includes turning large or small pieces, adding handles, glazing, or operating the retail store.

The original Arden Pottery made only large churns and pots, but a few items have been added over the years, including unglazed chicken roasters and glazed casseroles and cookware. The Browns are known also for their face jugs, large brown vessels with popping eyes, snarling mouths, and ears that rival Prince Charles's. Poured over these macabre visages are glossy brown glazes, often with drippy green edges that pour down a cheek or drool around the mouth.

PRICES: 50¢–$350. No commissions. Send a business-size SASE for the free catalog/brochure.

VISITORS: Yes.

LOCATION: On Rte. 25, halfway between Asheville and Hendersonville. P.O. Box 10, Arden, NC 28704; 704-684-2901. Take I-26 to the Arden exit/Rte. 25.

ASHEVILLE

Southern Highland Handicraft Guild Folk Art Center
APPALACHIAN CRAFTS

The verdict is in. After a bitter struggle, the skilled hands of Appalachia have triumphed over the long, plastic arm of modernity. The crafts of the past have not only survived, they've triumphed. For a while, however, it looked as if the skills developed by mountain residents for over 200 years would be replaced by trips to the discount store.

Hardship and isolation forced Appalachians to produce what they needed. Clothing and furniture, tools and toys, all were created by hand from local materials. When passable roads finally reached these communities, the flow of manufactured goods threatened the continuance of these handicrafts. Perceptive individuals, many of them church missionaries, realized in the 1920s that a concerted effort was required to preserve, improve, and market these unique crafts. In 1930 the Southern Highland Handicraft Guild was established to accomplish these goals.

From an initial membership of 30 craftspeople, the guild has grown to represent over 2,000 artisans from mountain counties in nine Appalachian states. Accepted only after passing a strict jurying process, members work in both traditional and contemporary crafts. The guild now offers an extensive educational and marketing program, sponsors four retail craft shops and two annual fairs, and administers the Folk Art Center.

Located in a striking modern building of native stone and wood, the center provides an excellent introduction to Appalachian crafts. The museum and exhibition gallery highlight crafts from all nine states, and the lobby provides space for artisans to demonstrate their skills. The center's Allanstand Craft Shop offers an excellent cross section of Appalachian crafts from brooms to whistles, marquetry to quilts.

Folk Center and Allanstand Craft Shop

PRICES: 50¢–$1,500+ (average, $10–$80). Accepts Mastercard, Visa.

OPEN: Daily, 9 A.M.–5 P.M. Closed Thanksgiving, Christmas, and New Year's Day. Craft demonstrations are held on weekends May–Oct., on weekdays on occasion. Free admission. Wheelchair accessible.

LOCATION: Milepost 382 on the Blue Ridge Parkway half a mile north of Rte. 70. Box 9545, Asheville, NC 28815; 704-298-7928.

Other Southern Highland Handicraft Guild Shops

PARKWAY CRAFT CENTER: located in an elegant mansion in Cone Memorial Park, Milepost 294, Blue Ridge Parkway, P.O. Box 367, Blowing Rock, NC 28605; 704-295-7938.

GUILD CRAFTS: 930 Tunnel Road, Asheville, NC 28805; 704-298-7903.

GUILD GALLERY: 501 State Street, Bristol, VA 24201; 703-669-0821.

Guild Fairs

Since 1948, the guild has sponsored annual fairs exhibiting and selling members' work. Now held twice a year, these popular (and packed) fairs also offer craft demonstrations and Appalachian entertainment.

EVENTS: Third weekend in July (Thurs.–Sat., 10 A.M.–9 P.M.; Sun., noon–6 P.M.) and third weekend in Oct. (Fri.–Sat., 10 A.M.–9 P.M.; Sun., noon–6 P.M.). Admission to both is $3.50 for adults, children under 12 free.

LOCATION: Asheville Civic Center, located just off I-240 on Haywood Street in downtown Asheville. For more information contact the Folk Art Center.

BANNER ELK

Edd L. Presnell
DULCIMERS

If central casting wanted a man to play the part of an Appalachian dulcimer maker, they would choose Edd Presnell. With his striking gray hair, long flowing beard, omnipresent pipe, and ready smile, Edd is the perfect portrait of a talented but self-effacing craftsman.

"I'm all trial and error, self-taught," Edd says. "I got interested in making dulcimers after looking at one my father-in-law made for my wife back in 1935. Now I make a real variety, offering my customers three-, four-, five-, or six-stringed instruments in two sizes. There's the standard size for personal playing or for accompanying folk songs and ballads. I also make a concert size, which has a longer string span, wider and deeper sound box, and more volume for auditorium playing."

All instruments are made with steam-bent sides, a hollow neck (for clearer tone), and rose-

Edd Presnell and his dulcimer. W. 6½"; D. 1¾"; L. 36". DAVID LUTTRELL

wood bridges and turning pegs. "I finish each one with a coat of tung oil," Edd adds, "then I hand rub them with wax. I also include a hand-carved wood pick, fret bar, and even an instruction book on how to tune and play the dulcimer."

PRICES: $115–300 +. Commissions accepted. Send a business-size SASE for the free catalog/brochure.

VISITORS: Yes.

LOCATION: Northwestern North Carolina, about 20 miles west of the Blue Ridge Parkway, 15 miles southwest of Boone. Rte. 3, Box 546F, Banner Elk, NC 28604; 704-297-2072. "Please call for directions and to make sure we're home."

BRASSTOWN

John C. Campbell Folk School
BRASSTOWN WOOD CARVING

Since 1925, the John C. Campbell school has offered short-term classes in a variety of traditional skills from log cabin building to pottery, woodworking, and folk dancing. But the school is best known for its Brasstown Woodcarvers, a cottage industry begun in the 1930s and still operating.

For over sixty years, every Friday has brought a steady stream of Brasstown Woodcarvers to the Campbell campus. Throughout the day, the school purchases the carvings completed during the previous week and distributes blocks of wood for the next week's work. "They carve realistic mountain animals, birds, and other figures in a variety of woods," says Ronald Hill, school director. "Most often they use black or white walnut, cherry, bass, or the unusual streaked buckeye wood."

"Probably the best known carver today," Hill adds, "is Hope Brown. She's been carving for almost fifty years and is known nationally for her cherubs, sleeping cats, and baby in the manger. She designs her own patterns, many of which are used daily in our classrooms." The oldest Brasstown carver is Ray Mann. Now in his mid-eighties, he carves realistic families of goats and sheep, oxen and mules. There are also squirrels and rabbits by J. A. Morris and crèche figures by Helen Gibson, a school instructor and second-generation carver.

In the lobby of Keith House, the school's administrative center, visitors can see a variety of Brass-

Brasstown Carvers (Nolan Beaver, Hope Brown, Martha Coffey, Helen Gibson, Larry Hatchard, Ray Mann): Crèche set. Basswood, buckeye, holly, and oak. COURTESY JOHN C. CAMPBELL FOLK SCHOOL

town carvings created over the last six decades. More recent carvings are sold through the school's craft shop, which also offers student work in a variety of media.

PRICES: $2–$500; Hope Brown's work, $15.75–$50. Accepts MasterCard, Visa.

OPEN: Mon.–Fri., 8 A.M.–5 P.M.; Sun., 1–5 P.M. Closed July 4th, Thanksgiving and the day after, Christmas, New Year's Day. Wheelchair accessible.

LOCATION: Southwestern tip of North Carolina. Rte. 1, Box 14A, Brasstown, NC 28902; 704-837-2275. From Asheville, take I-40 to Rte. 74, then Rte. 74 west to Murphy. Turn east on Rte. 64 and go about 5 or 6 miles and watch for the sign.

BRASSTOWN

Fred G. Smith
HAND-CARVED WOODEN BOWLS. SERVING TRAYS

"**I**f you get any of my pieces, don't just set them up to look at, *use them!*" Fred says emphatically. "Useful beauty" is how Fred describes the trays and bowls he has been carving for over fifty years. Starting with native Appalachian woods such as butternut, basswood, and black walnut, Fred roughs out each piece with mechanical tools, then gouges, shapes, and carves the final forms by hand. The inside of a characteristic piece smoothly highlights the grain while the outside retains the flowing marks of the carver's gouge, adding an appealing texture.

Fred G. Smith: Bowl. Butternut wood. H. 6"; L. 9½"; D. 4".
FOSTER A. DIONNE

Fred's special touch with wood began when he was a small child. "I whittled my own toys from native red cedar," he recalls. "Then later I made wagon wheels and sleds. In the 1930s I studied at the John C. Campbell Folk School to learn more about carving and marketing my work." Fred learned his lessons well. For years he has wholesaled his work throughout the country, even selling larger pieces to Georg Jensen in New York. "But I prefer to work directly with my customers, get to meet them," Fred says. "So now I just sell out of my home and by mail order."

PRICES: $12–$500. Commissions accepted "infrequently." There is no catalog/brochure, but Fred says, "Just call or write, tell me what you'd like."

VISITORS: Yes.

LOCATION: Southwestern tip of North Carolina, near the Georgia border. #1 Smith Road, Brasstown, NC 28902; 704-837-2274. Take Rtes. 19/129 or Rte. 64 to Murphy. Go east on Rte. 64. Following sign for Brasstown, turn right (this is on Rte. 66, which leads to Young Harris, Georgia). 1 mile east of Brasstown (4 miles west of Warne) look for directional signs to Smith Craft.

BURNSVILLE

Barbara Grenell
CONTEMPORARY TAPESTRIES

Barbara's three-dimensional tapestries resemble landscapes glimpsed through a train window, two separate panoramas seen by looking first forward then back. Displayed on angled panels resembling a folding screen, Barbara's tapestries offer two complete landscapes that can never be viewed from a single perspective. Instead, as the viewer walks from side to side, one scene disappears and is replaced by the second.

A painter turned weaver, Barbara gains much of her inspiration from the Blue Ridge Mountains outside her studio window. Each tapestry begins with a landscape sketch that she transfers to a larger drawing or watercolor, known as a "cartoon." She then cuts up the cartoon, placing it on the warp as a general outline for weaving. "For each tapestry, I hand-dye the cottons and wools to get the specific colors I need," Barbara notes. "And I use an eccentric or balanced weave, with the natural linen warp visible as an important element in the design."

PRICES: $1,000–$25,000 + . Commissions accepted. Brochure/slides free to people seriously considering commission work.

VISITORS: By appointment only.

LOCATION: Western North Carolina, about 32 miles northeast of Asheville. 1132 Hall's Chapel Road, Burnsville, NC 28714; 704-675-4073. Directions will be provided when appointment to visit is made.

Barbara Grenell: *Dawn Septet,* tapestry. Natural linen warp, custom-dyed cotton and wool design. H. 36"; L. 72"; D. 6". ROB GRENELL

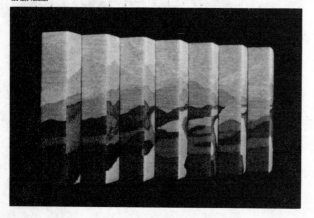

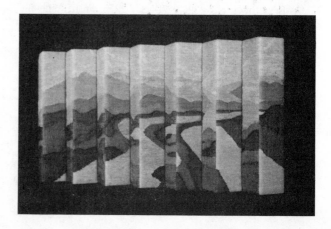

CHEROKEE
History and Background

A sophisticated tribe that established its own constitutional government and, under Sequoyah, developed a written language, the Cherokee Nation was tolerated until gold was discovered on its land in the 1830s. Greedy whites, abetted by the federal government, promptly robbed the Cherokees of their homelands, deporting the populace to Oklahoma via the harrowing Trail of Tears. A few courageous Cherokees, however, hid in the nearby Appalachian Mountains. Their descendants, and a few Cherokees who returned from Oklahoma, formed the nucleus of the reservation established in Western North Carolina.

Although nothing can erase a single tear spilled on the trail to Oklahoma, today's numerous trinket stands and assorted hype are perhaps at least a subtle form of revenge on today's predominately white tourists. Persevere. Beyond the ersatz Indian culture dished out along the highway are three highly recommended stops: Oconaluftee Indian Village, the Museum of the Cherokee Indian, and Qualla Arts & Crafts Mutual. All three are within walking distance of each other and should be visited in the order listed below.

CHEROKEE

Oconaluftee Indian Village
TRADITIONAL CHEROKEE CRAFTS

Situated in an area first occupied by the Cherokee over 10,000 years ago, Oconaluftee (which means "by the water") is a reconstructed 1750 Cherokee town, a "living museum" emphasizing period crafts. Visitors walk along secluded forest paths to small clearings where craftspeople demonstrate crafts in authentic settings. Near a brook, a dugout canoe is fashioned from a giant poplar tree. Farther along, men carve ceremonial masks once used in religious ceremonies or burn out the pith in river cane to create blowguns, arrows, and darts.

Craftswomen sit quietly in the shadow of a rhododendron thicket weaving baskets of white oak splits and river cane, natural dyes boiling nearby over an open fire. In another clearing, women finger-weave. Handling thirty-six to forty-eight different strands at a time, the women use no loom—a single long stick holds one end of the material. Down the path, pots are built from long coils of clay, allowed partially to dry, then stamped with a carved wooden paddle. After further drying, the pots are polished with a smooth wet stone and fired in an open fire.

Visitors can also learn about Cherokee myths and history at a replica squareground where ritual dances were once held, or hear details of past and present tribal government inside the seven-sided replica Council House.

OPEN: May 1–Oct. 25, daily, 9 A.M.–5:30 P.M. There is no museum shop, but the Qualla Arts & Crafts shop is close by. See the listing below. Admission is $6 for adults, $3 for children. Tours are given. Wheelchair accessible.

LOCATION: Just north of Cherokee on Rte. 441. P.O. Box 398, Cherokee, NC 28719; 704-497-2315.

MORE: Adjacent to the village is a botanical garden and nature trail including a hewn log house surrounded by a typical Cherokee vegetable garden.

Amanda Swimmer: Cherokee pottery. COURTESY CHEROKEE HISTORICAL ASSOCIATION

CHEROKEE

Museum of the Cherokee Indian
CHEROKEE CRAFTS, HISTORY

After visiting the Oconaluftee Indian Village, stop by the museum for a more thorough indoctrination into Cherokee crafts, clothing, and weaponry. Of particular interest is the Myth Keepers display, which provides an oral introduction to ancient legends. If you want to be truly steeped in this nation's history, view one (or all) of the six audiovisual shows that trace Cherokee history from ancient times to the present.

OPEN: Mid-June to Aug., Mon.–Sat., 9 A.M.–8 P.M.; Sun., 9 A.M.–5 P.M. Sept.–mid-June, daily, 9 A.M.–5 P.M. Closed Thanksgiving, Christmas, New Year's Day. There is a museum shop, but pass it by for Qualla Arts & Crafts, across the street. Admission is $3 for adults, $1.50 for children. Wheelchair accessible.

LOCATION: On Rte. 441. After leaving the Oconaluftee Indian Village, the museum will be on your right just before the highway. P.O. Box 770-A, Hwy. 441N, Cherokee, NC 28719; 704-497-3481.

CHEROKEE

Qualla Arts & Crafts Mutual, Inc.
EASTERN CHEROKEE CRAFTS

Now that you've seen Cherokee crafts being made in Oconaluftee Village and learned more about them in the museum, it's time to purchase some for your collection. This venerable craft shop, established in 1946, is largely responsible for keeping Eastern Cherokee crafts alive and viable in the twentieth century. Pass by all the other craft shops in town and look exclusively at Qualla.

The full range of Cherokee crafts is represented here. Among the more interesting (and most expensive) pieces are stone sculptures, baskets, and wood carvings. Look for sculptures covered with multiple animal, serpent, bird, and human forms said to represent the images present in the mind of the Cherokee people. Good purchases are the large river cane baskets, including those woven in the traditional "cross on hill" design and stained in butternut and bloodroot. River cane is also the material used by Rowena Bradley to weave intricate mats, often incorporating seven different designs in a single piece. Wood carving is another Cherokee specialty and includes the traditional "Booger mask" used by medicine men to ward off disease and the "Cyclops mask," which uses a knothole for one eye.

PRICES: $3–$1,000 (average, $3–$100). Accepts American Express, MasterCard, Visa. Send $2 for an excellent, 24-page, full-color catalog.

OPEN: Winter—daily, 8 A.M.–4:30 P.M. Summer—daily, 8 A.M.–8 P.M. Closed Thanksgiving, Christmas Day, and New Year's Day.

LOCATION: On Rte. 441, directly across the street from the Museum of the Cherokee Indian. P.O. Box 277, Cherokee, NC 28719; 704-497-3103.

FRISCO

Browning Artworks
CONTEMPORARY CRAFTS

Straddling a slender peninsula that begins in Virginia, Frisco is part of the Outer Banks, a narrow, 110-mile-long strip that seems to float offshore like a long, delicate string. Constantly shaped by winds and waves, the area's contours can change overnight. Sheltered by tall pines and bay trees on one of the last remaining coastal forests, Browning Artworks is located just a few miles south of the nation's tallest lighthouse.

Specializing in ceramics with practical purposes and pretty exteriors, this gallery is a crafts oasis in the middle of a souvenir desert. Ask to see the sculptural yet functional pieces by Clyde Gobble, especially his ovenproof chicken pot, which resembles a Jules Verne fantasy. Another stellar potter is Edward Brinkman, whose work is represented in the Smithsonian collection. Edward mixes and blends his own porcelain using feldspar, kaolin, and flint mined from the North Carolina mountains behind his studio. He then shapes, incises, imprints, and models the clay into everything from wall plaques to mirror frames.

PRICES: $5–$600 (average, $20–$30). Accepts MasterCard, Visa. Free mail-order catalog.

LOCATION: Outer Banks, off North Carolina's eastern shore. P.O. Box 275, Highway 12, Frisco, NC 27935; 919-995-5538. Take I-95 to the Rocky Mount (Rte. 64) exit, Rte. 64 east 154 miles to Manteo. Go south on Rte. 12 to the gallery, just south of the Cape Hatteras lighthouse. For a more adventurous approach, take I-95 to the Wilson (Rte. 264) exit, Rte. 264 east about 118 miles to Swan Quarter. Take the ferry from Swan Quarter (reservations are recommended) to Ocracoke Island. Drive to the north end of the island, then take the ferry to Hatteras. The gallery is north a few miles on Rte. 12.

KILL DEVIL HILLS

Tar Heel Trading Co.
CARVED WILDFOWL, DECOYS

Like everyone else, you'll want to know how the town got its name. Local lore suggests it comes from the moonshine made in the thickly wooded nearby hills. The brew is said to have been so strong "it could kill the devil."

If you're visiting the Outer Banks during the summer season, plan to drop by the Tar Heel Trading Company. Ignore the other crafts it carries and head straight for the carvings by Cecil and Evelyn McDowell and Curtis and Wayne Waterfield. The prize-winning McDowells create exact reproductions of waterfowl. Fully carved, their work is so realistic you may find yourself offering the birds a crumb of bread. No room in your suitcase? Then choose one of the Waterfields' miniatures. These realistic, indigenous shorebirds are hand-carved and hand-painted in meticulous detail.

PRICES: $1.50–$675; McDowell carvings, $325–$750; Waterfield carvings, $95–$325. Accepts American Express, Choice, MasterCard, Visa.

OPEN: Easter–Thanksgiving, daily, 9:30 A.M.–9:30 P.M. (mail-order accepted year-round). Wheelchair accessible.

LOCATION: Outer Banks, off North Carolina's eastern shore. P.O. Box 1036, Sea Holly Square, Kill Devil Hills, NC 27948; 919-441-6235. Take I-95 to the Rocky Mount (Rte. 64) exit, Rte. 64 east 154 miles to Manteo. Go north on Rte. 158 to Kill Devil Hills. Sea Holly Square is at milepost 9½, across from the Ramada Inn.

MORE: In 1903, the Wright brothers made their first sustained flight in a "heavier-than-air" machine near Kill Devil

Hills. A memorial and visitors' center at milepost 8 on Rte. 158 celebrates Wilbur and Orville's accomplishments.

LEICESTER

Ralph Gates
APPALACHIAN BROOMS

"After nine years as a systems engineer with Project Apollo at the Kennedy Space Center in Florida, I was burned out," says Ralph. "I needed something to support my family, and I wanted to work out of the house while the children were small." The answer? Handcrafting brooms using unbleached, undyed broomcorn.

"I layer the broomcorn, using the entire stalk, so it just cannot fall apart," Ralph explains. "I learned from the late Lee M. Ogle of Gatlinburg, Tennessee, who, in turn, learned from his grandmother. I also make the double broom he invented as a time- and laborsaving device. It's really two brooms in one. The broomstick forks at the bottom, each fork supporting a separate group of broomcorn which come together halfway down. One swath sweeps away a lot of dirt!"

Ralph Gates: Double broom.

In addition to double brooms, Ralph makes sweeping, hearth, cobweb, and children's brooms. All the handles are handworked from wood Ralph personally chooses. "A lot of the handles," Ralph says, "are made from wood that has been overgrown by honeysuckle vines. The vines cause the tree to spiral, leaving real interesting shapes."

PRICES: $8–$250. Commissions accepted. Send an SASE for the catalog/brochure.

VISITORS: Yes.

LOCATION: About 15 miles northwest of Asheville. Rte. 2, Box 138, Leicester, NC 28748; 704-683-9521. Please call for directions.

PENLAND

Penland School of Crafts
TRADITIONAL AND CONTEMPORARY CRAFTS

A trip to Penland is more a pilgrimage than a tourist outing. Established in 1923 to revive Appalachian weaving, Penland has grown into one of America's largest and most prestigious craft schools. The fairy godmother in the Penland saga was Miss Lucy Morgan, a determined and practical woman who decided that certain traditional skills would not die out if she had anything to say about it. Beginning with just three looms, the school blossomed under Miss Lucy's resolve and forty years of her leadership.

Focusing on pottery and weaving until the early 1960s, Penland now offers courses in the full spectrum of traditional and contemporary crafts. Every fall, spring, and summer, 100 students converge on this North Carolina mountaintop to attend courses taught by some of the country's most talented artisans. Although visitors may tour the campus, they are not allowed in studios during classes. As part of your tour, stop by the school's Ridgway Gallery to see exhibits of work by community craftspeople and the school's instructors, then visit the craft shop, which offers a good selection of Penland work.

PRICES: $5–$5,000 (average, $5–$150). No credit cards.

OPEN: Spring–fall sessions—Tues.–Sat., 9 A.M.–noon & 1–4 P.M.; Sun., 9–11 A.M. & noon–4 P.M. Wheelchair accessible.

LOCATION: Western North Carolina, about 65 miles northeast of Asheville. Penland School, Penland, NC 28765; 704-765-2359 (crafts shop, 704-765-6211). From Asheville, take Rte. 19/23 north 18 miles. Turn right on Rte. 19E toward Burnsville. 10 miles after Burnsville, look for signs, then turn left to Penland.

MORE: Bed and breakfast accommodations are available at the Chinquapin Inn, three tenths of a mile from Penland School. P.O. Box 145, Penland, NC 28765; 704-765-0064.

RALEIGH

North Carolina Museum of History
NORTH CAROLINA CRAFTS

Slated for a 1992 opening is an extensive new building that will house a variety of North Carolina exhibits and will include a separate Folk Art Gallery on the main floor. The new gallery will display both traditional and contemporary North Carolina crafts in metal, wood, textiles, ceramics, glass, and paper. Prior to 1992, visitors can see a portion of the museum's excellent pottery collection displayed in the first floor of the east wing of the old building.

A special pottery exhibit features some of the state's most famous potters, including many still operating today. A particular treat is the work by Walter Benjamin Stephen, whose glazes were among the most distinctive of the art pottery movement in the 1920s and 1930s. On display are examples of his American Cameo ware with its distinctive raised designs of covered wagons, buffalo hunts, and horseback riders. Equally unusual is the work of Ernest and Clara Hilton, whose favorite glazes were made from crushed Coca-Cola bottles, and the double-dipped and multicolored glazes found on North State Pottery pieces.

OPEN: Tues.–Sat., 9 A.M.–5 P.M.; Sun., 1–6 P.M. Closed Thanksgiving and Christmas. Museum shop on the premises. Free admission. Wheelchair accessible.

LOCATION: (until 1992) Between the Governor's Mansion and the Legislative Building. 109 East Jones Street, Raleigh, NC 27611; 919-733-3894. Take I-85 to Rte. 70 (Raleigh exit). Rte. 70 becomes Glenwood Avenue. Turn left on Jones Street to the museum. (NOTE: The new building will be on the Bicentennial Plaza between the State Capitol and the Legislative Building.)

SEAGROVE

Jugtown Pottery
TRADITIONAL POTTERY

Before inexpensive china and glassware replaced earthenware as the household standard, the country was dotted with potteries producing functional ware from local clay. Victims of "progress," the majority of these family-run businesses closed earlier this century. Today, Seagrove remains one of the few remaining hubs of traditional potteries. Scattered along Route 705, announced only by faded wood signs staked near the road, these hardy survivors operate out of well-weathered log cabins nestled in the forest.

Ironically, one of these, Jugtown, actually owes its existence to New York City. "In 1915," explains Jugtown owner Vernon Owens, "Jacques and Juliana Busbee became intrigued by an orange pie plate they purchased. Jacques traced its origin to Seagrove, then visited the area to see what else was being produced. Distressed to learn that many of the potteries were folding, he devised a counterattack. While his wife opened a successful New York tearoom, Jacques shipped her Seagrove pottery to use and sell. Later, to assure continued availability of this popular ware, the Busbees opened Jugtown Pottery."

Although Jugtown has gone through several owners since the Busbees, it continues to produce earthenware similar to the original work. "We make the traditional shapes including a line of Oriental vases and bowls which Mr. Busbee developed," says Vernon. "And we use a variety of glazes, colored ones for kitchenware, copper glazes ranging from red to turquoise, and salt-glazes including frogskin, which produces a slightly stippled green surface."

PRICES: $2–$100. No commissions. No catalog/brochure.

VISITORS: Mon.–Sat., 8 A.M.–5 P.M.

LOCATION: Central North Carolina, about 40 miles south of Greensboro. Rte. 2, Box 546, Seagrove, NC 27341; 919-464-3266. Take Rte. 220 south from Greensboro to Seagrove. Go left on Rte. 705 and travel for 6 miles, then take a left to Jugtown Pottery.

Jugtown Pottery, Vernon Owens: 1½-gallon jug. Salt-glazed, wood fired. JUAN M. VILLA

SEAGROVE

Westmoore Pottery
TRADITIONAL POTTERY

Not all traditional potters have a long personal history in ceramics. Indeed, some of the best are relative newcomers with a great deal of talent and a dedication to authenticity. This group of nouveau traditionalists includes David and Mary Farrell, who apprenticed with Jugtown owner Vernon Owens before opening Westmoore Pottery in 1977.

"We constantly do research in an effort to present a historically accurate product," Mary says.

Westmoore Pottery: Redware platter with pierced rim, slip-trail and sgraffito decoration. Diam. 17″. MARY L. FARRELL

"Most of our pottery is patterned after late seventeenth-, eighteenth-, and early nineteenth-century earthenware. We specialize in pieces used in North Carolina during that period, including ones made locally as well as those purchased from England, Germany, Pennsylvania, and New England."

In addition to redware, the Farrells make salt-glazed stoneware. "Our salt-glazed work varies tremendously in color from light gray to brown," Mary points out. "After decorating some with cobalt blue patterns, we fire all of them in a traditional 'ground-hog' kiln, stacking the pots in the old style, rim to rim. This practice leaves small, characteristic 'stacking marks,' smooth areas on the rim where the color varies slightly."

PRICES: $2.75–$300. Commissions accepted "sometimes." Send either an SASE or 25¢ for the catalog/brochure.

OPEN: Mon.–Sat., 9 A.M.–5 P.M. Closed for vacation July 17–31, Dec. 24–Jan. 16, and major holidays.

LOCATION: Central North Carolina, about 40 miles south of Greensboro. Rte. 2, Box 494, Seagrove, NC 27341; 919-464-3700. From Greensboro, take Rte. 220 south to Seagrove. Go left on Rte. 705 for about 7.5 miles, left on Rte. 1419. The pottery is located half a mile farther, on the left.

MORE: Another Seagrove ceramic stop worth making is the Potter's Museum, which houses a working pottery as well as displays of local work dating back to the mid-eighteenth century. The museum is located on Rte. 220 about 1 mile north of Seagrove.

SPRUCE PINE

Woody's Chair Shop
TRADITIONAL LADDERBACK CHAIRS

Back hurt when you bend over to tie your tennies or wingtips? Then order one of Woody's colonial slipper chairs. With seats only 14 inches off the ground, your shoestrings will be bowed in a flash.

Slipper chairs are only one variation offered by these fifth-generation chair makers. "I can remember watching my grandfather make these chairs," Arval Woody says. "I played around his shop as a child and just loved to watch the waterwheel that furnished the power for his tools. Although our ladderback styles have changed somewhat since then, we use the same shrink-fit methods employed over one hundred fifty years ago. We don't use any glue, just let the joints shrink as they dry. They won't ever come apart."

Arval Woody: Colonial American rocker. Seat, H. 17″; W. 21″. CRAIG PHOTOGRAPHY

Using clean, spare lines and basic colonial designs, the Woodys produce rockers and nesting stools as well as slipper, side, arm, and children's chairs. "And you need not be horrified if someone puts a foot on the rounds or accidentally overturns one of our chairs," Arval says. "Our finish will take it without chipping and scratching, because we finish each piece while it spins in a lathe. This hand rubbing equals several years of ordinary waxing and polishing. All you need to touch up a scuff mark is a little wax."

PRICES: $80–$240 + . No commissions are accepted. "We haven't been caught up on orders in over twenty years." Free catalog/brochure.

VISITORS: Yes.

LOCATION: Western North Carolina, about 55 miles northeast of Asheville. 110 Dale Road, Spruce Pine, NC 28777; 704-765-9277. Take the Blue Ridge Parkway to the Mineral Museum/Gillispie Gap exit. Go north on Rte. 226 for 2 miles. The shop is on the left.

WAYNESVILLE

Museum of North Carolina Handicrafts
TRADITIONAL NORTH CAROLINA CRAFTS

In 1951 the director of the North Carolina State Fair decided to establish an annual handicraft exhibit so fairgoers could see traditional craft demonstrations. Rebuffed by a state crafts group that thought an agricultural fair was not an appropriate crafts venue, he turned to Mary Cornwell, a county extension agent. Under her capable direction, the exhibit became so successful that eventually a location was sought for a year-round display.

The museum's collection includes work by master artisans from throughout the state as well as items made by early pioneer craftspeople. Among other items, there is a good selection of pottery, Cherokee crafts, porcelain "character" dolls, handwoven coverlets, dulcimers, marquetry, pewterware, and needlecrafts. There is even a miniature farmstead.

OPEN: May 15–Nov. 15, Wed.–Sat., 10 A.M.–5 P.M.; Sun., 2–5 P.M. Closed holidays. The museum shop sells local crafts. Admission is $2.50 for adults, $1.50 for children. Wheelchair accessible.

LOCATION: Southwestern corner of North Carolina, about 35 miles west of Asheville. 301 Shelton Street, P.O. Box 778,

Waynesville, NC 28786; 704-452-1551. Take I-40 west of Asheville to Clyde. Go south on Rte. 23 to the Waynesville/Rte. 276 exit. Rte. 276 becomes Pigeon Street. The museum is on the corner of Pigeon and Shelton streets, two blocks from City Hall.

WINSTON-SALEM

Craft Shop of Piedmont Craftsmen, Inc.
CONTEMPORARY SOUTHEASTERN CRAFTS

This highly selective gallery is sponsored by Piedmont Craftsmen, which admits new members from twelve Southeastern states only after a strict jurying process. Included in the group's North Carolina roster are Bob Trotman, a woodworker known for his "dancing table," a lacquered, tri-legged side table; Cynthia Bringle, whose raku has a distinct Oriental flair; and Stanley Mace Andersen, who specializes in festive majolica dinnerware. For something bizarre yet practical, see Chester Old's work. A Georgia craftsman, Chester creates functional lighting sculptures from tire rubber, air filters, wire, rocks, strips of metal, and cement. Let your imagination run wild—that's just what they look like.

PRICES: $3.50–$3,000 (average, $20–$100). Accepts American Express, MasterCard, Visa.

OPEN: Mon.–Fri., 10 A.M.–6 P.M.; Sat., 10 A.M.–5 P.M.; Sun., 1–5 P.M. Closed on major holidays. Wheelchair accessible.

LOCATION: Downtown Winston-Salem. 411 North Cherry Street, Winston-Salem, NC 27101; 919-725-1516. Take I-40 to the Cherry Street exit. The shop is approximately three blocks down Cherry, on the right side of the street. Free parking is available.

MORE: Winston-Salem is North Carolina's art center. Near the gallery is Salem SoHo, an arts and crafts community of studios and retail shops. Also worth visiting are the Museum of Early Southern Decorative Arts (located in the charming Old Salem area of town), 926 South Main Street, Winston-Salem, 919-722-6148; and the Southeastern Center for Contemporary Art, 750 Marguerite Drive, Winston-Salem; 919-725-1904.

SOUTH CAROLINA

Crisscrossed by a maze of interstates, South Carolina offers visitors easily accessible options from glorious azalea gardens and deep-sea fishing to the gentile charm of Charleston and its extensive collection of historic homes. To remind yourself of the state's many faces, take home a hammock to recall lazy vacation days, purchase one of the state's famous African-American sweet grass baskets, or treat yourself to contemporary ceramic or pine needle vessels. Try to squeeze in a trip to explore St. Helena Island's Sea Island crafts, or visits to galleries in Pendleton and Columbia.

COLUMBIA

Clay Burnette
LONGLEAF PINE NEEDLE VESSELS

"I use a material that is considered a nuisance by most Southerners," Clay says. "In fact, the main thing people around here do with longleaf pine needles is rake them up and haul them to the garbage dump. I take this rather insignificant material and transform it into a work of art. Like our lives, the materials are gifts from God. We just have to do something with them."

Using only 10-to-15-inch pine needles, hand-waxed linen thread, a large sewing needle, scissors, and a plastic gauge, Clay creates coiled, sculptured vessels, flowing forms that sometimes appear to spin like tops around their own centers. Using the needles' dark, stubby ends as both a textural and a design component, Clay staggers them to resemble dry-brush strokes, streaks them diagonally across a basket, or swirls them inside an elliptical basket as if they were the crest of a pine needle wave.

PRICES: $40–$1,000. No commissions. No catalog/brochure.

VISITORS: Not at the studio, but Clay manages the Carol Saunders Gallery (see following listing), where his work is on display.

Clay Burnette: Round platter. Longleaf pine needles. H. 3″; W. 14″; L. 16″.

COLUMBIA

Carol Saunders Gallery
CONTEMPORARY CRAFTS

Specializing in studio designer jewelry, Saunders Gallery also displays the work of a variety of nationally known artisans in all media. In jewelry, Ronald Pearson combines malachite and other semiprecious stones in delicate gold necklaces; Ken Loeber sculpts gold pins featuring unusually shaped natural pearls or crystalline gemstones. In textiles, Lee Malerich meticulously embroiders pieced fibers, turning them into abstract environments, and paper becomes an undulating three-dimensional art form in the hands of Nancy Albertson.

The gallery also shows the work of two very different but equally compelling basket makers. Clay Burnette forms fluid vessels by binding long-leaf pine needles with waxed linen, and Bryant Holsenbeck creates "Urban Baskets" from found objects. Sometimes resembling what your supermarket basket might look like after a nuclear attack, Bryant's work is nevertheless colorful and witty.

PRICES: $10–$2,000 (average, $50–$250). Accepts American Express, MasterCard, Visa.

OPEN: Mon.–Fri., 10 A.M.–5 P.M.; Sat., 11 A.M.–4 P.M. Not wheelchair accessible.

LOCATION: Central South Carolina. 927 Gervais Street, Columbia, SC 29201; 803-256-3046. Take I-20 or I-26 to I-126. Go right on Huger Street. Continue for about six blocks, then turn left on Gervais. The gallery will be on the north side of the street, one and a half blocks before the State Capitol Building.

MORE: Columbia's McKissick Museum has a crafts gallery with rotating exhibits that display Catawba Indian pottery, sea grass baskets, Southern quilts, wood carvings, and other regional crafts. It's located on the University of South Carolina campus. Take I-20 to Rte. 177; Rte. 177 becomes Bull Street. The museum is at the intersection of Bull and Pendleton streets.

Twenty miles southeast of Columbia, off Rte. 48, is Congaree Swamp National Monument, the last tract of virgin bottomland in the Southeast. Try the self-guided canoe trails, which wind in and out of this bluff-flanked bottomland.

EUTAWVILLE

Jeri Burdick
CERAMIC VESSELS

Like the South, Jeri's work combines the beauty of the earth with the jagged excesses of a neon society. "I use pretty common materials," Jeri says, "but I combine them in a unique expression influenced by my environment, especially the textures, shapes, light, and color I see in this part of South Carolina."

Forming sensuous sculptural vessels of earthenware and stoneware, Jeri adds tin-enamel glazes or pit-fires her work. Contrast, commentary, and highlights are sometimes provided by a row of leather buttons, the addition of fiber, or even bright crayon lines. Jeri also fashions impertinent ceramic cats that look like the product of an unholy alliance between modern architecture and a tomcat.

PRICES: $8–$2,500. Commissions accepted. No catalog/-brochure.

VISITORS: By appointment only.

LOCATION: South Carolina between Columbia and Charleston, about 13 miles northeast of I-26 near Lake Marion. P.O. Box 342, Eutawville, SC 29048; 803-492-7010. Directions will be provided when appointment to visit is made.

MORE: Jeri's work is also available through the Duke Street Gallery, Pendleton, SC (see Pendleton entry)

MT. PLEASANT

TRADITIONAL AFRICAN-AMERICAN
SWEET GRASS BASKETS

Using designs and techniques similar to those still found in West Africa, slaves at eighteenth-century Carolina rice plantations created large, flat, "fanner" baskets used to winnow rice seeds from the hull. Today their descendants use the same techniques, passed matrilineally from generation to generation, to create a variety of coiled baskets, from simple trivets and small bowls to intricate

Mt. Pleasant sweet grass basket stand. COURTESY MCKISSICK MUSEUM, UNIVERSITY OF SOUTH CAROLINA, COLUMBIA, S.C.

covered vessels and large baskets with lacy open-work.

This unique craft, which survived for decades, is now ironically threatened by encroaching housing developments and resort accommodations. Until recently the traditional materials were readily available in nearby marshes and swamps. Now concrete and blacktop cover much of this same area, and local basket makers must travel as far as Florida to harvest the necessary sweet grass and palmetto leaves. At least for the present, however, enough materials are gathered to continue production of these distinctive coil baskets.

Each basket begins with a bundle of sweet grass, tied in a knot. The ends are then wrapped (coiled) around the knot. A sharpened metal spoon handle is used to open a small hole in the grass through which a thin palmetto strip is pulled

to secure the coil. Grass is added and the coiling continues until the desired shape is completed. Sometimes bullrush is added for color or pine needles are incorporated as a contrasting design. Each basket, however, has characteristic curved coils dotted with diagonal palmetto strips.

Baskets sell from $5 to over $200 and can be purchased from family stands near Mt. Sterling or in downtown Charleston. Basket designs, shapes, and prices vary, so stop at several different stands to get a feeling for what is available. Note: Prices are firm and bargaining is considered an insult.

LOCATION: During most of the year, up to sixty family stands dot Rte. 17 from north of Charleston to Mt. Pleasant. In downtown Charleston, baskets are sold Mon.–Sat. from stands near the main post office at the corner of Meeting Street and Broad Street and near the Old Charleston Market at the corner of Market and State streets.

PAWLEYS ISLAND

Pawleys Island Hammock Co.
ROPE HAMMOCKS

Convert a couch potato! Next summer send the sofa out for cleaning, the television for repair. String up a Pawleys Island hammock between two trees, set out a pitcher of lemonade and an array of reading materials. This won't guarantee scintillating conversation, but at least your favorite "potato" will get an airing—unless, of course, you claim prior hammock rights.

First made in the late nineteenth century, the famous Pawleys Island rope hammocks are still entirely handmade by local craftspeople. The first one was made by Captain Joshua John Ward, a riverboat pilot who barged rice and supplies between nearby Georgetown and the great plantations of the South Carolina low country. His grass-filled mattress on the boat was uncomfortable and hot in the summer so he decided to make a cotton rope hammock to solve both problems. After trying several designs, he devised a style without knots and using wooden spreaders, still the way today's hammocks are made.

Travelers can visit the company's weaving room, where the hammocks are created from ropes of cotton or spun polyester spread with Carolina red oak stretcher bars. Not far away is the Original Hammock Shop, one of several outlets on the island. Hammocks range from a comfortable single-person 12-foot hammock ($103) to the deluxe "family" hammock, which is 60 by 84 inches ($128).

LOCATION: South Carolina coast, about 24 miles south of Myrtle Beach. The Original Hammock Shop, Highway 17 South, Pawleys Island, SC 29585; 803-237-3461. Take I-95 to the Manning (Rte. 521) exit, then Rte. 521 east to Georgetown. Go north on Rte. 17 to Pawleys Island.

MORE: The Original Hammock Shop is part of a complex of boutiques and restaurants. In fact, the town itself is a beach mall of shop-lined boardwalks, one of the oldest beach resorts on the East Coast. There is also a white sand beach (Litchfield) and an occasional moss-draped oak.

PENDLETON

Duke Street Gallery
CONTEMPORARY CRAFTS

Surrounding plantations as well as the entire town of Pendleton comprise one of the largest National Historic Districts in the country. It's a lovely area to explore, and the discoveries shouldn't stop until you've included the Duke Street Gallery in your tour. This gallery, owned by an art professor at nearby Clemson University, includes a good selection of work by South Carolina's most talented contemporary artists.

Hometown ceramist Michael Vatalaro produces functional plates that really deserve to be wall hangings. Using colorful glazes, swirls, and dots, he makes platter patterns that appear to have partially worn away, revealing compatible but clearly different designs underneath. Bob Chance, from nearby Greenville, produces raku work combining abstract expressionism and Southwestern design. Look also for Connie Lippert's subtle, woven wool rugs; Jeri Burdick's imaginative ceramic vessels; and the functional but exaggerated teapots by North Carolina's Kathy Triplett.

PRICES: $5–$500 (average, $25–$60). No credit cards.

OPEN: Tues.–Fri., 1–5 P.M.; Sat., 10 A.M.–5 P.M. Closed Christmas and July 4th. Wheelchair accessible.

LOCATION: Northwestern South Carolina, about 30 miles southwest of Greenville. 109 Duke Street, Pendleton, SC 29670; 803-646-3469. Take I-85 to the Rte. 76 (Anderson) exit, Rte. 76 north 7 miles, then bear right on Rte. 28 for almost 1 mile. Turn right on Duke Street. The gallery is just beyond the corner, marked with a wooden sign.

ST. HELENA ISLAND

Y. W. Bailey Museum
AFRICAN-AMERICAN SEA ISLAND CRAFTS

The Sea Islands stretch from Georgetown, South Carolina, to the Florida border. Isolated from the mainland until this century, the islands were once home to enormous rice and cotton plantations whose workers were African slaves. Because the slaves were numerous, constantly replenished by new arrivals, and virtually untouched by mainland white culture, many of their crafts and customs persisted and survived, even to the present day.

The Bailey Museum displays some of these crafts, including the famous Sea Island coiled baskets, quilts, and casting (shrimp) nets. There is also an exhibit of Mr. Sam Doyle's wonderful folk art, primitive paintings on scraps of tin and wood that capture St. Helena's past, people, and places. The museum is located on the grounds of the Penn Historic District, home of the Penn School, founded by northern missionaries in 1862 as the first school in the nation for freed salves.

OPEN: Mon.–Fri., 9 A.M.–5 P.M. Closed all major holidays. There is a museum shop, but it doesn't sell crafts. Free admission; donations accepted. Tours available. Wheelchair accessible.

LOCATION: Southeastern South Carolina, about 55 miles northeast of Savannah, Georgia. P.O. Box 126, Lands End Road, St. Helena Island, SC 29920; 803-838-2432 or 838-2235. Take I-95 to the Beaufort/Rte. 21 exit. Continue on Rte. 21 past Beaufort, across Lady's Island to St. Helena Island. Turn right on Lands End Road to the museum.

MORE: Several local craftspeople sell their traditional pieces. On St. Helena Island, Mrs. Lilly Singleton makes sweet grass baskets, and Mr. Rufus Fripp of Lady's Island creates the distinctive shrimp nets. Inquire at the museum for exact locations.

Experience Sea Island traditions and culture by attending the annual Penn Heritage Celebration. In addition to demonstrations of sweet grass basket weaving, net weaving, and boatbuilding, the event includes traditional Sea Island entertainment and mouth-watering cuisine such as oyster and shrimp pilau. The celebration is held the second weekend in Nov. Contact the museum for details.

TENNESSEE

If down-home country cooking, music, and crafts are your passion, make a beeline for Nashville, Tennessee. Start off the day with grits and red-eye gravy, make reservations for a night at the (new) Grand Ole Opry, then hop in your car to meet some of the region's talented traditional craftspeople.

Throughout the area, visitors will find crafts from twig furniture, handcrafted knives and guns, carved wood figures, and salt-glazed pottery to Cannon County's famous white oak baskets and oak chairs. Created for generations as subsistence barter items or as family necessities, these crafts owe their continued existence to collectors willing to pay up to 1,000 times what similar crafts cost in the 1920s and 1930s.

In the eastern part of the state, the Museum of Appalachia displays over 250,000 traditional and contemporary craft items, while area shops have more modest (but still intriguing) inventories. Contemporary crafts from unusually glazed ceramics and handmade briar pipes to whimsical textile sculptures and ornate forged-iron pieces can be found in Nashville's galleries and annual craft fairs, through individual artisans, or in Memphis's unique Ornamental Metal Museum.

BON AQUA

Al and Barbara Blumberg
Bon Aqua Pottery
SALT-GLAZED STONEWARE

Beginning in the twelfth century, potters used salt-glazes to produce a bright, hard surface that was popular in America during the eighteenth and nineteenth centuries. Al and Barbara now use this same process to create functional stoneware that ranges from light gray to creamy beige with cobalt blue designs.

Using their own clay blend, which includes primarily native Tennessee minerals, the Blumbergs make each piece individually. "We don't use molds or other shortcuts," Al says. "If there's a handle, we pull it by hand." Although they consult on shapes and designs, Al forms each pot and Barbara decorates them freehand. The cobalt designs include a heart, flower, or bird on smaller pieces, with elaborate lions, rabbits, and other animals on the large crocks. All are lined with Albany-slip glaze and are safe for use with all foods. In addition to these production items, the Blumbergs occasionally make face jugs, wonderful bulbous faces of people or animals complete with shiny white procelain teeth and eyes.

PRICES: $6.50–$78. No commissions. For the catalog/brochure, send an SASE to Bon Aqua Pottery, Rte. 1, Box 369-10, Bon Aqua, TN 37025.

VISITORS: No.

MORE: A good selection of Bon Aqua Pottery can be seen 12 miles east of Nashville at the Hermitage (4580 Rachel's Lane, Hermitage, TN 37076-1331; 615-889-2941), and, outside of Memphis, at Fields of Clover (2726 Bartlett Boulevard, Bartlett, TN 38134; 901-338-1810).

BYBEE

Akira Blount
TEXTILE SCULPTURES

Always wanted your own court jester, someone to be on call for a wry comment here, a tambourine tap there? Or perhaps you'd prefer a jovial eighteenth-century charwoman, always ready to sweep the floor, wash your clothes, and hand out friendly advice? Akira Blount has just what you need, exquisitely rendered 16-to-36-inch-tall soft-sculpture human forms who sit decoratively but decorously until you need them.

Using natural fabrics, found objects, and antique remnants, Akira creates more than just soft dolls, appropriately dressed. She endows them with personality. In one sculpture, a young turn-of-

Akira Blount: Fabric soft sculpture.

the-century womans grasps a basket (you can almost smell the fresh bread inside), and holds her hat against what seems to be a quickening wind. She looks slightly bemused, as if life is always a bit breezy for her.

Akira's mother and grandmother introduced her to dolls and taught her sewing and embroidery. But Akira's soft friends are her own imaginative creations, with personas flexible enough for purchasers to see in them what they wish.

PRICES: $150–$2,000. Commissions accepted. The price list is free; Polaroids are $1 each, refundable upon purchase.

VISITORS: Yes.

LOCATIONS: Eastern Tennessee. (NOTE: There is also a Bybee in central Tennessee; do not confuse the two.) Rte. 1, Box 334A, Bybee, TN 37719; 615-625-1160. "Finding me is an adventure in itself. Stop in Newport, Tennessee, off I-40, and call for directions."

CANNON COUNTY

A Directory of Folk Artists and Craftsmen

The preface to this directory says, "Generations of folk artists and craftsmen of Cannon County have hauled their handmade rockers, chairs, and baskets to markets across the U.S.A. This booklet invites you to come into their workshops and homeplaces in beautiful Cannon County, see their skilled hands at work, and take home with you a unique experience and a work of art."

Sponsored by the local Rural Area Development Committee, this thirty-page directory lists over sixty craftspeople: basket makers, quilters, woodcrafters, and other artisans who welcome visitors. A foreword provides insight into what it was like to be a craftsperson in the 1920s and 1930s, an afterword discusses the newcomers who have adopted these crafts.

To get a copy of this directory, send $3 to RAD Crafts Project, Rte. 1, Box 25, Bradyville, TN 37026; or call Arlin Hastings at 615-765-5682 for more information.

(NOTE: Cannon County is located in central Tennessee, southeast of Nashville.)

GATLINBURG

Arrowcraft Shop
TRADITIONAL AND CONTEMPORARY CRAFTS

Located at the northern entrance to the Great Smoky Mountains National Park, Gatlinburg is a popular resort area and a center for Southern Highlands handicrafts. The town owes its importance as a craft community to a craft show that originated in 1937 and to the Arrowmont School of Arts & Crafts, whose outstanding programs have drawn students here from throughout the country.

Visitors face the problem of how to determine which of the over fifty craft shops sell top-quality crafts rather than tacky souvenirs. The best suggestion is to visit the Arrowcraft Shop, which offers the work of over 300 regional craftspeople. Although it sells everything from honeysuckle brooms to ceramics and jewelry, Arrowcraft has been known since 1926 for its outstanding hand-loomed textiles. Working under the shop's weaving designer, Nella Hill, Arrowcraft's cottage weavers create table linens and scarves, afghans and blankets. Particularly attractive are tablecloths in the Whig Rose pattern and the Miss Olivia place mats.

PRICES: $2.50–$1,900 (average, $5–$250). Accepts Master-Card, Visa. Send $1.50 for the catalog, with color illustrations.

OPEN: Apr.–Nov., daily, 8 A.M.–8 P.M.; Dec.–March, daily, 8 A.M.–5 P.M. Closed Thanksgiving, Christmas, and New Year's. Wheelchair accessible.

LOCATION: Southeastern Tennessee. 576 Parkway, P.O. Box 567, Gatlinburg, TN 37738; 615-436-4604. The shop is located on the main street of Gatlinburg, Rte. 441.

MORE: After visiting Arrowcraft, stop by the Arrowmont School's gallery, located next door at 556 Parkway, Gatlinburg; 615-436-5860. The gallery is open Mon.–Sat., 8:30 A.M.–4:30 P.M.

GREENBRIER

Roy K. Pace
HANDCARVED WOODEN FIGURES

Carving human figures is an Appalachian tradition, and Roy is one of the masters. Each figure, from 9 inches to 5 feet tall, is carved from native Middle Tennessee woods such as yellow pine or mulberry, then finished either naturally or with watercolor. Roy's "friends," as he calls his figures, depict people from all walks of life: farmer, logger, sea captain, banjo player, even cowboys, Indians, and historical figures. On many of them, Roy adds special details. A blacksmith works at his forge, a worker carries his lunch pail, and Santa Claus has a doll sticking out of a coat pocket.

Roy is a retired construction worker and third-generation woodworker. One grandfather was a cabinetmaker, the other a logger. His father was also a cabinetmaker and carpenter by trade. But it wasn't until Christmas 1973, when Roy's son gave him a book on wood carving, that Roy tried his own hand at this traditional Appalachian craft. Now he carves over 150 different figures, adding more each year.

PRICES: $125–$1,150. Commissions accepted. No catalog/ brochures.

VISITORS: Yes.

LOCATION: 20 miles north of Nashville. Old Greenbrier Pike, R #4, Box 112, Greenbrier, TN 37073; 615-643-7967. Take I-65 to Hendersonville, then go west on Rte. 41. Roy's place is directly across the railroad tracks from the sawmill.

MORE: Roy's work is also available through the Tennessee State Museum Gift Shop, Polk Building, Nashville, Tennessee, and the Rock Castle Visitor's Center, Hendersonville, Tennessee.

JONESBOROUGH

Curtis Ray Buchanan
WINDSOR CHAIRS

Airy grace and heirloom durability are the distinctive features of the best Windsor chairs. "The durability," Curtis says, "comes from using green, unseasoned wood. As the wood dries, its natural contraction and expansion binds the joints. My chairs come with a lifetime guarantee to outlast either myself or the original owner." Working with the same materials, tools, and techniques used at the height of Windsor chair popularity in the eighteenth century, Curtis does everything himself, from cutting down the tree to applying the final coat of paint.

"The Windsor has always been made of several different woods," he explains, "so that is how I make mine. For the seats, I use two-inch pine planks carved for real comfort. Maple is best for the turnings since it allows good detail, and I use oak, hickory, or ash for the spindles and backs." In addition to making a variety of chair styles, Curtis also makes a continuous-arm settee, a courting bench, and even a chair with a writing arm.

Recently he completed four chairs commissioned for Thomas Jefferson's home in Monticello. "They're painted dark green and will be used in the garden's gazebo," Curtis says proudly. He is happy to accept special orders. "If you want one with different proportions," he notes, "or some extra detail work, like carved knuckles on the handhold, I'd be happy to make it."

PRICES: $500–$1,500. Commissions accepted. Send $2 and an SASE for the catalog/brochure.

VISITORS: Yes.

LOCATION: Eastern Tennessee. 208 East Main Street, Jonesborough, TN 37659; 615-753-5160. From I-81, take I-181 south to Johnson City, then Rte. 11E west to Jonesborough. Go left at the traffic light onto Boone Street, then left at the next stop sign onto Main Street. The house is the second on the right.

LIBERTY

Gregory K. Caffy
TWIG FURNITURE

Gregory's business card lists him as "Puppeteer, Artist, Craftsman, Actor, Teacher," and indeed his first love is performing with the puppets he makes. "But I don't sell them," he says. "I dislike seeing amateurs using my puppets and calling themselves puppeteers when all they can do is *shake* a puppet." Gregory does, however, sell the twig furniture he makes.

Taking advantage of the bends and forks that nature bestows on branches, Gregory combines them into rustic armchairs and small tables.

Gathering the maple, oak, and hickory limbs on his own property is part of the fun. "Making furniture," he admits, "is another excuse to wander around in the woods." Greg's living conditions are as rustic as his furniture, with no public utilities or running water. But he does keep an "office" a mile down the road with a telephone and answering machine.

PRICES: $50–$650. Commissions accepted, "but not repetitive production of the same chair over and over." No catalog/brochure.

VISITORS: Yes. By appointment.

LOCATION: About 60 miles east of Nashville and 15 miles north of I-40. Rte. 1, Box 107, Liberty, TN 37095; 615-563-8450 (answering machine only). "Because my place is so remote, I make appointments, a meeting place, then drive folks in."

MORE: Gregory's furniture can also be seen at Harold's Place, 204 East Main Street, Woodbury, TN 37190.

MEMPHIS

National Ornamental Metal Museum

Sitting on a bluff above the Mississippi River is an unusual museum with its own smithy, artist-in-residence, and annual "Repair Days." Opened in 1979, the museum exhibits fine metalwork from the past as well as pieces by contemporary craftspeople. Although the emphasis is on forged ironwork, exhibits also include copper catfish weathervanes, bronze sculptures, and one-of-a-kind jewelry.

In the smithy, visitors can watch daily demonstrations by the artist-in-residence, then purchase his work in the museum shop. Outside, guests can wander in the sculpture garden, rest on benches held up by cast-iron fish, or stand in a nineteenth-century pavilion to see a view once described by Mark Twain as "the finest between Cairo and New Orleans."

Each fall the museum sponsors Repair Days, a two-day event when the public is encouraged to bring in any metal object that needs repair work. For a small fee, the museum offers welding, soldering, retinning of copper cookware, and sharpening of everything from sewing scissors to lawnmower blades.

OPEN: Tues.–Sat., 10 A.M.–5 P.M.; Sun. noon–5 P.M. Closed major holidays. Admission is $1.50 for adults, $1 for seniors, 75¢ for children. Free admission Wed., 10 A.M.–noon. Tours available. First-floor galleries, smithy, and grounds are wheelchair accessible. The museum shop features items made in the smithy, jewelry, and other metalwork.

LOCATION: 374 West California Avenue, Memphis, TN 38106; 901-774-6380. From I-55 north, take the Delaware exit (12-C). Delaware curves under I-55 and dead-ends two blocks south at California. Turn right. The museum is next to the river, across from DeSoto Park.

MORE: During Repair Days, the work of a master smith is exhibited. Call museum for details and specific dates.

MURFREESBORO

Alvin and Trevle Wood
TRADITIONAL WHITE OAK BASKETS

As fourth-generation basket makers, Alvin and Trevle remember going into the woods with their grandparents to select and cut white oak trees. "We'd help split the tree," Alvin recalls, "begin whittling hoops, splints, and ribs, and then the weaving began. Someone would usually turn on the radio and we'd listen to George Burns and Gracie Allen while we weaved and visited. There were many times when there were no jobs or money, so we traded baskets at the country store for groceries and necessities."

Although Alvin and Trevle began basketmaking as children, they went on to other careers: Alvin as a builder and brickmason, Trevle as a nurse. "But after we sent our three daughters through college," Trevle says, "we both started working full-time on our baskets. In a time when life is so rushed, we find it very relaxing to sit and weave a basket." The Woods specialize in Appalachian egg baskets, including miniature ones from 1½ to 3 inches in diameter. They also make baskets to hold casserole dishes or pie plates, perfect for potluck dinners.

PRICES: $15–$300. Commissions accepted. Send an SASE for their information sheet.

VISITORS: Yes.

LOCATION: About 20 miles southeast of Nashville. 2415 East Main Street, Murfreesboro, TN 37130; 615-895-0391. From I-24, exit on Rte. 96 (Franklin Road). Follow Franklin, then turn right on Broad. Turn left onto Mercury, which then becomes East Main.

NASHVILLE

The American Artisan
CONTEMPORARY CRAFTS

Nashville may be the headquarters of the Opry and country music, but you won't know it in this sophisticated gallery. With every craft medium represented, there is something here for every taste. Of particular note is the work of Nashville ceramist John Cummings and his *sang-de-boeuf* (oxblood) glazes. Developed during China's Sung dynasty and rarely used today, this glossy, bright red glaze is particularly effective as it drips over John's geometrically patterned black-and-white vases.

PRICES: $15–$1,000 (average, $30–$300). Accepts American Express, MasterCard, Visa.

OPEN: Mon.–Sat., 10 A.M.–6 P.M.. Closed Christmas, New Year's Day, and July 4th. Wheelchair accessible.

LOCATION: 4231 Harding Road, Nashville, TN 37205; 615-298-4691. Take I-440 to the West End Avenue exit. Go south on West End, which becomes Harding Road, for 1.5 miles. The gallery is on the left, across from St. Thomas Hospital.

NASHVILLE

Tennessee Spring Crafts Fair
Tennessee Fall Crafts Fair

Both of these excellent fairs benefit the Tennessee Artist-Craftsmen's Association, the state's primary craft support and network organization. The Tennessee Spring Crafts Fair showcases over 150 of the state's top craftspeople. Later in the year, artisans from around the country are invited to the Tennessee Fall Crafts Fair, where visitors will find everything from handmade briar pipes to avant-garde jewelry. Both fairs have ongoing craft demonstrations and live music. The spring fair also offers a variety of ethnic food and the Kids' Tent, where children can try their own hand at a variety of crafts.

SPRING FAIR: First full weekend in May. Free admission. Located in Centennial Park, Nashville, on the lawn in front of the Parthenon replica. Take I-440 to exit 1 (Rte. 70S, West End). Proceed east about five blocks on West End Avenue. Centennial Park is on the left, across from Holiday Inn Vanderbilt.

FALL FAIR: Late Oct./early Nov. Admission is $3.50 for adults, $3 for seniors, children under 12 free. Located in the Nashville Convention Center, 600 Commerce Street, Nashville. Take I-40 to exit 209 (Broadway). Go east on Broadway about five blocks to 7th Avenue North, left on 7th for one block, then right on Commerce. The entrance to the Convention Center is on the right, just beyond the Stouffer Hotel entrance.

For more information on either fair contact the Tennessee Artist-Craftsmen's Association, P.O. Box 120066, Nashville, TN 37212; 615-382-2502.

NORRIS

Museum of Appalachia
TRADITIONAL APPALACHIAN CRAFTS

"**W**hen I was quite young, my grandfather gave my brother and me some of his pioneer relics. He said that sometime we ought to start a little museum of these 'old-timey things.' So I did," says John Rice Irwin, founder and operator of this museum, which is actually a re-created mountain village with over thirty-five structures. Crafts buffs will be most interested in the main display building, which exhibits over 250,000 items from past and present-day Appalachia. Also worth seeing is the Craft & Gift Shop, which sells the work of 150 local craftspeople.

OPEN: Daily, during daylight hours. Admission is $4 for adults, $2 for children 6–12, children under 6 free. Wheelchair accessible, except for some of the cabins.

LOCATION: 16 miles north of Knoxville. Box 359, Norris, TN 37828; 615-494-7680. From I-75 north, take exit 122 and follow the signs.

RUGBY

Rugby Commissary
TRADITIONAL APPALACHIAN CRAFTS

Visionaries often base their dreams on faulty logic, and Thomas Hughes was no exception. Concerned about British inheritance law, under which only eldest sons could inherit, leaving younger sons of the gentry with little money and few socially acceptable professions, Hughes wanted to help. His solution? Establish a town in Tennessee where scions of the wealthy could follow manual and agricultural trades. Predictably, these transplanted young men preferred cultural and recreational activities to manual labor, and another nineteenth-century utopia withered.

What remains are charming Victorian buildings, gardens, and a "gentlemen's swimming hole." The reconstructed general store now houses Rugby Commissary, an Appalachian crafts shop. Here, visitors can purchase traditional slatback or woven hickoryback chairs made by Willie Doss, a fourth-generation chair maker. There are also quilts by Ola Mae Ledbetter, wooden kitchen spoons by Karen Davis, and Daron Douglas's handwoven rugs. If you're musically inclined, look for Milford Blevins's walnut-and-maple dulcimers or buy your children one of his folk toys.

PRICES: $1–$400 (average, $10–$25). Accepts MasterCard, Visa.

OPEN: March–Dec., Mon.–Sat., 10 A.M.–6 P.M.; Sun., noon–6 P.M. Open weekends in Jan. & Feb. Closed Thanksgiving, Christmas, and New Years' Day. Wheelchair accessible.

LOCATION: Eastern Tennessee, about 70 miles northwest of Knoxville. P.O. Box 8, Rugby, TN 37733; 615-628-5166. From I-75, take Rte. 63 west to Rte. 27. Follow Rte. 27 south to Elgin, then Rte. 52 west to Rugby. From I-40, take Rte. 27 north to Elgin, then Rte. 52 west to Rugby.

MORE: Overnight guests can stay in one of two historic homes. Newbury House Inn, the colony's first boardinghouse, charges $47 per night for a double (in 1882 it cost $4.50–$6.50 a week). Pioneer Cottage, Rugby's first frame house, can be rented in its entirety for $56 a night. For reservations call 615-628-2441 or 615-628-2269.

SMITHVILLE

Appalachian Center for Crafts Gallery
TRADITIONAL AND CONTEMPORARY APPALACHIAN CRAFTS

This gallery is a one-stop introduction to the finest in Appalachian crafts. Part of a center that also offers craft classes and degree programs, the gallery represents craftspeople from throughout the thirteen-state Appalachian region. For sale are the best in traditional and contemporary wood, metal, fiber, clay, and glass. And they won't break your budget!

If you're looking for traditional crafts, consider the array of colorful, finely stitched quilts or the split white oak baskets of Estel Youngblood, a third-generation basket maker. More interested in contemporary work? Ask to see Curtis and Susan Benzle's dramatic, colored-clay jewelry or Curtiss Brock's highly prized blown glass. In either case, a decided plus in this gallery are the salespeople: friendly, knowledgeable folks who know how to assist you and when to leave you alone.

Located in the Upper Cumberland Mountains, the campus is in a wooded area on Center Hill Lake. The spacious and well-lighted gallery also has two exhibition spaces that feature crafts of national, regional, and historic interest.

PRICES: $2–$800. Accepts MasterCard, Visa.

OPEN: Daily, 9 A.M.–5 P.M. Closed Thanksgiving, Christmas week, and two days at the end of June for inventory. Wheelchair accessible.

LOCATION: About 75 miles east of Nashville, 120 miles west of Knoxville. Rte. 3, Box 430, Smithville, TN 37166; 615-597-6801. From I-40, take Rte. 56 south. Turn into the Crafts Center driveway on the south side of Hurricane Bridge. Follow driveway for 1 mile to the parking lot. The gallery is in the administration building.

SMITHVILLE

Josie Ann Jones
TRADITIONAL WHITE OAK BASKETS

While in Smithville stop by Josie's home to watch her make a basket. The fourth-generation basket maker in her family, she learned to make them by watching her mother. For over fifty years, Josie has been cutting down her own trees, splitting them into strips, then smoothing, scraping, and trimming the pieces until they're ready for weaving. Nice baskets at a very reasonable price.

PRICES: $40–$65. No commissions. No catalog/brochure.

VISITORS: Yes. But call for an appointment first.

LOCATION: Downtown Smithville. 733 West Main Street, Smithville, TN 37166; 615-597-1525. From I-40, take Rte. 56 straight into Smithville.

SNEEDVILLE

Rick Stewart
COOPERED BUCKETS AND CHURNS

Rick Stewart is probably the only craftsman in Tennessee who has a two-sided business card with one side in English, one in Japanese. A cooper who makes traditional Appalachian buckets, churns, and pitchers, Rick visited Japan in 1988 to study Japanese cooperage techniques. "We do things both alike and differently," Rick says. "We both make wood barrels and other items without any nails or glue, but there are important differences. The main one is shape. In Appalachia we want our pieces perfectly round, in Japan they make saki kegs and other items egg-shaped, but never round. It's a matter of tradition.

"My ancestors came to Tennessee from Scotland in the late 1700s," Rick continues. "I'm a fifth-generation cooper, and the items I make are identical to those made by my great-great-grandfather. Like them, I begin by choosing my own cedar and white oak trees, split the wood, then let it air-dry for a year. To make a bucket, I shape and taper the staves, using instinct to make them fit together perfectly. Then I groove and slide in the bottom, slip over bands of fresh white oak to bind the bucket, then add a handle."

One of only five coopers still practicing these skills in the United States, Rick is pleased that customers consider his items decorative. "After the 1920s and 1930s," he says, "coopered items were replaced by manufactured containers and *no one* churns their own butter anymore. But you could. All my pieces are still fully functional."

PRICES: $5–$125. Commissions accepted. Send an SASE for his catalog/brochure.

VISITORS: Yes.

LOCATION: Northeastern Tennessee, about 55 miles west of Kingsport, Rte. 1, Box 101, Sneedville, TN 37869; 615-733-2617. Take I-81 to the Rte. 25E exit (near Witt). Go north on Rte. 25E to Bead Station, left on Rte. 11W to Rte. 33, right on Rte. 33 to Sneedville. "Then just stop and ask anyone, they'll tell you how to find my place."

WOODBURY

Harold E. Woodward
KNIVES, SWORDS, AND GUN ENGRAVING

Harold couldn't afford to buy an authentic bowie knife, so he made one. Then he made more. It developed into a hobby, then a business. Now he is a member of the prestigious International Knifemakers Guild. True works of art, his knives are finely crafted, with gleaming blades, silver spacers, and custom-carved finger grooves on graceful handles. Some handles are made from warthog or walrus tusk, sambar staghorn or mastadon ivory, others from ebony, rosewood, or Jamaican dogwood.

A paraplegic due to a motorcycle accident, Harold was once a disc jockey, a St. Louis policeman, and a toolmaker. Now, in addition to hunting knives, he also makes fighting knives and swords. "I make real fighting weapons," Harold says, "not those cheap, imported imitations. Mine could really lop off a head or a limb." But generally they are ordered by people who reenact famous sword fights or battles. Recently Harold created an exact replica of Henry V's battle sword, including a handle of red leather wrapped with sterling silver wire.

Harold also engraves firearms, adding delicate leaves and sworls to the barrel of a pearl-handled Smith & Wesson automatic. But he isn't always in his shop making knives or engraving. "One thing that gets me out of here," he says, "is an opportu-

nity to go groundhog hunting. I can't resist trying to blow them off a nearby hillside!"

PRICES: $150+. Commissions accepted. His catalog/brochure costs $1.

VISITORS: Yes.

LOCATION: Central Tennessee, about 50 miles southeast of Nashville. Harold's Place, 204 East Main, Woodbury, TN 37190; 615-563-2229. Take I-40 to Murfreesboro, then Rte. 70S to Woodbury.

MORE: Harold also owns a shop that is a clearinghouse for local folk art and furniture.

WOODBURY

Ida Pearl Davis
Thelma Hibdon
WHITE OAK SPLIT BASKETS

If Cannon County, known as the "basket capital of the country," were ever to crown a basket queen, it would surely be Ida Pearl Davis of Woodbury. For over fifty years Ida's baskets have gained her recognition, from the blue ribbon she won at a 1938 county fair to her selection as a craft demonstrator at the Smithsonian's 20th Annual Festival of American Folklife in 1986. Although her baskets are now bought by collectors, they were born of necessity.

"I can trace basketmaking in my family back to my great-grandmother Adaline Barrett," Ida says. "But they made rough-looking baskets. They were ugly, looked like an old tooth sticking out. I learned from mammy. She and I, pappy and my brother, we'd go to the woods to look for poles [trees]. Sometimes we'd have to walk ten or twelve miles across hills and hollers to find the right one. We'd cut it down, bust it into slats right there, and make our splits.

"I made my first basket when I was six or seven years old. Baskets were all we had for survival. I remember my first basket was a little round egg basket. I traded it at the store for a tobaggan cap with a tassle. We traded baskets to get sugar, flour, coffee, shoes, cooking oil, thick domestic cloth, and dye to make clothes.

"The least the market gave us was thirty to forty cents a basket, that was in the 1930s. By the late 1940s, I got up to a dollar-fifty. But we didn't get paid in cash, just trade. We also took our baskets around to people's homes, trading them for meat,

Ida Pearl David and Thelma Hibdon: White oak split baskets, bushel (left) and peck (right). GARY GOOD

used clothes, turnips, anything we could get to eat or wear."

In later years Ida laid aside her basketmaking to work in a local textile plant hemming shirts but resumed her craft in the 1970s. Her daughter, Thelma Hibdon, now helps out. "Mostly I just finish up what mama starts," Thelma says. "She shapes the splits, starts a basket, adds all the ribs, then I just finish weaving them. Mama never taught us children to make baskets. She told us she'd often been made to feel ashamed of her basketmaking and she didn't want people to make fun of us. People aren't handing down this knowledge to their kids. There won't be families of basketmakers any more, just folks who learn it at craft classes.

"So I can't whittle the splits right. It takes a lot of talent. Sometimes they're brittle and will break, or so hard you can't hardly whittle it at all. Other times they're locky, your knife just jumps along; or they're eaty, that's when your knife just keeps on going down into the wood."

PRICES: $125–$400. Free price list.

VISITORS: Yes.

LOCATION: About 50 miles southeast of Nashville. Rte. 2, Box 167, Woodbury, TN 37190; 615-563-5445. Take I-24 to the Murfreesboro exit, then Rte. 70S 10 miles past Woodbury to Rte. 146. Go left (north) on Rte. 145; the house is the first one on the left.

WOODBURY

Lonnie "Don" Davis
Hoyte "Jake" Davis
TRADITIONAL OAK AND MAPLE CHAIRS

"Chairmaking has been our way of life for generations," says Don Davis. Although Don and his brother Jake have held other jobs, both started making chairs as children and now concentrate full-time on their craft. Jake produces swings, rockers, ladderback chairs, and various stools. Don adds children's and dining room chairs and footstools. "I cut the trees myself," Jake says, "then saw them at my own mill. I use either my own patterns or a customer's. And I guarantee them for comfort, durability, and appearance."

Don makes chairs the way his father and grandfather did. "I use the same primitive machinery," he explains. "Much of it isn't commercially available, so I make it myself from parts I pick up. You know, making chairs used to be a real necessity. When I was a young man, factory work just wasn't available. This was the only way I could support my family." Now Jake and Don continue a family tradition because they love the work and there is great demand. "Even from the governor," Jake notes. "In 1986, Governor Lamar asked us to make rocking chairs for a special state celebration."

PRICES: Don, $8–$65; Jake, $10–$60. Don accepts commissions; Jake doesn't. No catalog/brochure.

VISITORS: Yes.

LOCATION: About 50 miles southeast of Nashville.
   Don Davis, Rte. 2, Box 151, Woodbury, TN 37190; 615-563-4564. From Woodbury, go 8 miles east on Rte. 70S, turn left onto Rte. 146. Go 1.25 miles; there is a sign in the yard.
   Jake Davis, Rte. 2, Box 156, Woodbury, TN 37190; 615-563-4498. From Woodbury, go 8 miles east on Rte. 70S, turn left onto Rte. 146. Go 2 miles, then turn left on Todd Road. The house is the first one on the right.

MORE: Don and Jake's sister, Josie Ann Jones, is also a craftsperson. See her entry under Smithville, Tennessee.

GREAT LAKES

   Dangling like jewels surrounding a watery torso, the Great Lakes states glitter with recreational possibilities, luring travelers with their sparkling metropolitan areas. Less well known are the talented artisans who exhibit in regional galleries or permit customers to visit their studios. Although there are some outstanding contemporary craftspeople in each state, the primary craft attractions are traditional items created by Native Americans or by the descendants of immigrant populations who settled in the region's industrial centers, lumber camps, and dairylands. Of particular note are Scandinavian and East European craft legacies, as well as a smattering of traditional Amish, American colonial, and nineteenth-century work. For purposes of this book, Minnesota, admittedly a Great Lakes state, is included in the western edition under Mid-America.

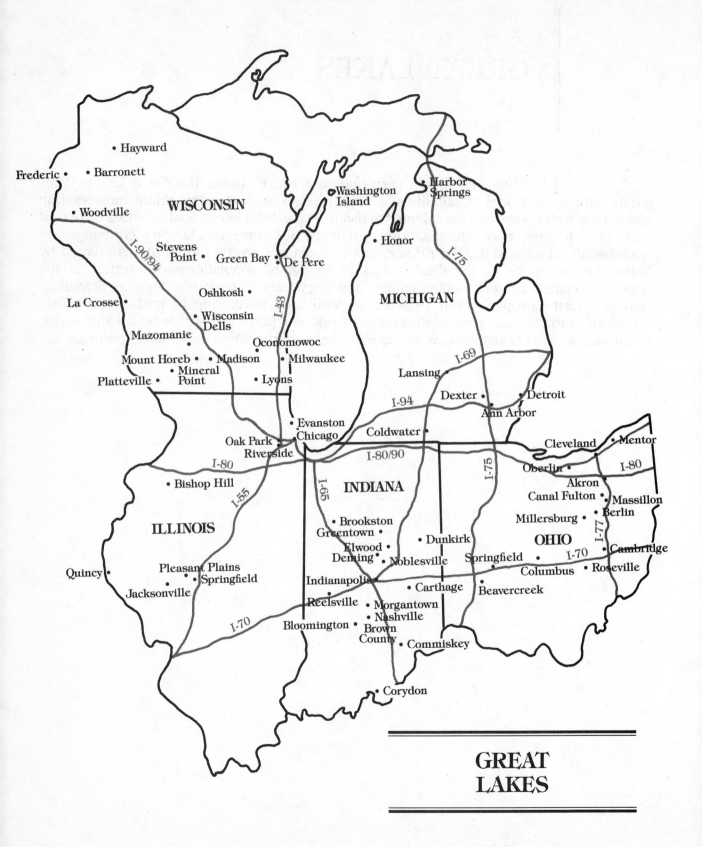

GREAT LAKES

ILLINOIS

If you equate Illinois only with Chicago, let crafts draw you out of the state's megalopolis. Set your course for central and western Illinois to see fantasy papercuttings, copperware, and Bishop Hill Colony crafts, or to attend traditional craft festivals in Pleasant Plains. In the Chicago area, choose between top-notch contemporary galleries, glasswork, forged-iron pieces, reproduction canoes, a multiethnic festival in nearby Evanston, or a nostalgic look at architectural and functional crafts by Frank Lloyd Wright.

BISHOP HILL

Bishop Hill Heritage Museum
COLONY FURNITURE AND TEXTILES

Bishop Hill Colony was a short-lived utopian experiment by Swedish immigrants seeking religious freedom. Founded by Erik Jansson in 1846, it flourished briefly, but dissolved in 1861 after Jansson's murder and increasing dissension among the remaining trustees. Colonists earned 40 percent of their income by selling crafts, including tin-, silver-, gold-, and blacksmithing products; furniture; and textiles.

Some of these crafts are displayed in the Steeple Building, one of the original colony structures. The most interesting items on exhibit are Bishop Hill furniture and textiles. Colony furniture, like Shaker work, emphasized simple, functional lines. To the careful observer, obvious differences include leg detailing and the use of surface embellishments such as paint which resembles fancy graining. Colony textiles on display include woven rag rugs in soft grays and browns, and linen tablecloths and runners.

OPEN: Daily, 9 A.M.–5 P.M. Closed Thanksgiving, Christmas, and New Year's Day. The museum shop offers local crafts.

Admission is $1.50 for adults, $1 for seniors, 50¢ for children. Wheelchair accessible on the first floor only.

LOCATION: Northwestern Illinois, about 50 miles northwest of Peoria. Bishop Hill Heritage Association, Bishop Hill Road, P.O. Box 1853, Bishop Hill, IL 61419; 309-927-3899. Take I-74 to Rte. 17 (north of Galesburg), Rte. 17 east to the junction with Rte. 34, Rte. 34 east several miles to the Bishop Hill turnoff on the left.

CHICAGO

Chiaroscuro
CONTEMPORARY CRAFTS

Chiaroscuro, named for the Italian word referring to the interplay of light and dark in works of art, is a relatively new gallery in Chicago's artsy River North area. "Our main interests," says Ronna Isaacs, gallery co-owner and former archivist for Chicago's Museum of Contemporary Art, "are to introduce neophyte collectors to emerging artists and to create a nonintimidating and affordable gallery experience."

Most appealing are the gallery's functional crafts made to sit on, dress in, or eat from. Starting with whimsical furniture, look for Craig and Judy Carey's fishy chairs and bunny settees. The chair has a brown wormholed seat, seaweed-colored arms and braces, a ravenous blue fish on the back, and squiggly blue worms dangling everywhere. Suspended carrots mark another Carey creation. This time it's a settee with three huge white rabbits on the back.

In the nonfunctional category, don't miss James Van Deurzen's fluid glass sculptures or Jill Bosckay's brightly colored vessels made from intersecting ceramic planes posed atop high-tech metal legs. In glass, look at (and inside of) James Van Deurzen's sculptural pieces.

PRICES: $20–$650 (average, $30–$70). Accepts American Express, MasterCard, Visa.

OPEN: Mon.–Sat., 10 A.M.–5:30 P.M. Closed all legal holidays. Not wheelchair accessible.

LOCATION: River North gallery area. 750 North Orleans, Chicago, IL 60610; 312-988-9253. From downtown Chicago, take Michigan Avenue north to Chicago Avenue. Go west down Chicago Avenue to Orleans Street. The gallery is on the southwest corner.

CHICAGO

Ralph C. Frese
BLACKSMITHING, CANOES

Ralph C. Frese's business card reads "Blacksmithing, Welding, Canoe Builder, Environmentalist, Historian, Lecturer." Although he's a master at all six, it's the last two that make a visit to his shop memorable. If you ask him a question about his work, any question, you're likely to receive a full introduction to its history and development. "I *want* customers to ask questions," Ralph says, "about the trade of blacksmithing, about the heritage of the canoe, about the traditions and fabrication of any item I make."

A fourth-generation blacksmith, Ralph creates candlesticks and fireplace tools and particularly delights in making historic reproductions. With a national reputation for authenticity, Ralph's commission work has included a replica of a 1740 French cannon for Fort de Chartres, French military "pole arms" for a fife and drums corps, and a wrought iron throne for a theater production of *St. Joan.*

Some customers, however, are more interested in Ralph's *voyageur* canoes, reproductions of boats once used by French-Canadian fur traders. "Through my involvement in Scouting I decided it would be fun to re-create these canoes," Ralph explains. "So in 1956 I started experimenting with fiberglass. I eventually devised a way to simulate the original birch bark construction. I make the frames from wood and lash the joints with plastic rope in the same way vines and roots were once used. A fiberglass hull is added, then covered with fabric resembling birch bark. To complete the illusion, I add daubs of real pitch."

Popular with outdoor enthusiasts, Ralph's canoes also star in historic reenactments. Two were used in the 300th anniversary celebration of Joliet and Marquette's discovery of Illinois, while eight others had paddle-on parts in the television miniseries "Centennial."

PRICES: Blacksmith items, $1 and up; canoes, $1,681–$10,769; history lessons, free. Commissions accepted. Send an SASE for his catalog/brochure.

VISITORS: Yes. Mon.–Sat., 9 A.M.–5 P.M.

LOCATION: Portage Park area of Chicago. 4019 North Narragansett Avenue, Chicago, IL 60634; 312-777-1489. Take I-90 to the Irving Park Road exit. Go west on Irving Park for 3 miles to the intersection with Narragansett Avenue. Turn right; the shop is 183.5 feet down on the right (look for canoes out front).

CHICAGO

Illinois Artisans Shop
CONTEMPORARY AND TRADITIONAL CRAFTS

The fog may come in on little cat feet, but this shop pounces like a puma, dazzling by design, captivating through quality. Now representing over 350 Illinois artisans, the gallery juries in an additional fifty to seventy craftspeople each year. Concerned that the sheer numbers imply a ragtag conglomeration of mediocrity? Don't be. There's a piece of fine workmanship here for every pocketbook—and almost every taste.

Among the best? Lisa Nelson's wall hangings made from canvas strips wrapped in silk, cotton, wool, and metallic fibers; Char Wiss's contemporary coiled baskets; rough stoneware vessels with smooth, lacquered surfaces by Sarah Jo Hermanson; and Judy Walter's vibrant quilts featuring vel-vet-and-satin highlights and subtle bas-relief stitchery.

Each month the shop sponsors a day of craft demonstrations featuring six or more artisans working in a particular medium or theme. Visitors may find demonstrations of paper arts, folk and ethnic weaving, jewelrymaking, or perhaps crafts that incorporate Illinois bird motifs.

PRICES: 90¢–$5,000 (average, $35–$200). Accepts American Express, MasterCard, Visa.

OPEN: Mon.–Fri., 9 A.M.–5 P.M. Closed all holidays. Wheelchair accessible.

LOCATION: State of Illinois Center. 100 West Randolph Street, Chicago, IL 60601; 312-917-5321. The State of Illinois Center, a spectacular glass building, is in the heart of Chicago's Loop.

Ken Loeber: Brooch. Forged and fabricated 14K gold. H. 1¾"; W. 3"; D. ½". RALPH GABRINER

CHICAGO

Ken Loeber
CONTEMPORARY JEWELRY

Dona Look
WOVEN WOOD VESSELS

Residents of northern Wisconsin, master craftspeople Ken Loeber and Dona Look sell their one-of-a-kind pieces through a few top galleries, including Perimeter, in Chicago. Masters in their media, Loeber and Look create highly individualized work definitely worth going out of your way to see.

Some of Ken's beguiling brooches resemble pieces of crumpled gold tissue paper floating through air, whipped-around pieces of shiny black coral, or balancing like an acrobat atop a freshwater pearl. Another piece appears to be a rippled gold potato chip draped over a green crystal. "I purposely make my pieces appear very frail and thin," Ken explains. "I forge and texture 14K gold to make it look like each piece has been formed by chance or accident."

His expert craftsmanship, however, is no accident. "I started off in sculpture," Ken says, "but found that my work was getting progressively smaller and smaller. Finally I realized that it was best worn rather than presented as sculpture." Other wearable Loeber work includes production jewelry of forged, folded, and fabricated sterling silver or vermeil. For pure silliness, Ken also offers real Lake Michigan gizzard shad, dipped in resin, ready to give your ensemble a fishy allure.

Ken's wife, Dona, begins her creative work by gathering birch bark and grasses from northern Wisconsin forests, then weaving them into vessels of uncommon precision and beauty. Although remnants of the traditional baskets she once made can be glimpsed in their graceful lines and fundamental forms, Dona's vessels surpass their functional attributes to appeal as sculpture. A vessel may suggest a Shaker "cat's head" basket, but Dona subtly gives it new definition, banding it with a strip of white birch, embellishing the rim with tightly looped silk (see color plate #12).

PRICES: Ken's production jewelry, $24–$250; Ken's 14K gold one-of-a-kind work, $300–$9,000; Dona's vessels, $300–$3,000. No commissions. There is a catalog/brochure of Ken's production jewelry only. To request this mail-order catalog, send $1 (refundable with order) to Loeber/Lowe, P.O. Box 204, Algoma, WI 54201.

VISITORS: No.

LOCATION: Loeber and Lowe's one-of-a-kind items are available through the Perimeter Gallery, 750 North Orleans, Chicago, IL 60610; 312-266-9473. The gallery is open Tues.–Sat., 10:30 A.M.–5:30 P.M. From downtown Chicago, take Michigan Avenue north to Chicago Avenue. Go west down Chicago Avenue to North Orleans Street; the gallery is on the southwest corner.

MORE: While visiting the Perimeter Gallery, look also for realistic ceramic slice-of-life sculptures by Jack Earl, and hauntingly colored ceramic vessels by Toshiko Takaezu.

EVANSTON

Annual Evanston Ethnic Arts Festival

Purchase Lithuanian wood crafts, Hmong embroidery, Japanese origami, or African-American ceramics. Attend a piñatamaking workshop, or try your hand at Mayan pottery or Turkish paper marbling. Everywhere you turn at this annual "affirmative action" arts festival, you will be able to sample over twenty-five cultures that thankfully have not yet melted into the American amalgam.

When your shopping bag is full, enjoy a cross-cultural entertainment mélange: West Indian dance, a Mexican guitar solo, Balkan rhythm bands, or a Black American poetry reading. Forget breakfast so you will have room for ethnic foods like Jamaican sodas, Laotian satay, Ethiopian lentils, and Italian ices. Want to leave your own imprint? Each year festival sponsors give participants that opportunity. It may be a "festival weaving," where everyone can add several threads to a community tapestry, or a "festival mural," where guests can contribute their own splash of color.

EVENT: Third weekend of July, Sat. & Sun., noon–6 P.M. Free admission.

LOCATION: Lakefront area. Dawes Park, Sheridan Road, between Church and Davis streets. Take I-94 to the Dempster Street exit. Take Dempster Street east about 5 miles to Forest Avenue. Go left on Forest and continue about five blocks to Dawes Park at Church Street and Sheridan Road.

MORE: For information contact the Evanston Arts Council, 927 Noyes Street, Evanston, IL 60201; 312-491-0266.

EVANSTON

Mindscape Gallery, Inc.
CONTEMPORARY CRAFTS

The oldest and largest "crafts only" gallery in the Midwest, Mindscape represents over 350 artisans. In addition to glass, jewelry, and ceramics, Mindscape offers a good selection of crystalline pottery, sculpted handmade paper work, and unusual textiles.

If you think felt is only for hats and Christmas decorations, ask to see Lynda Lowe Oren's wall pieces. Using comparatively unknown felting and dying techniques, Lynda creates vividly colored yet softly textured work. One piece may depict a muted landscape glistening with the first light of day, another appears as a symbolic map, filled with Indian signs and suggestions of flowing water and a land mass.

Need something to perk up your home or office decor? Try one of Ron Mazonowski's dull pot/bright bird combos. Ron begins subtly, with large-scale terra-cotta vessels, perfectly formed, delicately incised and textured. Perched on top of each piece, however, is a colorful, life-size ceramic parrot or macaw, meticulously detailed, waiting for a magic word to give it breath.

PRICES: $10–$10,000 (average, $25–$350). Accepts American Express, Diners Club, MasterCard, Optima, Visa.

OPEN: Tues. & Wed., Fri. & Sat., 10 A.M.–6 P.M.; Thurs., noon–9 P.M. Call for details on extended holiday hours. Wheelchair accessible.

LOCATION. Downtown Evanston. 1521 Sherman Avenue, Evanston, IL 60201; 312-864-2660. Take I-94 to the Dempster Street exit, Dempster Street east to Sherman. Go left on Sherman four blocks to the gallery.

ILLINOIS CITY

Carol Nelson
TRADITIONAL BASKETS

Carol really has a handle on basketmaking. Although most basket makers add handles almost as an afterthought, a necessity worth attaching but artistically irrelevant, Carol makes them an integral part of each work. Her handles may sport a cut-out heart or a pierced apple design, woven herringbone, cross-stitch, or complicated double-layered designs.

The baskets themselves are well designed and competently crafted, formed in over thirty-five different styles, from berry and "buttocks" to market and field. Most appealing, however, are Carol's "fowl" baskets. They are used today to hold yarn, paperbacks, or even lunch, but their original purposes were much more colorful.

Carol Nelson: Pigeon basket with folk art weaving on handle. Diam. 10″.

Back then, families shared a good broody hen and carried her between homesteads in this type of basket. I also make a Goose Basket twenty-three inches tall and thirteen inches in diameter. When a live goose was plucked for its down, the head was placed inside this deep basket to prevent it from nipping its tormentor."

PRICES: $6–$750+. Commissions accepted. Accepts MasterCard, Visa. Send $2.50 for the catalog/brochure.

VISITORS: No. Mail order only.

MORE: Send correspondence about the catalog to Carol Nelson, Walnut Creek Baskets, Box 84, TC8, Illinois City, IL 61259-0084. If you have questions, call 309-791-0194.

"My covered Pigeon Baskets were used during the 1800s to transport small animals to market and pigeons to 'shoots,'" Carol explains. "The circular-shaped Hen Baskets are copies of ones used prior to the age of electricity and automatic incubators.

JACKSONVILLE

Howard Maguire
PAPER CUTTINGS

Picture your favorite fairy tale. Now imagine each elf, prancing unicorn, castle, and handsome prince

Howard Maguire: Papercutting.
CHRIS MAGUIRE

portrayed in intricate detail by mere cuts on a piece of white paper. Fantasy? Not if you contact Howard Maguire. Using only an X-acto knife and paper, Howard creates images that could illustrate the finest child's book, from two unicorns dueling in a garden to a storybook princess awaiting her fate in the world's most elaborate gazebo.

A factory worker at Capital Records by day, Howard snips away his nights and weekends, weaving paper dreams. "Initially I was interested in learning how to stencil," Howard recalls. "So I got a book out of the library to teach myself that craft. But a small chapter at the back of the book discussed papercutting, which sounded much more interesting. At first I just folded my paper in half, cutting both sides at once but rarely doing more. Now I've started to cut several layers of different-colored paper at the same time, weaving them together to form a three-dimensional effect. Soon I plan to make my own paper, especially rough-textured styles, and move toward a type of cut sculpture."

PRICES: $10–$100 +. Commissions accepted. No catalog/brochure.

VISITORS: Yes. By apointment only.

LOCATION: Western Illinois, about 30 miles west of Springfield. 1840 Plum, Jacksonville, IL 62650; 217-243-3845. Directions will be provided when appointment to visit is made.

OAK PARK

Frank Lloyd Wright
WRIGHT FURNITURE AND CRAFTS

Oak Park is *the* place to learn about both Frank Lloyd Wright's distinctive architecture and the furnishings he designed for it. Twenty-five of his buildings can be found here, along with the home and studio he occupied from 1889 to 1909.

Wright's home and studio include unusual slantback chairs, tables, and many other furnishings and architectural details. If you'd like to have some Wright reproductions in your own home, two catalogs offer everything from stained-glass win-

dows and panels to dinnerware, vases, and even woven fabrics and wallpaper.

OPEN: For information on tours of Wright buildings, contact the Oak Park Visitor Center, 158 North Forest Avenue, Oak Park, IL 60301; 312-848-1978. The Wright home and studio (951 Chicago Avenue, Oak Park, IL 60302; 312-848-1976) is open for tours daily. Admission is $4 for adults, $2 for seniors and children 10–18.

A catalog of reproduction Wright windows and ceiling panels, as well as scarves, posters, and notecards with Wright motifs, is free. For a copy, contact the Visitor Center. Another catalog, produced by Archetype Associates, offers reproduction Wright furniture, textiles, wallcoverings, and accessories. To order it, send $7 to FLW Catalog, P.O. Box 4736, Chicago, IL 60680-4736.

PLEASANT PLAINS

Clayville Folk Arts Festivals
TRADITIONAL CRAFTS

Dolls made from apples, cornhusk, and hickory nuts, and buttons of shell and antler are just some of the traditional crafts that distinguish Clayville's biannual craft festivals. More interested in needlework? Stop by to watch hoop quilting, huck weaving, pierced cardboard embroidery, and tatting on the grounds of a restored 1820s brick inn and farmhouse, now used as a rural life museum. A third festival, held every June, features traditional quilts and fiberwork.

EVENTS: For specific information about dates, hours, and admission, contact the Clayville Rural Life Center.

LOCATION: 12 miles west of Springfield. Clayville Rural Life Center, Beardstown Road, Box 175, Pleasant Plains, IL 62677; 217-626-1132. Take I-72 to Springfield's West Jefferson exit (Rte. 97). Go west on Rte. 97 to the junction with Rte. 125. Follow Rte. 125 to Clayville.

QUINCY

Paul E. Rakers
COPPERSMITH

Extremely malleable, copper can be hammered, forged, stamped, and shaped without cracking. Used both decoratively and for functional items since the fifth century B.C., copper is most often found today in industrial components and gourmet

Paul E. Rakers: Copper coffeepot and scoop.

RIVERSIDE

Frances and Michael Higgins
FUSED AND ENAMELED GLASS

Using glass instead of bread, enamel in place of cold cuts, Frances and Michael create sandwiches for the eye, not the tummy. Since 1948 these partners in marriage and art have created fused-glass objects from dangling earrings to a 500-square-foot curtain of linked glass.

"First we coat flat sheets of clear glass with microlayers of color enamels," Michael says, "then fix them in an initial firing. Next, we take these enameled sheets and cut out our designs, two pieces of each shape and size, often in different colors. On the bottom piece, color side up, we put additional decoration. Then we lay on the top piece of glass, color side down. We set this 'sandwich' on a mold of clay or stainless steel, then fuse the glass together at about fifteen hundred degrees Fahrenheit. As the glass softens, it assumes the shape of the mold."

"One of the most complex pieces we've ever done," adds Frances, "was a doublet of interior windows in a church complex. That work displayed over seventy-eight Christian symbols in thirty-eight panels. But we also do residential windows, bowls, and table tops—even mobiles. And we're never sure exactly how a piece will turn out. The cold colors are quite different from their appearance after firing, but by then they're completely sealed in. We have no chance to change anything."

PRICES: $3–$4,000. Commissions accepted. Send an "SASE for general leaflet only, no catalog."

VISITORS: Yes.

LOCATION: Just west of Chicago. 33 East Quincy Street, Riverside, IL 60546; 312-447-2787. Take I-55 to the First Avenue north exit. Continue to the fourth traffic light (Forest Avenue) and go right. Continue past a water tower, veering right onto Longcommon Road. Cross the railroad tracks, then turn left on East Quincy. The glass studio will be on your right. (CAUTION: If you park in Riverside after dark on streets lighted only by (dim) gaslight, leave on your parking lights or risk a ticket!)

cookware. In the late 1800s, however, it was the metal of choice for everything from sheathing the Massachusetts capitol dome to common household items.

Although Paul Rakers hasn't yet received a call from the governor of Massachusetts, he does recreate nineteenth-century domestic copperware from wash boilers and coal buckets to cookware, vases, and lanterns. "My father was a metalsmith for over sixty years," Paul says. "I grew up watching him make metal items, then later served a four-year apprenticeship under him. Although I earn my living by installing metal roofs and heating and air-conditioning systems, at night I pick up my eighty- and ninety-year-old tools and create over forty different copper items."

For an interior accent, choose one of Paul's table lamps with pierced copper shades, or a copper sconce perfect for holding long fireplace matches or dried flowers. Outside, let one of Paul's hummingbird, buffalo, or angel yard ornaments chase birds from your vegetable crop—or at least confuse the neighbor's cat.

PRICES: $4–$200. Commissions accepted. No catalog/brochure.

VISITORS: Yes. Evenings and weekends; please call first.

LOCATION: Western Illinois, along the Mississippi River, about 20 miles north of Hannibal, Missouri. 3512 North 12th, Quincy, IL 62301; 217-223-9394. Directions will be provided when you call.

INDIANA

Like spokes in a wheel, Indiana's interstates fan out from Indianapolis, speeding through rolling hills, past lakes, and into river valleys. Slow down the blur of scenery by taking time to visit some of the state's talented craftspeople. Within only a few miles of the freeways you will find traditional craftsmen working in copper and leather, artisans creating graceful baskets, utilitarian stoneware, outrageous ceramic animals, and even top-notch handmade paper. For a peaceful respite from highway monotony, plan an afternoon in woodsy, picturesque Brown County, home to many Indiana craftspersons and artists. And if glass is your passion, stop by a few of the many production glassworks initially drawn to the area for its abundant supply of natural gas. For even more traditional crafts, visit Pioneer Village at the Indiana State Fair, held during the last two weeks of August in Indianapolis.

BLOOMINGTON

The Gallery
CONTEMPORARY CRAFTS

Utilitarian ceramics don't have to be boring, and the Gallery's Indiana artisans prove this. Gail Russell's ash and copper-red glazes, Scott Frankenberger's unusual shapes, and Alan Patrick's brushwork give new definition to porcelain and stoneware. Even more unusual, Nell Devitt's, nonfunctional raku pieces often incorporate string, wood, or copper wire to provide striking surface textures.

PRICES: $3.50–$1,500 (average, $20–$100). Accepts American Express, MasterCard, Visa.

OPEN: Tues.–Sat., noon–5:30 P.M.; Sun., 3–5 P.M. Closed Mon., Thanksgiving, Christmas, New Year's. Not wheelchair accessible.

LOCATION: 109 East 6th, Bloomington, IN 47401; 812-336-0564. From Court House Square, go half a block east on 6th Street.

BROOKSTON

Kathryn and Howard Clark
Twinrocker Handmade Paper

In 1971 Kathryn Clark asked why the San Francisco press where she printed lithographs didn't use handmade paper. "Because there isn't any," was the response. Accepting the challenge, the Clarks founded Twinrocker and became leaders of a revived papermaking movement. Relocating to the Clark family's Brookston farm in 1972, they built a papermill, with much of the equipment invented by Howard, a former mechanical engineer.

The emphasis here is *handmade*. Envelopes are *hand*-scored and folded, then glued individually with a brush. Made from twenty-five different plants, most papers contain cotton, linen rag, or abaca (banana leafstalk), with additional fibers such as coconut or cornhusk, flower petals, or metallic threads.

Visitors can watch a variety of fine papers being made, from stationery and invitations to paper for drawing, watercolor, and nonsilver photography as well as archival, conservation, and other specialty uses. Need paper of a particular size, color, surface, thickness, or watermark? The Clarks will design it specially for you.

PRICES: 67¢–$32+ per sheet; set of 25 4″×5″ swatches, $7.50.

VISITORS: Mon.–Fri., 8 A.M.–5 P.M.

LOCATION: Between Indianapolis and Chicago. 100 East 3rd Street, Brookston, IN 47923; 317-563-3119. 10 miles east of I-65, on Rte. 18, just east of the railroad tracks.

MORE: Twinrocker also sells papermaking supplies, offers workshops, and provides "studio services" to help artists solve their paper needs. After browsing at Twinrocker, stop next door at the Klein Brot Haus. "It's a unique German bakery," says Kathryn, "which is to bread what we are to paper—handmade and unusual."

Susan Wyke Frost: *Schmaigle,* fantasy creature. Porcelain. H. 4″; W. 5¼″; D. 3¾″.

BROOKSTON

Susan Wyke Frost
FUNCTIONAL AND DECORATIVE PORCELAIN

If you're tired of teddy bears and fuzzy bunnies, you might want to adopt one of Susan's creatures. Totally out of the running in the cuddly sweepstakes, these 6-inch to 8-inch bizarre animals fix you with a glassy stare and *dare* you to come closer, some with claws that could only be used for unspeakable acts. A winged beast with a come-hither look is obviously not interested in romance, an uncomely frog relative has suspiciously bubbly protrusions, and a pigged-out pig is too fat to move and proud of it!

Although Susan's weird little folks may populate a child's nightmare, she also creates works of pure grace and beauty. Influenced by Fabergé, Susan creates highly decorated porcelain eggs with rows of colorful raised dots, and vases studded with ceramic shapes resembling carefully set precious jewels. The common thread between her romantic pieces and her weird menagerie is the amount of detail and careful crafting that goes into each work.

PRICES: $8–$600. Commissions accepted, depending on what is requested. No catalog/brochure.

VISITORS: Yes.

LOCATION: Between Indianapolis and Chicago. 114 West 3rd Street, P.O. Box 433, Brookston, IN 47923; 317-563-3711.

Take I-65 to the Brookston exit (Rte. 43 from the south, Rte. 16 from the north). Continue to downtown Brookston. The studio is on the corner where Rtes. 43 and 18 connect.

BROWN COUNTY

Since the turn of the century, the vast forests, rolling hills, covered bridges, log cabins, and rustic isolation of Brown County have attracted craftspeople and artists. Located in central Indiana, not far from Indiana University in Bloomington, the area still lures artisans for both the inspiring natural beauty and the strong crafts marketplace. Nashville, in the heart of Brown County, has over 200 shops and hosts over seven million visitors annually. The mere numbers tend to overwhelm the locals, whose favorite graffiti is "Flatlanders go home." Despite this, warm camaraderie exists among artisans, along with a genuinely friendly atmosphere and a wonderful potpourri of quality work. See the Nashville listing below for a recommended local gallery.

Since parking in Nashville can be difficult, you may want to stay within walking distance of the shops. The Allison House B&B is a comfortable old Victorian home (P.O. Box 546, Nashville, IN 47448; 812-988-0814). For something more unusual, try the Story Inn, a combination old dry goods store, gas station, restaurant, and inn with friendly hosts, antiques, and great food (P.O. Box 64, Nashville, IN 47448; 812-988-2273).

CARTHAGE

Michael Bonne
TRADITIONAL COPPERSMITH

Michael Bonne's only concessions to the twentieth century are electric lights and a propane soldering torch. In all other respects, his workshop is an authentic 1880s Indiana sheet metal shop. Located in an 1850s log cabin that Michael found and re-built, the shop has walls filled with nineteenth-century tools and patterns. "When I first bought these old tools," Michael recalls, "I didn't know their names or how to use them. I had to sit down and experiment until I figured them out."

Now Michael makes over eighty copper items, reproductions of everyday goods from the eighteenth and nineteenth centuries. Visitors can watch

Coppersmith Michael Bonne and his nineteenth-century workshop. TERESA L. BONNE

him fashion huge wash-boiling tubs, baking pans and cookie cutters, watering cans, and tankards. To make sure no one resells his work as antique, Michael signs each one with the date, his mark, and a saying. On the bottom of large washtubs he writes "Grandma Hazel kept her socks in one" . . . because she did!

Michael's illustrated catalog also gives advice. One hint came from an 1820s copper-cleaning recipe, which he realized was really a recipe for ketchup. His advice? "The best way to clean copper is to apply ketchup liberally. After a few minutes rinse well and towel dry." Michael goes through five to six gallons of ketchup a week.

PRICES: $1.50 (small heart mold)–$60 (lantern)–$1,000+ for very large pieces. Commissions accepted. The catalog costs $3.

VISITORS: Mon.–Sat., 10 A.M.–5 P.M.; other days/times by appointment.

LOCATION: About 20 miles east of Indianapolis, RR #1, Box 177, Carthage, IN 46115; 317-565-6521. From I-70, go south on Rte. 109 to Knightstown, left on U.S. 40, right on S.R. 140, right on Carthage Road to the shop, on the left.

MORE: Michael demonstrates his skills at the Indiana State Fair's Pioneer Village. Last two weeks of Aug.; Fairgrounds, 1202 East 38th Street, Indianapolis; 317-927-7524.

COMMISKEY

Gerald Manning
BLACKSMITH

Betty Manning
COUNTRY CRAFTS

Gerald's and Betty's crafts are steeped in family history. The farm where they live and work, Stream Cliff, has been in Betty's family for over 100 years. Built in 1836, this Federal-style farmhouse was raided during the Civil War by Morgan's Raiders, a Confederate unit of 3,000 men who came north to gain provisions for the South. Now Gerald provisions modern homes with his hand-forged items. Although he began blacksmithing by using his grandpa's forge to make shoes for the family horses, he now makes graceful but practical fireplace sets, dinner bells, chandeliers, and candlesticks, most incorporating a heart motif.

Betty creates a variety of "country crafts": cornhusk dolls, pixielike wood-carved Santas, apple-head dolls, primitive paintings of country scenes, and herbal wreaths. The wreaths are made from plants in the Mannings' three herb gardens. Dedicated to Betty's grandmother, a quilter, each of the three gardens is done in a familiar quilt pattern. One garden is Grandmother's Fan, another Dresden Plate, and the third a crucifix with a heart within a square.

PRICES: Gerald's work, $3–$100; Betty's work, $3–$85. Gerald accepts commissions; Betty does so sometimes. No catalog/brochure.

VISITORS: By appointment only. Call 812-346-5859 after 6 P.M.

LOCATION: Between Indianapolis and Louisville, Kentucky. Stream Cliff Farm, RR #1, Commiskey, IN 47227. Please call for directions.

MORE: The Mannings' studio is open several weekends in the spring and each weekend during Nov. & Dec.; call for specific dates/times.

DEMING

Steven M. Lalioff
TRADITIONAL LEATHERWORK

Sometimes in the back of an antique shop you can find a dusty old trunk, its leather cracked and mildewed, the paper lining yellow and crumbling. Its appearance and smell evoke ghosts of the people who once owned the trunk and the goods they transported. These trunks are difficult to find, almost impossible to restore, but it is now possible to purchase new ones from Steven Lalioff.

Steven apprenticed to the harness and saddle maker in Colonial Williamsburg after college, then returned to Indiana to reproduce leather items made originally from 1750 to 1850 (see color plate #13). "All my construction methods are accurate to the period of time I'm making," Steven notes. "I use the same materials—vegetable-tanned leather, linen cord, solid brass, and steam-bent trunk frames. I hand-stitch all items and line trunk interiors with either original eighteenth- or nineteenth-century newspapers, handprinted cloth, or hand-grained painting I do myself."

Steven also makes leather-bound chests, fire-buckets, portmanteaus, saddlebags, doctor's bags, leather map cases, and tavernware (mugs, dice cups, noggins). "I make one-of-a-kind items.

They're all so labor-intensive that I avoid burnout by always making new items or changing old ones."

Visitors can watch Steven at work in the rebuilt log cabin where he lives. "I did the entire cabin," he points out, "to resemble a craftsman's home of the early nineteenth century."

PRICES: $4–$1,200. Commissions accepted "if it's something I have the mental energy to do." No catalog/brochure.

VISITORS: By appointment only.

LOCATION: 25 miles north of Indianapolis. RR 1, Box 324C, Cicero, IN 46034; 317-877-0314. Take I-465 (the Indianapolis loop) to Rte. 31. Go north on Rte. 31 for 13 miles to Deming/ Rte. 226, east on Rte. 226 to Deming. The cabin is 1,000 yards behind the old Masonic Lodge.

MORE: Steven demonstrates his skills at the Indiana State Fair's Pioneer Village. Last two weeks of Aug.; Fairgrounds, 1202 East 38th Street. Indianapolis; 317-927-7524.

INDIANAPOLIS

Artifacts Gallery
CONTEMPORARY CRAFTS

Twenty minutes from downtown Indianapolis is Broad Ripple Village, a small community with galleries, boutiques, and ethnic bistros clustered near a central canal. After visiting the canal's resident ducks and geese, stop by Artifacts Gallery to see Joe Rohrman's poignant ceramic commentary on contemporary life. In one grouping, four homeless men huddle around a trashcan fire for warmth while they watch two men emerge, well-fed, from a nearby diner. For something in a lighter vein, pin on one of Joe Lee's sculptured pins, perhaps his flying pig.

PRICES: $5–$2,000 (average $25–$350). Accepts American Express, MasterCard, Visa.

OPEN: Mon.–Wed. & Sat., 10 A.M.–5 P.M.; Thurs. & Fri., 10 A.M.–9 P.M.; Sun., noon–5 P.M. Closed all federal holidays. Wheelchair accessible.

LOCATION: 6327 North Guilford Avenue, Indianapolis, IN 46220; 317-255-1178. From downtown Indianapolis, take College Avenue north, past Kessler Boulevard. Turn right onto Ripple Avenue, left onto Guilford. There is a parking deck two blocks down on the left.

MORGANTOWN

Suzanne Hickey
BASKETS

Heart, elbow, and fanny; key, tote, and loom are just some of the basket styles Suzanne creates. Made of reed splints, cornhusks, maple limbs, and iris leaves, these functional baskets often sport soft pastels woven in geometric designs. "I create many of my own dyes from walnut and pecan shells, tree bark, and also blossoms from marigolds, petunias, and irises," Suzanne notes. "And my husband helps by cutting oak and ash boards for basket handles."

"I started making baskets," Suzanne recalls, "when my daughter asked for baskets of flowers on the table at her wedding reception. I took a two-day basket workshop and made every one myself." Later she taught herself how to make Appalachian egg baskets from the famous book *Foxfire I*. Thousands of baskets later, Suzanne now teaches courses herself and also does commissions: "People send me wallpaper samples and tell me what size basket they'd like. Then I come up with a design and color that will look nice." Ask to see her straw hats, cornhusk dolls ("We farm several acres of corn right out the front door"), and her collection of old baskets.

PRICES: $10–$100. Commissions accepted. No catalog/brochure.

VISITORS: It's best to call or write first for an appointment.

LOCATION: About 30 miles south of Indianapolis. R #2, Box 361, Morgantown, IN 46160; 812-597-4617. From Indianapolis, take Rte. 37 south. East of Martinsville, take Rte. 252 east to Morgantown. At the four-way stop in Morgantown, turn left and go 1 mile to the house, the only one on the left side of road.

MORE: Suzanne's work is also available through the Brown County Craft Gallery (Nashville, IN 47448; 812-988-7058) and the Indianapolis Museum of Art Gift Shop (1200 West 38th Street, Indianapolis, IN 46208; 317-923-1331).

NASHVILLE

Brown County Craft Gallery
CONTEMPORARY AND TRADITIONAL CRAFTS

If you want a flavor of what Brown County artisans create, visit this co-op gallery, the only shop in Nashville exclusively representing local craftspeople. Although there is fine work in every medium, some of it is particularly appealing. Jack Brubaker and Susan Showalter's hand-forged metalwork uses natural oxides to bring out the pinks and purples of copper, the yellows and browns of brass. Their steel, copper, and brass cala lily candlesticks appear more fluid than the lighted candles that top them. Tom Kemerly's "wall jewelry" gives you a choice: leave it framed on your wall or take it down and wear it. Look also for Larry Pejeau's pottery, which recalls Oriental watercolors, and Rob Mills's wood furniture with brass detailing.

PRICES: $1–$200 (average, $10–$45). Accepts American Express, MasterCard, Visa.

OPEN: Apr. 1–Jan. 1, daily, 10 A.M.–5 P.M.; Jan. 1–March 31, Fri.–Wed., 10 A.M.–5 P.M. Closed Christmas and New Year's Day. Not wheelchair accessible.

LOCATION: Central Indiana. Van Buren and Main streets, P.O. Box 13, Nashville, IN 47448; 812-988-7058. From Rte. 65 in Columbus, turn west on Rte. 46. At the first light in Nashville, turn north on Rte. 135 (Van Buren). The gallery is at the next stoplight, above the Hobnob Restaurant.

NOBLESVILLE

Conner Prairie
1836 LIVING HISTORY MUSEUM

In 1934 pharmaceutical heir Eli Lilly purchased the dilapidated 1823 William Conner frontier home, later restoring and opening it to the public. On the same site, fifty-three years and $10 million later, Conner Prairie is one of the better "living history museums" that now dot the country. Although it includes the requisite blacksmith and pottery shop, the real gem is the Loom House. Here visitors can watch textile experts re-create period blankets and coverlets for use in the historic buildings. Nearby is a dye garden whose plants are used to re-create the exact colors favored by nineteenth-century weavers. The best purchases at Conner Prairie are the pillows and sacks made from remnant ends of these period textiles.

While you're staring at dye pots, spinning wheels, and looms, let your children wander over to the Pioneer Adventure Center, where they can weave on an authentic loom, carve wood, or try their hand at gunsmithing, basketry, or soapmaking.

OPEN: May–Oct., Tues.–Sat., 10 A.M.–5 P.M.; Sun., noon–5 P.M. Nov., Wed.–Sat., 10 A.M.–5 P.M.; Sun., noon–5 P.M. Open Memorial Day, July 4th, and Labor Day; closed Thanksgiving and Christmas. Admission is $6 for adults, $5.50 for seniors, $3.25 for children, children under 5 free. Partially wheelchair accessible.

LOCATION: 6 miles north of the I-465 loop, 13400 Allisonville Road, Noblesville, IN 46060-4499; 317-776-6000. From I-465, take the Allisonville Road exit. Connor Prairie is on the left, 4 miles south of Noblesville.

MORE: Candlelight tours in Dec., Hearthside Suppers Jan.–March. Call for details. Special exhibits annually (folk art, quilts, other crafts).

REELSVILLE

Richard and Marj Peeler
STUDIO POTTERS

"I really love the feel of clay," Marj says. "I like to throw it, pound it, roll it, add clay to clay, distort, incise, stamp, and cut it. Although I've been a potter for over forty years, I still want to try out new ideas." Since 1946, Marj and Richard Peeler have produced utilitarian and decorative stoneware, much of which is thrown by Richard and decorated by Marj.

Influenced by American Indian pots, inspired by Japanese and Mexican craftsmen, the Peeler's pottery often incorporates references to weaving, feathers, and basketry. Some of their more ornate pots resemble a river bottom, frozen in time, filled with pebbles and fossil fish. Equally unusual are Richard's abstract fantasies, intricate towers with multiple arches and cornices, seemingly the constructs of an architect gone mad.

PRICES: $2–$3,500. Commissions sometimes accepted. No catalog/brochure.

VISITORS: Anytime (including Sat. & Sun.).

LOCATION: 40 miles west of Indianapolis. R. 1, Box 320, Reelsville, IN 46171; 317-795-4370. Take I-70 to Rte. 231, Rte. 231 to Cloverdale. At the yellow flasher, turn right on Burma Road, left on Rte. 243. Take the first right and continue until it ends in a T intersection. Turn left and follow the road to Peeler Pottery signs on the right.

MORE: Richard and Marj's work is also available through the Indianapolis Museum of Art Gift Shop, 1200 West 38th Street, Indianapolis, IN 46208; 317-923-1331.

Indiana Glass

In the late nineteenth century, two discoveries led to the establishment of glass factories throughout central Indiana: natural gas and abundant quantities of suitable sand. With a reliable fuel source to heat furnaces up to 2,600°F, factories began producing all types of glass products, including the first optical glass successfully made in this country. Although most of the gas fields were depleted by the first decade of the twentieth century and many factories moved or shut down, some small family operations persist and are well worth a visit.

CORYDON

Zimmerman Art Glass

Bart Zimmerman's grandfather moved here to take advantage of the natural gas supply. Although the gas is gone, Bart and his family continue to produce a line of handcrafted glass paperweights, ashtrays, and vases. Visitors can watch third-generation glass artists individually sculpting items by building layer upon layer of clear and colored liquid glass that has first been heated to 1,800°F.

PRICES: $4–$250.

VISITORS: Tues.–Sat., 9 A.M.–3 P.M.

LOCATION: 31 miles east of Louisville, Kentucky. P.O. Box 292, Corydon, IN 47112; 812-738-2206. From I-64, take Rte. 135 south to Corydon's business district. Rte. 135 becomes North Capitol Avenue. Take a left on Chestnut, right on Mulberry, left on Valley Road to Zimmerman's.

DUNKIRK

The Glass Museum

Worth a stop if you are in the area, this museum features over 3,000 pieces of American glass from eighty-five factories in central Indiana and elsewhere. Ask to see the twenty-five leaded glass windows, the array of hanging lamps, and a fine collection of Depression glass.

OPEN: May 1–Nov. 1, Mon.–Sat., 10 A.M.–5 P.M. Free admission; donations accepted.

LOCATION: 14 miles northeast of Muncie. 309 South Franklin, Dunkirk, IN 47336; 317-768-6809. From Muncie, take Rte. 67 north to Albany, then Rte. 167 north 5 miles to Dunkirk.

ELWOOD

In 1886 the first gas well was drilled in Madison County. Four years later, a special train brought 365 glassblowers from Pittsburgh to work in a new Elwood plant. Factories making window glass, plate glass, and lamp chimneys sprang up. But some gas was wasted, even more was pumped to Chicago and Indianapolis, and the wells dried up. Now gas is brought in from West Virginia and Texas. Elwood is 30 miles northeast of Indianapolis. Take I-69 north to Rte. 28, then go west on Rte. 28 for 15 miles to Elwood.

ELWOOD

St. Clair Glass

John B. St. Clair came to America from Epinal, France, in 1890. Working at an Elwood plant, he made glass chimneys by day and developed unique paperweights in his spare time. Later, he began a small factory in the backyard of his home, also making ashtrays, penholders, and small doorstops. Today his five sons continue the family glass art. A specialty is the rose paperweight—a perfect pink rose encased in a glass globe.

OPEN: Mon.–Thurs., 9 A.M.–3 P.M. Closed holidays.

LOCATION: 408 North 5th Street, Elwood, IN 46036; 317-552-5045.

ELWOOD

House of Glass

Joe Rice, owner of the House of Glass, is a nephew of John B. St. Clair. A third-generation glassworker, Joe still makes his own crystal glass from silica sand, soda ash, lime, feldspar, and other materials. Using old-world techniques, a full line of paperweights and lamps are produced. Many of the items appear to be exotic underwater flowers frozen in an orb of clear ice.

PRICES: $10 and up.

OPEN: Mon.–Fri., 9 A.M.–5 P.M.

LOCATION: R 3, Box 153, Elwood, IN 46036; 317-552-6841. Located on Rte. 28, just west of Elwood.

ELWOOD

Peacock Glass Works Inc.

Continuing the glass tradition of John B. St. Clair, the five employees of Peacock Glass Works continue to make paperweights from simple designs to intricate internal patterns. Look also for their bird, turtle, apple, and pear paperweights, which have bright sparks of color.

PRICES: $12–$30. No commissions. Need information? "Just ask."

VISITORS: Mon.–Fri., 9 A.M.–3 P.M.

LOCATION: 505 North 12th Street, Elwood, IN 46036; 317-552-6759.

GREENTOWN

Greentown Glass Museum

The Indiana Tumbler and Goblet Co. operated in Greentown from 1894 to 1903. Although its primary product was crystal clear and translucent colored glass, it is best known for its "chocolate" and "golden agate" pieces. These unusual opaque glass colors were based on secret formulas created by resident glass chemist Jacob Rosenthal. The museum displays these items as well as a variety of Greentown Glass animal dishes and mugs.

OPEN: May 31–Sept. 2, Tues.–Fri., 10 A.M.–noon, 1–4 P.M. March 1–Oct. 31, Sat. & Sun., 1–4 P.M. Closed Easter. Free admission; donations accepted.

LOCATION: 60 miles north of Indianapolis. 112 North Meridian, Greentown, IN 46936; 317-628-7818. From Indianapolis, take Rte. 31 north to Kokomo, then Rte. 22 east 8 miles to Greentown.

MICHIGAN

Shaped like a giant child's mitten, Michigan lives up to its (somewhat silly) state motto: "If you seek a pleasant peninsula, look around you." With its population concentrated in the lower third of the state (primarily Detroit), the state has a great deal of remote country to lure visitors, particularly along the four Great Lakes that lap its shores. Pull yourself away from boating and fishing long enough to sample local crafts from exquisite Native American ceramics and Pewabic Pottery's renowned architectural tiles to an eclectic selection of glasswork, jewelry, carved natural stones, wall hangings, and cedar "fans."

Armchair travelers may want to order *Gifts for All Seasons: Michigan Gift Guide,* a catalog of items made by Michigan artisans (and factories). The offerings vary, from inexpensive knickknacks to top-notch snowshoes, handcrafted fly rods, and fine furniture. For a free copy, write to the Office of Michigan Products Promotion, Michigan Department of Commerce, P.O. Box 30004, Lansing, MI 48909.

ANN ARBOR

Ann S. Epstein
CONTEMPORARY WALL HANGINGS

Ann's wall hangings resemble colorful Rorschach tests that summon each viewer's fears and fantasies. Stretching over several panels, they appear as evocative landscapes, infrared space photography, or X rays of emotional hot spots. In one, the viewer seems to peer through unwashed windows (or rusting screens), seeing a last glimpse of daylight wash over an urban skyscape. Another hanging suggests burning buildings, their outlines blurred by heat and suffering. In a calmer mood, five panels suggest a remote lake at sunset. Surrounded by dark marsh, rimmed with orange reeds; the lake is turned by the sun into a pool of lemon custard.

A psychologist as well as a talented artisan, Ann might find these descriptions to be deeply meaningful. "I took my first weaving course at the local Y when I was working on my doctorate in psychology," Ann says. "I immediately knew I'd found my medium. In fact, ten years after completing my doctorate, I returned to earn an M.F.A. in textiles. Now, as a developmental psychologist, I evaluate educational programs for children and their families; as an artist I use color and structure to convey emotional states and the universal concerns of struggle, joy, and growth."

To create her suggestive pieces, Ann uses complex twill weaving with cotton yarns she hand-dyes using ikat techniques. "Ikat," Ann explains, "is a method where the yarn is tied at various places before being dyed. Since the dye is unevenly absorbed, the yarn produces unusual patterns and contrast."

PRICES: $100 per sq. ft.; most ready-made pieces start at $2,200. Commissions accepted. No catalog/brochure.

VISITORS: Yes. By appointment only.

LOCATION: Southeastern Michigan. 2316 Walter Drive, Ann Arbor, MI 48103; 313-996-9019. Directions will be provided when appointment to visit is made.

MORE: Ann's work is included in many private and public collections. One piece can be seen in the lobby of Chicago's Executive Hotel, at 51 East Wacker Drive.

COLDWATER

Shirley M. Brauker
NATIVE AMERICAN POTTERY

If you're traveling in the Midwest and Michigan is not in your itinerary, change your plans. Located about 17 miles north of I-80/90, between Chicago and Toledo, is one of this country's finest Native American potters. Reflecting Indian motifs and often "telling a story," Shirley's vessels and wall shields include deep-relief detailing as well as contrasting textures and forms. Finished with iron oxide stains, they resemble fine wood carvings more than pottery.

Some of Shirley's vessels use open areas and elaborate sculpture to define or suggest intricate details (see color plate #14). In one vessel, the bottom half is a smooth, pleasingly plump form. Rising above it is an elaborate frieze, a deeply three-dimensional forest scene that includes a bear investigating a hollow log. Even more complex, a 24-inch wall shield shows a beaver near tangled foreground branches while the background suggests a stream and distant moon.

In addition to openwork carvings, Shirley creates story jars that use pictures and symbols carved in high-relief to reflect tribal legends. Like a richly embroidered Chinese robe, the vessels use design to convey realistic forms as well as abstract ideas. *Bearwalk* portrays a popular Woodland tribal legend about an Indian shaman who could turn himself into a bear. The pot shows him in mid-transformation.

A member of the Grand River Band of the Ottawa Indian Nation, Shirley studied pottery while earning her M.F.A. but depends on Native American traditions for her inspiration. "My work is dedicated to Native American art," she says, "and to our ancestors, who left a rich culture for everyone to enjoy and learn from. All my designs are meant to emphasize not only this external beauty but also the inner spirit as well."

PRICES: $25–$500. Commissions accepted. Send an SASE for her catalog/brochure.

VISITORS: Yes. Please call first.

LOCATION: South-central Michigan, 17 miles north of I-80/90, about 38 miles south of Battle Creek. 1044 Silver Road, Coldwater, MI 49036; 219-351-3858. Directions will be provided when you call.

MORE: Shirley's work is also available in the Lower Peninsula shops of Indian Hills (1581 Harbor Road, Petoskey) and Made in Michigan (311 East Lake, Petoskey); also in the Upper Peninsula shop Laughing Loon (Crafts of the North), Land's End, Box 145, Copper Harbor.

DETROIT

Pewabic Pottery
HISTORIC POTTERY MUSEUM
CONTEMPORARY CERAMICS GALLERY

Originally a china painter, Mary Chase Perry Stratton became one of the Arts & Crafts Movement's most emphatic proponents, introducing Michigan residents to the movement's major precept of combining beauty and utility in objects of everyday life. Working with Horace Caulkins, who created the Revelation Kiln, Stratton experimented with a number of different ceramic glazes and firing techniques. In 1903 Stratton and Caulkins founded Pewabic Pottery, taking its name from a Chippewa Indian word meaning "copper-colored clay."

In continuous production from 1907 to the present, Pewabic has always specialized in architectural tiles for both private homes and public buildings, from the National Shrine of the Immaculate Conception in Washington, D.C., to the 1987 "People Mover Station" in New York's Times Square. In addition to contemporary tiles for commercial and residential applications, Pewabic continues to produce functional and decorative vessels as well as reproductions of popular tiles, including a series of fable and fairy tale tiles created for the children's section of Detroit's public library.

Located in a 1907 building designed to resemble an old English inn from Kent, Pewabic is more than an operating pottery. Visitors will also find a museum filled with works by Stratton and her followers: vases, commemorative tiles, and architectural moldings made during the pottery's eighty-year life. Not one to let modern ceramics pass it by, Pewabic also houses a gallery that features contemporary functional, sculptural, traditional, and experimental ceramic work by artisans from throughout the country. Look for John Glick's dinnerware, Mary Roehm's wood-fired porcelain vessels, painterly sculptural forms by Susanne Stephenson, and unique soda-fired porcelainware by Sarah Coote.

PRICES: Individual tiles, $9–$60; installations, vessels, $250–"unlimited."; gallery crafts, $10–$2,500 (average, $75–$125). Commissions accepted. Free catalog/brochure.

OPEN: Tues.–Sat., 10 A.M.–5 P.M.

LOCATION: 10125 East Jefferson Avenue, Detroit, MI 48214; 313-822-0954. Take I-75 to I-375 (business spur). Take the Jefferson Avenue exit and continue east. The pottery is on the left, just past Cadillac Boulevard.

DETROIT

Karen Sepanski
SLUMP-CAST GLASSWORK

Some of Karen's light fixtures resemble complex ice carvings, designs beginning to liquefy but not yet drip. In contrast, her bas-relief panels evoke clear patterns in the sand, or abstract, see-through, relief maps.

"I use a variety of techniques including fusing and etching," Karen says, "but most of my work is slump-cast. First I make a mold, usually from clay or plaster, then I place blanks of glass over the top and fire them until they 'slump' into the molds." The results are fluid pieces that look as if they are ready to melt again, changing like chameleons when your back is turned. Particularly attractive as

hanging light fixtures and sconces, Karen's slump-cast work is sometimes available as decorative platters and bowls.

PRICES: $75 and up. Commissions accepted. Send an SASE for her catalog/brochure.

VISITORS: Yes.

LOCATION: 2827 John R Street, Detroit, MI 48201; 313-832-4941. Directions will be provided when you call.

DEXTER

Pat Garrett
CONTEMPORARY JEWELRY

Precious and not-so-precious metals and stones complement and imitate each other in Pat's striking jewelry. "I often see images in the stones," Pat says, "which I carry over into the metalwork designs. Much of the metal I use is yellow, rose, or green 14K gold, but I also use copper extensively. The stones range from tourmaline and topaz to garnet,

Pat Garrett: Earrings. Sterling silver, 14K gold, tourmalines, dreuzy chrysocholla, freshwater pearls. L. 3″. BILL PELLETIER

agate, and even cameos. I also use a stone called dreuzy, which is a quartz crystal layer on top of a mineral which gives it color."

Many of Pat's earrings, brooches, and pendants incorporate several different stones in a single piece. A brooch may resemble delicate tropical leaves resting on an onyx stalk; while a pair of earrings look like wind-whipped fronds secured against destruction by jewels that both anchor and glimmer.

A nationally recognized artist, Pat's coast-to-coast one-person shows have been held in such top-notch galleries as the Elements in Greenwich, Connecticut, and California's Del Mano Arts Gallery in Los Angeles. Pat also served as a juror in both 1980 and 1987 for the prestigious American Crafts Enterprise crafts fairs.

PRICES: $95–$6,200. No commissions. No catalog/brochure.

VISITORS: Yes. Tues.–Fri., 9 A.M.–5:30 P.M.; Sat., 9 A.M.–3 P.M.

LOCATION: Southeastern Michigan, about 8 miles west of Ann Arbor. Pat Garrett & Friends, 8107 Main Street, Dexter, MI 48130; 313-426-4599. Take I-94 to the Baker Road exit. Go north on Baker Road to the T intersection. Turn left onto Main Street. The studio is about one block farther, on the left.

MORE: Pat's work is also available in Michigan through the Detroit Gallery of Contemporary Crafts (301 Fisher Building, 3011 Grand Boulevard W, Detroit, MI 48202; 313-873-7888) and the Selo/Shevel Gallery (329 South Main Street, Ann Arbor, MI 48104; 313-761-6263).

HARBOR SPRINGS

Boyer Glassworks
CONTEMPORARY ART GLASS

The top of Michigan's Lower Peninsula is uppermost in many travelers' minds for its year-round recreational offerings and beauty. Although the area is dotted with typical tourist craft shops, one shop that merits a stop is Boyer Glassworks.

Only a glass window divides this gallery from the huge furnace where Harry Boyer creates his molten images. Visitors can watch him fashion everything from vases and paperweights to handmade marbles. Even your children will enjoy seeing Harry pull a vase from the furnace, then shape it with charred wooden blocks or dip hot

glass into patterns of colored glass chips to form decorative vases and bowls. The gallery sells this colorful art glass as well as pieces by local potters, metalsmiths, and other artisans.

PRICES: $5–$1,250 (average, $40–$75). Accepts American Express, MasterCard, Visa.

OPEN: Mon.–Sat., 10 A.M.–5 P.M.; at other times by appointment. Closed major holidays. Wheelchair accessible.

LOCATION: About 40 miles southwest of Mackinac Bridge, which links Michigan's Upper and Lower peninsulas. 207 North State Street, P.O. Box 733, Harbor Springs, MI 49740; 616-526-6359. Take I-75 to Rte. 68 (Indian River exit). Go west on Rte. 68 to Rte. 31, south on Rte. 31 to Rte. 119. Follow Rte. 119 to Harbor Springs where it becomes Main Street, then State Street. The glassworks is across the street from the post office.

HONOR

Don Stiles
PETOSKEY STONE CARVINGS

"Michigan is the only place in the world where you can find Petoskey stone," Don says. "The name comes from a beach where the stones are often found. They were formed during the Devonian period, which began four-hundred-fifty-million years ago and lasted for sixty-million years. During this time coral colonies called *Hexagonaria anna* grew locally in the warm seas, sometimes reaching up to eight feet in diameter. Each polyp was a living creature sharing a wall with its neighbors. After the coral died, the walls filled with limestone mud and petrified over eons of time."

The mottled stones show white polyp walls filled with granular centers ranging from light beige to black. Starting with one of these small coral colonies, Don shapes poised and polished animals from bears and ducks to rabbits and frogs. Among the most appealing are turtles whose polyp-dotted backs realistically imitate an actual turtle shell.

PRICES: $20–$1,200. Commissions accepted. Send an SASE for Don's catalog/brochure.

VISITORS: Yes. By appointment only.

LOCATION: Northwestern Lower Peninsula, about 32 miles southwest of Traverse City. Rte. 1, Box 72-A, Honor, MI 49640; 616-325-3723. Directions will be provided when appointment to visit is made.

MORE: Don's work is also available through the Artisan's Gallery (2666 Charlevoix Avenue, Petoskey), Made in Michigan (311 East Lake Street, Petoskey), and the Blanford Nature Center (1715 Hillburn NW, Grand Rapids).

If you are in the Honor/Traverse City area, you should also see Frank Ettawageshik's traditional Ottawa Indian pottery. Frank uses the same type of clay, shape, decoration, and open-pit firing as his prehistoric ancestors once did. See this work at Pipigwa Pottery, P.O. Box 71, Karlin, MI 49647-0071; 616-263-7141. Karlin is located near Green Lake, south of Rte. 31 and Interlochen.

LANSING

Glen Van Antwerp
CEDAR FAN CARVINGS

"Around the turn of the century lumbering was one of Michigan's major industries," Glen says. "During long winter evenings in remote camps, the lumbermen had little to do, so they often turned to wood carving to pass the time. My grandfather, like his own father and grandfather before him, were all Michigan lumberjacks. One of the folk arts he learned was carving cedar fans. Later he taught me how to make them.

"I create all my fans from a single piece of wood, from three-and-a-half-inch basic birds with outstretched wings and tail to fourteen-inch peacocks complete with the spread fan tail and head fan. I even make fencepost fans from old wea-

Glen Van Antwerp: Peacock fan. Cedar. H. 14″; W. 17″; D. 8″.
HAROLD MILLER

thered split-rail posts. The weathered wood still shows on the base, but the top is transformed into a fan with up to sixty-four blades.

"Everything starts with a piece of northern white cedar which I get from land that has been in my family for many years. I start with a rough block, cutting a deep notch in each side to make a narrow point. Above this point will be the fan, below it is the rest of the bird or other carving. I split the fan by peeling off thin layers with a knife, keeping them attached at the base. Next I soak the fan in water to make it soft and pliable, then spread it open, interlocking the notched blades."

PRICES: $10–$150. Commissions accepted. Send an SASE for Glen's catalog/brochure.

VISITORS: Yes. Please call first.

LOCATION: South-central Michigan, between Detroit and Grand Rapids. 912 Sparrow Avenue, Lansing, MI 48910; 517-482-6258 (it's best to call between 6 and 7 P.M.). Please call for directions.

OHIO

Ohio's reputation as a deep pocket of industrial Middle America is accurate but incomplete. Scattered throughout the state are rolling hills and bucolic countryside, even the simple farms of Amish and Mennonite communities. Crafts reflect this mingling of old and new, from contemporary work displayed in classy Cleveland galleries or created by innovative artisans working in textiles and aluminum to traditional baskets, furniture, bandboxes, theorem paintings, and Amish textiles. Travelers can also visit an array of festivals featuring traditional crafts or drop by glass and ceramic centers dating back to the nineteenth century.

AKRON

Don Drumm
ALUMINUM CRAFTS

"Don started college studying pre-med," says his wife, Lisa, "but made his contribution to humanity by getting out of medicine. He ended up majoring in art, then later worked for an industrial design firm. Along the way he learned the foundry process and how to work with sand-cast aluminum. Now he creates a wide variety of aluminum items from casseroles and platters to candleholders, sculptures, and Jewish ceremonial pieces.

"In producing his work, Don develops an original and, when the image is satisfactory, it is put onto a matchplate similar to a three-dimensional print plate a graphic artist might use. The sand of the mold is then packed around the plate, the plate is removed, and molten aluminum is poured into the resulting cavity. The casting is then trimmed, filed, and buffed to produce the finished object."

PRICES: $38–$100. Commissions accepted. A catalog/brochure is available.

VISITORS: Mon.–Fri., 10 A.M.–6 P.M.; Sat., 10 A.M.–5 P.M.

LOCATION: Northeastern Ohio. 437 Crouse Street, Akron, OH 44311; 216-253-6268. Take I-77/76 to the Rte. 8 exit. Take Rte. 8 to the first exit on Exchange Street. Turn left on Exchange, left on Spicer Street, right on Crouse.

BEAVERCREEK

Barbara and Norbert Hala
TRADITIONAL BASKETS

If you can't travel to Nantucket for a lightship basket, to a Shaker museum shop for a traditional cheese basket, or to Appalachia for a sturdy egg basket, visit the Halas', where Barbara and Norbert re-create these and other traditional baskets. Although interested in authenticity, their location makes some adjustments necessary. "Since we don't have ready access to native woods," Norbert explains, "we have to be content with using commercially produced weaving supplies. But we make our own natural black walnut dyes, which give our pieces an antique appearance."

"We try to take the extra steps needed to produce exceptional baskets," Barbara adds. "For ex-

245

Barbara and Norbert Hala: Market baskets with stenciled pattern. (Left, with geese stencil) H. 12″; W. 9″; L. 13″. (Right, with Amish buggy stencil) H. 14″; W. 11″; L. 17″. FRANK ESTERLIN

ample, many basket weavers will use only ten to twenty spokes in an Appalachian-style basket, but we put up to fifty in the same size basket. We also do extra weaving on many of the handles. And although every basket is decorative, each is strong enough to be used for its original purpose—from holding eggs to carrying two pies to a church supper."

The Halas also create New York apple baskets, Cape Cod berry baskets, and even woven doll cradles. Another specialty is rectangular market baskets stenciled with colorful figures from rocking horses and sheep to sleighs and Amish buggies.

PRICES: $8–$145. No commissions. Send a business-size SASE for their catalog/brochure.

VISITORS: Yes. "Call to make sure we're home."

LOCATION: Just east of Dayton. 1641 Etta Kable Drive, Beavercreek, OH 45432; 513-429-3937. Take I-70 or I-75 to I-675. Take exit 17 (Fairfield Road) and proceed 2.5 miles south to Suburban Drive. Turn left on Suburban, then go about five blocks to Hillside. Turn right on Hillside. Go one block to Etta Kable Drive and turn right. The house is the first on the right.

BERLIN

Kaufman Gallery
CONTEMPORARY MENNONITE CRAFTS AND AMISH FOLK ART

The largest Amish community in the world lives in Holmes County, Ohio, not Pennsylvania. Although Holmes has become a bit touristy over the years, it still has some outstanding attractions, including quality Mennonite and Amish crafts. One gallery worth visiting is Kaufman's, specializing in both contemporary Mennonite work and traditional Amish crafts.

Kaufman's most unusual items are Amish "shoe rugs" made by the ultraconservative Schwartzentruber Amish. Meant for wiping your shoes upon entering the house, these 1½-by-2-foot rugs are made from scraps of clothing material, reflecting this group's preference for bright colors. The Schwartzentruber also create miniature Amish quilts, often incorporating over 200 pieces of fabric in a single 10-by-12-inch work.

Although most of the gallery's Amish crafts are made locally, contemporary pieces are created by Mennonite artists from throughout the country. Look for Lynn Lais's elegant ceramics with delicate calligraphic decoration and Barbara Fast's handmade paper constructions, which include references to more traditional Mennonite crafts such as quilting.

Located in an 1879 Victorian bracketed Italianate house, the gallery also offers a special treat to travelers: overnight accommodations in two-room suites on the second floor. The Victorian bedrooms and sitting rooms are furnished with local crafts and original art.

PRICES: $25–$900 (average, $200–$300); overnight lodging, $60–$80/night. Accepts MasterCard, Visa.

OPEN: Gallery—Tues.–Sat., 1–5 P.M. Closed Thanksgiving, Christmas, and New Year's Day. Wheelchair accessible. Accommodations—Daily, year-round.

LOCATION: Northeastern Ohio, about 35 miles southwest of Canton. #4786 State Route 39, Box 185, Berlin, OH 44610; 216-893-2842. Take I-77 to the Strasburg exit (Rte. 250), Rte. 250 past Strasburg to Wilmot. Go left on Rte. 62 to Berlin. The gallery is located on the main street, at the junction of Rtes. 62 and 39.

MORE: To watch groups of Amish and Mennonite women quilting, stop by Helping Hands, located on the main street of Berlin (216-893-2410). For an introduction to local Amish, Mennonite, Lutheran, and Reformed Church cultures and their crafts, visit the German Culture Museum in nearby Walnut Creek (216-893-2510). During August, stop by the Ohio Mennonite Relief Sale & Auction, featuring quilts and other crafts made by Ohio and Pennsylvania craftspeople. For details contact the Relief Sale, Box 62, Kidron, OH 44636; 216-682-5263 or 216-852-4651.

CAMBRIDGE

Ohio Glass

If you're a glass nut, you'll probably want to veer off I-70 or I-77 for a brief stop at Cambridge. Like neighboring West Virginia and Indiana, Ohio was an early-twentieth-century glass-manufacturing center. Although most operations were large factories, some produced glass now considered collectible.

For a glance at Ohio's glass history, stop by two local museums. The Degenhart Paperweight and Glass Museum displays a variety of Ohio glassware. The Cambridge Glass Museum focuses on items made locally from 1902 to 1954, including dinnerware, fancy hand-painted pieces, jardinieres, and satin-etched glass. If that's not enough, and your kids like factory tours, drop by one of the

still-operating companies: Mosser Glass or Boyd's Crystal Art Glass Co.

DEGENHART PAPERWEIGHT AND GLASS MUSEUM: Days open vary, but always include Sat., 10 A.M.–5 P.M., and Sun., 1–5 P.M. Admission is $1.50 for adults, $1.25 for seniors, children under 18 free. SR 22, Cambridge, OH 43725; 614-432-2626.

CAMBRIDGE GLASS MUSEUM: Mon.–Sat., 1–4 p.m. Admission is $1.50 for adults, $1 for seniors, children under 12 free. 812 Jefferson Avenue, Cambridge, OH 43725; 614-432-3045.

FACTORY TOURS: Mosser Glass, 614-439-1827; Boyd's Crystal Art Glass, Co., 614-439-2077.

MORE: If you still haven't had enough, visit the National Heisey Glass Museum in Newark, about 40 miles east of Columbus. Manufacturer of fine glassware from 1896 to 1957, Heisey is known for its pressed glass, colonial patterns, figurines, and colored glass (pastels, cobalt, and tangerine). There's even a glass mailbox on display. 6th Street Park, 6th and Church Streets, P.O. Box 4367, Newark, OH 43055; 614-345-2932.

CLEVELAND

Sylvia Ullman/American Crafts
CONTEMPORARY CRAFTS

A transit power generation station may not say "gallery space" to you, but this one works well, especially the second floor's 40-foot ceiling, which displays a variety of mobiles and suspended crafts. Back on eye level, fine craftsmanship, the innovative use of color, and abstract design link this gallery's otherwise disparate pieces. Many items also seem to have subtle, and possibly unintended, humor.

In Holly Kenny's woven wall hangings, a burst of raffia often provides an appealing contrast to an otherwise carefully ordered piece. In one work, a cascade of raffia looks as if someone's unkempt, teal-green dog got its tail caught in a subtle black-and-purple weaving. Playing tricks on your eyes in another medium, Richard Schneider's ceramics contradict their basic shapes by plopping you visually down amidst jagged orange lines or polka-dotted rectangles. Richard's wife, Patricia Hughes-Schneider, creates large vases that act as ceramic canvases for pastel abstractions.

PRICES: $5–$20,000 (average, $75–$150). Accepts Master-Card, Visa.

OPEN: Mon.–Sat., 10 A.M.–6 P.M., Sun. (Oct.–May), 1–5 P.M. Closed all legal holidays. Not wheelchair accessible.

LOCATION: Shaker Heights, east of downtown Cleveland. 13010 Larchmere Boulevard, Cleveland, OH 44120; 216-231-2008. From downtown Cleveland, take Rte. 87 (Shaker Boulevard) to East 130th. Turn right at the stop sign and continue to Larchmere. The gallery is one block north of Shaker Square.

MASSILLON

Jack B. Robinson
COUNTRY FURNITURE REPRODUCTIONS

"When I was a boy during World War II, I made little wooden toys to sell to our neighbors at Christmastime," Jack recalls. "As an adult, I became a carpentry apprentice, graduating to journeyman in only four years. I helped build churches, homes, did a lot of restoration work, even some architectural furniture. But it was a trip to the Ford Museum which got me interested in early craftsmen and their furniture. I started making a few pieces for my family, and my children liked the work so much they said I should try selling it. Been doing just that since 1978."

Using seventeenth- and eighteenth-century tools and techniques, Jack reproduces period furniture and accessories. "I use curly maple, wormy chestnut, walnut, and cherry for my pieces," Jack says. "I make everything out of three-quarter-inch boards, no plywood or modern gimmickry, even use a chisel and mallet for all my dovetail work. If the originals used nails, I use cut nails. I even finish my pieces to make them look used."

In addition to cupboards, tables, dry sinks, and other large furniture, Jack makes some unusual items: bed steps, Bible and diaper boxes, twine winders, and even tricorn hat boxes.

PRICES: $10–$1,000 +. Commissions accepted. A catalog/brochure is available.

VISITORS: Yes.

LOCATION: Eastern Ohio, about 10 miles west of Canton. American Country Reproductions, 8760 Beatty Street NW, Massillon, OH 44646; 216-832-5641. Please call for directions.

MORE: Jack's work is also available through the Country Barn, 5541 Butterbridge Road NW, Canal Fulton, OH 44614; 216-854-4758.

MILLERSBURG

Rastetter Woolen Mill
HANDWOVEN RAG RUGS AND CARPETING

The Smithsonian has knocked twice at the door of this fifth-generation woolen mill. In 1971 Ralph Aling, grandfather of present owner Tim Rastetter,

Rastetter Woolen Mill: *Smithsonian Brick and Block,* patterned rug. W. 27"; L. 54".

was asked to demonstrate rug weaving at the Smithsonian's Folk Festival. Seventy-five-year-old Ralph took along $300 worth of rugs, sold them all, and returned with a full year's worth of orders. In 1983 the Smithsonian called again, this time inviting Tim to be one of 100 craftspeople (and the only weaver) to exhibit at the annual Spring Craft Show. Repeating his grandfather's success, Tim took along $10,000 worth of rugs, sold out, and came home with a staggering pile of new orders.

What's the appeal? Colorful, handwoven rugs in a variety of patterns, materials, and sizes, from small, braided wool rugs to full-size carpets. Patterns may be stripes, plaids, the wonderfully random "hit-n-miss," or the Smithsonian Brick and Block design, named after pieces Ralph created during his 1971 Smithsonian visit. Made from new wool or wool rags, cotton rags, or acrylic blanket remnants, many rugs are woven in double layers with lofts up to 1 inch. Have your own favorite rag pile? Ask the Rastetters to transform it into a custom-made rug.

In the tradition of a true family operation, Tim and his wife, Maureen, are joined on weekends by their children, Vanessa and Timmy. Even Ralph, now in his nineties, comes in to do a bit of weaving now and then and chat with the customers.

PRICES: $8.50–$432 +. Commissions accepted. Send a business-size SASE for the catalog/brochure.

OPEN: Feb.–May, Wed.–Sat., noon–5 P.M.; June–Dec., Tues.–Sat., noon–5 P.M. Closed all of Jan.

LOCATION: Northwestern Ohio, about 42 miles southwest of Canton. 5802 S.R. 39, Millersburg, OH 44654; 216-674-2103. Take I-77 to the Strasburg exit (Rte. 250), Rte. 250 past Strasburg to Wilmot. Go left on Rte. 62. The mill is located 4.5 miles east of Millersburg, on the south side of the highway.

MORE: Staying overnight? Consider the Inn at Honey Run, a contemporary inn filled with handmade Amish furnishings, quilts, and other crafts. 6920 County Road 203, Millersburg, OH 44654; 216-674-0011 (800-468-6639 in Ohio).

OBERLIN

Deborah Banyas
FABRIC SCULPTURE

Just lost your best friend? Suffering from the empty-nest syndrome? Feel a need to expand your circle of acquaintances? Talk to Deborah. She can

supply you with instant companions who are guaranteed not to raid the refrigerator but who may give you a reputation as the neighborhood eccentric.

Using fabric, paint, and assorted doodads, Deborah creates yard-tall animal folk who thoughtfully bring their own furniture, and sometimes even rugs, when they move in. Always dreamed of having a pet goat? Deborah's creation is somewhat garishly attired in a red-and-black shirt, pedal pushers, and a red tie. Sitting in an overstuffed red chair, this content goat gently pats a pet alligator (see color plate #15).

Rather have a turquoise deer? This upright figure, known as *Blue Squaw*, sweetly offers you her favorite red snake. Of course, her mother dresses her rather oddly. Feathers sprout from her head, and she wears a Nouveau Punk costume with beaded leather top, jester-inspired short skirt, and bell-topped black boots.

Prefer something risqué? Purchase *Love Birds*. Snuggled on a love seat, these spiffily dressed birds look as if they were interrupted in a moment of passion. The female has one leg draped over the chair arm and (blush) her bodice is untied, revealing a prominent blue private part.

Humor, childhood fantasies, and a rejection of "normal" art forms, all combine to make Deborah's work unusually appealing. "Although each piece looks rather straightforward technically," Deborah notes, "they're really complex. In order to get my forms to stay in the right position I have to use armatures, counterweights, straps, tucks, and extremely tight stuffing." Whatever the process is, the results are charming but rather impertinent new family members who delight in being the centers of attention.

PRICES: $45–$3,000. No commissions. No catalog/brochure.

VISITORS: Yes.

LOCATION: North-central Ohio, about 40 miles west of Cleveland. 22 Carpenter Court, Oberlin, OH 44074; 216-775-2238. Take I-90/80 (the Ohio Turnpike) to exit 8. Take Rte. 57 south to Elyria, then go west on Rte. 113 about 6 miles to the junction with Rte. 58. Take Rte. 58 south 6 miles to Oberlin. Take the first driveway on the right past College Street (next to the gas co.). The studio is in the stucco building with the turquoise door, behind the gas co.

ROSEVILLE

Ohio Pottery and Ceramic Center
MUSEUM AND POTTERY

Eal Run, Possom Hollow, Breadless, Poverty Hollow, and Henpeck are a few of the over forty-one different nineteenth-century potteries that once operated within four miles of Roseville. Run by farmers during the winter season, the potteries used locally mined clay prepared by horse-powered mills. In 1885 steam power replaced horses and some potteries began year-round operations. When art pottery became popular, twenty-two local companies produced this decorative work. The Ohio Pottery and Ceramic Center documents local ceramic history with displays in five different buildings that include exhibits of art pottery and utilitarian ware as well as currently produced items.

OPEN: Apr. 15–Oct. 1, Wed–Sat., 10 A.M.–6 P.M.; Sun., noon–5 P.M. Closed holidays. A museum is on the premises. Admission is $1 for adults, 50¢ for children. Wheelchair accessible.

LOCATION: East-central Ohio, about 10 miles southwest of Zanesville. Ceramic Road (Rte. 93), Roseville, OH. The mailing address is Box 200, Crooksville, OH 43731; 614-697-7021. Take I-70 to Zanesville, then go south on Rte. 22 to Moxahala Park, south on Rte. 93 to Roseville.

MORE: The center sponsors an annual pottery festival the third weekend in July, Thurs.–Sat. Visitors will enjoy watching potters working in the on-site studio, taking tours of Robinson-Ransbottom Pottery (one of the largest in the world), and seeing a Miss Pottery Queen contest.

SPRINGFIELD

Eileen Sherrard
BANDBOXES

Pretend you are a fashionable lady living in the American Federal period (1800–1850). How would you transport your latest finery when traveling? Where would you store your handkerchiefs and imported gloves at home? No, no, you wouldn't use a Bloomie's shopping bag or recycled Tupperware. You'd choose instead a bandbox. Sturdy but lightweight, these prettily papered cardboard boxes were the early nineteenth century's answer to many storage problems.

Eileen carefully sews together pieces of 60-pt. cardboard to form a box and lid. She then covers them with period wallpaper, perhaps a delicate pastel flower pattern or a romanticized design showing a young woman walking her dog. Eileen's boxes come in every size and shape, from small round trinket boxes to large, six-sided boxes perfect for storing your favorite childhood teddy bear.

PRICES: $25–$125 ($325 for graduated sets). Commissions accepted. No catalog/brochure.

VISITORS: Yes.

LOCATION: Western Ohio, about 50 miles west of Columbus. 2404 Lagonda Avenue, Springfield, OH 45503; 513-399-3453. Please call for directions.

TROY

Nancy Rosier
THEOREM PAINTINGS

If art-by-the-numbers and black velvet paintings generally make you gag, set aside your prejudices for a moment to learn about the craft that probably spawned them both. Theorem paintings, so named because they were painted according to a formula, were produced by early-nineteenth-century schoolgirls to re-create designs provided by their teachers. Most often portraying still lifes, theorem paintings were a respected craft used to decorate fine homes of the past.

"I reproduce theorems found in major museum collections," Nancy says, "But I also create original and custom designs. Following traditional practices, I first analyze the design I want to copy and divide it into numbered parts. Next I cut stencils to correspond to the numbers and place them on cotton velveteen. I rub or brush oil paint through the openings to form the painting, sometimes adding a few details freehand. To keep an authentic 1800s look, I make my own frames, either false-grained or black with bronze stenciling.

"Antique theorems are a rare find today," Eileen adds, "because many were done on fabrics which

Nancy Rosier: Reproduction antique theorem. H. 20″; W. 16″.
WILLIAM ROSIER

deteriorated long ago. The museums have all the good ones. The next best thing is a fine reproduction, like the ones I make." Eileen's catalog illustrates over thirty of her designs, from baskets of fruits and vegetables to bouquets of flowers, a rocking horse, and even a slice of watermelon.

PRICES: $35–$225. Commissions accepted. Write to Eileen at 2366 Rockingham Drive, Troy, OH 45373. Send $1 for her catalog/brochure, which features black-and-white illustrations; color photos are available for a small, refundable fee.

VISITORS: Mail order is preferred, but Eileen will see customers by appointment; call 513-335-3761.

Ohio Craft Festivals and "Homecomings"

Ohio craft shows reproduce faster than bunnies. Every year brings new additions, particularly historical fairs, eager to find their niche among collectors and tourists. They vary so tremendously in quality and appeal that only a Buckeye craft groupie could keep them all straight. Listed below are a few you might want to sample if you're in the right town at the right time.

BERLIN

Der Dutch Peddlar
TRADITIONAL CRAFTS

Known as a "Homecoming," since that is how the Amish refer to their seasonal festivals, Der Dutch Peddlar is a twice-yearly event with good-quality crafts, including some fine Amish quilts and dolls. Craft demonstrations, apple butter making, and sheep shearing will appeal, especially to your children.

EVENT: Third Thur.–Sat. in July & fourth Fri./Sat. after Labor Day in Sept. Contact the sponsors for specifics. Admission is $3 for adults, $2.50 for seniors and children 12–18.

LOCATION: Amish Farm, Rte. 39, 1 mile east of Berlin, about 35 miles southwest of Canton. Take I-177 to the Dover/Rte. 39 west exit. Follow Rte. 39 west for about 20 miles to the Amish Farm.

MORE: For information contact Down Home Publications, 5515 CR 407, P.O. 418, Millersburg, OH 44654; 216-674-9631.

CANAL FULTON

Yankee Peddler Festival
TRADITIONAL CRAFTS

Seventy-five acres of festival space, seven entertainment stages, and ninety-three food booths tell you this is not going to be an intimate fair. It is, however, well done, with great pains taken to see that (almost) everything fits into the Colonial America theme. Craft booths must be "rustic," exhibitors must dress in colonial garb, and crafts must be traceable to colonial times. Buy your own butter churn, pierced tinware, quilts, or even a violin, then sample "old-fashioned" food, including sarsaparilla, lemonade, Amish cheese, and apple fritters.

EVENT: Last three weekends in Sept. Sats. & Suns., 11 A.M.–7 P.M. Admission is $6 for adults, $4.50 for seniors, $1.50 for children.

LOCATION: Clay's Park Resort, Canal Fulton, about 25 miles south of Akron. Take I-76 to Rte. 21, Rte. 21 south to Rte. 93. Follow Rte. 93 south, away from Canal Fulton. Clay's Park will be on the left.

MORE: For information contact the Yankee Peddler Festival Association, 4046 State Road, Medina, OH 44256; 216-239-2554.

MENTOR

Little Mountain Folk Festival
Yesteryear Festival
TRADITIONAL AND CONTEMPORARY CRAFTS

Sponsored by the local historical society, these two festivals celebrate the area's heritage. Little Mountain Folk Festival, held every July, is the larger of the two. Featuring over ninety artisans, the event includes a sprinkling of ethnic crafts by local Irish, Ukrainian, and Hungarian artisans. There's also entertainment by groups such as Buddy Herak's Tamburitzans and tummy-pleasing traditional and ethnic foods. The Yesteryear Festival is a harvest-time event featuring fruits of the harvest, old-time farm machinery, and log cabin crafts such as whittling, basketweaving, and blacksmithing.

EVENTS: The Little Mountain Folk Festival is held the last weekend in July. Sat., 10 A.M.–7 P.M.; Sun., noon–7 P.M. The Yesteryear Festival is held the first weekend in Oct. Sat., 10 A.M.–5 P.M.; Sun., noon–5 P.M. Admission is $3 for adults, $2 for children.

LOCATION: (both events) Lake County History Center, 8610 King Memorial Road, Mentor, about 25 miles east of Cleveland. Take I-90 to the Rte. 44 (Chardon) exit. Go south on Rte. 44 to King Memorial Road, right on King Memorial Road. The center is on the left, at the junction with Little Mountain Road.

MORE: For information contact the Lake County Historical Society, 8610 King Memorial Road, Mentor, OH 44060; 216-255-8979.

SPRINGFIELD

The Fair at New Boston
PIONEER CRAFTS (1780–1818)

A re-created early American trades fair, this annual event features not only colonial crafts but also medicine shows, battle reenactments, a surgeon's tent, melodramas, and a Woodland Indian camp. The emphasis here is on craft demonstrations (sales are secondary) by costumed artisans. In addition to craft booths, wandering "mongers" sell their wares from baskets or wooden boxes, and "blanket traders" purvey their goods from, of course, a blanket spread on the ground.

Intent on keeping the festival strictly authentic, the sponsors jury *everything*, even entertainers, food, and artisans' costumes. Participating artisans are warned not to wear modern eyeglasses, smoke only clay pipes (preferably in the woods), and, no matter how hot the day, men are to keep their coats and hats on, women must at least wear a chemise over- and underskirts, a bodice, and a mobcap. This strict adherence to tradition may give artisans heatstroke, but it permits visitors to step back in time, hear hurdy-gurdy players and balladeers, and snack on period treats such as corn oysters, fried pies, and sausage-on-a-stick.

EVENT: Labor Day weekend. Sat. & Sun., 10 A.M.–6 P.M. Admission is $4 for adults, $2 for children.

LOCATION: George Rogers Clark Park, 3 miles west of Springfield, about 50 miles west of Columbus. The park is at the corner of Rtes. 4 and 369.

MORE: For information contact the George Rogers Clark Heritage Association, 818 North Fountain Avenue, P.O. Box 1251, Springfield, OH 45501; 513-324-0657.

WISCONSIN

Wisconsin, vacationland for many Midwesterners, is often unexplored by East Coast or West Coast travelers. To rectify this situation, choose a craft itinerary that takes you across southern Wisconsin and up along Lake Michigan to the tip of Door County's peninsula, or strike northwest through Wisconsin Dells and Woodville. Whichever route you choose, you will find ethnic crafts from Norwegian wood carving and Polish papercutting to Yugoslavian and Czech Easter eggs; Oneida, Menominee, or other Wisconsin tribal arts; duck decoys or whirligigs; and striking contemporary crafts.

In addition to the entries listed below, if you're interested in Amish crafts and a back road adventure, look for handmade signs advertising quilts, bentwood rockers, and produce along highways in three areas: 1. About 28 miles southeast of La Crosse, along Rte. 33 between Cashton and Ontario take a circular route south of Cashton along Rte. 27, east on Rte. P and north on Rte. D. 2. About 15 miles southeast of Stevens Point, along a circular route beginning on Rte. A south of Amherst continuing west on Rte. 54, north on Rte. J, and east on Rte. B. 3. About 48 miles northeast of Madison between Cambria and Pardeeville. From Madison, take Rte. 151 northeast to Beaver Dam, then Rte. 33 to Cambria. Amish crafts can be found along Rte. 33 and Rte. P, both of which connect Cambria and Pardeeville.

BARRONETT

Phillip Odden and Else Bigton
NORWEGIAN WOOD CARVING AND FURNITURE

Else and Phillip met at the famous Hjerleid carving school in Dovre, Norway. "Else was born in Norway," Phillip says, "but I grew up on a Wisconsin dairy farm. I really didn't want to farm, so I wandered the world trying my hand at a variety of things. In Norway I met a distant cousin who is a master carver and I knew I'd found my niche." While at Hjerleid, Else majored in cabinetmaking and Phillip in carving. "Although one of us may fashion an entire piece from start to finish," Else says, "generally I'll do the initial design and cabinetry while Phillip concentrates on carving and ornamentation."

"We specialize in three carving styles," Phillip continues. "My favorite is the robust Medieval Viking style, which often includes animals and people. Else's specialty is the Acanthus leafage of the Baroque period. But we also do some pieces in a Rococo style. We work with butternut, pine, birch, or basswood to fashion everything from small plate racks to large *Fram Skaps* [hutches]."

"One of our most unusual pieces," Else says, "is the *Kubbe Stol*, a traditional Norwegian chair. We start with a large basswood log, hollow it out, and create the basic shape. Then we season it for a year. After that we finish shaping it, then cover the chair with carving, each time using a different design." Visitors will also find elaborately carved corner cupboards (*Hjorne Skap*) with backs of solid wood and hanging cupboards (*Henje Skap*) with carved, pierced doors.

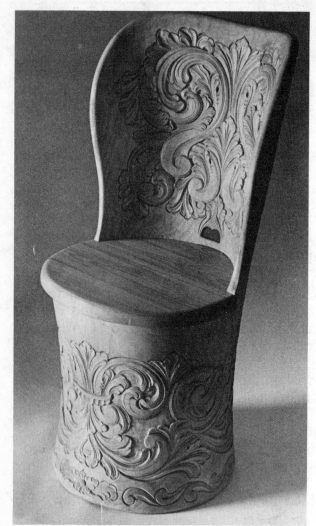

Phillip Odden and Else Bigton: *Kubbe Stol.* Carved from solid basswood log. H. 35″; Diam. 19″.

PRICES: $25–5,000. Commissions accepted: "Sixty to eighty percent of our work is by commission." Send an SASE for their catalog/brochure.

VISITORS: Yes. By appointment only.

LOCATION: Northwestern Wisconsin between Duluth, Minnesota, and Eau Claire, Wisconsin; about 90 miles northeast of Minneapolis. Box 66, Highway 63, Barronett, WI 54813; 715-822-3104. Take I-94 to the Rte. 63 exit (Baldwin). Go north on Rte. 63 to Barronett. The shop is located along the highway.

MORE: Phillip & Else's work is also available through Norsk Hasflid (a shop operated by Phillip's parents), Box 87, Highway 63, Barronett, WI 54813; 715-822-8747.

DE PERE

Oneida Nation Museum
TRADITIONAL CRAFTS

A member of the six-nation Iroquois Confederacy, the Oneida tribe moved from New York to Wisconsin in the 1820s. The Oneida are by tradition a matrilineal society, so the women continued to till the fields, own their own homes, and choose the chiefs. Once in Wisconsin, they also helped support their families by making beaded souvenirs.

Museum visitors will see examples of this intricate beadwork as well as other Oneida/Iroquois crafts such as war clubs, lacework, cornhusk dolls, and a variety of shopping, fruit picking, and floursifting baskets. Children will enjoy the museum's "hands-on" exhibit, where they can touch baskets and beadwork, heft a war club, and try out drums, dance bells, and rattles.

Although small, the gift shop carries some interesting items, including traditional "courting flutes," melodious, low-toned, wood instruments Oneida men once used to serenade the women they loved.

OPEN: Apr.–Oct., Mon.–Sat., 9 A.M.–5 P.M. Closed Sat. Nov.–March. A museum shop is on the premises. Admission is $1 for adults, 50¢ for children. Wheelchair accessible.

LOCATION: Northeastern Wisconsin, 6 miles southwest of Green Bay. P.O. Box 365, Oneida, WI 54155-0365. Take I-43 to Rte. 172 west. Continue to the end of Rte. 172. This will lead you to Highway E. Turn left onto Highway E and continue for 4.5 miles to Highway EE. Turn right onto Highway EE. The museum is one block farther.

MORE: See the listing under Green Bay, below, for other Oneida crafts.

FREDERIC

Sigvart Terland
WOODEN SHOES

I grew up in Norway," Sigvart says, "and my father taught me to make wooden shoes when I was nine years old. His father taught him the same skills at that age and now it became my responsibility to make shoes for the family." In 1926 Sigvart emigrated to the United States, moving eventually to Washington, D.C., where he became a metallurgist for the Navy. "I retired thirty-four years later," he says, "and moved to Frederic, where my wife grew up. Once again I began to carve wooden shoes. I use birch and special tools made by a Norwegian blacksmith. And I still make the shoes the same way our family has for generations. Sometimes I also create replicas of Viking ships."

PRICES: Wooden shoes, $45–$50; Viking ships, $50. No commissions. No catalog/brochure.

VISITORS: Yes. Please call first for appointment.

LOCATION: Northwestern Wisconsin, about 72 miles northeast of Minneapolis, 82 miles southwest of Duluth. Box 355, 304 Birch Street, Frederic, WI 54837; 715-237-8852. Directions will be provided when appointment to visit is made.

(NOTE: Although Mr. Terland, an active senior citizen in his eighties, crafts a number of pairs of wooden shoes each year, he does not have a large stock on hand. If you want to talk with a fine craftsman, and possibly place an order, be sure to visit with him. If, however, you are merely interested in owning a pair of wooden shoes, visit a more commercial place such as the Wooden Shoe Factory in Holland, Michigan [616-396-6513].)

GREEN BAY

Sheila S. Smith
ONEIDA/IROQUOIS CLOTHING AND BEADWORK

After our tribe moved to Wisconsin in the early nineteenth century," Sheila recounts, "they became Christianized and lost many of their customs. My father was always very interested in preserving Oneida culture, and I picked up a similar concern. One day I decided to redo the beadwork on a traditional outfit I owned but found almost no one remembered the techniques. I ended up doing a lot of research, which led to an interest in all traditional Oneida/Iroquois clothing."

Today Sheila re-creates both men's and women's clothing, including overdress skirts and leggings, ribbon shirts, aprons, moccasins, beaded purses, and feather headdresses. She also makes fancy dress outfits with satin skirts and beaded yolks and cuffs. "One of these traditional outfits was worn by our museum director at Reagan's 1984 Presidential Inaugural Ball," Sheila recalls proudly. "But not all of my work is traditional. I also create contemporary Indian fashions which incorporate silk screen-

ing and other techniques that aren't part of my heritage."

PRICES: $50–$4,000. Commissions accepted. No catalog/brochure.

VISITORS: Yes. By appointment only.

LOCATION: Northeastern Wisconsin. 966 Willard Drive, #7, Green Bay, WI 54304; 414-498-8512. Directions will be provided when appointment to visit is made.

HAYWARD

Ricky and Cathy Barber
BUCKSKIN CLOTHING

Nothing can compare to the softness, warmth and subtle smokey odor of authentically prepared buckskin clothing. It's like wrapping yourself up in the fragrance of a winter campfire, the memories of America's distant generations.

Members of the Lac Courte Oreilles Band of Lake Superior Chippewa Indians, Ricky and Cathy prepare deerskin using the time-honored methods of their ancestors. "We soften the skin with deer brains," Cathy explains. "Then we smoke it with punk wood for color and aroma. When the process is complete, we create pouches, dresses, vests, moccasins, belts, gloves, leggings, and other items. We decorate each piece with traditional floral or geometric beading patterns."

Visitors during the summer or on warm fall days may be able to watch the Barbers tan the deer hides. At other times the couple may be sewing a pair of fringed leggings, lining a buckskin vest, or creating colorful beaded patterns on the soft side flaps of a moccasin.

PRICES: $3–$700. Commissions accepted. No catalog/brochure.

VISITORS: Yes. Please call first.

LOCATION: Far northwestern Wisconsin, about 70 miles southeast of Duluth, Minnesota. Buckskin Arts, Rte. 5, Box 5392-C, Hayward, WI 54843; 715-634-5240. Directions will be provided when you call.

MORE: The Barbers' work is also available through the Turtle Island Stopping Place, on the Lac Courte Oreilles Indian Reservation. The shop also sells a variety of Ojibwe crafts, including birch bark and black ash baskets, "dance sticks," and other traditional items. The shop is open daily (except Christmas and New Year's Day), 9 A.M.–5 P.M. RR #2, Box 2900, Hayward, WI 54843; 715-634-4128. It's located in the reservation's commercial center, 10 miles southeast of Hayward, at the junction of County Trunk Roads K and E.

LA CROSSE

Touch the Earth
WINNEBAGO BASKETS AND OTHER NATIVE AMERICAN CRAFTS

Although Touch the Earth offers a variety of Indian crafts, from Acoma to Zuni, its Winnebago baskets are particularly notable. Made from black ash splints, these durable and attractive baskets are known for their colorful horizontal and vertical stripes. Some also sport ash curlicues that act as pretty pointed feet or decorations on lids and rims.

"We are proud of our Winnebago baskets," says owner Ron Klemmedson. "An old story says that as long as Winnebago women make baskets, their people will not want for anything. Unfortunately, most of the productive basket makers are older now, and very few young people are learning the craft. In fact, the production of quality Indian crafts from our area is very limited. People find better pay

Marie and Velma Lewis: Winnebago sewing baskets. KATHRYN MCMAHON

elsewhere, and the best crafts are generally made for private or ceremonial use."

While here, ask to see intricately beaded pipestone stemwork by Lorraine Carrimon (Winnebago), as well as fine pipestone pipes and carvings by Lee and Myron Taylor (Sautee) and those by Pete Musil (Sisseton).

PRICES: Winnebago baskets, $12–$75; other items, $8–$625. Accepts Discover, MasterCard, Visa.

OPEN: Mon.–Fri., 10 A.M.–5 P.M.; Sat., 10 A.M.–3 P.M.. Closed all national holidays. Not wheelchair accessible.

LOCATION: Western Wisconsin, along the Mississippi River. 220 Main Street, La Crosse, WI 54601; 608-785-2980. Take I-90 to downtown La Crosse. The shop is one block from the Radisson Hotel, two blocks from the Civil Center.

LYONS

Sidonka Wadina-Lee
CZECHOSLOVAKIAN EASTER EGGS

"I was taught to make Czechoslovakian Easter eggs from the time I was first old enough to comprehend what that meant and how to do it," says Sidonka. "Both of my grandmothers were from Slovakia, and they taught me the various techniques. In fact, my Grandmother Birksadsky once said to me: 'You are the future—you must carry on the traditions for me when I am gone.' So I do, and I also teach the crafts to my own children."

The most unusual eggs Sidonka creates are *Kraslice*. Made from goose or duck eggs, they are painted or shellacked, then decorated with flattened pieces of straw arranged in intricate geometric and star shapes. Sidonka also makes Blue Onion eggs, covered with delicate blue ink flower patterns, and Bratislava eggs, decorated with hand-painted flowers in bright pinks, yellows, and greens. Wax-dyed eggs, hand-painted woodenware, and wheat weaving are just a few of the other traditional crafts at which this woman of many talents excells.

PRICES: $5–$300. Commissions accepted. No catalog/brochure.

VISITORS: Yes.

LOCATION: Far southeastern Wisconsin, about 22 miles from the Illinois border, about 8 miles northeast of Lake

Geneva. 1468 Church Street, Lyons, WI 53148; 414-763-4332. Take I-90 to I-43, I-43 northwest to Rte. 12. Go south on Rte. 12 to the Rte. 36 exit, north on Rte. 36 to Lyons. The house is about half a block southeast of Rte. 36.

MAZOMANIE

Stephanie Lemke
YUGOSLAVIAN EASTER EGGS

Stephanie's unusual eggs, called *Pisanica,* are created entirely with colored threads woven around an egg. No glue is used to keep the threads in place, and only one knot at the top of each egg secures the designs. At the top and bottom of each egg, and in a row around the middle, are colorful God's Eye diamond shapes, sometimes in various hues of blue or in vibrant multicolors, at other times in orange or pastels.

"We use spring colors in making these traditional Yugoslavian eggs," Stephanie explains. "I learned this craft as a child, from my mother. When we made them together she used the opportunity to impose strict morals. 'No matter where you go,' she would say, 'or what you do, God's eye is watching you.' The craft itself is a very ancient one, passed down through many, many generations. I think people in this country find the *Pisanica* interesting because it's so different from American dyed eggs. I'm proud to say that one of my eggs is part of the official White House Easter egg collection."

PRICES: $7–$15. Commissions accepted. No catalog/brochure.

VISITORS: Yes.

LOCATION: South-central Wisconsin, about 15 miles northeast of Madison. 214 West Hudson, Mazomanie, WI 53560; 608-795-4303. Please call for directions.

MILWAUKEE

Katie Gingrass Gallery
CONTEMPORARY CRAFTS

Milwaukee is one of America's great undiscovered cities. It also oddly resembles a giant industrial beer garden, mixing German heritage, sophisticated manufacturing, and hops. Almost required for visitors are brewery tours and samples, followed by a tour of the house that hops built, the gigantic thirty-seven-room Pabst mansion. Before you foam at the mouth from your beery circuit, take a cultural detour to Katie Gingrass's superb contemporary crafts gallery.

In a well-designed space that shows off each item to its best advantage, Katie Gingrass and partner Pat Brophy display crafts from unusual contemporary baskets to stunning jewelry. Look particularly for large sculptured clay vessels by Don Reitz, who uses colorful surfaces as a backdrop for sgraffitoed images. Also of interest are hand-carved painted birds and animals by William Jauquet, a self-taught folk artist. Jauquet's large swans and flamingos, small long-horned bulls, and horses on wheels are both captivating and well executed.

PRICES: $25–$5,000 (average, $100–$500). Accepts American Express, MasterCard, Visa.

OPEN: Mon.–Sat., 10 A.M.–5 P.M. Closed all major holidays. Wheelchair accessible.

LOCATION: Downtown Milwaukee. 714 North Milwaukee Street, Milwaukee, WI 53202; 414-289-0855. Take I-794 to the Plankington exit. Continue straight on St. Paul over the river

Stephanie Lemke: Yugoslavian Easter egg. Chicken egg and thread. RICHARD MARSH

to Milwaukee Street. Turn left on Milwaukee; go four blocks to gallery.

MILWAUKEE

Ryszarda Klim
WYCINANKI *(POLISH PAPERCUTTINGS)*

"***W**ycinanki* is a very old Polish craft," Ryszarda explains. "Originally the cuttings were made by villagers using colorful paper and sheep shears. They pasted the cuttings on the whitewashed walls of their homes as decoration. The designs themselves often represent different holidays or just the Pole's love of nature. There's quite a lot of symbolism in them too. For example, the traditional round *wycinanki* shape stands for the sun, while roosters represent rural life. The colors used are always strong and basic. The background is usually black with colors layered on top."

Although Ryszarda was born in Poland and lived there for thirty-five years, she didn't learn *wycinanki* until after she emigrated to the United States. "As a child," Ryszarda recalls, "I learned

Ryszarda Klim: *Wycinanki.* Diam. 14". RAY M. IGNATOWSKI

needlework and *pajaki,* a type of rye straw decoration. But I didn't really focus on *wycinanki* until my children returned from a visit to Poland with several examples. Now I make *wycinanki* the traditional way, except I can't find sheep shearing scissors, so I use regular ones. It is also difficult to find some of the papers, especially black, so sometimes I 'make' my own with special ink. But I still use one piece of paper, folded many times and cut."

PRICES: $25–$100. Commissions accepted. No catalog/brochure.

VISITORS: Yes.

LOCATION: 2989 South Mabbett Avenue, Milwaukee, WI 53207; 414-483-9985. Take I-94 to the Howard Avenue exit. Go right on Howard to Howell Avenue, left on Howell Avenue to Oklahoma Avenue, right on Oklahoma to Mabbett Avenue, left on Mabbett for one block.

MILWAUKEE

Julian Orlandini
ORNAMENTAL PLASTERWORK

"**I**'m the faceless crafter who makes the nice shapes but remains unknown," Julian says. "And that's as it should be." In fact, Julian comes from an extended family of skilled craftsmen who have left their mark but not their names on buildings throughout Europe and the United States.

"My father was born in Lizano, Italy, into a family of stonemasons and glassblowers," Julian says. "He came to the United States in 1912, apprenticed with an ornamental plasterer in Philadelphia, and opened his own shop in Milwaukee in 1936. When I was five I started to help him by mixing plaster and cement. Although I considered becoming an architect, I finally returned to the wonderful scrolls and high-relief designs of decorative plasterwork.

"The 1940s and 1950s weren't a good time for our business," Julian recalls. "Everything was stark, modern, no room for such beautiful details. But recently there's a renewed interest in elegant surroundings. People want my intricate moldings and cornices, corbels, rosettes, columns, and even entire ceilings. For each one I begin by carving a plaster model. Then I cover the model with a type of gelatin to form a mold, and fill the mold with plaster of paris. In comparison to machine-made pieces, mine have sharply defined detail and each commission is unique."

PRICES: $10–$100,000. Commissions accepted. No catalog/brochure.

VISITORS: Yes.

LOCATION: 633 West Virginia Street, Milwaukee, WI 53204; 414-272-3657. "Please call for directions, to make sure I'll be in the shop and not up on a scaffolding somewhere."

MILWAUKEE

Fran Rubenstein
CONTEMPORARY FLOORCLOTHS

Packed dirt floors that were raked daily or bare board floors were de rigueur for early American homes, even the most prosperous ones. Although Americans today take carpeting for granted, prior to the Industrial Revolution carpets were expensive and were more often hung on walls than walked upon. The alternative was painted floorcloths, heavy canvas covered with layers of painted patterns. Colorful, decorative, and durable, they graced the finest homes, including the White House during Thomas Jefferson's presidency. Once factories were able to produce inexpensive carpets, the use of painted floorcloths declined and the craft died out until it was revived by artists during the last decade.

"Almost ten years ago I moved into a new house," Fran recalls. "As I was furnishing it, I fell in love with a $10,000 Persian rug. Financially that was out of the question, so I decided to create a painting for my floor. This turned out to be both practical and affordable. Although at the time I thought I was inventing a whole new concept, I later realized that eighteenth- and nineteenth-century homeowners used this same solution."

Fran does not, however, make reproduction floorcloths. Hers are dashing splashes of color from abstract pastels to tropical-colored flower patterns. "I use heavy canvas," Fran says, "then paint with acrylics. When I'm done I coat it with several layers of clear acrylic and add a nonskid backing. You end up with a painting you can walk on. It's perfect for a home with young children. You can have a light-colored floor covering and it will actually stay that way!"

PRICES: $140–$1,500. Commissions accepted. "I have a book of photos available for $175; $125 of that is refundable with minimum first order of rugs equal to or exceeding $500 wholesale."

VISITORS: Yes. Preferably during the week. Please call first.

LOCATION: Divine Inspirations, 7841 North 47th Street, Milwaukee, WI 53223; 414-354-3544. Take I-43 to Teutonia North, Teutonia North to Parkview. Go west on Parkview to 47th Street.

MINERAL POINT

Crafts Community

Steep hills, narrow streets, and a distinctive Cornish heritage mark this unusual town. Drawn by area lead mines, Cornish miners and craftsmen flocked to Mineral Point during the 1830s but largely abandoned the town when gold was discovered in California. During their stay, however, they constructed solid limestone homes and left a tradition of craftsmanship that continues today. In addition to visiting reconstruction homes and sampling Cornish pasties and saffron cake, travelers can drop by over thirty artisans' studios from weavers to leathersmiths, clockmakers to potters.

Some of the craft studios are located in Shake Rag Alley, an area named after the white rags a miner's wife would hang outside her home to signal the mine's windlass operator. He in turn would relay a message to the woman's husband that he was needed for dinner or an emergency. Today the narrow alley is punctuated with flower gardens and includes the original cabinet, blacksmith, and pottery shops.

At the far end of Shake Rag Street, visitors will find the Looms, a textile museum, gallery, and school. Featuring weaving equipment used from the early nineteenth century to the present day, the Looms also has a fine collection of pre–Civil War coverlets. Demonstrations of a jacquard loom and other equipment make this a special stop. Don't miss the unique weavings for sale in the gallery. Many of these items are special studies by Looms staff, including pieces designed on a computer but woven on antique looms.

OPEN: Studio hours vary. The Looms is open May 1–Oct. 15, daily, 10 A.M.–4 P.M. Museum admission is $3 for adults, $1.50 for children.

LOCATION: Southwestern Wisconsin, 48 miles southwest of Madison. Take I-90 to the Rte. 18 (Madison) exit, Rte. 18 west to Dodgeville, then go south on Rte. 151 to Mineral Point.

MORE: For information contact Shake Rag Alley (18 Shake Rag Street, Mineral Point, WI 53665; 608-987-2808) or the Looms (Box 61, Shake Rag Street, Mineral Point, WI 53565; 608-987-2277).

MOUNT HOREB

Wisconsin Folk Museum

If you're in the Madison area, plan to see this new museum. Established only in 1986, the museum nevertheless has a good start-up collection of traditional Wisconsin folk crafts. Look for rosemaling, Ukrainian-style decorated eggs, and Norwegian wood carving.

Featured crafts include Adolph Vandertie's stick whittlings, which are carved from a single stick of basswood and include linked chains or multiple balls encased in cages. Always a favorite, whirligigs by John Bambic are particularly appealing: a pig spins on a spit while a butcher sharpens his knife, a carpenter's saw spins while another carpenter planes, and a gypsy makes tame bears "dance."

OPEN: May 1–Labor Day, daily, 10 A.M.–5 P.M. Day after Labor Day–Christmas, weekends, 10 A.M.–5 P.M. Closed Dec. 26–Apr. 30. The museum shop sells traditional crafts such as Polish-style papercuttings and Indian basketry. Admission is $1.50 for adults, 75¢ for children. Tours by appointment only. Not wheelchair accessible.

LOCATION: Southern Wisconsin, about 17 miles west of Madison. 100 South Second Street, Mount Horeb, WI 53572; 608-437-4742. Take I-90 to the Rte. 18 (Madison) exit, Rte. 18 to the Mount Horeb exit. The museum is half a block south of the downtown stoplight.

OCONOMOWOC

Rich Riemenschneider
DUCK DECOYS

From the top of Rich's mailbox to the bottom of his basement, there's no question what craft has held his attention since 1927. The mailbox sports a single decoy, the basement holds over 400 duck, goose, and swan decoys that Rich refers to as the Duck Hunter's Hall of Fame.

"I got started carving as a boy," Rich says. "First I made ducks from soap my mother gave me. Then, when I was fourteen, my uncle said he'd take me duck hunting if I'd caulk his skiff and replace the heads of some decoys. That gave me the incentive I needed. I've been carving ever since, creating over two-thousand heads and five-hundred bodies. I've made decoys of every duck and wildfowl that uses the Mississippi Flyway. That's over thirty-nine different species, from mergansers and scaups to buffleheads and grebes."

Rich's decoys have the artistic flare of fine art but are fully functional. Although most are made from white cedar or pine, practicality dictates that some feather crests be leather to prevent breakage during use. An innovative craftsman, Rich also uses a variety of painting techniques. For example, to create a loon's distinctive checks, he first coats a piece of net with black paint, then snaps it against the duck's white undercoating.

PRICES: $50–$1,200. Commissions accepted. No catalog/brochure.

VISITORS: Yes.

LOCATION: Southeastern Wisconsin, between Milwaukee and Madison. 37935 Genesee Lake Road, Oconomowoc, WI 53066; 414-965-2513. Please call for directions.

OSHKOSH

Gerald F. Hawpetoss
MENOMINEE BEADWORK, DANCE REGALIA

Gerald Hawpetoss explains, in his own words, how his heritage and art are inseparable from each other or from his life's purpose:

"I am the last practitioner of Great Lakes Native American material culture. I know of no one else who has the skills and mythological belonging to the crafts. Others may try, but they lack correct techniques and ideologies that must accompany the artifacts, and their work is improper. I specialize in the arts attributed to the Grand Medicine Society, mainly Menominee in origin. My floral works depict the works of God. I use no lines to draw my design. The work is done on hides I tan myself. I gather and dye the porcupine quills using only natural dyes.

"I had no choice but to learn these crafts. It was my parents' command that I separate myself from the rest of the world and create, to help our nation survive. Among other items, I construct marriage and funeral moccasins (see color plate #16). It is my duty to deliver death and mourning attire upon request. I inherited this craft; only I can properly incorporate the details.

"My grandmother told me: 'We were hired by the chief families, the British, the French, and finally the Americans, to make red hides for war, moccasins, while other tribal members were hired to fight. Now you must provide these items when someone asks, especially death moccasins. We are so poor, my mother went to her grave in rewashed moccasins. You must not let this happen.'

"This was also my grandmother's way of telling us that we should keep His works alive, so the Menominee will never die. No one can ever pay us enough for the time it takes to create these pieces. That's why it is abandoned by some family members. Even I cannot demand my children learn these skills because I want them to be able to compete in present-day society."

PRICES: $15–$1,000. Commissions accepted. No catalog/brochure.

VISITORS: Yes. Please call for an appointment.

LOCATION: Eastern Wisconsin, about 56 miles southwest of Green Bay. 341 Saratoga Avenue, Oshkosh, WI 54901; 414-235-3701. Directions will be provided when appointment to visit is made.

PLATTEVILLE

David Lory
TURNED WOOD BOWLS

David's ⅛-inch turned wood bowls are unusual because they are functional as well as decorative.

You can use them to toss a salad or serve a stew, then wash them in soapy water and put them on the mantle as a work of art. "The secret," David says, "is the way I finish them. Although a lot of work goes into choosing just the right burl or tree crotch, aging it, then turning the bowl on my lathe, the real difference is what happens next.

"First I bake a newly turned bowl in the oven at one hundred fifty degrees for five to seven hours," David explains. "This removes all the moisture and also slightly warps the bowls into pleasing shapes. After baking I put on five coats of a specially formulated epoxy which really penetrates the wood. Final sanding is done by my wife, Suella, who starts with a chemical sandpaper, then uses increasingly fine steel wool, pumice, and rottenstone. The results are bowls which are not only thin and beautiful, but are guaranteed for a lifetime of normal use."

PRICES: $30–$400. Commissions accepted. No catalog/brochure, "but I send out a list of available sizes and their prices."

VISITORS: Yes.

LOCATION: Southwestern Wisconsin, about 23 miles northeast of Dubuque, Iowa; 70 miles southwest of Madison. 5604 Southwest Road, Platteville, WI 53818; 608-348-6344. Take I-90 to Rte. 18/151 (Madison exit), Rte. 18/151 west to Dodgeville, then Rte. 151 south to Platteville. Continue 2.2 miles south of Platteville, then turn left on Southwest Road. The house is .25 mile farther, the first driveway.

WASHINGTON ISLAND

Edward Larson
WIND TOYS AND PICTURE QUILTS

Wisconsin resembles a giant mitten with Door County, a pastiche of gentle hills, acres of cherry orchards, excellent salmon fishing, and even night skiing, as the thumb. The real gem, however, is Washington Island, which floats between Green Bay and Lake Michigan, just off the mainland tip. In addition to wandering the bucolic countryside, island visitors can meet one of Wisconsin's most unusual and prolific craftsmen, Edward Larson.

Humor and politics link the disparate expressions of Ed's creativity, which ranges from

Edward Larson: *Flying Icarus,* whirligig. H. 10'; W. 14'; D. 5½'.

whirligigs and folk sculpture to elegant picture quilts, wood snakes, and polka-dot rocking chairs. Even if you're not of the liberal persuasion, you can't help laughing at Ed's three-tiered whirligig *MX Missile System,* which shows a somewhat bewildered Ronald Reagan pushing the button to fire the system.

A former toy designer and department chairman at the Chicago Art Institute school, Ed also creates picture quilts such as *Fight of the Century,* which depicts him knocking out Muhammad Ali. "I design the quilts myself," Ed says, "but then I find a quilter who is willing to share in the creation and sale of the finished work. My inspiration for all my designs, in quilting or wood, comes from a combination of childhood fantasies, politics, Will Rogers, Jesus Christ, and Woody Guthrie."

PRICES: $500–$5,000. Commissions accepted. No catalog/brochure.

VISITORS: Yes.

LOCATION: Far northeastern Wisconsin, about 85 miles northeast of Green Bay. Washington Island, WI 54246; 414-847-2451. Take I-43 to Rte. 42 (at Manitowoc) or Rte. 57

(at Green Bay). Go north on Rte. 42 or 57 to Sturgeon Bay, then continue north on Rte. 42 to tip of peninsula. Take the ferry from North Port. On Washington Island, drive north on Swenson Road. The house is at the end of the road.

WISCONSIN DELLS

Parson's Indian Trading Post
NATIVE AMERICAN CRAFTS

One of Wisconsin's prime tourist attractions, the Dells is a 15-mile-long, 150-foot-wide channel cut by the Wisconsin River, and lined with unusual sandstone formations. The surrounding tourist hoopla, however, is eminently forgettable with one exception—Parson's Indian Trading Post.

Founded in 1925, Parson's offers beadwork, quillwork, jewelry, and other Native American crafts. Worth your attention are the more expensive, high-end items, particularly the top-quality basketry. Look especially for blue-and-brown Winnebago baskets by Helen Lonetree, miniature baskets by Lauren Little Wolf, and picnic baskets by Margaret Decorah, the last Winnebago creating these large pieces.

PRICES: $1–$20,000 (average, $10–$20); baskets, $8–$96. Accepts American Express, Discover, MasterCard, Visa.

OPEN: Every day of the year, 8 A.M.–9 P.M. Wheelchair accessible.

LOCATION: Central Wisconsin, 56 miles northwest of Madison. 370 Wisconsin Dells Parkway, Box 34, Wisconsin Dells, WI 53965; 608-254-8533. Take I-90/94 to exit 87 or 92. Follow signs into Lake Delton, Wisconsin. The shop is located right on Wisconsin Dells Parkway.

MORE: For more Winnebago and other Native American crafts, visit the Winnebago Indian Museum and its gift shop, 3889 North River Road (Rte. 13), Wisconsin Dells, WI 53965; 608-254-2268.

WOODVILLE

Dave Woodworth
CELTIC HARPS, HAMMER DULCIMERS

"Hammer dulcimers and Celtic harps are among man's oldest instruments," David says. "There are Middle Eastern drawings and descriptions of the hammer dulcimer which date to 2500 B.C. Harps go

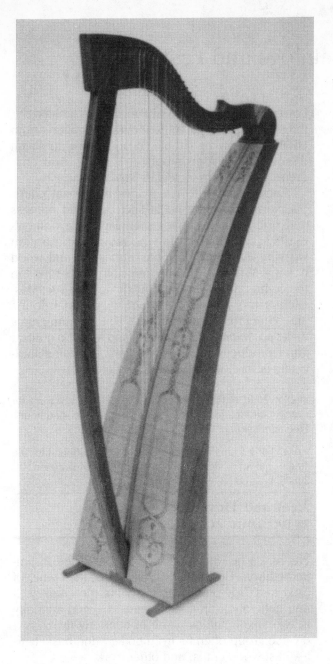

back even further. In fact, versions of both instruments can be found in nearly every country in the world."

A furniture and cabinet maker for five years, Dave made his first dulcimer as a surprise for his wife. "Actually the surprise was on me," Dave recalls. "She showed no interest in playing it and I did. I've been making them ever since. I also fashion harps with soundboards and sound boxes which curve from top to bottom. This makes the design very strong and stable, which is important in the Midwest, where humidity varies so widely. I also use a cherry-and-maple laminate that has fourteen layers of hardwood."

PRICES: Finished harps, $500–$1,200; finished dulcimers, $325–$625; kits, $175–$400. Commissions accepted. Send an SASE for his catalog/brochure.

VISITORS: Yes. "But please call first to make sure I'm at the shop."

LOCATION: Western Wisconsin, 24 miles east of the Minnesota/Wisconsin border, 6 miles from I-94. Heartland Strings, Rte. 1, Box 248, Woodville, WI 54028; 715-778-5561. Directions will be provided when you call.

Dave Woodworth: Celtic harp.

National Crafts Catalogs and Festival

The Guild: A Sourcebook of American Craft Artists
CONTEMPORARY CRAFTS

Whether you are decorating a new home, refurbishing your corporate offices, or merely looking for an unusual accent piece, the Guild Sourcebook offers a stunning array of crafts by some of America's most talented artisans (each of whom pays $1,400 for a listing). Published first in 1985, the Sourcebook is intended to connect craftspeople with interior designers and architects throughout the country. Individuals, galleries, and museums, however, also use this stunning compilation to purchase or commission artwork directly from the artisans.

Published annually, the Sourcebook includes excellent color photographs and brief, informative write-ups on the work of over 400 craftspeople. Distributed free to over 10,000 architects and interior designers, the Sourcebook has a retail cost of $60, which is definitely a bargain for craft collectors. Look for contemporary lighting and neon; vessels and baskets; furniture and cabinetwork; textiles, fabrics, tapestries, and quilts; floor coverings; paper and mixed media; and tiles and mosaics, as well as architectural wood, metal, and glass works.

An appendix lists artists both alphabetically and by home state, and includes a compilation of contemporary craft galleries in forty-two states.

To order the Sourcebook, send check for $60 to Kraus Sikes Inc., 150 West 25th Street, New York, NY 10001; 212-242-3730.

National Folk Festival
TRADITIONAL CRAFTS

Sponsored since 1934 by the National Council for the Traditional Arts, the National Folk Festival celebrates the music, crafts, stories, and dance passed down through time by America's families, communities, and ethnic groups. Held in different locations (perhaps one year at the Cuyahoga Valley National Recreation Area in Ohio, the next year at Lowell National Historical Park in Massachusetts), the festival presents authentic traditional arts from cowboy poetry and tobacco auctioning to Cajun dance music, Amish bonnet making, and children's games from Georgia's Sea Islands.

Each year ten to twenty-five traditional craftspeople demonstrate skills such as Ohio harness and bridle making, traditional Japanese women's crafts, Czechoslovakian bookbinding, Laotian weaving, Abnaki Indian basketmaking, and wood carving. Visitors are often treated to crafts found in the communities surrounding the festival site: Massachusetts's Azores craftsmen create mandolins and other musical instruments, Hmong immigrants make *paj ntaub* (flower cloth), and an Ohio quilters guild produces a variety of work including intricately embroidered patterns.

EVENT: Held at the end of July. Contact the sponsors for specific information concerning location, dates, and hours. Free admission.

MORE: For information contact the National Council for the Traditional Arts, 806 15th Street NW, #400, Washington, DC 20005; 202-639-8370.

Neat and Tidy
TRADITIONAL, FOLK CRAFTS

Serving a network of collectors interested in limited editions of traditional folk crafts, the owner of Neat and Tidy publications scours the country to find authentic, top-quality items. Offered annually in two small catalogs, and in quarterly flyers, is a diverse group of crafts from pottery and baskets to textiles, wood crafts, and other work.

Crafts might include original papercuttings by Claudia Hopf, "People Jars" adapted from a mid-nineteenth-century Pennsylvania potter, elaborately decorated salt-glazed stoneware, ice fishing decoys or old-fashioned cloth dolls. Foltz Pottery redware plates are another popular item, created using 200-year-old methods. The red clay is rolled like dough and shaped over antique molds. Edges are then decorated or crimped like a pie.

The cost for the catalog is $2; the flyers are free. To get on Neat and Tidy's mailing list, send your name, address, and the type of traditional crafts you collect to Jan Mallow, Neat and Tidy, 27 Pine Brook Road, Spring Valley, NY 10977. For more information call 914-356-0446.

Source Directory of American Indian, Eskimo & Aleut Owned/Operated Arts & Crafts Businesses

Published by the Indian Arts & Crafts Board, part of the U.S. Department of the Interior, this Source Directory includes over 300 Native American craftspeople, artists, and shops. Listed by state, each entry mentions typical items created or sold by the person or business. Although entries are not juried according to quality, excellent black-and-white photos help directory users sort out what may be of interest to them. Included in the Source Book is everything from traditional arrowheads, drums, beadwork, clothing, and Navajo rugs to contemporary jewelry, pottery, and baskets. There's also a smattering of fine arts, including paintings and sculpture.

For a free copy write to the Indian Arts & Crafts Board, U.S. Department of the Interior, Room 4004-MIB, Washington, D.C. 20420; or call 202-343-2773.

Craft Event Calendar

SEPTEMBER
   Annual Appalachian Arts & Crafts Festival. Beckley, West Virginia, p. 139.
   Craftproducers Market Craft Show. Stowe, Vermont, p. 65.
   Der Dutch Peddler. Berlin, Ohio, p. 251.
   Fair at New Boston. Springfield, Ohio, p. 252.
   Hopkinton Colonial Craft Festival. Ashaway, Rhode Island, p. 49.
   Traditional Craft Days. Oneida, New York, p. 80.
   Ukrainian Festival. Pittsburgh, Pennsylvania, p. 122.
   Wildfowl Carvers & Collectors Festival. New Orleans, Louisiana, p. 186.
   Yankee Peddler Festival. Canal Fulton, Ohio, p. 251.

EARLY FALL
   Kentuck Festival. Northport, Alabama, p. 148.

OCTOBER
   Annual Fall Craft Festival. Pleasant Plains, Illinois, p. 230.
   Blue Ridge Folklife Festival. Ferrum, Virginia, p. 127.
   Indian & Pioneer Heritage Fair. Ridgeland, Mississippi, p. 193.
   Pennsylvania Traditional Crafts & Folk Art Sale. Stouchsburg, Pennsylvania, p. 124.
   Southern Highland Handicraft Guild Fair. Asheville, North Carolina, p. 197.

OCTOBER/NOVEMBER
   Tennessee Fall Crafts Fair. Nashville, Tennessee, p. 217.

NOVEMBER
   Craftproducers Market Craft Show. West Dover, Vermont, p. 65.
   Vermont Handcrafters' Fall Craft Fair. Burlington, Vermont, p. 54.

NOVEMBER/DECEMBER
   Celebration of American Crafts. New Haven, Connecticut, p. 12.

DECEMBER
   Chimneyville Crafts Festival. Jackson, Mississippi, p. 190.

GLOSSARY

Albany-slip: a glaze often used in early American pottery made from a clay found near Albany, New York. Varying from dark brown to black, the glaze is used on high-fired ceramic work.

cloisonné: decorative enamelwork (most often jewelry) created by forming designs on metal plates using thin metal strips, then filling in the spaces with molten enamels. The work is often characterized by very colorful, intricate designs.

cochineal: a red dye made from the bodies of dried female cochineal insects found primarily on cactus in Mexican deserts.

colcha embroidery: once used to decorate bedspreads (*colcha* in Spanish) and other household goods, this work consists of long, parallel stitches, tacked down either randomly or in a pattern, used now by Colorado Hispanics to create intricate pictorial tapestries.

crotch-veneered: thin sheets of wood (veneer) taken from just below where a tree forks, resulting in intricate grain patterns.

earthenware: low-fired, comparatively coarse-grained pottery that is usually red or tan and somewhat porous.

Favrile: a trademark glass developed by Louis Comfort Tiffany to resemble long-buried, ancient Roman glass. Used most often in vases, Favrile is known for its iridescent, metallic colors and delicate designs created by spraying metallic salts onto hot glass.

finger-weaving: a form of Native American weaving that uses no loom or shuttle. Instead, yarns hang freely from a pole and alternate as weft or warp. Designs are most commonly chevrons or lightning zigzags.

fraktur: a very ornate handwriting (surrounded by symbolic decorations) used to create birth and marriage certificates and other family documents. Developed originally in sixteenth-century Germany, the craft continues today in Pennsylvania German communities.

glass, blown: glass that has first been reduced to a molten state resembling glue or gelatin, then formed by blowing air into the glass through a long tube.

glass, lampworked: glass tubing and cane that has been softened over a lamp (such as a Bunsen burner) just to the point where it can be worked into various shapes.

glaze: a liquid emulsion including finely ground minerals that is applied to the surface of ceramicware prior to final firing and produces distinctive colors and patterns depending upon the minerals used.

greenware: term applied to pottery that has not been fired.

Indian pawn: also known as "dead pawn" or "old pawn," is a term applied to Indian jewelry pawned at shops or trading posts, not redeemed by its owner, and now available through retail sale. Indian pawn sometimes affords purchasers the opportunity to acquire old, high-quality pieces seldom for sale. The items can, however, just as easily be junk. Depend only on personal expertise or the advice of a reputable dealer to distinguish the two.

jacquard loom: developed in the nineteenth century by Joseph-Marie Jacquard, this loom used a rotating, punched-card system enabling hand weavers to easily and rapidly create intricate patterns.

neriage: a type of ceramic construction where colored clays are wedged together in a pattern, then sliced or cut and applied as surface decoration.

porcelain: a type of clay that, when fired, becomes hard, nonporous, translucent, and white.

raku: a type of hand-built, low-fired, relatively soft, lead-glazed pottery originally made in Japan and used as tea bowls.

repoussé: a type of metalwork where the design is hammered in from the back so the pattern is raised from the background surface.

rive: a process used to form laths, boards, shingles, or splits for basketry by splitting logs with a sharp tool or by concussion.

rosemaling: a colorful Scandinavian type of painting incorporating flowers, scrolls, and other stylized designs and used as decoration on various household objects from cutting boards to chests of drawers.

rya rugs: long-pile Scandinavian-style rugs often incorporating bright colors and abstract designs.

salt-glaze: a hard, glassy glaze used on ceramics and formed by throwing salt into the kiln during its peak temperature.

scrimshander: another word for a person who creates scrimshaw, carved whalebone or ivory that is often colored by rubbing ink or paints into the cut surfaces.

sgraffito: ceramic decoration where a clay surface is covered by a colored (often light yellow) slip, then incised with decorations or writing that reveals the colored surface below. This process is traditionally used as one type of decoration in Pennsylvania German redware.

slip: clay diluted with water and used as a surface decoration or glaze on ceramics.

slip-trailed: a decorative process used often in Pennsylvania German redware where a slip is decoratively trailed across the surface, leaving a raised design.

spalted wood: wood invaded by fungi and microorganisms that produce colorful, mottled patterns in addition to the natural grain pattern.

stoneware: all clay pottery (except porcelain) that is fired at a high temperature, is hard and nonporous, and is either gray, tan, or reddish in color.

treenware: functional wood cooking and serving utensils formed most often from attractively colored woods in naturally curvilinear shapes.

trompe l'oeil: a French term meaning "deceives the eye" and refers to paintings on flat surfaces that, because of the skillful use of shading and other illusionary techniques, make the viewer think they are seeing an actual three-dimensional object. For example, a painting of a fence in front of a garden would make viewers believe they could actually cross over the fence to pick the flowers.

vitreous: a glassy, hard, impermeable glaze or surface.

INDEX

CRAFTS

CRAFTSPERSONS

CRAFT SHOPS, GALLERIES, AND MUSEUMS

Craft Report Card

Use this form to comment on existing entries you've visited or to suggest craftspeople, places, and events for the next edition. For suggested additions, provide as much information as possible, including a description of the craft(s). If they're available, attach brochures, snapshots, or other illustrations.

( ) Comment on existing entry   ( ) Suggested new entry

Name (craftsperson, place, or event): _____

Address (MUST be included): _____

_____ Zip _____

Telephone: (_____) _____.

Your comments:

(Optional)

Your name: _____

Address: _____

Telephone: (_____) _____.   E

Return this form to: Suzanne Carmichael, P.O. Box 7604, Tacoma, WA 98407-0604.

THANK YOU!